ARMOR ATTACKS

ARMOR ATTACKS

THE TANK PLATOON

An Interactive Exercise in Small-Unit Tactics and Leadership

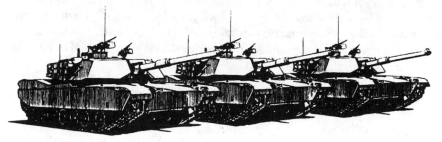

John F. Antal

Foreword by Gen. Richard E. Cavazos, USA (Ret.)

PRESIDIO

The views expressed in this book are my own and do not necessarily reflect the position or policies of the Department of the Army or the Department of Defense. The characters in this book are fictional, and any resemblance to any other person, living or dead, is pure coincidence.

Copyright © 1991 by John F. Antal

Published by Presidio Press
31 Pamaron Way, Novato, CA 94949

Library of Congress Cataloging-in-Publication Data

Antal, John F., 1955-
    Armor attacks : the tank platoon : an interactive exercise in small-unit tactics and leadership / John F. Antal
      p. cm.
    ISBN 0-89141-383-9
    1. War games. 2. Tank warfare. I. Title.
U310.A57 1991
355.4'8—dc20   91-16420
                                   CIP

Typography by ProImage

Printed in the United States of America

This book is dedicated to the superb officers, noncommissioned officers, and soldiers who serve America in the armor and mechanized forces of the United States Army and the United States Marine Corps. Together with fellow soldiers, sailors, airmen, and marines, they protect America in peace and war.

If you want to know when the war is coming, just watch the U.S. and see when it starts cutting down its defense. It's the surest barometer in the world.

Will Rogers

Americans fully understand the requirements of the football field or the baseball diamond. They discipline themselves and suffer by the thousands to prepare for these rigors. A coach or manager who is too permissive soon seeks a new job; his teams fail against those who are tougher and harder. Yet undoubtedly any American officer, in peacetime, who worked his men as hard, or ruled them as severely as a college football coach does, would be removed.

But the shocks of the battlefield are a hundred times those of the playing field, and the outcome infinitely more important to the nation.

The problem is to understand the battlefield as well as the game of football. The problem is to see not what is desirable, or nice, or politically feasible, but what is necessary.

From the book *This Kind of War* by
T. R. Fehrenbach © 1963

Contents

Maps

Diagrams

Acknowledgments

I would like to thank the U.S. Army Training Support Center; the Chief of Public Affairs, Headquarters, Department of the Army; and *Armor Magazine* for authorization to use selected drawings to illustrate *Armor Attacks*.

Technical data for this book was drawn totally from open sources. The definitions in the glossary come from the 1985 edition of U.S. Army *Field Manual 101-5-1, Operational Terms and Graphics*.

Every writer needs a devil's advocate, in this respect I was particularly lucky to have the advice and assistance of many positive critics. I want to thank Majors Lance Betros, Paul Bonney, Gary Coleman, Harold Coyle, Gail Dezhel, Brad Naegle, and James Womack for their assistance and critical analysis. My special thanks goes to General (Retired) Richard E. Cavazos for taking the time to write the foreword for this book.

Lastly, and most importantly, I want to express my sincere thanks to my wife, Angel. Without her love, support, encouragement, and understanding, this book would never have been written.

John F. Antal
22 June 1990

Foreword

Everyone's hope is for a peaceful, more gentle world. Yet, just as we welcome the extraordinary events in the Eastern Bloc countries, we also know how any situation can dramatically go sour. Soldiers prepare for the worst.

Major John Antal's *Armor Attacks* is both stimulating and instructional. It is an excellent exercise for small unit leaders. To those not familiar with Army combat units, I recommend it as a superb example of the enormous complexity of the modern battlefield, of how very much we expect of young Privates, Specialists, Buck Sergeants, and 2nd Lieutenants. To those who have worn the uniform, it should be comforting that the thread of selfless service, the belief in DUTY, HONOR and COUNTRY, are as imbued in this generation of soldiers as they were in our time.

Major John Antal has provided us a war game designed to sharpen tactical thinking. It came from a bright young officer who has spent his entire time in the Army with troops in the field. Twice a tank company commander, twice a tank battalion operations officer, and now a graduate of the Command and General Staff College at Fort Leavenworth, Kansas. His assignments have been perfect and what I urge young officers to have—"duty time where the rubber meets the road."

Armor Attacks is most real! What many war stories overlook is the human dimension of war. The terrible fear, the shattered nerves, the lack of sleep that erode courage, judgment, and the ability to shoot quick and straight. So while the "war game" is very interesting, it should not be treated as merely a "fun" exercise by soldiers, but as a serious professional development opportunity. I believe that is why it was written.

What I value most in war are officers of courage, tenacity, guile and cunning. Guile and cunning because we should bait and entrap the enemy to frustrate, confuse and frighten him. Guile and cunning

Foreword

are the natural products of young leaders of imagination. Here is a work of most admirable imagination. Professional competence is required to decide correctly. Yet the best decisions are inhibited by the press of time. In *Armor Attacks,* the reader must ACT NOW! No other profession is so demanding nor is failure more punishing. This indeed is war.

I enjoyed reading *Armor Attacks.* It is a modern day *Defense of Duffer's Drift* and much more. Finally, and above all, here is a work that subtly, yet in truth, captures the terrible work members of our Armed Services are willing to shoulder. We should acknowledge that service with deep gratitude.

Richard E.Cavazos
General (Ret), U. S. Army

General Richard E. Cavazos, United States Army (Retired), is a decorated combat veteran of both the Korean and Vietnam Wars. He has commanded every echelon of command in the United States Army, including command of the 9th Infantry Division at Fort Lewis, Washington, and III Corps at Fort Hood, Texas. He assumed command of the U.S. Army's largest command, the U.S. Army Forces Command at Fort McPherson, Georgia, in 1982.

He has twice been awarded the nation's second highest combat decoration, the Distinguished Service Cross; has twice been awarded the Silver Star; and wears twenty-nine other combat awards. He is also Airborne Ranger qualified and wears one star on his Combat Infantryman's Badge.

Preface

Armor Attacks: The Tank Platoon is an interactive fiction designed to
let you, the reader, decide the ending. You are in command of an American
tank platoon in combat in the Middle East. At the end of each section
you will be required to make a decision. Your skill, foresight, and luck
will determine life or death, victory or defeat. To play the role of the
tank platoon leader you will need only three things: this book, a pair
of six-sided dice, and all the tactical expertise that you can muster!
Each tactical decision that you make impacts on the future course of
the battle. Make your decisions wisely!

This book can be challenging and educational even if you have never
seen a tank. You will become 2d Lt. Samuel Jaeger. You are twenty-
two years old, a product of the Army Reserve Officer Training Corps
program and the United States Army Armor School.

Jaeger commands 3d Platoon, A Company, in a tank battalion of a
U.S. mechanized infantry division. Alpha Company is a typical U.S.
Army tank company and consists of fourteen M1 tanks and approximately five officers and fifty-seven enlisted soldiers. Normally, tank
battalions are cross attached with infantry, forming a company team
that consists of a combination of tank platoons and mechanized infantry platoons. In the first mission of *Armor Attacks: The Tank
Platoon*, Alpha Company is "pure" and has no attached mechanized
infantry. For the second mission, Jaeger's platoon is combined with
an M3 cavalry fighting vehicle–equipped scout platoon to fight the
counterreconnaissance battle during a task force defense.

Immediately following the preface is a section explaining crew positions
and responsibilities on the M1A1 tank. In order to make decisions that
take into account the tank's capabilities, the reader should become
thoroughly familiar with these positions.

At the end of the book, pages have been included which will allow
the reader to keep track of decisions made. Enter the number of each
section selected in the next circle as you make the choice. In general,
the more directly you proceed through the choices to victory, the better.

Preface

If you find yourself going back to sections you have already been through, you should try a different approach to the problem.

The sounds of exploding artillery have been coded to indicate the nearness of the exploding rounds. Sound effects printed all in capital letters are intended to represent artillery exploding close by. Those printed in small letters denote explosions at a distance.

Crew Positions on the M1A1 Abrams Tank

The leadership and tactical principles that apply to a tank platoon apply universally to almost all types of combat. The more you know about tank platoon operations, however, the more correct your decisions should be. The glossary and weapons-data sections at the end of the book will assist you in understanding modern military terms and weapons.

As the tank platoon leader you will be in charge of four M1 Abrams tanks. The M1 Abrams is one of the best tanks in the world. It is a fully tracked, low-profile, land combat assault weapon system possessing armor protection, shoot-on-the-move capability, and a high degree of maneuverability and tactical agility. The four-man crew has the capability to engage the full spectrum of enemy ground targets with a variety of accurate point and area fire weapons.

Each M1 tank weighs sixty tons. The power to drive the M1 tank comes from a 1,500-horsepower Avco-Lycoming turbine engine. The tank can maintain a maximum speed on level terrain of forty-four miles per hour. The cruising range on one tank of fuel is approximately 275 miles, or eighteen hours of operation. The M1 tanks are also equipped with special armor, which makes the M1 the most survivable tank on the battlefield.

The M1 Abrams tank is armed with an M68 105mm rifled cannon that is accurate and lethal enough to destroy most enemy tanks with just one round. In addition, each tank has one .50-caliber machine gun located at the tank commander's hatch and two 7.62mm machine guns, one at the loader's hatch and one coaxially mounted with the main gun. The M1 tank has a crew of four men: tank commander, gunner, loader, and driver. There are sixteen men assigned to each tank platoon (four per tank times four tanks equals sixteen).

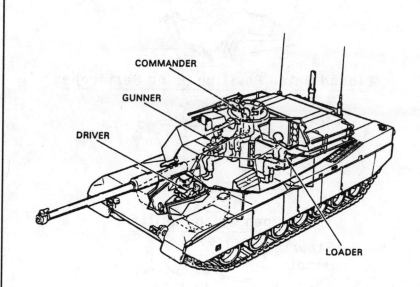

COMMANDER

GUNNER

DRIVER

LOADER

M1A1 ABRAMS TANK

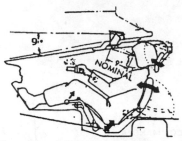

Closed Hatch Position Using Periscopes

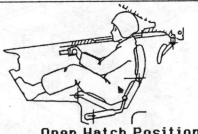

Open Hatch Position

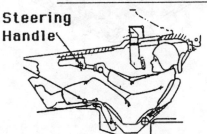

Steering
Handle

Closed Hatch for
Night Vision Device

The Driver's Station

The Driver

The driver controls the maneuver and speed of the tank. He moves the tank as directed by the tank commander. The driver sits in a reclining position in the front of the hull surrounded by his controls.

The driver's controls on the M1 tank are unique and simple to use. A T-bar acts as the steering mechanism to direct the tank left or right and also acts as the accelerator control. The T-bar was designed to eliminate the need for a separate accelerator pedal. The hand throttles utilize a motorcycle-style grip that can be operated with either hand, or both hands, as the situation warrants. Push-to-talk buttons are located on the hand throttle housing to permit the driver to key his intercom without removing his hands from the steering controls.

The interior of the driver's station was designed to be functional and to reduce crew fatigue. Panel lights, rather than gauges, provide the driver with a quick assessment of each critical function (such as vehicle master power, engine automatic start, and release of parking brake). Automotive gauges and displays (such as engine/transmission parameters, fuel status, electrical system voltage) are grouped together into a single functional representation to provide easy monitoring by the driver.

The driver, totally protected by a heavy protective hatch, looks through telescope vision blocks during the day, or a passive night vision viewer at night, to maneuver the tank. During the hours of darkness the driver's passive electronic viewer effectively turns night into day, allowing the driver to see in near-total darkness without any external means of illumination.

The Loader

The loader is usually the junior member of the crew. Loaders hold the rank of private or specialist fourth class. The loader's job is to open the tank ammo door, grab the forty-pound tank round from the protected ammo storage area, and load the gun as fast as possible. A good loader can load a round in four to five seconds.

The loader's station is designed to minimize the complexity of work required by the loader. The loader sits in a seat on the left side of the turret. The basic sequence for loading a round into the M68 cannon is as follows:

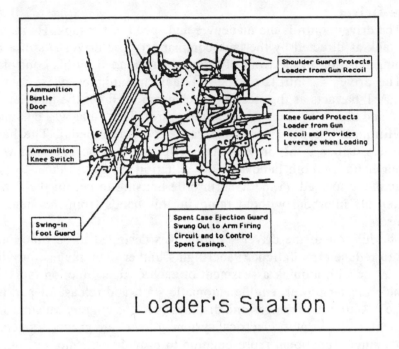

Loader's Station

1. The loader opens the ammunition compartment door by activating a knee switch with his right knee. The door opens and the loader pulls a spring-loaded tab to release the round from the honeycomb storage compartment.
2. The loader extracts a round and begins to turn toward the gun.
3. The door starts to close two seconds after the gunner removes his knee from the switch. This door protects the crew from the explosion of their own ammunition in the event that the tank is hit by a projectile.
4. The loader swivels on his seat as he swings around toward the breech. The loader rams the round into the gun with his closed fist. The breech snaps shut after being triggered by a round.
5. The loader then arms the gun by turning and pulling out the spent ejection case guard. After accomplishing this the loader yells "UP" to inform the tank commander and gunner that the gun is loaded and ready to fire.

The Gunner

The gunner is the heart of the tank. He performs the tasks of surveillance, target acquisition, and target engagement in a moving tank. He is usually a sergeant or a senior specialist fourth class. He operates the tank fire control system and fires the main gun and coaxially mounted machine gun on the order of the tank commander.

Equipped with an accurate laser range finder, a digital computer that applies all ballistic data to the guns automatically, and an extremely high resolution thermal target sight, the M1 has earned a reputation as having the finest fire control system of any tank in the world. The gunner's fire control system allows him to see targets out to 3,000 meters and to accurately range to these targets within plus or minus five meters.

The gunner's primary sight, or GPS, provides a wide range of daylight vision alternatives. The daylight sight provides a dual-power

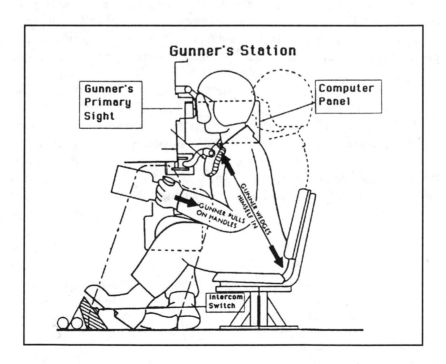

Gunner's Station

Gunner's Primary Sight

Computer Panel

GUNNER WEDGES HIMSELF IN

GUNNER PULLS ON HANDLES

Intercom Switch

Preface

capability: a wide-angle mode for area surveillance (three power) and a high magnification mode for target identification and gun laying (ten power).

The M1 tank's parallel-scan thermal imaging system (TIS) provides the tank commander and gunner the ability to observe targets, day or night, based on the difference in temperature of the target and its surrounding background. Any hot or cold object that emits heat or cold (reflected radiation) is easily distinguished by the M1 tank's thermal sights. The thermal sights can be a decisive advantage in fast-moving tank combat by making it easy for the gunner to detect targets that would appear camouflaged to nonthermal tank sights. The fire control system makes it easy for the gunner on an M1 tank to hit targets at extreme ranges.

The Tank Commander

The tank commander is the brain of the tank and is usually a sergeant or higher ranking soldier. The tank commander (or TC) is an experienced tanker who has worked his way up through the ranks from the loader's, to the driver's, to the gunner's position before he is given the responsibility of becoming a tank commander. The tank commander commands the movement of the tank and directs the firing of the main gun by giving orders over the tank's intercom. The TC can also transmit and receive radio messages over the tank's FM radio system.

The M1's fire controls allow the tank commander to override the gunner and fire both the tank cannon and coaxial machine gun from the TC's position. His commander's weapons station provides the means for the commander to slew, track, and position his weapon with a minimum of effort. The turret is moved by a powerful turret motor that slews the turret as directed by the tank commander or gunner. The tank commander has override capability of the gunner's controls. The effectiveness of any tank commander is dependent on how quickly he can acquire a target and lay the gun.

Normally the tank commander will fight from the open protected posture, where his overhead hatch will be slightly raised above the cupola, protecting him from overhead fires but allowing him to peek out with unrestricted vision. This ability to see while still being protected is vital in tank battles.

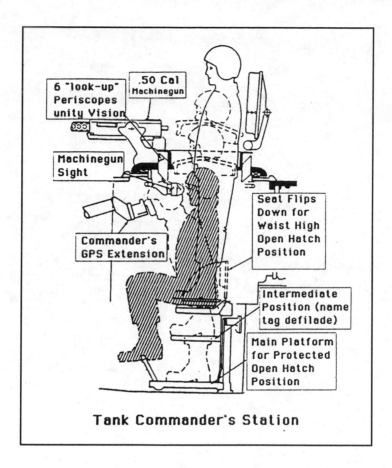

Tank Commander's Station

Your challenge is to survive and win on the modern battlefield. The enemy is skilled, determined, and eager to beat you. The fate of your platoon and the success of your company depend on your decisions and your actions. ARE YOU READY? If you are, read on!

Introduction

In spite of everything, or maybe because of it, America went to war in the closing years of the twentieth century. Events in the 1990s took on a terrible velocity that defied peaceful solutions. This kind of thing had happened before. In 1914 the world had stumbled into war, and a generation was lost in the trenches. Twenty-two years later the West, fearing the enormous casualties of the First World War, appeased Nazi Germany until war became inevitable. In both situations, good men had attempted to keep the peace and had failed.

In the 1990s the situation was much the same. Most of the nations of the world became involved in a long and bloody conventional war. Technology had changed tremendously since 1914. The means to wage war and opportunities to maintain the peace had progressed a hundred times that available to the belligerents of Flanders Field and Tannenburg. But man had not changed. Greed, nationalism, and fear still ruled man's psyche. As in 1914, no one could control the situation. The brightest minds of the time, the best statesmen, and the men of purest intention were unable to stop the relentless push toward war.

The "unsolvable" problems of the Middle East ignited the spark that created the blaze that engulfed the entire world. The warning signs had been clearly visible for years, but almost everyone had chosen to ignore them. A growing world dependency on oil produced from the Arabian Gulf, the instability of the Gulf regimes, and the never-ending feud between Arab and Jew finally erupted. Responding to the defense of its Middle Eastern allies, the United States deployed ground combat forces to the Middle East. American soldiers once again found themselves on foreign soil, fighting against a well-trained and well-equipped enemy.

Why the war started, and how it could have been avoided, was a matter for politicians and statesmen. To the soldier who became the sharp edge of America's foreign policy, the intricacies of high-level politics and the reasons why international diplomacy had collapsed were purely academic questions. The point was that diplomacy had failed and war had started. The point was that the United States now sent soldiers to achieve what talk alone could not secure. To these soldiers

Introduction

war was up close and personal. Like it or not, it was a matter of kill or be killed.

For more than forty years America had maintained an expensive military force to prevent the outbreak of a third world war. In spite of the bloody wars in Korea and Vietnam and sharp, short conflicts in such places as the Dominican Republic, Grenada, Libya, and Panama, the American strategy of deterrence had largely succeeded. But when deterrence fails, policymakers are faced with two simple possibilities—fight or run.

The Americans and their allies decided to fight rather than surrender their national interests. They fought in difficult desert terrain, hampered by a long supply line that required all the sea and air transport capability that the United States could muster. Outnumbered, the American forces depended on superior training and their ability to employ combined arms to win battles.

The first major battle of the war was fought at a nameless road junction in an isolated desert valley. Despite the Americans' deployment for war, the initial battle came as a surprise. In the battle of the Valley of Tears, casualties on both sides were heavy. During this battle both the Americans and the enemy learned the hard and terrible lessons of modern war. For many, these lessons were their last.

The battle of the Valley of Tears had been the first real test of American mechanized arms since the Second World War. But weapons were much more lethal now than they had been during World War II. Tanks were better armored and had heavier guns. Infantry rode in protected infantry fighting vehicles and carried an array of sophisticated weaponry that could kill almost anything that moved on the battlefield. Artillery, always the greatest killer in modern war, had a new arsenal of improved munitions that could wipe out square kilometers of territory. Added to these improvements in conventional firepower and mobility was the increased capability of tactical air power and the horrible specter of chemical warfare.

Before the war many people who should have known better thought that air power and precision-guided munitions would win wars without the necessity for close ground combat. Such push-button warfare had been the dream of academic strategists since the dawn of the technological age. But modern conventional war is a complicated thing and no one arm alone can force a decision on an opponent. One needs only to understand that the Korean War and the Vietnam War, both fought by America with near total air supremacy, could not be won by the mere application of air power. In the final analysis, war is still won or lost by men who must face their enemy in close combat and force him to run or die.

These factors put a premium on effective tactical leadership and unit training. Expert strategy and operational brilliance can arrange the conditions for victory, but tactical effectiveness must secure it. As in the past, the quality of the ground tactical units can decide the fate of campaigns. Highly trained units, led with skill and determination, can now wield more mobile firepower than ever before in the history of warfare. The side that can effectively employ mobile combined arms forces can, therefore, create the opportunity to defeat a force several times its own size.

The first battle of the war had been a close-run affair, but the Americans had prevailed based on their skillful employment of combined arms. The enemy was defeated at the Valley of Tears and the Threat forces were given a bloody nose. The Threat, defeated but not destroyed, pulled back in good order to strong defensive positions. They dug in, prepared their defenses, and waited for the Americans to make the next move. Now the initiative rested with the Americans, and if this war was ever to end, the Americans would have to attack.

MAP SYMBOLS

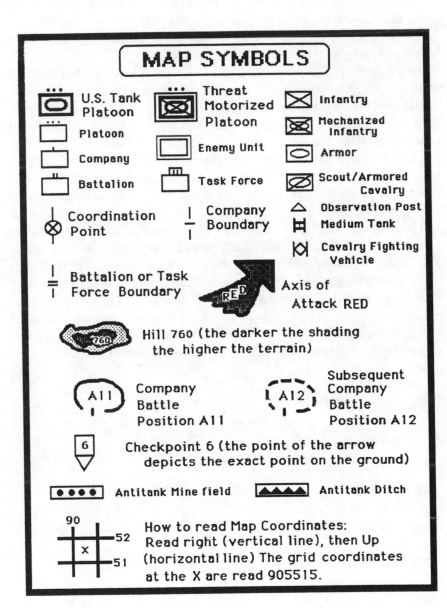

U.S. Tank Platoon

Platoon

Company

Battalion

Coordination Point

Battalion or Task Force Boundary

Threat Motorized Platoon

Enemy Unit

Task Force

Company Boundary

Axis of Attack RED

Infantry

Mechanized Infantry

Armor

Scout/Armored Cavalry

Observation Post

Medium Tank

Cavalry Fighting Vehicle

Hill 760 (the darker the shading the higher the terrain)

Company Battle Position A11

Subsequent Company Battle Position A12

Checkpoint 6 (the point of the arrow depicts the exact point on the ground)

Antitank Mine field

Antitank Ditch

How to read Map Coordinates:
Read right (vertical line), then Up
(horizontal line) The grid coordinates
at the X are read 905515.

Section 1

"God, it's hot!" 2d Lt. Sam Jaeger grumbled out loud. He licked his dry lips, reached for his canteen, and unscrewed the black plastic cap. The warm water that tumbled into his dry mouth was a welcome relief, in spite of the strong, bitter taste caused by the iodine purification tablets.

Jaeger wondered if he would ever get used to this god-awful desert. The days were fire and the nights were too cool to enjoy. The burning sun bore down on everything, making any type of shade a precious commodity. The dust was everywhere—coating your uniform, your skin, in your hair, your food. There was no escaping the dust.

To the north, buzzards circled ominously, searching for the day's meal. Jaeger quickly ducked into the shade of a tarp that had been rigged to the side of his company commander's M1 Abrams tank.

Madsen, a tall, good-looking young lieutenant, shrugged, answering Jaeger's unfocused question. "You'll get used to it. Just keep drinking plenty of water." Madsen paused for a few quiet moments. "I think we attack tomorrow."

Madsen's comment hung in the air, unanswered. Jaeger replied with a silent glance, trying to look confident. Jaeger had joined Alpha Company only seven days ago . . . a lifetime ago. In that time he had developed a strong respect for 2d Lt. John Madsen. You could count on him. Solid. No nonsense. Madsen's platoon had led the company road march for the past two days. You didn't get to lead in Alpha Company unless you knew your stuff.

The road march had been dusty, hot, and monotonous. Thirteen of the company's tanks had arrived at their designated assembly area position. One had broken down due to a faulty engine fuel pump. The road march had been conducted over 100 tiring kilometers of dust and sun, interrupted by an occasional strafing enemy aircraft. Luckily, no one had been hurt. The company's air defense team had even managed to hit and destroy one enemy aircraft with a Stinger missile. So far, things were looking good.

Jaeger's mind went blank as he leaned against the side of the big M1 tank and stared out at the desert landscape. He was tired. The desert

Section 1

was so different from anything he had ever experienced. The heat took a lot out of you. He thought about his home in Stillwater, Minnesota. He dreamed of ice water. Gallons and gallons of ice water.

Captain Russell, the company commander, and three lieutenants and an NCO walked up to the lean-to and joined Jaeger and Madsen. For a few moments no one said a word. All eyes were on Russell. Bleary eyed, dust streaked, and sweaty, the young officers waited for their commander to begin his briefing.

"OK. Take a seat. Get out your maps and listen," the captain announced. The five officers and one NCO quickly took their places and opened their notebooks.

Jaeger unfolded his map, which was protected by a shiny acetate map case, and prepared to receive tomorrow's attack order. He looked at the faces of the men around him. All except Captain Russell and the first sergeant were his age. The executive officer (XO), 1st Lt. Rick Shields, was a capable twenty-six-year-old who had been with the company since it deployed from the States. Shields had worked well as Russell's second in command and was a veteran of the battle of the Valley of Tears.

Madsen, who had personally destroyed three enemy T-72 tanks in that battle, was in charge of 1st Platoon. Second Lieutenant Joseph Williams, a tall, black ROTC graduate, was in command of 2d Platoon. Williams was also new to the unit and, like Jaeger, had not yet experienced combat.

Lieutenant Rogers, an artilleryman, was the company's new addition. Rogers was the company fire support officer, in charge of field artillery support and coordination. "Top," 1st Sgt. "Wild Bill" Brock, the epitome of the tough, leather-faced, professional noncommissioned officer, rounded off the group. He was Russell's right arm and handled all the company's logistical and supply needs.

"First let me introduce Lieutenant Rogers," Russell said, his gaze at Rogers full of firmness and expectation. "He is our new fire support officer, and I expect a lot of accurate artillery fire support from him. He will monitor the company command frequency and will call for fire from battalion mortars and 155mm artillery automatically, based upon your spot reports and his best judgment. Don't waste time calling for artillery and don't tie up my command frequency asking for mortar fire." Russell then opened up his map, clipped it to a wooden board with metal clips, and continued.

2

"I received the operations order from battalion a few hours ago. I will now issue you the company order. As you should know, we are now located in our assembly area at grid LK892462. Save your questions for the end of my briefing and follow with me on your maps as I talk you through tomorrow's mission." Captain Russell's tone left no mistaking that he was serious and demanded everyone's complete attention.

"Situation: We are up against elements of an enemy motorized rifle division. We will be attacking into the enemy's security zone. The security zone, for those of you who haven't seen it in real life, is the first belt in the enemy's defenses. The enemy is defending in our battalion's zone of attack with a reinforced motorized rifle company. He seems pretty well spread out, and we anticipate that he is trying to delay us until their reinforcements arrive from the east. We can expect to see at least a reinforced motorized rifle platoon in our company zone of attack: approximately three BMPs and one T-72 tank." Captain Russell paused to let that piece of information sink in.

"The battalion intelligence officer says that we may be up against the T-72M1, the best tank the enemy has sent against us so far. The T-72M1 has the same 125mm gun as the original T-72 but has a TPD-2-49 laser range finder instead of the older coincidence range finder found on earlier versions. The gunner's sight is a passive image intensification sight, which will allow them to fire at night without artificial illumination. The T-72M1 also sports improved laminated armor and a triple stack reactive armor array. This reactive armor will defeat our antitank missiles, and our tank HEAT (high explosive antitank), but you still can take them out with tank main gun sabot rounds."

Russell looked at his tank platoon leaders as if searching for a reaction. Jaeger, Madsen, and Williams, focused on the details of Russell's briefing, made notes in their combat notebooks without any sign of emotion.

"Their BMP infantry fighting vehicles are probably BMP-2s," Russell continued. "Each BMP has a 30mm cannon and carries the AT-4 or AT-5 antitank missile. That gives the enemy a reach of about four kilometers with the AT-5, so take that into account. The BMPs are also reported to have improved appliqué armor, which makes them tougher to kill but should be no problem for our 105mm guns. One BMP has already been spotted on the eastern edge of Objective Eagle at grid coordinates LK943538. That is the only location I have right now on the enemy.

Section 1

"Doctrinally, the enemy will deploy a reinforced motorized rifle platoon approximately five kilometers forward of the motorized rifle company strongpoint. Depending on the terrain and time constraints, the Threat security zone commander will position squads ten to fifty meters apart in dug-in positions with connecting trenches. You can expect dummy positions and alternate firing positions prepared for each vehicle.

"They are usually pretty well spread out in the security zone, so there is a good chance that we can flank them and get them to move," Russell said as he paced in front of his map. "When faced with encirclement or decisive engagement, the forces of the security zone are often ordered to withdraw under cover of artillery fire and return to the main defensive area. Our job is to see that this doesn't happen.

"The Friendly Situation: Battalion will attack across Phase Line August tomorrow at 0425 to clear enemy forces up to Phase Line December. The battalion's mission is to destroy all enemy forces between these phase lines so that 2d Brigade can exploit our success and continue the attack north. Before morning nautical twilight (BMNT) starts at 0530, so we will begin the attack in the dark." Captain Russell paused to let his lieutenants observe the map. "We have Task Force 2-7 to our left and Team Charlie, Task Force 3-69, to our right.

"Mission: Alpha Company attacks 020425 June to destroy enemy forces in zone and to prevent the enemy from withdrawing past Phase Line December," Russell explained. "I want you to orient on the enemy, not the terrain. Objective Eagle is for orientation only. Seizing Objective Eagle, seizing the ground, is not necessary. My intent is to find the enemy platoon, pin it down with the supporting fires from 1st and 2d Platoons, and let 3d Platoon roll up their flank, before they can escape to the north. I want to find the enemy's flank and attack him one enemy vehicle at a time. I don't want to see any mad cavalry charges, but when you move, move fast.

"Execution:" Captain Russell paused as his lieutenants carefully scanned their maps and took notes (see Map 1). "First let me talk you through the terrain for tomorrow's attack. The ground is dominated by three key terrain features: Hill 766 (LK895503), Hill 740 (LK940880), and Hill 790 (LK960540). A deep wadi, wide enough to move at least one tank through, goes southwest to northeast in the eastern portion of the company zone. The small hill at LK935535 is designated as Objective Eagle.

4

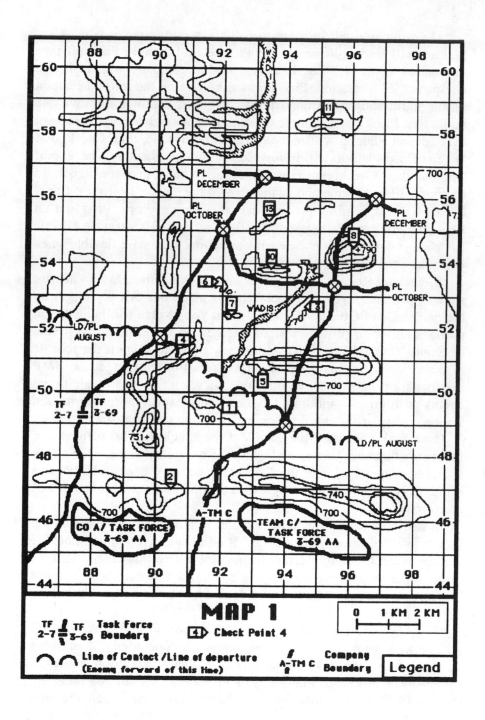

Section 1

"The company will move out of this assembly area at 0400. First Platoon will lead, followed by 2d Platoon and then 3d Platoon. Two kilometers south of Phase Line August the company will deploy to company "V" formation. First Platoon will be on the left, 2d Platoon on the right, and 3d Platoon trailing. We will continue to move due north. First Platoon will move to Checkpoint Four and then to Checkpoint Six. Second Platoon will move to Checkpoint One, then Checkpoint Seven. Third Platoon will follow 2d Platoon and occupy Checkpoint One and then Checkpoint Four, on order. When I give the signal, 3d Platoon will follow me and swing around the enemy's weakest flank, left or right, depending on how the situation develops. First and 2d Platoons will provide support fire for 3d Platoon's assault. All this can change depending on the enemy situation, so remain flexible when you plan your platoon operation.

"Lieutenant Rogers," the captain said, looking straight into his fire support officer's eyes, "I expect you to place our priority target on the north side of Objective Eagle. I want you to plan for the battalion mortar platoon to provide a smoke screen on the east and west side of Eagle. You and I will plan additional targets to support the scheme of maneuver after this briefing. Make sure that you target the BMP that battalion has identified on Eagle. If we pinpoint any additional enemy positions, I want those targeted, too. I expect more information on the enemy at the intelligence update at battalion at 0300."

The captain discussed the details of the attack with his officers and made sure that each understood what was necessary to make the attack a success. The location of the T-72 tank and the other two BMPs was critical to their attack planning. Not knowing their exact location was dangerous.

"Based on what I know now, I prefer to attack the enemy from the western side of the company zone," Russell said without emotion. "If we can avoid the rough terrain in the east where this deep wadi cuts through the company zone and can attack the enemy where he's not looking, we can gain the advantage. It all depends on finding the enemy before he finds us.

"I will be with 1st Platoon, trailing their last, far left tank. The XO will be with me on my left." Captain Russell concluded. "If anything happens to me, the XO will be in charge, then the platoon leaders in order—1st Platoon, 2d Platoon, and 3d Platoon. I want you all at my tank at 0320 for the intelligence update. After the order, the first

6

sergeant will go over the details of service support and resupply. The time is now 1346. What are your questions?"

"Sir," Jaeger asked, "do we know of any enemy mine fields or obstacles?"

"The enemy has been in position only since this morning. You can count on at least two shallow point mine fields in front of the platoon position, mostly antitank mines, for a total of about twenty mines in each mine field. We don't have a fix on any of their exact locations," Russell answered. "The battalion is sending scouts forward. If I get any more information you all will be the first to know. Good question, Jaeger, any more?"

"Yes, sir," Madsen asked with a grin. "When do we go forward to look for ourselves?"

"I'll take all of you forward in my maintenance M113 at 1600," Russell ordered. "Be here on time! I have limited space in the APC and I will only have room for platoon leaders, so don't bring anyone else. I expect to go to the high ground on the southwest side of Hill 766 (LK895504). The battalion has a scout observation post near the crest of the hill. From there we can see most of the battle area. I'll have you back at this location at 1945. Bring your maps, binoculars, and an M-16 rifle. There have been some reports of enemy dismounted patrols in the area. If we get into any trouble, I don't want to fight it out with pistols! Lastly, don't carry any written orders or map overlays with you when we go to Hill 766. Anything else?"

There were no more questions. Lieutenant Jaeger copied the commander's graphics onto his map and headed back to his tank. He was greeted by his gunner, Sgt. Tony Colwell, who was a veteran of the fighting at the Valley of Tears.

"What's the story, L. T.?" Sergeant Colwell asked eagerly.

"You were right, Colwell," Jaeger said, "we attack tomorrow. Let's get cranked up and back to the platoon. We have work to do!"

America had been at war now for two and a half months. Second Lieutenant Sam Jaeger arrived a few days after the fighting at the Valley of Tears. He had been with Alpha Company for only one week. Now he was preparing his platoon to go into battle for the first time. Events were happening so fast. Was the world really at peace only a few months ago? Those days seemed like a faraway dream.

After the battle of the Valley of Tears, replacements were rushed from the United States and units were brought up to full strength. Jaeger's 3d Platoon had been filled with some of these replacements and a smattering of veterans. Luckily, his platoon had more than its share of excellent soldiers. As Jaeger directed his tank back toward his platoon area, he mentally reviewed the personalities of the leaders in his platoon (see Diagram 1 for vehicle numbers and radio call signs).

1st Mission

Vehicle Type	Vehicle Number	Commander	Radio Call Signs
M1 TANK	A31	2d Lieutenant Sam Jaeger	R47
M1 TANK	A32	Staff Sergeant Jerry Johnson	Red 2
M1 TANK	A33	Sergeant Joseph Ramos	Red 3
M1 TANK	A34	Platoon Sergeant William Riley	Red 4
Other Important Characters			
M1 TANK	A66	Captain Kurt Russell	D20

Diagram 1

Platoon Sergeant William Riley—tank commander of A34. This tough Irish-American tanker was the heart and soul of the platoon. The men trusted him unflinchingly. He could run the platoon without a platoon leader and had been in charge of the platoon before Jaeger had joined the unit. Jaeger, fresh from the States, had yet to earn Riley's complete trust and confidence. Riley's actions over the past few days had revealed that he was still a little unsure of his "green" lieutenant's capabilities. Nevertheless, Riley had gone out of his way to assist Jaeger.

Riley had seventeen years of experience in the U.S. Army and had soldiered on every tank in the army's inventory, including the older M60 tanks, the M1 tank with the 105mm gun, and even the newer 120mm M1A1 tank. He had even served as a gunnery and tactics instructor at Fort Knox, the U.S. Army Armor Training Center. He knew his tank gunnery backward and forward and trained his platoon accordingly. He was a competent, proven professional.

Riley had joined the unit two years before the war and had been a platoon leader ever since. He had distinguished himself as a platoon leader (officers were in short supply, and units were thrown together as soon as they off-loaded from the ships) during the battle of the Valley of Tears. He had personally destroyed six enemy T-72 tanks and two enemy BTRs. He was a leader of the old style; he led by example.

Staff Sergeant Jerry Johnson—"Hot Rod" to his friends. Johnson was the tank commander of A32 and acted as Jaeger's wingman. Impulsive. Independent. Renowned for his ability to push his M1 tank to the limit of its speed capability. A hero to his crew, Johnson was a twenty-seven-year-old native of Cincinnati, Ohio. He came from a middle-class black family with no military heritage. He joined the army, over his family's objections, to get out of working in his father's grocery store. He found that he loved the army, and he enjoyed being a gunner on an M1 Abrams tank even more. He served as Platoon Sergeant Riley's gunner in the battle of the Valley of Tears, and took all the credit for the kills that they scored that day. He seemed eager to show everyone how well he could perform as a tank commander and had been vigorously training his new gunner. His loyalty to Riley was unceasing. His respect for his new platoon leader was a bit more reserved.

Sergeant Joseph Ramos—tank commander of A33. No combat experience. Ramos arrived in the unit at the same time as Jaeger, replacing a tank commander who had been wounded in battle. A sharp-looking soldier, Ramos was largely an enigma. A twenty-three-year-old native of San Juan, Puerto Rico, he had been in the army for only four years. Quiet and withdrawn, he had adapted to his new surroundings quickly and had taken good care of his three men. He was Riley's wingman, a placement that suggested that Riley wanted to keep a close eye on him. All in all, with a little training, Ramos should prove to be a good tank commander.

Sergeant Tony Colwell—gunner of A31, the platoon leader's tank. Colwell was a twenty-three-year-old, sandy-haired Californian who was the tank commander of A31 before Jaeger arrived. One of the four combat veterans in the platoon, Colwell was unflappable. A quick and intelligent soldier, Colwell was purposely picked by Riley to be the platoon leader's gunner. Riley knew that his new green lieutenant would need all the help he could get inside the turret once the action started. Colwell was the obvious choice. A weight lifter and an avid swimmer, Colwell had a personality that fit perfectly into this supporting role as Jaeger's main assistant. He looked upon this responsibility as a personal challenge, and took good care of "his lieutenant" and the other two members of the crew. The rest of the crew of A31 consisted of the driver, PFC Warren Jones, a seventeen-year-old New Yorker, and the loader, SP4 Travis Curn, of Lampasas, Texas.

The short ride in A31 from the company command post to his platoon assembly area caked Jaeger with dust from the top of his tanker's helmet (combat vehicle crew helmet, or CVC) to the pockets on his battle-dress uniform. Upon reaching his platoon, Jaeger ordered the driver to halt. He directed Colwell to take over as tank commander, drive the tank into a hide position, and then join him at Riley's tank. After giving these directions he took off his CVC, put on his Kevlar helmet, grabbed his map, and hopped off the tank. He headed in the direction of his platoon sergeant's tank, arriving there just in time to see Riley checking the maintenance reports of the other two tank commanders, under the shade of another makeshift lean-to.

"I'm glad you are all here," Jaeger said, trying to sound confident. "I just got tomorrow's mission from the old man. We will be attacking tomorrow morning."

"Johnson, Ramos! Go back and get your maps and make sure you bring a notebook. Put your gunners in charge of getting those maintenance items checked. Be back here for the lieutenant's warning order in five minutes. Now move!" Riley bellowed, and turned to wink at his platoon leader. Johnson and Ramos took off obediently, on the double.

"So what's the plan, Lieutenant?" Riley asked, looking directly at Jaeger.

"I'm not sure yet," Jaeger replied rather hesitantly. "I just received the company commander's operations order and I haven't had a chance to put together a platoon order yet."

"It's your ball game, Lieutenant," Riley reminded him. "Johnson and Ramos will be back in a few minutes. What do you want us to do?" Riley, looking a little tense, reached for his canteen to take a gulp of water.

The sun beat down. Sweat soaked the young lieutenant's battle-dress uniform. Jaeger looked at his platoon sergeant and then looked down at his watch. The air was heavy, making it hard to breathe. A pesky fly buzzed around Jaeger's head. Reacting quickly, he caught it in his right hand and vengefully put an end to its life. This tiny success, however, did not solve his problem.

Jaeger's mind wandered as he looked out at the horizon. It's already 1430. In less than one hour and thirty-five minutes I must be back at the old man's tank to go on reconnaissance. Tomorrow's battle and the lives of my men may be decided by my ability to prepare an effective platoon plan. Riley and the rest are not too sure of me. I have got to prove to them that I know how to lead this platoon. I must earn their respect if I am going to get everyone through this alive. If I hesitate, and they interpret that hesitation as fear, I will never gain their confidence. I must decide now!

Karummph! The muffled crash of distant Threat artillery punctuated Jaeger's last thought. Time was pressing and the war wouldn't wait.

If Jaeger chooses to prepare his operations order right now, to make the most of his planning time, go to Section 2.

If Jaeger delays his order preparation and asks for advice from Platoon Sergeant Riley, go to Section 3.

Section 2

Hell, Jaeger thought. I didn't spend four years in ROTC and a year training in army schools for nothing. I can handle this. Time is critical. I can't afford to waste a minute! The most important thing is to show some confidence and show everyone that I know what I am doing!

"Sergeant Riley," Jaeger ordered, "when the rest of the men get here, have them take a seat and I will have a warning order for them in five minutes. While you are waiting, get a complete report from them on our ammunition and fuel status."

"Yes, sir!" Riley grinned. "That's the ticket, Lieutenant! I always wanted a platoon leader who could take charge. But you don't have to worry about the fuel and ammunition. I personally inspected each tank just thirty minutes ago. We are all loaded, topped off with fuel, and set to go."

"Oh, of course," Jaeger muttered. "I'll be ready in a few moments."

Riley looked at his platoon leader curiously, as if waiting for additional instructions. Jaeger ignored the look and sauntered over to his tank and took a seat on a large white rock on the shaded side of A31. Sergeant Colwell, who was busy helping the crew put up the final section of their desert camouflage net, looked over at Jaeger, puzzled.

"Sir," Colwell announced, like a small puppy trying to please, "can I help you with anything?"

"No," Jaeger retorted. "I've got to get some planning done, so don't let anyone disturb me."

"Yes, sir," Colwell answered. "Meanwhile I will send Jones over to the platoon sergeant's tank to see if they have any chow for us. Do you want some?"

"No . . . no time for chow now," Jaeger replied, already consumed in his work.

Colwell shot one glance at Private Jones, and the private took off at a slow walk. Halfway to Sergeant Riley's tank, Jones picked up the pace, inspired by the muffled sound of several more artillery shells exploding five to six kilometers north of 3d Platoon's assembly area.

Jaeger mentally listed the tasks that he needed to accomplish. His mind began to stray as the thought of Colwell's offer of food registered in his busy head.

I haven't had a decent meal in forty-eight hours and I haven't had a good night's sleep since I arrived in this godforsaken place, Jaeger thought. But food will have to wait. The men are depending on me. I have got to figure out what to do!

Jaeger began writing in his notebook. The lack of any type of breeze, and the heat of the June desert sun, made this task all the more difficult. He looked at his notes, analyzed his map, and began jotting down his warning order.

The purpose of a warning order was to give his subordinates time to make the necessary plans and preparations for combat. Jaeger knew that it was critical to get the warning order out early, but he didn't want to forget anything important. After fifteen minutes of scribbling in his notebook, he walked back over to Riley's tank. There, in the shade of a tank tarp, Riley, Johnson, and Ramos were studying their maps, eating MREs, and waiting for their lieutenant.

"OK, gentlemen, here it is. Look at your maps, listen up, and take notes." Jaeger began to read his warning order to the men. "The company task organization remains the same.

"Mission: Alpha Company will attack tomorrow at 0425 to destroy enemy forces in zone," Jaeger briefed in a calm and steady voice, trying a little too hard to look confident and in control. "We can expect to be up against at least a reinforced platoon, probably three BMP-2s and one T-72 tank. Our earliest time of movement from here is approximately 0410 tomorrow morning. We will move from here in column in the following order: my tank A31, Johnson in A32, Riley in A34, and lastly Ramos in A33. After I return from the reconnaissance with Captain Russell, I will write the platoon operations order. I will issue the platoon operations order to you here after I have completed it. I want everyone to put on MOPP II prior to departure from this assembly area. I'll leave a copy of my warning order here with Sergeant Riley for you all to copy. The time is now . . . ," Jaeger paused to look down at his watch, "1515. Are there any questions?"

The tank commanders looked at each other nervously without saying a word. The thought of chemical warfare added to their unease. No one enjoyed the idea of putting on the chemical protective MOPP suits.

MOPP stands for mission oriented protective posture and involves various stages of wearing charcoal-lined chemical protective clothing, protective mask, rubber boots, and rubber gloves. The chemical protective suits are extremely hot and uncomfortable, but they are also the only protection from Threat chemical weapons. The bad guys hadn't used any chemical munitions yet, but how long they would show such .enlightened restraint was anybody's guess.

"Lieutenant," Riley announced seriously, "you need to get started on your operations order. I will take care of the rest of the details.

We will be ready for you at 2100. Give me your map and I will have all the tank commanders copy the company attack plan graphics."

"Roger that," Jaeger replied triumphantly, knowing that he had accomplished his first task. "I will be at my tank if you need me."

The time went by quickly. Jaeger used every minute to write down everything he could think of to develop a good plan. He analyzed the mission, listed all the tasks that he knew would have to be accomplished, and war-gamed several possible ways the enemy might try to defend the terrain in Alpha Company's zone of attack. His problem was tricky because, as the company assault force, he could be employed several different ways.

Jaeger wrote feverishly. The sun and the incessant buzzing of flies made it difficult to concentrate. Jaeger focused his energy and tried to visualize what the best course of action should be.

Soon it was time to go to the rendezvous with Captain Russell. Jaeger had finished the situation, mission, and most of the execution paragraph of his platoon operations order. Well, he thought confidently, the order is almost done. The reconnaissance will shed more light on the matter.

He quickly gathered up his papers and told Johnson to start the tank. Grabbing a handle on the rear deck with one hand and putting his foot on the tank sprocket, he climbed aboard his big M1. He walked over to the turret and lowered himself into the tank commander's station. Exchanging his Kevlar helmet for his CVC helmet, he checked his intercom system, made sure that the crew was ready to move, and ordered the driver to move to Captain Russell's location.

Go to Section 4.

Section 3

"Platoon Sergeant," Jaeger asked sincerely, "I need your help. What should we do first?"

"Lieutenant, I knew that you were a smart officer the moment I met you!" Riley beamed a grin from ear to ear. "The emphasis is on the *we*—this has got to be a team effort! Here is my advice: First take a few moments to collect your thoughts and backward plan your available time. Time is our most valuable resource. We can't lose a minute! Start with the crossing of the line of departure [LD] and work your way back in time to the present.

"A simple time plan will organize your actions and help us get the important things done first. If we plan well we can get ready and get everyone rested prior to tomorrow's battle. Your time line should list all the things we have to do and those things we need to coordinate with the other platoons, the company FIST, and the company commander.

"Then give us the best Armor School–style warning order you can. Take about ten minutes to prepare your warning order. In your order tell us everything you know about tomorrow's mission. Once Johnson and Ramos know what to get ready for, they can do the rest.

"I suggest that you give the warning order from up there," Riley said, pointing to the hill to the north, "on the side of Hill 722. From up there, everyone can see at least a part of tomorrow's ground. A quick look at the ground will be a valuable investment of our available time.

"While that is going on," Riley explained, "I will get my gunner, SP4 Harrison, to make us up a terrain model of our area of operations. I have spent a lot of time training him to make terrain models and he is getting pretty good at it! I'll make sure that the model is straight by the time you issue the operations order. If you have to issue the operations order in the dark, the terrain model will come in handy to help everyone visualize what you want us to do.

"Once you start preparing your operations order, write down the basic points and explain the rest. We give oral operations orders at the platoon level; *there is no time for written orders!* I'll take care of the service support paragraph; you just worry about how we are going to fight this battle and how our platoon will fit into the company's plan."

Jaeger stared in amazement, letting all this information sink into his tired brain. He truly admired Riley and was relieved to have such a well-trained platoon sergeant.

"Your order must be clear!" Riley said, pausing for emphasis. "Everyone must know exactly what to do and what everyone else is expected to do. You won't get that kind of communication by writing out long

15

plans. You have to look them in the eye, tell them, and see the lights go on in their heads to make sure they really understand. Our lives depend on that!

"I will prepare a sleep and maintenance plan to get everyone ready. I will inspect the platoon at 1900 tonight to make sure that everyone does what he is told. I'll also figure out how we will leave this assembly area, in the dark, and make it to our crossing location at the line of departure. Sergeant Johnson will prepare and mark a route in the daylight to make sure that we leave here in an organized fashion when we have to move out in the dark tomorrow morning.

"Lastly," Riley continued, "I'll send my loader, SP4 Nelson, to fetch Sergeant Colwell to attend your warning order. The platoon leader's gunner needs to be well informed. It is his job to brief your crew and get them ready. You are too busy to baby-sit them."

"Sergeant Riley," Jaeger smiled with admiration for his platoon sergeant, "if you weren't so ugly, I'd kiss you! I'll be ready with the warning order in ten minutes. See to it that everyone is here and prepared to listen."

"Wilco, Lieutenant," Riley replied, looking as though he had just adopted a new son. "Don't worry, you are not alone. We are a good platoon, and we will all be around tomorrow evening if we just do our jobs and work as a team."

With that last comment, Jaeger sat in the shade of the platoon sergeant's tank and quickly focused his entire attention on developing a time line, using a backward planning process:

TIME LINE

LIGHT DATA	TIME	ACTION	COORDINATION & PLATOON PREPARATION
		1 June	
Daylight	1500	Issue warning order	PSG & TCs start parallel planning
" "	1530	Make tentative plan	Precombat checks
" "	1545	Depart for company CP	Platoon sgt creates terrain model
" "	1600	Conduct recon with co commander	Mark routes to LD, boresight
" "	1900	Return from recon to company & coordinate artillery with FIST	TCs, observe route to LD

TIME LINE

LIGHT DATA	TIME	ACTION	COORDINATION & PLATOON PREPARATION
		1 June	
" "	1930	Return to platoon assembly area	Platoon sgt inspects platoon
Sunset	2025	Make decision & complete plan	
EENT	2100	Issue oral order with sketch map	Brief all tank commanders. Conduct briefback and rehearsal over the terrain model
40% Illum	2400	Change frequencies on all radios	As per CEOI
		2 June	
40% Illum	0320	Intelligence update at company CP	Enemy locations
40% Illum	0330	Stand-to	Start engines, muzzle ref up date
0% Illum	0340	Moon set (no illumination)	
0% Illum	0410	3d Platoon departs assembly area	25 km/hr
0% Illum	0425	Alpha Company attacks / crosses PL August	
0% Illum	0440	Approximate time that 3d Platoon crosses PL August	
BMNT	0530	Continue the attack	
Daylight	0605	Sunrise / continue the attack	
" "	1100	Approximate time to reach PL December	

Precious time slipped away. Jaeger jotted down the main points of his warning order. The broiling sun and the incessant buzzing of flies made it difficult to concentrate. Struggling through these distractions, Jaeger forced himself to deal with the task at hand.

Finally, he completed the order. Glancing at his watch he realized that he had only two minutes to spare! He was ready. Johnson, Ramos, and Colwell arrived and started studying their maps. Each tank commander copied the company graphics from Sergeant Riley's map.

Riley motioned to Jaeger and the small group started the short climb up to the vantage point on the east side of Hill 722. Jaeger led, fol-

Section 3

lowed by Riley, Johnson, Ramos, and Colwell. It took almost seven minutes to complete the climb.

"OK, men, this is far enough," Jaeger puffed, as beads of sweat streaked down his face. The hot air was heavy. Jaeger paused a few moments to catch his breath.

"From this vantage point we can see all the way to the line of departure. Let me take a few minutes to orient you to the terrain." Jaeger scanned the area with his binoculars. He pointed out to his men the key geographical features and the general layout of the battlefield.

Karrummp! Karrummp! Karrummp! Three 122mm artillery shells slammed into Hill 730, approximately five kilometers to their front.

"It looks like the bastards want us to know they are still around, Lieutenant," Riley stated.

"Yeah, they probably think someone is using Hill 730 as an observation post," Johnson said, pointing at the white-gray puffs of smoke left behind by the Threat artillery shells.

"Let's get on with it before they decide to try our hill!" Jaeger announced seriously. "Pull out your maps and listen up."

The soldiers lay on their bellies, looking down at the valley. Tomorrow's battlefield. The thought of it hit Jaeger like a jolt of electricity. Calming himself, he concentrated on the task at hand. I must set a good example for the men! Jaeger started his briefing.

"The company task organization remains the same," Jaeger said, attempting a calm and steady voice. "The company is organized as a pure tank company, four tanks per platoon with three platoons. Add the company commander's tank and XO's tank and that gives us a total of fourteen M1s. We also have three M113 APCs—one with a Stinger air defense team, one FIST-V for the FIST, and one medical evacuation vehicle . . . if they all work tomorrow morning.

"Probable Mission: Alpha Company will attack tomorrow at 0425 to destroy enemy forces in zone. Against our company we can expect at least a reinforced platoon, probably three BMPs and one or two T-72 tanks. Only one enemy BMP has been identified so far. You can't see it from here but I have posted it on my map. It is at LK943538.

"Our earliest time of movement from here is approximately 0410 tomorrow morning," Jaeger continued. "We will move from here in column in the following order: my tank A31, Johnson in A32, Riley in A34, and lastly Ramos in A33. We will follow behind 1st and 2d Platoons in a company "V" formation. We will move to traveling overwatch formation just short of the line of departure, Phase Line

18

August. The company commander's intent is to use 1st and 2d Platoons to find the enemy, then employ them as a base of fire while we maneuver as his assault force to attack the enemy's flank. I will issue the platoon operations order to you at Sergeant Riley's tank at 2100, an hour after I return from the recon with Captain Russell. I want everyone in MOPP II at stand-to. You can keep your chemical suits unzipped due to the heat until we cross the line of departure, PL August."

The tank commanders looked at each other nervously. No one enjoyed the idea of putting on the chemical protective MOPP suits. MOPP stands for mission oriented protective posture and involves various stages of wearing chemical protective gear. It was hot enough in the desert without having to wear a charcoal-lined sauna suit! Everyone had learned to wear the MOPP suit in training. As hot and uncomfortable as the suits were to wear, not a soldier in the platoon wanted to be caught in a Threat chemical attack without one.

"The time is now 1520." Jaeger looked at each of his tank commanders, the determination on his face unmistakable. "Any questions?"

"Sir, how do we plan to move from here to the line of departure, over there?" Johnson asked the lieutenant and pointed to the low ground east of Hill 730.

"Don't forget," Jaeger reminded, "we will have 1st Platoon to our left and 2d Platoon to our right. I intend to trail 2d Platoon by 400 to 600 meters and use the high ground, there," Jaeger pointed at Hill 700, "as a firing position to cover the company's move across the LD. From this point we will try to maintain the company "V" formation and use the local ground to our advantage. I'll get a better picture of how the company will attack after I get back from the reconnaissance with Captain Russell. We will cover those kinds of things, and how we'll deal with the enemy, in detail during the operations order."

Johnson nodded in approval. Ramos quickly marked his map with a grease pencil and stared at the area that Jaeger was describing. Sergeant Riley scanned the horizon to the north with his binoculars. Each of them studied the terrain with hungry eyes, searching for every bit of ground that could provide cover during tomorrow's battle.

"Anyone else have a question?" Jaeger asked, waiting for each tank commander to motion his answer.

"All right," Riley barked, "you heard the man. We're wasting daylight! I want everything combat ready by 1900. I'll be by to inspect and you had better be perfect! If you haven't got the graphics on your map, copy mine and brief your crews. I want every man to know what is going to happen. Let's get cracking!"

"Lieutenant," Riley whispered as the other tank commanders scurried down the hill, "I will make sure that everything is ready for combat. I am proud of you. You issued that warning order like a real pro. We will be ready for you at 2100."

"Thanks," Jaeger replied triumphantly, knowing that he had accomplished his first task. "I will be at my tank if you need me."

The sun was high in the sky. Jaeger and Riley walked down the hill silently, each in his thoughts. Returning to his tank, Jaeger used every minute to work on his operations order.

Soon it was time for the rendezvous with Captain Russell. Confident that he was off to a good start, Jaeger walked over to Sergeant Riley's tank and handed him a copy of the time line. Riley reviewed it and nodded with a wide grin.

"Lieutenant, you may make it yet!"

"You can count on it!" Jaeger exclaimed. "Make sure that every tank is boresighted before the sun sets. I want everyone shooting straight and true tomorrow."

"Check," Riley answered. "I've already got that scheduled."

"I'm headed for the old man's tank," Jaeger said. "I'll be back as soon as I can."

Jaeger decided to walk to Captain Russell's location, only 900 meters away, rather than take his tank. He grabbed his loader's M-16 rifle, checked the action, and stuffed two thirty-round magazines into his BDU trouser side pocket. He slung his binoculars around his neck, took his map in his free hand, and headed off in the direction of the company commander.

"We will expect you around 1930 tonight. I'll alert the OP/LPs," Riley announced as the lieutenant jaunted off. "Don't forget the password. I don't want to be responsible for getting my new lieutenant shot by one of his own sentries!"

"You sure know how to brighten up a fellow's day," Jaeger replied, cradling the M-16 in his arms. "Just make sure that the soldier on duty at the western edge of the perimeter is aware that I am on his side." Jaeger smiled and moved out to the west at a quick walk.

I think I'm getting the hang of this, Jaeger thought.

Go to Section 5.

Section 4

The commander of Alpha Company, Capt. Kurt Russell, was an impressive officer. His appearance wasn't anything extraordinary. On the contrary, he was really very normal looking. It was more the way he handled himself. He had a calm confidence that was infectious. A thoroughly professional officer, he had earned a reputation in the battalion as a tough fighter and a hard taskmaster. His personality was like a finely tuned watch—organized and set on a definite motion.

"The attack tomorrow is a deliberate attack along a narrow and rather shallow zone," Captain Russell explained to his lieutenants. "I know that most of you will be experiencing combat for the first time. Tomorrow's battle should give you a taste of what lies ahead. Stay alert and pay attention and we will beat those bastards and live to tell about it! Now, everyone in the APC."

Lieutenant Shields led Madsen, Williams, and Jaeger into the M113 armored personnel carrier. Captain Russell hopped up the front slope and squirmed down into the vehicle commander's open hatch. He quickly stowed his Kevlar helmet and put on the APC's CVC helmet. With his hands on the .50-caliber machine gun, he cocked the handle and fed the ammunition into the gun. Placing the machine gun on safe, he ordered the driver to close the M113 ramp and prepare to move. Once the ramp was closed he ordered his driver to move out. Russell shouted to his lieutenants, standing in the open hatch behind him, to hang on. Jaeger bounced hard against the side wall of the APC as the vehicle jerked forward.

The recon party traveled without incident, moving slowly to avoid creating a large dust cloud with the tracks of the APC. The lieutenants stood silently in the back of this square aluminum "taxi," scanning the desert from all sides of the vehicle. The APC moved to the south side of Hill 751 (LK895482) and, under Russell's direction, drove along the east side of the hill to a drop-off point just southeast of Hill 766.

"OK, drop the ramp!" Russell shouted at his driver as the APC jerked to a halt. "Everybody out!"

Section 4

The lieutenants ran from the rear of the M113 with M-16s in hand and took up hasty firing positions on the right side of the carrier. Captain Russell gave some quick instructions to his driver and grabbed his helmet and rifle to join the group. The driver cut the engine and took over the machine gun position in the vehicle commander's hatch, ready to support the officers with .50-caliber machine gun fire in case of trouble.

"Follow me," Russell ordered quietly. "Remember, somewhere up here is a battalion scout observation post, so don't get trigger-happy. Let's go."

Russell led the group up the hill. Jaeger was third in line and doing his very best to keep up with the hard-charging captain. How they had the nerve to call this guy the old man he would never know.

The hill was steep and the climbing was difficult. Each man carried the usual thirty pounds or so of equipment: rifle, helmet, ammunition, water, binoculars, map case, and other essentials of the trade. Everyone was sweating profusely and panting from the rigors of the climb. The captain seemed oblivious to all this and kept up a steady pace.

Finally Russell motioned silently for everyone to freeze. Jaeger clearly heard the bolt of an M16A2 rifle slam forward. They all hit the ground and took up prone firing positions.

"Peach." An unseen voice sounded off with the challenge of the day.

"Jockey," Russell answered back.

The rest of the party peered up, rifles at the ready, waiting for any false move that would signify danger.

"Advance one to be recognized," the unknown voice said.

Captain Russell moved forward and convinced the battalion scout team that was holding this little piece of the desert that they were on the same side. He then signaled for the rest of the officers to come to the vantage point.

"Sorry for the precautions, sir," a tough-looking scout sergeant said, "but we did have some visitors last night." The scout motioned to two bodies of enemy soldiers, partially covered with a poncho, lying in a dried pool of blood not fifteen feet from their positions. "I guess they thought this was a good position, too!"

"I understand, Sergeant," Russell said without emotion. "Now, daylight's a-wasting. Let's get down to business."

The platoon leaders gathered around their commander, crouching behind cover. Together they crawled to the crest of the hill to look down at the valley.

"I want 1st Platoon to move on the left, hugging the south side of the hill we are on while 2d Platoon moves along the west side of the small rise at Checkpoint One. Jaeger, I want your platoon to provide overwatch of the line of departure from that hill. As soon as 1st and 2d Platoons get to the area between the high ground at Checkpoint Four and the wadi near Checkpoint Five, you will move from overwatch to traveling overwatch. That means you follow behind us and continue to cover our ass as you move. You got that?"

"Roger, sir. What about the wadi?" Jaeger asked. "If the enemy is in there we will have a tough time getting at him."

"If they are there, we will plaster them with artillery and shoot them as they try to come up the sides," Russell said thoughtfully, pointing at the wadi with his right hand. "If necessary, I will move 2d Platoon against them, establish a base of fire, and try to maneuver you against the enemy's right flank. If that happens, the wadi will separate you from the rest of the company, but we would have them pretty well boxed in.

"Battalion thinks that the enemy will have a security outpost or a platoon position on Objective Eagle. Battalion scouts sighted that BMP there earlier this morning. From here I can see why. Eagle is the key terrain in our zone. All the other hills are too steep for use as fighting positions. Eagle offers the best defensive positions. The BMP was probably in a night firing position and has since moved back into a reverse slope hide position. That should put the main enemy strength on the east side of Eagle. Rogers, make sure you target that BMP position!"

"I already have, sir," Lieutenant Rogers said nonchalantly.

"How about air recce?" Lieutenant Madsen asked.

"Nothing for us," Russell replied. "The air force is busy fighting for the skies. Our helicopter boys are dedicated to our west, where the division is placing its main effort. We can't expect much more help. Our job is to clear out this area and be prepared to move farther north on order.

"Now I am going to draw you a quick diagram of how the enemy would defend if they do in fact have a platoon on the hill at Eagle." (See Diagram 2.)

"The enemy normally defends with each motorized rifle platoon in a strong point with three squads, dug in around their BMP-2s. Each BMP has a three-man crew—commander, a driver, a gunner—and a six-man infantry squad. The BMP-2 has a 30mm cannon and carries

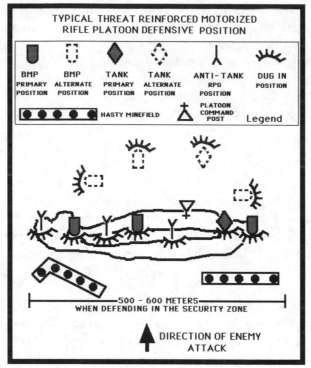

TYPICAL THREAT REINFORCED MOTORIZED
RIFLE PLATOON DEFENSIVE POSITION

BMP PRIMARY POSITION

BMP ALTERNATE POSITION

TANK PRIMARY POSITION

TANK ALTERNATE POSITION

ANTI-TANK RPG POSITION

DUG IN POSITION

HASTY MINEFIELD

PLATOON COMMAND POST

Legend

500 – 600 METERS
WHEN DEFENDING IN THE SECURITY ZONE

DIRECTION OF ENEMY ATTACK

Diagram 2

either an AT-4 Spigot man-portable missile launcher or the AT-5 Spandrel missile launcher, mounted on the BMP. The 30mm won't penetrate the armor of your M1 tank, but the Spigot and the Spandrel can cause some damage. Watch out for them! The range of the Spigot is 2,000 meters. The Spandrel has a reach of 4,000 meters.

"Each squad also will have several RPG-16s and RPG-18s with the dismounted troops. The RPG-16 has an effective range of about 500 to 800 meters. There is usually one RPG-16 per squad. The RPG-16 won't penetrate our tanks' frontal armor, but it will definitely stop you if you get hit in the track or rear. The RPG-18, much like our LAW [light antitank weapon], has an effective range of only about 200 meters. In short, we should be up against three BMPs and one or two T-72s— a possible total of eight or nine major antitank weapon systems.

"If he sets up like his doctrine reads," Russell continued, "he will disperse his BMPs 75 to 100 meters apart, with three BMPs forward.

The infantry squads dig in forward of the BMPs. The platoon commander's BMP will either be in the center of this formation or somewhere behind the others in a dug-in observation post location where he can control the battle. Any tanks will be dug into a firing position up front with the BMPs. The enemy will position their tanks along the area where they feel most threatened by enemy armor.

"The main thing I want you all to remember is that we are here to kill the enemy, not seize real estate." Russell looked as determined as if he were made of stone. "I don't give a damn if we take this hill or that. Once we find the enemy, use the ground to get the best firing positions. Then form a firing line and plaster him with fire. Once we've got him pinned, I'll move 3d Platoon against one of his flanks. If we try to take these guys on frontally, and wander into their fire sacks, they can cause us a great deal of damage.

"We don't have the luxury of having any attached infantry, so watch out for that wadi. We will use artillery and smoke to disrupt his antitank missile fire, and to kill his infantry. Remember, your greatest advantage over those bastards down there is your mobile firepower. We have got to pick him apart one vehicle at a time without becoming targets ourselves!

"Jaeger." Russell leaned over to his new lieutenant. "You are going to have to plan this just right. We have got to figure a way to flank these guys with minimal losses. Make your plan with that in mind. Don't forget, these guys may be spread out thin, but they usually have platoons to their flanks that interlock fires. Don't stray too far or you will wind up in another enemy platoon's fire sack!"

It took twenty more minutes at the OP (observation post) before everyone was satisfied that they had seen all there was to see. It took another forty-five minutes before they returned to the company assembly area.

The sun was setting. The desert had an eerie beauty about it as the sun set. The combination of relief from the oppressive heat, and the colorful pink to orange painted sky, was bewitching. On the slow ride back, Jaeger almost forgot the war . . . almost.

Back in the assembly area each platoon leader made his final coordination with the company FIST and Captain Russell before rushing back to their platoons. Russell ordered 1st and 2d Platoons to move in close together and form a night defensive perimeter. This would allow each platoon leader to be within 500 meters' walking distance to attend the early-morning intelligence update.

Section 4

Jaeger walked around in the failing light between sunset and night looking for his camouflaged tank. It appeared that his crew was a little too good at camouflage. After a ten-minute search from one position to another, he was finally challenged by Specialist Curn, his loader, who was alert and on watch. The rest of the crew, Colwell and Private Jones, were fast asleep, lying on the M1's flat engine deck.

"Colwell!" Jaeger cried angrily. "Get everyone up right now and let's get back to the platoon!"

"Ah . . . what . . . YES, SIR!" Colwell answered, rather annoyed, wiping the sleep from his eyes and nudging Private Jones. "We will be ready in a few minutes."

Jaeger and Curn quickly began tearing down the tank camouflage net as Colwell and Jones rapidly packed their gear onto the tank's bustle rack. Within minutes Jones started the tank's engine. The high-pitched whine of the turbine could be heard for quite a distance. After a confusing ten-minute night drive, Jaeger arrived back in his platoon assembly area at 2105.

Jaeger jumped off his tank and walked over to Sergeant Riley's tank. Riley, sitting under an improvised lean-to made of tank tarps and main gun cleaning staffs, looked up as Jaeger entered the covered shelter. Riley had been studying a map with his flashlight and munching on a MRE orange nut cake.

"I just got back," Jaeger announced, looking hungrily at the food that Riley was eating. "Got any MREs for a hungry platoon leader? I haven't eaten all day!"

"Sure, Lieutenant," Riley said, throwing Jaeger a brown rectangular plastic bag. "You have got to start taking better care of yourself! I inspected each tank and we are as ready as we will ever be. Ramos and Johnson have a general idea of what will happen tomorrow and are ready for your operations order. Everyone boresighted their tank main guns before sunset. How did the recon go?"

"It was good to get a look at the ground, but I don't know much more about the enemy than we did earlier." Jaeger ripped open the MRE bag and began to devour cold beef stew. It was awful, and marvelous. It was amazing how good anything could taste when you were really hungry.

"I will need some time before I'm ready to issue the operations order. Get the tank commanders together and have them stand by while I finish the order," Jaeger said between gulps of stew.

"Well," Riley said deliberately, "sit down here and do your planning. I will fetch the other tank commanders as soon as you are ready."

Time was pressing. Jaeger finished his dinner and eagerly attacked the writing of his operations order. The meal had helped renew his strength and the cool desert night was a huge relief from the heat of the day. If he could issue this order before midnight, maybe he could get some badly needed sleep. Sleep . . . the word itself tempted him like a siren. Who was it who once said, "no human knows how sweet sleep is but a soldier"? He couldn't remember.

Jaeger tried to concentrate on his map. From what he had learned from the reconnaissance, and from what Captain Russell had told him, he had the following options: (A) Attack along the right flank, hitting the enemy from east to west; (B) Attack along the left flank, hitting the enemy from west to east; (C) Attack up the center, providing overwatch, and maneuver to either flank on order of the company commander. Which way was best? Jaeger had to decide.

If Jaeger chooses Option A (Map 2), go to Section 6.

If Jaeger chooses Option B (Map 3), go to Section 8.

If Jaeger chooses Option C (Map 4), go to Section 7.

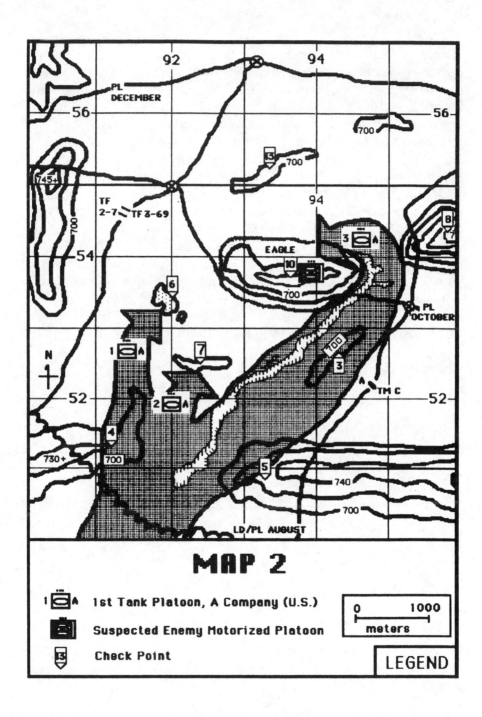

MAP 2

1 🔲A   1st Tank Platoon, A Company (U.S.)

▣   Suspected Enemy Motorized Platoon

▽   Check Point

0 ____ 1000
meters

LEGEND

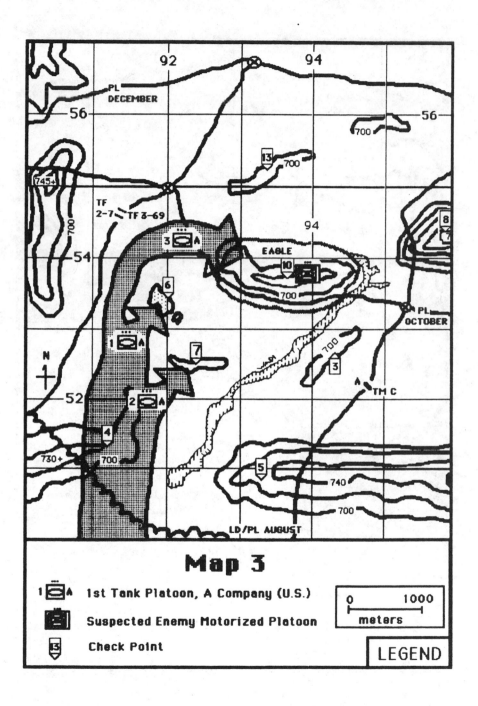

Map 3

1 ☐ A — 1st Tank Platoon, A Company (U.S.)

☐ — Suspected Enemy Motorized Platoon

🛡 — Check Point

0 — 1000
meters

LEGEND

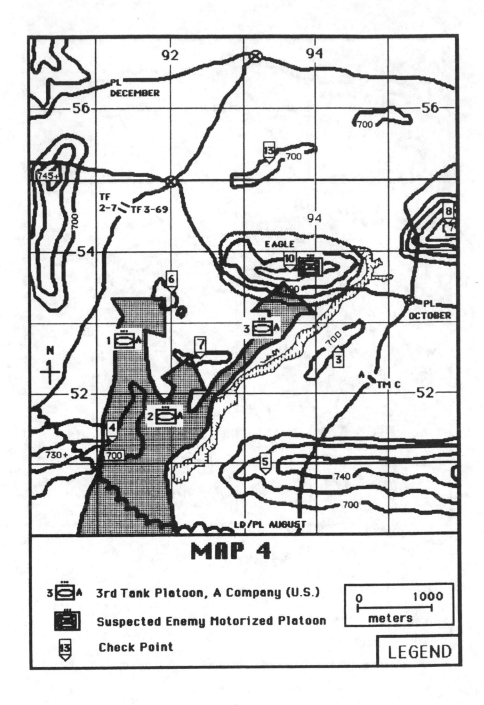

MAP 4

3 [⊞] A   3rd Tank Platoon, A Company (U.S.)

[⊞]   Suspected Enemy Motorized Platoon

[13]   Check Point

0   1000
meters

LEGEND

Section 5

Standing five feet nine inches tall, Capt. Kurt Russell, the commander of Alpha Company, was an impressive officer. What he lacked in height he more than made up for in energy. Russell had earned a reputation in the battalion during the battle of the Valley of Tears as a good tactician and a tough fighter. He was a determined commander who fought hard to get the mission done and to keep his men alive.

"Tomorrow's attack is a deliberate attack along a narrow and rather shallow zone," Captain Russell explained to his lieutenants. "I know that most of you will be experiencing combat for the first time. Tomorrow's battle should give you a taste of what lies ahead. Stay alert and pay attention and we will beat those bastards and live to tell about it! Now, everyone in the APC."

Lieutenant Shields led Madsen, Williams, and Jaeger into the M113 armored personnel carrier. Russell hopped up the front slope and squirmed down into the vehicle commander's hatch. He quickly stowed his Kevlar helmet and put on the APC's CVC helmet. With one hand on the .50-caliber machine gun firing grip, he cocked the handle, feeding the ammunition into the gun. Placing the machine gun on safe, he ordered the driver to close the M113 ramp and prepare to move.

Once the ramp was closed he ordered the driver to move out. Russell shouted to his lieutenants, who were standing in the open hatch behind him, to hang on. Too late to react, Jaeger bumped hard against the side wall of the APC as it jerked to life and headed off to Hill 766.

The recon party traveled without incident, moving slowly to avoid creating a large dust cloud with the tracks of the APC. The lieutenants stood silently in the back of their aluminum "taxi," scanning the desert from all sides of the vehicle. The APC moved to the south side of Hill 751 (LK895482) and, under Russell's direction, drove along the east side of the hill to a drop-off point just southeast of Hill 766.

The desert had an eerie beauty about it that haunted Jaeger and made his mind wander. For a minute he forgot the war.

"OK. Drop the ramp!" Russell shouted at his driver. "Everybody out!"

Section 5

The lieutenants ran from the rear of the M113, with M-16s in hand, and took up hasty firing positions on the right side of the carrier. Captain Russell gave some quick instructions to his driver and grabbed his helmet and rifle to join the group. The driver cut the engine and took over the machine gun position in the vehicle commander's hatch that Russell had just exited.

"Let's go," Russell ordered quietly. "Remember, somewhere up there is a battalion scout observation post, so don't get trigger-happy! Follow me!"

Russell led the group up the hill. Jaeger was third in line and did his best to keep up with the hard-charging captain. How they had the nerve to call this guy the old man, Jaeger didn't know.

The hill was steep. The climbing was difficult. Each man was weighed down by the usual thirty pounds or so of equipment—rifle, helmet, ammunition, canteens, binoculars, map case, and other essentials of the trade.

At last, they reached level ground. Russell motioned silently for everyone to freeze. The lieutenants hit the ground and took up prone firing positions, their M-16s pointed out in all directions.

"Peach." An unseen voice sounded off with the challenge of the day.

"Jockey," Russell answered back.

The rest of the party peered up, rifles at the ready, waiting for any false move that would signify danger.

"Advance one to be recognized," the voice said.

Captain Russell moved forward, and convinced the battalion scout team of his identity. He then signaled for the rest of his officers to come to the vantage point.

"Sorry for the precautions, sir," a tough-looking scout sergeant said, "but we did have some visitors last night." The scout motioned to two dead enemy soldiers, partially covered with a poncho, lying in a dried pool of blood not fifteen feet from their positions. "I guess they thought this was a good position, too!"

"That's perfectly all right, Sergeant," Russell said with a nod of his head. "Now, daylight's awasting! Let's get down to business.

"I want 1st Platoon to move on the left, hugging the south side of the hill we are on while 2d Platoon moves along the west side of the small rise due west of Checkpoint One. Jaeger, I want your platoon to provide overwatch as the other platoons cross the line of departure. Find a good location behind 1st and 2d Platoons where you can provide suppressive fire and still move to either flank on my order. As soon as 1st and 2d Platoons get to the area between Checkpoint Four and the wadi at LK921508, you will move from overwatch to traveling overwatch. That means you follow behind us and continue to cover our ass as you move."

"Yes, sir. What about the wadi?" Jaeger asked. "If the enemy is in there, we will have a tough time getting at him."

"If they are there, and that would offer them a couple of good keyhole shots at us," Russell said thoughtfully, "I will move 2d Platoon against them, establish a base of fire, and try to maneuver you on a firing line against the enemy's right flank. If that happens, the wadi will separate you from the rest of the company.

"Battalion thinks that the enemy will position something on Objective Eagle. Battalion scouts sighted that BMP there earlier this morning. From here I can see why. Eagle is the key terrain in our zone. All the other hills are too steep to fight from. Eagle offers the best defensive positions in our area. The BMP was probably in a night firing position and has since moved back into a reverse slope hide position. That could put the main enemy strength on the east side of Eagle. Rogers, make sure you target that BMP position!"

"Wilco," Lieutenant Rogers said nonchalantly.

"How about air recce?" Lieutenant Madsen asked.

"Nothing yet," Russell replied. "The air force is busy. We can't count on anything from them right now. Our OH-58D helicopter boys are to our west, where the division is placing its main effort. We can't expect much more help. Our job is to clear out this area with what we have.

"This is how an enemy platoon would defend if they were on Objective Eagle." Russell used a stick to make his diagram in the dirt. (See Diagram 2.) "They normally defend with each motorized rifle platoon in a strong point with three dismounted infantry squads, dug in around their BMP-2s.

"Each BMP carries nine men—commander, gunner, driver, and dismounted squad that usually has six men. The BMP-2 has a 30mm cannon, an AT-4 Spigot man-portable missile launcher, or a mounted AT-5 Spandrel missile launcher. The 30mm won't penetrate the armor of your M1 tank, but the Spigot and the Spandrel can kill you. The range of the Spigot is 2,000 meters. The Spandrel has a reach of 4,000 meters."

"That means they can engage us as soon as we cross Phase Line August," Jaeger interrupted.

"That's right, Sam," Russell said. "You're catching on pretty fast.

"Each Threat squad will have several RPG-16s and RPG-18s with the infantry. The RPG-16 has an effective range of about 500 to 800 meters. There is usually one RPG-16 per squad. The RPG-16 won't penetrate our frontal armor, but it will definitely stop you if you get hit in the flanks or rear.

"The RPG-18, much like our LAW [light antitank weapon], has an effective range of about 200 meters. In short, we could be up against as many as three BMP-2s and one or two T-72s—a total of eight or nine antitank weapon systems.

"If he sets up like he has been taught by his doctrine," Russell continued, "he will disperse his BMPs about 75 to 100 meters apart, with three BMPs forward with their squads dug in around them. The platoon commander's BMP will either be in the center of this formation or somewhere behind the others in a dug-in observation post location where the platoon leader can control the battle. The tanks will be dug into a firing position up front with the BMPs. The enemy will position their tanks along the area where they feel most threatened by enemy armor.

"The main thing I want you all to remember is that we are here to kill the enemy." Russell looked as determined as if he were made of stone. "I don't give a damn if we take this hill or that hill. Once we find the enemy, use the ground to get the best firing positions and plaster him with fire. Once we have him pinned, I'll move Jaeger's platoon against his flank. If we try to take these guys on frontally, and wander into their fire sacks, they could kick our ass. We don't have the luxury of having any attached infantry, so watch out for the wadi. We will use artillery and smoke to disrupt his antitank missile fire and to kill his infantry. Remember, your greatest advantage over the bastards down there is our mobile firepower. We have got to pick them apart one vehicle at a time!

"Jaeger." Russell leaned over to his new lieutenant. "You are going to have to plan this just right. Stay flexible . . . I'm not sure how this is going to work out. We have got to figure a way to flank these guys with minimal losses. Make your plan with that in mind."

It took twenty more minutes at the vantage point before everyone had seen all they needed to. It took another forty-five minutes before they returned to the company assembly area. The sun was setting and each platoon leader made his final coordination with the company FIST and Captain Russell before quickly rushing back to their platoons. Russell ordered 1st and 2d Platoons to move in closer for a night perimeter. This would allow each platoon leader to be within walking distance of the early-morning intelligence update.

Jaeger walked back to his platoon assembly area in the dark. He had been careful to note the azimuth from his tank to the company commander's position when he left at 1530. Now he merely applied the back azimuth on his compass, 180 degrees opposite of his original direction, and he easily found his platoon perimeter. He was correctly challenged by Private Jefferson, the loader on Sergeant Ramos's tank, who was on guard, alert and waiting for the arrival of his platoon leader.

Jaeger, M-16 rifle in hand, walked over to Sergeant Riley's tank. Riley was sitting under an improvised lean-to made of ponchos and tank tarps. Inside this covered shelter, Riley was busy studying a map with his flashlight and making final corrections on the terrain model. The time was 2055.

"Welcome back, Lieutenant," Riley greeted, looking up from his terrain model. "Everything is ready on this end. Take a seat, grab an MRE, and I'll send for the rest of the tank commanders. How did the recon go?"

"I got a really good look at the ground. We have definitely located one BMP-2 position. We are pretty sure that they have a platoon position on Objective Eagle. Eagle offers them one good firing position!" Jaeger replied as he ripped open the MRE bag and began to devour cold beef stew. "I will need about ten minutes' time to organize my thoughts."

"No problem, sir. The terrain model is ready. The tank commanders have their maps posted with the company graphics. Every tank is boresighted and I checked their precombat preparations. The route is marked with blue chem lights from the assembly area to the first checkpoint, Checkpoint Two."

"Good job, Sergeant Riley," Jaeger grinned.

Time was pressing. Jaeger finished his dinner and eagerly jotted down the major points of his plan. The meal helped renew his strength and the cool desert night was a huge relief from the heat of the day. He planned to issue an oral order, rather than waste time by producing a written operations order that no one would have time to read. If he could issue his order quickly, then he might be able get some badly needed sleep.

Sleep . . . the word itself tempted him like a siren. But he had to finish his plan, brief his platoon, and make sure that everything was ready before he dared shut his eyes. He remembered the words of John S. Mosby, the famous Confederate light cavalry leader of the American Civil War: "No human being knows how sweet sleep is but a soldier."

Jaeger studied his map and the terrain model. From what he had learned from the recon, he really had only three options: (A) Move behind 2d Platoon, provide overwatch, and attack along the right flank, possibly using the wadi, attacking enemy forces on Eagle from east to west; (B) move behind 1st Platoon, provide overwatch as directed, attacking enemy forces on Eagle from west to east; or (C) plan for both attacks and decide which option to execute after the 0320 intelligence update with Captain Russell. Which way was best? Jaeger had to decide!

If Jaeger chooses Option A (Map 5), go to Section 10.

If Jaeger chooses Option B (Map 6), go to Section 11.

If Jaeger chooses Option C (Map 7), go to Section 9.

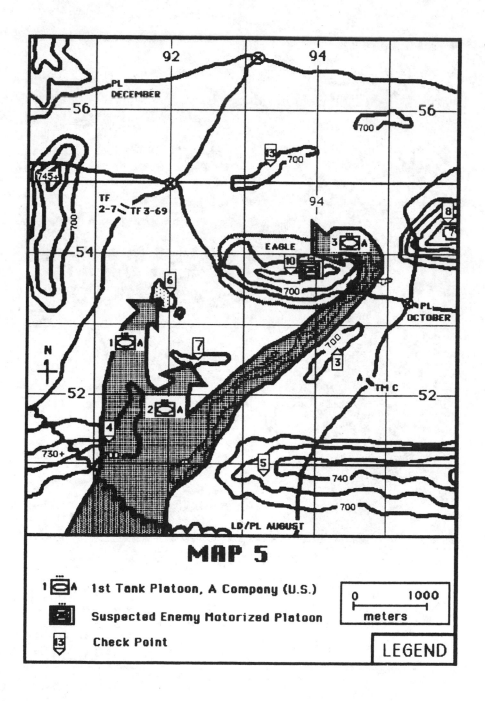

MAP 5

1 🔲 A   **1st Tank Platoon, A Company (U.S.)**

🔲   **Suspected Enemy Motorized Platoon**

🔲   **Check Point**

0   1000
meters

LEGEND

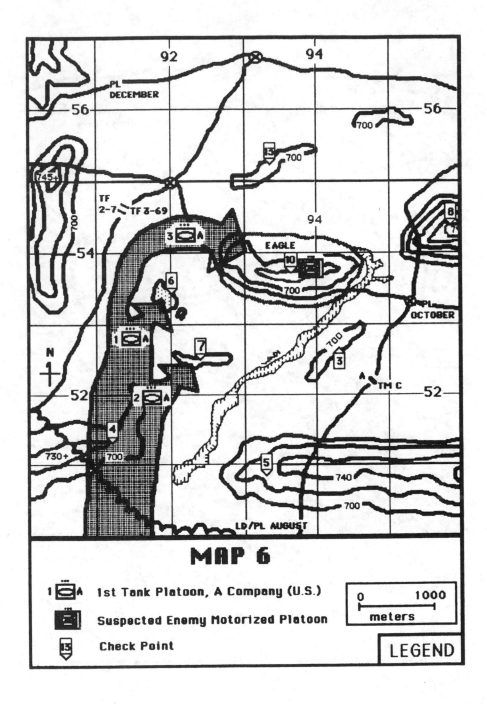

MAP 6

1 [A] 1st Tank Platoon, A Company (U.S.)

[ ] Suspected Enemy Motorized Platoon

[15] Check Point

0   1000
meters

LEGEND

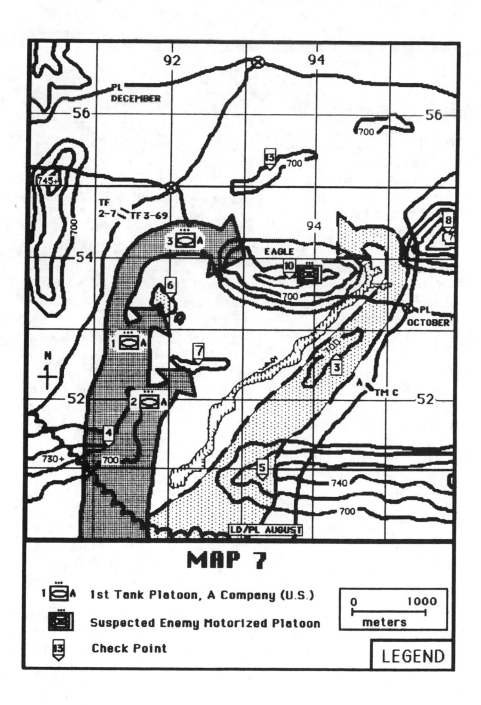

MAP 7

LEGEND

1 ⬭A   1st Tank Platoon, A Company (U.S.)

⬛   Suspected Enemy Motorized Platoon

⬇   Check Point

0   1000
meters

Section 6

The night was unnaturally quiet. Jaeger was tired. At 2310 he finished writing his order, on a specially arranged packet that he had previously made for writing operations orders. Each packet contained three carbon copies for every original he penciled. With this technique he could issue a written copy of the order to each of his tank commanders.

As soon as all the tank commanders had assembled, Jaeger began his briefing. He read each paragraph of the operations order and described the concept of the operation in great detail. He displayed his battle plan on his map with grease pencil so that his tank commanders could understand what he wanted each of them to do.

"We don't have much time," Jaeger said as he addressed his tired NCOs. "The plan is simple. As 1st and 2d Platoons move forward, we will trail behind 2d Platoon on the right. We will overwatch the company's move from Checkpoint One, then from Checkpoint Five, and then from Checkpoint Three. The assault will be made, on my order, attacking northeast and around the wadi. We will attack the enemy from east to west."

Jaeger, staring with bloodshot eyes at the dimly lit map, wondered if anyone was listening. His tank commanders had performed well during the past few days, but now they were going into combat. *If only there was more time!*

"Lieutenant, let me see if I have this straight," Riley said, marshaling his strength to stay awake. "We will follow 2d Platoon on the right, and then move around their right, on your order, to assault Objective Eagle. We will attack from east to west, and we should be faced with three BMPs and one tank."

The other tank commanders suddenly appeared to understand. Most of them had not closed their eyes for more than a few hours in the past couple of days. Riley, understanding the psychology of late-night briefings to dead-tired soldiers, knew the importance of repetition and mental reinforcement.

"That's correct," Jaeger emphasized, raising his voice slightly. "And we will have 1st and 2d Platoons providing us supporting fires during the assault."

"Let's hope they shoot straight tomorrow . . . straighter than they did at the Valley of Tears!" Johnson added sarcastically. Ramos winced and looked at his watch. Jaeger, supported by Riley, asked a few more pertinent questions, to make sure that Johnson and Ramos understood tomorrow's operation.

The briefing seemed to take forever. Jaeger finished his at 0120. The tired tank commanders finished explaining everything to their weary tank crews at 0200. Sergeant Riley put the platoon on 50 percent security and told everyone not on guard to get some sleep. Stand-to, the designated time for everyone in the platoon to be up and ready to fight, was set for 0330.

Jaeger had done all he could do. In less than two and a half hours he would be leading his platoon into battle for his first time. But now he needed to get some rest before the 0345 intelligence update with Captain Russell. Colwell had already laid out a folding cot for his exhausted platoon leader. Jaeger gladly accepted this kindness and quickly crashed into a deep sleep.

"L. T.!" Colwell shouted as he shook his platoon leader. "The old man is on the radio and wants to speak to you right now!"

"What! . . . Huh. . . . Colwell, what's going on?" Jaeger mumbled, eyes still closed, hoping that this was all just a bad dream and he would find himself back at home in Minnesota.

"The old man is on the radio and wants to speak to you right now!" Sergeant Colwell repeated. "It sounds pretty urgent, Lieutenant. You better get to the radio ASAP!"

Colwell jumped back to the tank commander's station to continue to monitor the radio. Jaeger stumbled out of his cot and groped in the darkness for his gear and helmet. Moving like a man returning from the grave, he hoisted his tired body up onto the turret of the tank and reached for the CVC helmet from Sergeant Colwell.

"Delta Four Seven, this is Romeo Two Zero. Over." Jaeger heard the familiar voice of Captain Russell in the earphones of his CVC helmet. Jaeger looked down at his watch; it was 0245.

"Romeo Two Zero, this is Delta Four Seven," Jaeger replied.

Section 6

"We have a change in plans, orders group in fifteen minutes at my location." Russell's voice was curt and to the point. "Do you understand, Delta Four Seven?"

"Roger, Romeo Two Zero. On my way. . . ."

"Colwell," Jaeger cried, "get over to Sergeant Riley's tank and wake up everyone. Tell Riley that I am going to an orders group meeting at the old man's position."

Jaeger grabbed his map and headed off into the dark in the direction of the company commander. In the distance he heard the sound of artillery explosions and the easily recognizable steady *Tungkt . . . Tungkt . . . Tungkt* of a Bradley 25mm chain gun.

Jaeger was the last of the three platoon leaders to arrive at Captain Russell's tank. Disoriented after his rude awakening, Jaeger walked around in the dark for some time. Finally, he stumbled into the company first sergeant. Sergeant Brock led him to the commander's tank. There, under another improvised lean-to, the commander was briefing his platoon leaders, using a flashlight to illuminate the map with white light.

"Glad you could make it, Jaeger," Russell said sarcastically, taking a sip from his GI-issue canteen cup. The lean-to smelled wonderfully of hot coffee. God! How I wish for a cup of hot coffee, Jaeger thought.

"I called this meeting early because the situation has changed. Let me get you up to speed. The battalion's scouts have identified an enemy tank platoon in the Charlie Company zone to our right. I've been eavesdropping on the scout platoon radio net and from what I can gather they think that the enemy has a reserve tank company somewhere in range to reinforce the enemy positions in our zone. So far it looks like the scouts have clearly identified two BMPs at LK932540 and one tank near the high-ground vicinity of LK928537.

"A scout M3 cavalry fighting vehicle got to the southeast side of Hill 790 at LK960544, found no enemy, and then hit a mine," Russell continued. "The survivors are now occupying an observation post on Hill 790 and should give us some good intelligence by daylight. From what intelligence the scouts have gathered and from other sources from higher, battalion figures that the enemy doesn't intend to withdraw their security forces into the main defensive belt.

"This means that the enemy is on Eagle with at least a reinforced BMP platoon and that they will fight until they are captured or killed. They are strong on the western portion of Eagle. We know where two

BMPs and one tank are. We will have to find the other BMP." Russell paused, giving everyone time to follow him on the map.

"I don't like this situation any more than the rest of you," Russell said solemnly. "Damn it! If only the enemy had been sighted earlier. If we go the way we have planned we probably will drive right into the center of an enemy fire sack!"

Russell stopped talking. The air was tense as the officers grouped around the map and waited for his decision. Seconds passed and no one said a word. Russell sat silently, studying the map.

"We don't have a choice. We have to change our plans. Madsen, move out at 0350. Williams, you follow with 2d Platoon. Jaeger, you follow behind 2d Platoon. Their main strength is on the left. According to what the scouts report, we should flank them to the right, where they are the weakest. I want 1st Platoon to provide support fire from Checkpoint Five, while I move 2d and 3d Platoons forward to Checkpoint Three.

"Williams," Russell said, pointing at the 2d Platoon leader, "I want you to drop off at Checkpoint Three, form a firing line, and fire on Objective Eagle from there. Give me everything you have."

Williams nodded.

"Jaeger," Russell paused for added emphasis, "you will then come with me as we swing around them from the northeast and clear their positions from east to west.

"We may have to dig them out one by one. I hope to avoid this by assaulting their flank and making them move to alternate positions," the tired company commander said. "If they start to move out of their holes, then we have them. The point here is to deny them the use of their prepared positions and to make them fight us in the open as they move to alternate positions. I will provide smoke and artillery fire on Eagle before we cross the LD.

"The enemy may try to counterattack us," Russell continued, his lieutenants somewhat dazed by the quickness of his decision to change plans one hour before the attack. "If he counterattacks, he will most likely hit us with his entire reserve tank company. If you see dust trails moving from the north, call me ASAP! Battalion has a FASCAM artillery mine field available. I've planned for it, and we may have a chance to get it if we have a good target. Brief your men and make sure that you are ready. The time is now 0330. Any questions?"

There was another long, quiet pause. There were no questions. Who had time for questions? Time was pressing. So much to do!

Jaeger, wearing his chemical protective clothing, hot, tired, and scared, was deep in thought. They would be in battle in a few minutes. The enemy lay waiting for them only eleven kilometers away. His life, and the lives of his men, would depend on how he reacted in the next few hours.

"OK, then," Russell said, sensing their apprehension. "You will all do fine. Trust in your training and use the ground well. Let's take them out one at a time. Get back to your platoons and stay on the radio net. Let's go!"

Go to Section 13.

Section 7

Jaeger was tired. He squinted as he tried to read the map under the dim light provided by his small, blue-filtered flashlight. At 2310 he finished his operations order. Ingeniously he had made three detailed carbon copies. Each tank commander would get a written copy to study with his crew.

Jaeger described each paragraph of the operations order and read the concept of the operation in great detail. He displayed his battle plan on his map with thick grease pencil lines. His tank commanders crowded over his shoulder to see the map as best they could.

The plan was simple. He based it on the speed and on-the-move firing capability of the M1 tank. As 1st and 2d Platoons moved forward, Jaeger's platoon would trail between 1st Platoon on the left and 2d Platoon on the right. He would provide overwatch of the company's move across Phase Line August from the short halt, and then continue in traveling overwatch in the center rear of the company "V". The assault could be made, on order of Captain Russell, by moving around either flank as 1st and 2d Platoons laid down a base of fire. All his platoon would have to do was to follow the leader and do as he did.

Jaeger finished his briefing at 0120. The tank commanders finished briefing their crews at 0200. Sergeant Riley put the platoon on 50 percent security and told everyone to get some sleep. Stand-to, the time when everyone in the platoon was expected to be up and ready to fight, was set at 0330.

Jaeger had done all he could do. In less than two and a half hours he would be leading his platoon into battle for the first time. Now he needed to get an hour or so of rest before the intelligence update at 0345 with Captain Russell. Colwell laid out a folding cot for the tired platoon leader and Jaeger gladly accepted this kindness and quickly crashed into a deep sleep.

"L. T.!" Colwell shouted as he shook his platoon leader. "The old man is on the radio and wants to speak to you right now!"

"What!.. Huh.... Colwell, what's going on?" Jaeger mumbled, eyes still closed, hoping that this was all just a bad dream and he would find himself back at home in Minnesota.

"The old man is on the radio and wants to speak to you right now!" Sergeant Colwell repeated. "It sounds pretty urgent, Lieutenant. You should get to the radio ASAP!"

Colwell jumped back to the tank commander's station to continue monitoring the radio. Jaeger stumbled out of his cot and groped in the darkness for his gear and helmet. Moving like a zombie, he hoisted his tired body up onto the turret of the tank and reached for the CVC helmet from Sergeant Colwell.

"Delta Four Seven, this is Romeo Two Zero. Over." Jaeger heard the familiar voice of Captain Russell in the earphones of his CVC helmet. Jaeger looked down at his watch: 0245.

"Romeo Two Zero, this is Delta Four Seven," Jaeger replied.

"We have a change in plans, orders group in fifteen minutes at my location," Russell said in a curt voice. Russell then acknowledged that Jaeger heard and understood the message and signed off the air.

"Colwell," Jaeger cried, "get over to Sergeant Riley's tank and get everyone up and ready to move. Tell Riley that I am going to the old man's position for an orders update." Jaeger grabbed his map and headed off into the dark in the direction of the company commander's night command post. In the distance Jaeger heard the sound of artillery explosions and the easily recognizable steady *Tungkt . . . Tungkt . . . Tungkt* of a Bradley 25mm chain gun.

Jaeger was the last lieutenant to arrive at Captain Russell's tank. He was a sorry sight. Unshaven, bleary eyed, and crumpled, he walked around in the dark for some time. Finally, he stumbled into the company first sergeant. Sergeant Brock took the young lieutenant in tow and led him to the meeting place. There, under another improvised lean-to, the commander was briefing his platoon leaders.

"Glad you could make it, Jaeger," Russell said sarcastically, taking a sip of coffee from his GI-issue canteen cup. The small lean-to smelled wonderfully of hot coffee. God! How I wish for a cup of hot coffee, Jaeger thought.

"I called this meeting a few minutes early in order for you to have more time to brief your men. Let me get you up to speed. The battalion's scouts think there is a tank platoon in the Charlie Company zone to our right. I've been eavesdropping on the scout platoon radio net and from what I can gather that probably means the enemy has a reserve tank company in range to reinforce the enemy in our zone. So far it looks like the scouts have clearly identified two BMPs at grid coordinates LK932540 and one tank near the high-ground vicinity of Objective Eagle at LK928537. A scout M3 cavalry fighting vehicle got to the southeast side of Hill 790 at LK960544, found no enemy, but then hit a mine. The survivors are now occupying an observation post on Hill 790 and should give us some good intelligence once it is daylight. From what intelligence the scouts have gathered and from other sources from higher, battalion figures that the enemy doesn't intend to withdraw their security forces into the main defensive belt.

"This means that the enemy is on Eagle with at least a reinforced BMP platoon and that they may fight until they are captured or killed. They are strong on the western portion of Eagle. We know where two BMPs and one tank are. We will have to find the other BMP. They also have a fairly extensive mine field located just north of Checkpoint Six." Russell paused for everyone to follow him on the map.

"I don't like this situation any more than the rest of you," Russell said solemnly. "Damn it! If only the enemy had been sighted earlier.

If we go the way we have planned we could land right in the center of an enemy fire sack!"

Russell stopped talking. The air was tense as the officers crouched around the crowded map and waited for his decision. Seconds passed. No one spoke.

"We don't have a choice," Russell said, breaking the heavy silence. "We have to change our plans. Madsen, move out at 0350. Williams, you follow with 2d Platoon. Jaeger, you follow behind 2d Platoon. According to what the scouts reported, we can flank them to the right, where they are the weakest. Their main strength is on the left. I want 1st Platoon to provide support fire from Checkpoint Five, while I move 2d and 3d Platoons forward to Checkpoint Three.

"Williams," Russell said, pointing at the 2d Platoon leader, "I want you to drop off at Checkpoint Three, form a firing line, and provide fire on any enemy you see on Objective Eagle. Give me everything you have." Williams nodded.

"Jaeger," Russell paused for added emphasis, "you will then come with me as we swing around the enemy from the northeast and clear their positions from east to west. We will have to dig them out one by one. If they start to move after we have flanked them, then they are ours. The whole point here is to deny them the use of their prepared positions and make them fight us in the open as they move to alternate positions. I will provide smoke and artillery fire on Eagle before we cross the LD.

"The enemy probably will try to counterattack us," Russell continued, his lieutenants somewhat dazed by the quickness of his decision to change plans one hour before the attack. "If he counterattacks, he will most likely hit us with his reserve tank company as soon as he finds out where we are coming from. If you see dust trails moving from the north, call me ASAP! Battalion has a FASCAM artillery mine field available, and we may have a chance to get it if we have a good target. Brief your men and make sure that you are ready. The time is now 0330. Any questions?"

There was a long, quiet pause. There were no questions, but the tension was obvious. Time was pressing, and now the plan had changed. So much yet to do! Jaeger, wearing his chemical protective clothing, was hot, tired, and scared. The enemy lay waiting for him only eleven kilometers away. He would be in battle in a few minutes, and his life and the lives of his men would depend on how he acted in the next few hours.

"OK, then," Russell said, sensing their apprehension. "You will do fine. Trust in your training, use the ground well, and we will take them out one at a time. Get back to your platoons and stay on the radio net. Let's go!"

Go to Section 14.

Section 8

Of the three possible options, Jaeger felt certain that the left flank attack held the best chance for success. The ground on the west side was more open and better suited to armor than in the east. The eastern part of the company's zone was dominated by Hill 790. In addition, the wadi that cut the company zone in half could be a real obstacle. Jaeger decided to base his plan on attacking the enemy from west to east.

The night was filled with an eerie silence, as if nature had forced a temporary truce on the desert. The occasional machine gun bursts and artillery explosions he had heard earlier were gone. Maybe everyone was asleep, Jaeger mused to himself.

Thankful for the respite and enjoying the relative coolness of the desert night, Jaeger planned his operations order. He wrote carefully and finished his task at 2330. Ingeniously he had made three copies of his order by using carbon paper, a trick he had learned at the Armor Officers' Basic Course. Each tank commander would now have a written copy of the order to study with his crew.

At 2345, the weary tank commanders assembled for the operations order under Sergeant Riley's makeshift tent. Jaeger recited his detailed order, step by step. He explained the concept of the operation in great detail. He displayed the drawing of his battle plan on his map. His tank commanders crowded over his shoulder to see the map as best they could.

The plan was simple. They would leave their present position, hugging the side of Hill 766 and trailing behind Lieutenant Madsen's 1st Platoon. The platoon would then maneuver from Checkpoint 4 to Checkpoint 6, providing overwatch at each position for the company. On the company commander's order, the platoon would then assault north and then east to sweep Eagle of enemy forces.

Ramos began to nod off as Jaeger continued explaining the concept.

"Stay awake and pay attention," Riley bellowed.

Jaeger finished his briefing at 0135. His tank commanders, in turn, finished briefing their crews by 0200. Sergeant Riley put the platoon on 50 percent security and told everyone to get some sleep. Stand-to, the time designated for everyone in the platoon to be up and ready to fight, was set for 0330.

Jaeger had done all he could do. In less than two and a half hours he would lead his platoon into battle for the first time. At least his tired men would get an hour or so of much needed sleep. It wasn't enough, but it was all they were going to get. Sleep was as critical now as ammunition. A tired platoon would make too many mistakes.

Jaeger needed to get some rest before the 0320 intelligence update with Captain Russell. Riley had slept earlier and volunteered to stay alert while the lieutenant rested. Colwell had already laid out a folding cot for his tired platoon leader. Jaeger laid down on the cot, under the cool desert sky, with only a poncho liner for cover, and fell instantly asleep.

"L. T.!" Colwell shouted as he shook his platoon leader. "The old man is on the radio and wants to speak to you right now!"

"What . . . huh . . . ?" Jaeger couldn't believe this was happening. It had seemed only seconds ago that he had lain his tired body down to catch some rest. "Doesn't that guy ever sleep?" he muttered out loud, shaking off his weariness and steadying himself as he stumbled out of his warm cot.

Colwell jumped back to the tank commander's hatch to continue to monitor the radio. Jaeger staggered to his feet and groped in the darkness for his gear and helmet. Moving like a zombie returning from the grave, he hoisted his tired body up onto the turret of the tank and reached for the CVC helmet from Sergeant Colwell. Shivering in the cold desert air of the pitch-black night, he wondered if he was ready for battle. A chill raced down his spine as he placed the helmet on his head and adjusted the microphone.

"Delta Four Seven, this is Romeo Two Zero. Over." Jaeger heard the familiar voice of Captain Russell in the earphones of his CVC helmet. Jaeger looked down at his watch; it was 0255.

"Romeo Two Zero, this is Delta Four Seven," Jaeger replied, trying to sound alert.

"We have a change in plans, orders group in fifteen minutes at my location," Russell said, short and to the point. Russell then acknowledged that Jaeger heard and understood the message and signed off the air.

"Colwell," Jaeger took off his CVC helmet and whispered to his gunner, "get over to Sergeant Riley's tank and get everyone up. Tell Riley that I am going to an orders group meeting at the old man's position. As soon as I get back I will need to see all the tank commanders." Jaeger grabbed his map and headed off into the dark in the direction of the company commander's position. In the distance he heard the fresh sound of artillery explosions and the easily recognizable steady *Tungkt . . . Tungkt . . . Tungkt* of a Bradley 25mm chain gun.

Jaeger was the last lieutenant to arrive at Captain Russell's tank. He was a sorry sight. Unshaven, bleary eyed, and crumpled, he had walked around in the dark for some time and had finally stumbled into the company first sergeant, who led him to the commander's tank. There, under another improvised lean-to, the commander was briefing his platoon leaders over a map using flashlights for illumination.

"Glad you could make it, Jaeger," Russell said sarcastically, taking a sip of coffee from his GI-issue canteen cup. The smell of coffee filled Jaeger's tired senses. How wonderful it smelled. God! How I wish for a cup of hot coffee, Jaeger thought.

"I called this meeting a few minutes early in order for you to have more time to brief your men. Let me get you up to speed. The battalion's scouts have identified a tank platoon in Team Charlie's zone to our right. I've been eavesdropping on the scout platoon radio net and from what I can gather that means that the enemy has a counterattack force, possibly with as many as thirteen tanks, in range to reinforce the enemy in our zone. So far it looks like the scouts have clearly identified two BMPs at grid coordinates LK932540 and one tank near the high-ground vicinity of Objective Eagle at LK928537. A scout M3 cavalry fighting vehicle got to the southeast side of Hill 790 at LK960544, found no enemy, but then hit a mine. The survivors abandoned their vehicle and are now occupying an observation post on Hill 790. They should give us some good intelligence once it is daylight. From what the scouts have gathered, and from other sources from higher, battalion figures that the enemy doesn't intend to withdraw their security forces into the main defensive belt.

"This means that the enemy is on Eagle with at least a reinforced BMP platoon and that they may fight until they are captured or killed. They have a fairly extensive mine field located just north of Checkpoint Six. They are, therefore, strong on the western portion of Eagle. We know where two BMPs and one tank are. We will have to find the other BMP." Russell paused for everyone to follow him on the map.

"I don't like this situation any more than the rest of you," Russell said solemnly. "Damn it! If only the enemy had been sighted earlier. If we go as planned we could drive right into the center of an enemy fire sack!"

Russell stopped talking. The air was tense as the officers crouched around the map and waited for his decision. Seconds passed and no one spoke.

"We don't have a choice," Russell said finally, breaking a long silence. "We have to change our plan. Madsen, move out at 0350. Williams, you follow him with 2d Platoon. Jaeger, you follow behind 2d Platoon. According to what the scouts report, we should flank them to the right, where they are the weakest. Their main strength is on the left. I want 1st Platoon to provide support fire from Checkpoint Five, while I move 2d and 3d Platoons forward to Checkpoint Three.

"Williams," Russell said, pointing at the 2d Platoon leader, "I want you to drop off at Checkpoint Three, form a firing line, and provide suppressive fire on any enemy you observe on Objective Eagle. Give us everything you have."

Williams nodded.

"Jaeger," Russell paused for added emphasis, "you will then come with me as we swing around them from the northeast and clear their positions from east to west. We may have to dig them out one by one. If they start to move after we flank them, then they are ours. The whole point here is to deny them the use of their prepared positions and make them fight us in the open as they move to alternate positions. I will provide smoke and artillery fire on Eagle before we cross the LD.

"The enemy may try to counterattack us," Russell continued, his lieutenants somewhat dazed by the quickness of his decision to change plans one hour before the attack. "If he counterattacks, he will most likely hit us with his reserve tank company as soon as he figures out where we are coming from. If you see dust trails moving from the north, call me ASAP! Battalion has a FASCAM artillery mine field available, and we may have a chance to get it if we have a good target. Brief your men and make sure that you are ready. The time is now 0330. Any questions?"

There was a long, quiet pause. There were no questions, but you could hear, almost feel, the panic in the air. Time was pressing. The plan had changed and there was so much to do!

Jaeger, wearing his chemical protective clothing, was hot, tired, and scared. He would be in battle in a very short time. The enemy was only eleven kilometers away. His men depended on him to make the right decisions. Was he ready? Could anyone ever really be ready to go to war?

"OK, then," Russell said, sensing their apprehension. "You will all do fine. Trust in your training and use the ground to your advantage. Take advantage of that M1 tank that we have been bragging about for so long. Brief your people quickly and keep 'em calm. Get back to your platoons and stay on the radio net. Let's go!"

Go to Section 12.

Section 9

"I don't have enough information on the enemy to develop just one course of action," Jaeger said as he looked at the terrain model that Sergeant Riley had so painstakingly created.

"The commander wants to hit the enemy in their weakest spot and then drive that advantage against their prepared defenses. To support the commander's intent, I will have to develop two courses of action and prepare everyone for both. The commander's intent must guide my planning."

"It seems, Lieutenant, that you have already figured this one out," Riley said with a smile. "We will have to develop a plan that we can change at the last moment to assault from the east flank or the west flank. It all depends on where the reconnaissance finds the enemy."

"This is it, then," Jaeger announced confidently, stabbing at his map with his flashlight (see Map 7). Get everyone together and I will issue the order."

The night was unnaturally quiet. At 2110 Jaeger was finished writing down the main points of his operations order. He used the terrain model that Sergeant Riley had ordered to be made. The terrain model was worth a thousand words. Eagerly his tank commanders listened to their lieutenant show them how they would leave their present position, and conduct one of two different attacks based upon where the enemy actually was.

The concept was simple: You had to understand that the enemy had a mind of his own. Jaeger knew that it was a process of seeing your options, creating new options, and shifting rapidly among those options as the situation changed.

"The enemy situation is always changing," Jaeger started his briefing to his tank commanders as they watched him move them across the battlefield on the terrain model. "The enemy will do what he wants to do, not what we want him to do. We, therefore, must plan based upon the enemy . . . and where he will be tomorrow morning, not where he is now. This means that we will have to plan two courses of action for tomorrow's attack.

"First the left flank attack." Jaeger traced a move along the terrain model with a stick. "We will depart the assembly area at approximately 0413, after the last tank in 1st Platoon leaves. We will then move north, hugging the side of Hill 766 and trailing behind Lieutenant Madsen's 1st Platoon. First Platoon will then maneuver from Checkpoint Four to Checkpoint Six. We will stay 400 meters behind them, providing overwatch. The company commander will fire artillery and smoke on Objective Eagle at 0435. Second Platoon, on our right, will move to Checkpoint Seven and provide support fire on enemy positions that

53

are identified on Objective Eagle. First Platoon, in front of us, will move to Checkpoint Six and provide support fire from there. On order, we will move to the northwest, around 1st Platoon, and attack the enemy on Eagle from west to east.

"If we attack the right flank," Jaeger continued, the eager eyes of his soldiers peering up at him, "we will merely reverse this plan. Again, we will depart the assembly area at approximately 0413, after the last tank in 1st Platoon leaves. As 1st and 2d Platoons move forward, we will trail behind 2d Platoon on the right. We will overwatch the company's move and trail 400 meters behind 2d Platoon. Second Platoon will then move to provide support fire from somewhere near Checkpoint Five. First Platoon will then continue and provide support fire from Checkpoint Three. We will then continue northeast and assault through Eagle from east to west.

"Seizing Objective Eagle is not important," Jaeger emphasized. "Getting the enemy to leave their prepared defenses is the key. If we can attack him where he is not prepared, we should knock him out as he begins to move. In either case, after the enemy is cleared from Eagle, we must reconsolidate quickly and take up hasty defensive positions in preparation for any enemy counterattack."

By seeing the terrain model, the tank commanders could visualize their mission. Jaeger and Riley drilled each tank commander on his duties concerning the attacks and asked them a series of "what if" questions to ensure their understanding. Sergeant Riley and Jaeger were working together like a well-oiled machine. Jaeger then walked each tank commander through the action, covering both options, until everyone clearly understood what was expected.

Jaeger finished his briefing at 2230. The tank commanders finished briefing their tired crews by 2300. Most of these soldiers had not slept more than four hours in the past two days. Sergeant Riley put the platoon on 50 percent security and told everyone to get some sleep. Stand-to, the designated time when everyone in the platoon was expected to be up and ready to fight, was set for 0330.

Jaeger had done all he could do. In less than four and a half hours he would be leading his platoon into battle for the first time. At least the weary soldiers of 3d Platoon would get two to three hours of much needed sleep. Sleep was as critical now as ammunition. A tired platoon would make too many mistakes.

Jaeger himself needed to get an hour or so of rest before the 0320 intelligence update with Captain Russell. Riley had slept earlier and would stay alert while his lieutenant rested. Colwell laid out a folding cot for the tired platoon leader and Jaeger gladly accepted this kindness. With Sergeant Colwell alert, standing guard, the young lieutenant quickly crashed into a deep sleep.

"L. T.!" Colwell shouted as he shook his platoon leader. "The old man is on the radio and wants to speak to you right now!"

"What . . . huh. . . . Doesn't that guy ever sleep?" Jaeger muttered out loud, half unconscious. "Tell him I will be right there."

Half dressed, Jaeger stumbled out of his cot like a drunken cripple. Regaining his senses, he climbed up onto the turret of his tank. Shivering in the cold desert air, he wondered about the reality of war in the pitch-black desert night, dreaming about what it would be like to be warm and rested. He reached for his CVC helmet from Sergeant Colwell, placed the helmet on his head, and adjusted the microphone.

"Delta Four Seven, this is Romeo Two Zero. Over." Jaeger heard the familiar voice of Captain Russell in the earphones of his CVC helmet. Jaeger looked down at his watch; it was 0255.

"Romeo Two Zero, this is Delta Four Seven," Jaeger replied.

"We have a change in plans, orders group in fifteen minutes at my location," Russell said in a curt voice. Russell then acknowledged that Jaeger heard and understood the message before signing off the air.

"Colwell," Jaeger cried, "get over to Sergeant Riley's tank and wake up everyone. Tell him I am going to an orders group meeting at the old man's position." Jaeger grabbed his map and headed off into the dark in the direction of the company commander's tank. In the distance he heard the sound of artillery explosions and the easily recognizable steady *Tungkt . . . Tungkt . . . Tungkt* of a Bradley 25mm chain gun.

Jaeger had noted the azimuth to the company CP earlier, and quickly found his way to Russell's tank. He arrived there in about six minutes and met the company first sergeant, "Wild Bill" Brock, standing outside the improvised shelter.

Brock offered Jaeger a hot cup of coffee and led him into the commander's lean-to. Eagerly, Jaeger took the coffee and downed a gulp of the hot liquid. He held the warm canteen cup lovingly, savoring every sip. The caffeine revived him after his short but deep sleep, bringing his body and mind to full alert status. Jaeger mused that few people back home would understand the luxury of a hot cup of coffee, served in a metal cup, and consumed as if it were your last.

Jaeger let his eyes adjust to the dim lighting of the commander's lean-to. The makeshift tent wasn't very roomy, and you had to crouch or sit to avoid hitting the ceiling. But the lean-to served as an excellent briefing tent where the commander could use white light to illuminate the map of the area of operations. The purpose of the lean-to was to provide the company commander a place to brief his officers without giving away the position to the enemy.

As Jaeger entered the lean-to, Captain Russell was briefing Lieutenant Rogers (company FIST) and Lieutenant Shields (company XO) over a map using a blue-filtered flashlight.

"Jaeger, come over here and take a seat," Russell said, motioning to the ground next to his tank track. "The others will be here shortly." Soon Madsen and Williams arrived and took up a position opposite their commander. The group included all the platoon leaders, the company XO, the first sergeant, the FIST, and the company medic NCO. The air inside the lean-to was warmed by the addition of these men. The smell of coffee, human sweat, and dirt was thick in the cramped confines, where each leader was only inches away from the other.

All this somehow reminded Jaeger of the days when he and his father had gone deer hunting in the woods near his home in Minnesota. He had spent many a cold night in a cramped deer stand with his Dad, waiting for an unsuspecting deer to walk by. But this was not a deer hunt, and Minnesota was another world away.

"I called the intelligence update a few minutes early in order for you to have more time to brief your men," Russell started off, taking a sip of steaming coffee from his metal canteen cup.

"Let me get you up to speed. The battalion's scouts have identified a tank platoon in the north of Charlie Company's zone, moving somewhere off to our right. I've been eavesdropping on the scout radio net and from what I can gather this means that the enemy has a reserve tank company five to seven kilometers northeast of Checkpoint Seven. That puts them in range to counterattack in our zone." The platoon leaders stared at their commander's map, marking their maps as he spoke.

"In addition," Russell said, raising his voice for added effect, "a scout M3 cavalry fighting vehicle got to the southeast side of Hill 790 at LK960544. He reported no enemy on Hill 790. Unfortunately, the scout hit a mine on the northeast side of Hill 790 and lost his track. The survivors are now occupying an observation post on Hill 790 and should give us some good intelligence once it is daylight.

"Now," Russell continued, "here is the picture in our zone. From what intelligence the scouts have gathered, and from other sources from higher, battalion figures that the enemy doesn't intend to withdraw its security forces into the main defensive belt.

"This means that the enemy is on Eagle with at least a reinforced BMP platoon and that they will fight until they are captured or killed. They appear to have a fairly extensive mine field located just north of Checkpoint Six. They are, therefore, strong on the western portion of Eagle.

"I don't like this situation any more than the rest of you," Russell said solemnly. "Damn it! If only the enemy had been sighted earlier. If we go the way we had planned we could be attacking right into the center of their fire sack!"

Russell stopped talking. The air was tense as the officers crouched around the map and waited for his decision. Seconds passed and no one spoke.

"We don't have a choice. We have to change our plans. We know where two BMPs and one tank are. We will have to find the other BMP. We will have to change our plan to attack them in the east.

"Madsen," Russell faced his lieutenant, pausing to let everyone follow him on their maps, "move out from this assembly area at 0350. At twelve miles per hour you should cross the LD at exactly 0425. Williams, you follow with 2d Platoon. Jaeger, I want you to follow behind Williams. According to what the scouts report, we should flank them to the right. The east side of Eagle is where they are the weakest. Their main strength, one T-72 and two BMPs, is on the western side of Eagle. I want 1st Platoon to provide suppressive fire from Checkpoint Five, while I move 2d and 3d Platoons forward to Checkpoint Three.

"Williams," Russell said, pointing at the 2d Platoon leader, "I want you to drop off at Checkpoint Three, form a firing line, and provide suppressive fire on anything that lives on Objective Eagle. Give me everything you have."

Williams nodded.

Section 9

"Jaeger." Russell looked Jaeger straight in the eye, as if looking for any sign of hesitation from his newest platoon leader. "You are the main effort. You will come with me as we swing around Eagle from the northeast and clear the Threat positions from east to west. We may have to dig them out one by one. We will have one critical advantage. If they move, we will kill them as they leave their holes. If they don't move, you can shoot them in the ass because their positions are oriented to the south. Don't forget, we are flanking them to make them move out of their holes! If they start to move after we have flanked them, then we have them. As they move, I expect 1st and 2d Platoons to smash them with accurate main gun fires. The whole point here is to deny the bad guys the use of their prepared positions and make them fight us in the open as they move to alternate positions or try to withdraw. I will provide smoke and artillery fire on Eagle before we cross the LD.

"The enemy may try to counterattack us," Russell continued, his lieutenants somewhat dazed by the quickness of his decision to change plans one hour before the attack. "If the enemy counterattacks, they will most likely hit us with their reserve tank company as soon as they find out where we are. If you see dust trails moving from the north, call me ASAP! Battalion has a FASCAM artillery mine field available, and I have planned two possible targets for it with the FIST. We may get a chance to use it if we have a good target. Brief your men and make sure that you are ready. Check your CEOIs and frequencies before you leave. The time is now 0330. Any questions?"

"Sir," Jaeger asked, unfolding his map. "I request permission to get with the FIST and plan a few more artillery targets behind and to the northeast of Eagle. With a good smoke screen, we can isolate any enemy on Eagle, and cut him off from his support to the north."

"Good. Rogers, see to it and show me what you come up with for final approval," Russell answered, grinning slightly as if he was now convinced that he had picked the right platoon leader for the assault force. "Any other questions?"

There was a long, quiet pause. There were no questions, but you could hear the gears working in each leader's mind. Time was pressing. So much to do! Each officer, wearing his chemical protective clothing, was hot, tired, and scared. They would be in battle in a few minutes and their lives and the lives of their men would depend on how smart and tough they would be against the enemy that lay waiting for them only eleven kilometers away.

"OK, then," Russell said, sensing their apprehension. "You will do fine. Trust in your training, shoot straight, and use the ground well. Our goal is to break up the strength of their defense by taking out their vehicles and antitank weapons one at a time. Get back to your platoons and stay on the company radio net. Let's go!"

Go to Section 14.

Section 10

Jaeger intuitively felt that the right flank attack held the best chance for success. The ground on the eastern side of the company's zone of attack was more restricted, but the high ground at Checkpoint Five and Checkpoint Three offered excellent firing positions on Objective Eagle.

The eastern part of the company's zone was dominated by Hill 790. If Hill 790 could be rendered ineffective by concentrated artillery and mortar fire, the back door to the enemy's position could be opened. In addition, the wadi on the eastern side cut the company zone in half, and might be used as a covered route that a few bold tank commanders could take to get behind Eagle without being seen. To reassure himself, Jaeger spent a few minutes mentally war gaming the options with Sergeant Riley.

"We don't have much time," Jaeger said as he addressed his eager NCOs. "The plan is simple. We will depart the assembly area in traveling formation at approximately 0413, after the last tank in 2d Platoon leaves. I will lead, Johnson will be to my left, Riley behind Johnson, and Ramos behind me. As 1st and 2d Platoons move forward, we will trail about 400 meters behind 2d Platoon on the right. The company commander will leapfrog platoons forward to various checkpoints to provide overwatching fires for the lead platoon. Second Platoon will then move to provide support fire from somewhere near Checkpoint Five. On order, 1st Platoon will then move to Checkpoint Three and provide support fire from there.

"By this time," Jaeger said, pointing to the terrain model, "we will have the wadi to our left. Use this wadi to help you navigate and keep your tank oriented northeast. Keep alert for enemy in the wadi and for the opportunity to use the wadi as a covered route to get behind Objective Eagle.

"Don't go into the wadi unless I order you to or unless you absolutely have to avoid enemy fire," Jaeger continued. You could almost hear the concentration of his tank commanders as they carefully listened to Jaeger explain the plan. "Once we get around the wadi we will change direction and move west. The assault will be made, on my order, by moving northeast and around the wadi or by going into the wadi and following it to get behind Eagle. In this manner we will attack the enemy from east to west, and roll up his positions on Eagle one at a time.

"We will assault through Eagle from east to west," Jaeger repeated, the eager eyes of his soldiers trained on him, "and we will be supported by both 1st and 2d Platoons as we make the assault. I have coordinated with the company FIST to plan an artillery target on Hill 790 in case the enemy tries to hamper us from there.

"Seizing Objective Eagle is not important! Clearing out the enemy by making them leave their prepared defenses is the key. If we can attack him where he is not prepared, we should knock him out as he moves to meet us. In either case, after the enemy is cleared from Eagle, we must reconsolidate quickly and take up hasty defensive positions, facing north, in preparation for any enemy counterattack."

By seeing the terrain model, the tank commanders could visualize their mission. Jaeger and Riley drilled each tank commander on his duties concerning the attacks and asked them a series of "what if" questions to ensure their understanding. Sergeant Riley and Jaeger, working together like a well-oiled machine, began to feel that infectious confidence that comes when a team begins to pull together for a common purpose.

Jaeger finished his briefing at 2230. The tank commanders brought their crews to the platoon sergeant's tank and briefed each crew member using the map and terrain model. The crews were electrified by the thought of action. Each soldier was alert and attentive as their tank commanders explained what would be expected of them in tomorrow's battle. Everyone was nervous at the thought of action, but Jaeger's calm manner focused their attention on the task at hand.

Most of the soldiers had not slept more than four hours in the past two days. The terrain model helped them concentrate and sped up the briefings. Finally, at 2320 the tank commanders had finished briefing their crews. Sergeant Riley put the platoon on 50 percent security and told everyone to get some sleep. Stand-to, the designated time when everyone in the platoon was expected to be up and ready to fight, was set at 0330.

Jaeger could do no more. In less than four and a half hours he would be leading his platoon into battle for the first time. At least the weary soldiers of 3d Platoon would get two to three hours of much needed sleep. Sleep was as critical now as ammunition. A tired platoon would make too many mistakes.

Jaeger himself needed to get an hour or so of rest before the 0320 intelligence update with Captain Russell. Riley had slept earlier and would stay alert while the lieutenant rested. Colwell had laid out a folding cot for Jaeger and, with Sergeant Colwell alert and standing guard, the young lieutenant quickly fell into a deep sleep.

"L. T.!" Colwell shouted as he shook his platoon leader. "The old man is on the radio and wants to speak to you right now!"

"What . . . huh . . . ?" Jaeger muttered out loud, half unconscious. "Tell him I will be right there."

Half dressed, Jaeger jumped out of his cot and grabbed his gear. Shaking off the sleep, he climbed up onto the turret of his tank. Shivering in the cold desert air of the pitch-black night, he wondered about the reality of war. He wondered if he would ever be warm and rested again. He wondered if he had forgotten anything . . . if he would be ready for today's battle. Reaching for the CVC helmet from Sergeant Colwell, he placed the helmet on his head and adjusted the microphone.

"Delta Four Seven, this is Romeo Two Zero. Over." Jaeger heard the familiar voice of Captain Russell in the earphones of his CVC helmet. Jaeger looked down at his watch; it was 0255.

"Romeo Two Zero, this is Delta Four Seven," Jaeger replied.

"We have a change in plans, orders group in fifteen minutes at my location," Russell said in a curt voice. Russell then acknowledged that Jaeger heard and understood the message and signed off the air.

Section 10

"Colwell," Jaeger cried, "get over to Sergeant Riley's tank and get everyone ready to go. Tell him I am going to an orders group meeting at the old man's position."

Jaeger grabbed his map and headed off into the dark in the direction of the company commander's position. In the distance he heard the sound of artillery explosions and the easily recognizable steady *Tungkt . . . Tungkt . . . Tungkt* of a Bradley 25mm chain gun.

Jaeger arrived at Captain Russell's tank in about six minutes. On the way he met the company first sergeant, "Wild Bill" Brock, who offered him a hot cup of coffee and led him to the commander's tank.

Jaeger eagerly took the coffee, holding the cup lovingly, enjoying each sip. The caffeine revived him after his short but deep sleep, bringing his body and mind to full alert status. Jaeger mused that few people back home would understand the luxury of a hot cup of coffee, served in a metal cup, and consumed as if it were your last hot meal on earth.

Jaeger entered the commander's improvised lean-to and let his eyes adjust to the low lighting. Captain Russell was standing next to a dimly lit map briefing his FIST, Lieutenant Rogers, and Lieutenant Shields (the company XO).

"Jaeger, come on over here and have a seat," Russell said, motioning to the ground next to his tank track. "The others will be here shortly."

Soon Madsen and Williams arrived at the lean-to and took up a position opposite their commander. The group included all the platoon leaders, the company XO, the first sergeant, the FIST, and the company medic NCO.

The air inside the lean-to was warmed by the addition of these men. The smell of coffee, sweat, and dirt left an aroma in the small confined area that reminded Jaeger of the days when he and his father went deer hunting in the woods near his home in Minnesota. But this was not a deer hunt, and Minnesota was another world away.

"I called this update a few minutes early in order for you to have more time to brief your men," Russell started off, taking a sip of steaming coffee from his metal canteen cup. "Let me get you up to speed. The battalion's scouts have identified a tank platoon in the north of Charlie Company's zone to our right. I've been eavesdropping on the scout radio net and from what I can gather this means that the enemy has a reserve tank company somewhere five to seven kilometers northeast of Checkpoint Seven. That puts them in range to reinforce the enemy in our zone." The platoon leaders stared at their commander's map and hurriedly took notes.

"In addition," Russell said, raising his voice for added effect, "a scout M3 cavalry fighting vehicle got to the southeast side of Hill 790 at LK960544. He reported no enemy on Hill 790. Unfortunately, the scout hit a mine on the northeast side of Hill 790 and lost his track. The survivors are now occupying an observation post on Hill 790 and should give us some good intelligence once it is daylight.

"Now," Russell continued, "here is the picture in our zone. So far it looks like the scouts have clearly identified two BMPs at grid coordinates LK932540 and one tank near the high-ground vicinity of Objective Eagle at LK928537.

"This means that the enemy is on Objective Eagle with at least a reinforced BMP platoon. We know where two BMPs and one tank are. We will have to find the other BMP." Russell paused for everyone to follow him on the map. "The enemy, therefore, is strong on the western portion of Eagle.

"I don't like this situation any more than the rest of you," Russell said solemnly. "Damn it! If only the enemy had been sighted earlier. If we go the way we had planned we could be attacking right into the center of an enemy fire sack!"

Russell stopped talking. The air was tense as the officers huddled around the map and waited for his decision. Seconds passed and no one spoke.

"We don't have a choice," Russell said, breaking the silence. "We have to change our plans. We will have to attack them in the east.

"Madsen," Russell said, pausing to let everyone follow his discussion as they studied the map, "move out from this assembly area at 0352. At twenty kilometers per hour you should cross the LD at exactly 0425. Williams, you follow with 2d Platoon.

"Williams," Russell said, pointing at the 2d Platoon leader, "I want you to drop off at Checkpoint Three and from there provide suppressive fire on anything that lives on Objective Eagle. Give me everything you have."

Williams nodded.

"Jaeger, I want you to follow behind Williams. According to what the scouts report, we should flank them to the right. The right side of Eagle is where they are the weakest. Their main strength, one T-72 and two BMPs, is on the left. I want 1st Platoon to provide support fire from Checkpoint Five, while I move 2d and 3d Platoons forward to Checkpoint Three.

"Jaeger." Russell looked Jaeger straight in the eye, as if looking for any sign of hesitation from his newest platoon leader. "You are the main effort. You will come with me as we swing around Eagle from the northeast and clear the Threat positions from east to west. We will have to dig them out one by one. Don't forget, we are flanking them to make them move out of their holes! If they start to move after we have flanked them, then we have them. As they move, I expect 1st and 2d Platoons to smash them with accurate main gun fires. The whole point here is to deny the bad guys the use of their prepared positions and make them fight us in the open as they move to alternate positions. I will provide smoke and artillery fire on Eagle before we cross the LD.

"The enemy may try to counterattack us," Russell continued, his lieutenants somewhat dazed by the quickness of his decision to change plans one hour before the attack. "If the enemy counterattacks, they will most likely hit us with their reserve tank company as soon as they find out where we are. If you see enemy tanks moving from the north, call me ASAP! Battalion has a FASCAM artillery mine field available, and we may get a chance to use it if we have a good target. Brief your men and make sure that you are ready. Check your CEOIs and frequencies before you leave. The time is now 0330. Any questions?"

"Sir," Jaeger asked, unfolding his map. "I request permission to get with the FIST and plan a few more artillery targets behind and to the northeast of Eagle. With a good smoke screen, we can isolate any enemy on Eagle, and cut him off from his support to the north."

"Good. Rogers, see to it and show me what you come up with for final approval," Russell answered, grinning slightly as if he was now convinced that he had picked the right platoon leader for the assault force. "Any other questions?"

There was a long, quiet pause. There were no more questions, but you could hear the gears working in each leader's mind. Time was pressing. So much to do! Each officer, wearing his chemical protective clothing, was hot, tired, and scared. They would be in battle in a few hours and their lives and the lives of their men would depend on how smart and tough they could be against an enemy that lay waiting for them only eleven kilometers away.

"OK, then," Russell said, sensing their apprehension. "You will all do fine. Trust in your training, shoot straight, and use the ground well. Our goal is to break up the strength of their defense by taking out their vehicles and antitank weapons one at a time. Get back to your platoons and stay on the company radio net. Let's go!

Go to Section 13.

Section 11

Of the three possible options—attack left, center, or right—Jaeger intuitively felt that the left flank attack held the best chance for success. The ground was more open and better suited to armor than in the east. The eastern part of the company's zone was dominated by Hill 790. In addition, the wadi that cut the company zone in half could be a real obstacle. To reassure himself, Jaeger spent a few minutes mentally war gaming the options with Sergeant Riley.

"If we get separated from the rest of the company by that wadi," Riley said, pointing at the map, "we might get caught in an enemy fire sack without any hope of direct support from the rest of the company. The bad guys used the wadi to their advantage the last time I fought them. They would wait until we got within range and then hit us with concentrated RPG and antitank fire."

"What about using the wadi as an avenue of approach?" Jaeger exclaimed. "The wadi is wide enough for two tanks and would offer us excellent cover from their direct fire weapons. We could get on their flank without them even knowing it!"

"Using a defile that has not been carefully reconnoitered is a risky business," Riley said seriously. "The gamble is that the enemy would not consider the wadi as an avenue of approach and would not mine or defend it. That banks on them being pretty stupid. With a couple of well-placed mines and a few RPGs, the enemy could bottle us up in the wadi and have us for breakfast!"

"I was worried about the same thing," Jaeger replied thoughtfully. "I guess you are right. But if we go down the middle we are sure to be right in the center of their fire sack!"

"It seems, Lieutenant, that we need to look at another option," Riley said with a smile. "How about the left side? If we move fast, from Checkpoint Four to Checkpoint Six, we could get around their western flank and use the good tank country in the western half of our zone."

"The old man is leaning that way, too. This is it, then," Jaeger announced confidently, stabbing at his map with his flashlight (see Map 6). "We will need some artillery support and smoke, but the left-hand option seems the best. Get everyone together and I will issue the order."

The night was unnaturally quiet. At 2110 Jaeger finished planning and issued his operations order. He used the terrain model that Sergeant Riley had prepared; it was worth a thousand words. Each tank commander listened eagerly as their lieutenant showed them how they would leave their present position, hugging the side of Hill 766 and trailing behind Lieutenant Madsen's 1st Platoon. The platoon would then maneuver from Checkpoint 4 to Checkpoint 6, providing overwatch at each position for the rest of the company.

At Checkpoint 6 Jaeger planned to call for artillery smoke to land behind Eagle, isolating the enemy from any support from the north. On Captain Russell's order, Jaeger would then move 3d Platoon to the north in platoon wedge formation. He would lead on the right, with Johnson following to his right rear. Ramos would be to his left, with Riley trailing to the left rear of Ramos. On Jaeger's order, the platoon would form on line, for maximum firepower forward, and sweep the objective.

Then each tank would move to positions on the south side and center of Eagle. From there, each tank would seek defensive positions and prepare for a possible enemy counterattack.

By seeing the model and walking through their expected actions, the tank commanders gained a clear concept of what they had to do. Jaeger went into great detail to explain the different formations, and each tank's relative position, as they made the assault across the miniature terrain of the battlefield model. Jaeger and Riley drilled each tank commander on his duties concerning the attack and asked them a series of "what if" questions to ensure their understanding. Sergeant Riley and Jaeger were now working together like a well-oiled machine. The tank commanders understood their mission and were ready.

Jaeger finished his briefing at 2230. The tank commanders finished briefing their crews by 2300. Sergeant Riley put the platoon on 50 percent security and told everyone not on guard to get some sleep. Stand-to, the designated time when everyone in the platoon was expected to be up and ready to fight, was set at 0330.

Jaeger was ready. He had done everything possible. The preparation phase was now over. From here on life or death would depend on how well Jaeger and his platoon could react in combat. In less than four and a half hours he would be leading his platoon into battle for the first time.

At least the tired men of 3d Platoon would get two to three hours of much needed sleep. Sleep was as critical now as ammunition. A tired platoon would make too many mistakes.

Now Jaeger himself needed to get an hour or so of rest before the 0320 intelligence update with Captain Russell. Riley had slept earlier and would remain alert while the lieutenant rested. Colwell laid out a folding cot for his tired platoon leader and, under the partial protection offered by the side of his M1 tank, Jaeger quickly fell into a deep sleep.

"L. T.!" Colwell shouted as he shook his platoon leader. "The old man is on the radio and wants to speak to you right now!"

"What . . . huh. . . . Doesn't the old man ever sleep?" Jaeger muttered out loud, shaking off his weariness and steadying himself as he jumped out of his warm cot. "Tell him I will be right there."

Half dressed, Jaeger climbed up onto the turret of his tank. Shivering in the cold desert air, he wondered if he was ready for today's battle. A chill raced down his spine with the thought of combat, but he suppressed it and got on to the business at hand. He reached for the CVC helmet from Sergeant Colwell, placed the helmet on his head, and adjusted the microphone.

"Delta Four Seven, this is Romeo Two Zero. Over." Jaeger could hear the familiar voice of Captain Russell in the earphones of his CVC helmet. Jaeger looked down at his watch; it was 0255.

"Romeo Two Zero, this is Delta Four Seven," Jaeger replied.

"We have a change in plans, orders group in fifteen minutes at my location," Russell said in a curt voice. Jaeger then acknowledged the message before signing off the air.

"Colwell," Jaeger took off his CVC helmet and whispered to his gunner, "get over to Sergeant Riley's tank and wake up everyone. Tell him that I am going to an orders group meeting at the old man's position. I'll be back in about fifteen minutes and I will need to see all the tank commanders."

Jaeger grabbed his map and headed off into the dark in the direction of the company commander's tank. In the distance he could hear the sound of sporadic artillery explosions and the easily recognizable steady *Tungkt . . . Tungkt . . . Tungkt* of a Bradley 25mm chain gun.

Jaeger arrived at Captain Russell's tank in about six minutes. On the way he met the company first sergeant, "Wild Bill" Brock, who offered him a hot cup of coffee from his ever-present thermos. Brock led Jaeger to the commander's tank.

Jaeger had eagerly taken the coffee. He held the warm cup lovingly, savoring every sip. The caffeine revived him after his short but deep sleep, and brought his body and mind to full alert status. It was amazing what a positive effect a simple cup of coffee could have.

Jaeger entered the commander's improvised lean-to and let his eyes adjust to the dim lighting under the tarp. Captain Russell was looking at a map, briefing Lieutenant Rogers and Lieutenant Shields.

"Jaeger, come on over here and take a seat," Russell said, motioning to the ground next to his tank track. "The others will be here shortly."

Soon Madsen and Williams arrived and sat opposite their commander. The standard orders group included all the platoon leaders, the company XO, the first sergeant, the FIST, and the company medic NCO. The air inside the cramped lean-to was warmed by the addition of these men. The smell of coffee, unwashed bodies, and dirt left an aroma that Jaeger would probably never forget.

"We have to move fast. Things have changed," Russell started off, taking a sip of steaming coffee from his metal canteen cup. "Let me get you up to speed. The battalion's scouts have identified a tank platoon in the Charlie Company zone to our right. I've been eavesdropping on the scout platoon radio net and from what I can gather the enemy has a reserve tank company in range to counterattack in our zone.

"So far it looks like the scouts have clearly identified two BMPs at grid coordinates LK932540 and one tank near the high ground in the vicinity of Objective Eagle at LK928537. A scout M3 cavalry fighting vehicle got to the southeast side of Hill 790 at LK960544, found no enemy, but then hit a mine. These scouts abandoned their vehicle and are now occupying an observation post on Hill 790. They may give us some good intelligence once it is daylight.

"This means that the bad guys are on Objective Eagle with at least a reinforced BMP platoon. We know where two BMPs and one tank are. We will have to find the other BMP and the T-72." Russell paused for everyone to follow him on the map.

"I don't like this situation any more than the rest of you," Russell said solemnly. "Damn it! If only the enemy had been sighted earlier. If we go the way we had planned we could drive right into the center of their fire sack!"

Russell stopped talking. The air was tense as the officers crowded around the map and waited for his decision. Seconds passed and no one said a word. Russell sat silently for several moments, studying the map.

"We don't have a choice," Russell announced, breaking the silence. "We have to change our plans. Madsen, move out from this assembly area at 0352. At twelve kilometers per hour, that will put you across the LD at exactly 0425. Williams, you follow with 2d Platoon. Jaeger, you follow behind Williams. According to what the scouts reported, we should flank them to the right. The right side of Eagle is where they are the weakest. Their main strength, one T-72 and two BMPs, is on the left. I want 1st Platoon to provide support fire from Checkpoint Five, while I move 2d and 3d Platoons forward to Checkpoint Three."

"Williams," Russell said, pointing at the 2d Platoon leader, "you will then drop off at Checkpoint Three, form a firing line, and provide suppressive fire on Objective Eagle from there. Give me everything you have."

Williams nodded.

"Jaeger," Russell paused, noticing the hesitation in Jaeger's eyes, "you will then come with me as we swing around Eagle from the northeast and clear their positions from east to west. Don't get too close to them, just move behind the position and shoot them as they move. If they move after we flank them, then we will kick their ass. The whole point here is to deny the bad guys the use of their prepared positions. We must make them fight us in the open by forcing them to move to alternate positions. I will provide smoke and artillery fire on Eagle before we cross the LD.

Section 11

"The enemy may try to counterattack us," Russell continued, his lieutenants somewhat dazed by the quickness of his decision to change plans one hour before the attack. "If he counterattacks, he will most likely throw his entire reserve tank company at us. If you see dust trails moving from the north, call me ASAP! Battalion has a FASCAM artillery mine field available, and we may get a chance to use it if we have a good target. Brief your men and make sure you are ready. The time is now 0330. Any questions?"

Jaeger's heart sank. The confidence he had felt earlier had vanished. He had assumed from his study of the ground that the best avenue to attack Eagle would be the left flank. That was where the best tank country was. Now, with less than an hour before the attack, the company commander had changed plans! All his efforts had been wasted!

Jaeger must now attack from east to west because the latest intelligence on the enemy showed the weak spot on the east side of Eagle. Jaeger hadn't considered the enemy adequately in his planning. Was there enough time to make a new plan?

There was a long, quiet pause. There were no questions, but you could hear the gears working in each leader's mind. Time was pressing. So much to do! Each officer, wearing his chemical protective clothing, was hot, tired, and scared. They would be in battle in a few hours and their lives, and the lives of their men, would depend on their leadership. The enemy was out there waiting, only eleven kilometers away.

"OK, then," Russell said, sensing their apprehension. "You will do fine. Trust in your training, use the ground well, and we will take them out one at a time. Get back to your platoons and stay on the radio net. Let's go!"

Go to Section 15.

Section 12

The night was black. There was no moon.

Rushing back as fast as he could, Jaeger returned to his platoon. He arrived at 0351. It was very quiet. Only the muffled sounds of soldiers preparing for combat stirred the otherwise peaceful desert at sleep. The company was going to move out in a few minutes. He had to issue instructions fast!

Jaeger ran over to Riley's tank and motioned for him to come down from the turret and meet with him on the ground. Platoon Sergeant Riley, efficient as ever, had everyone up, manning their tanks and ready to go. Riley, sensing the need for all tank commanders to gather for last-minute orders, had sent his loader to bring Ramos and Johnson to A34.

"We have a change in plans," Jaeger said gloomily. "Instead of attacking behind 1st Platoon and hitting Eagle on the left flank, the commander has decided to move us behind 2d Platoon and attack Eagle from the east!"

"Why the change, Lieutenant?" Riley asked, a bewildered expression on his face. "I thought he wanted to use the good tank country on the western part of our zone to assault Eagle."

"Well, we guessed wrong," Jaeger replied bitterly. "It seems that the enemy doesn't want to play their part and let us take the easy approach. The enemy has most of his strength on the western side of Eagle—two BMPs and one T-72. The battalion scout platoon radioed in those locations at 0300. The commander had to change the plan or risk leading us into an ambush. The question is, how do we pull this off?"

Ramos ran up, panting from his sprint in combat gear to the platoon sergeant's tank. A few seconds later, Johnson arrived. Riley looked at Jaeger. It was 0400!

"All right, listen up . . . our plan has changed. We don't have much time," Jaeger announced with a faked confidence that was not inspiring.

Jaeger knew that he had to take charge of the situation. He realized, more than ever before, that the success of his platoon and the lives of his men rested on his shoulders.

"We are moving out in about ten minutes. We will follow 2d Platoon from the assembly area. We will move in column—A31, A32, A34, and then A33. We are going to attack the right flank of Eagle, assaulting from east to west. Two BMPs and one T-72 are on the western side of Eagle. Follow me, and do as I do. Are there any questions?"

The loud, high-pitched whine of 1st Platoon's M1 tanks, moving off at the start point, shocked the group into action. First Platoon was already moving! Alpha Company was on its way toward Phase Line August, the line of departure. North of August the enemy was waiting to kill them.

Jaeger motioned for everyone to mount up and keep an eye out for the signal to move out. The tank commanders scrambled back to their vehicles. Each tank started its engine and waited for the signal to move out.

Jaeger peered through the blackness with night-vision goggles. He waited for the last tank in 2d Platoon to pass the start point on the northeast edge of the company assembly area.

Time ticked away. Jaeger pulled off his CVC helmet to listen for the sound of 2d Platoon's engines. The only thing he could hear was the whine of his M1 tank engine.

This was taking too long. Second Platoon should have passed by now, Jaeger thought. What was wrong? He searched the horizon with his thermal gun sight but saw only empty landscape. Second Platoon was nowhere in sight.

"Where are they?" Jaeger said over his intercom. "Colwell, scan the horizon for 2d Platoon."

Colwell traversed the main gun and viewed the area to their east with his thermal sight.

"I can't see anybody, sir," Colwell replied.

Jaeger couldn't use his radio and break listening silence. The fatigue of the past forty-eight hours and the fear of losing contact with the rest of the company gripped Jaeger like a vise. What was he supposed to do?

Jaeger ordered Private First Class Jones, his driver, to move out. Second Platoon must have moved out on time and he just didn't see them, Jaeger thought. Jaeger was determined to catch 2d Platoon as fast as possible.

The A31 moved forward quickly. The rough terrain to the east explained why they missed 2d Platoon. From Jaeger's old position he couldn't see more than 300 meters.

Jaeger wished now that he had taken the time to recon his route from the assembly area to the start point. He looked back and saw Johnson following right behind, less than twenty-five meters away. Johnson was following too close. It appeared that the fear of getting separated was greater, at this time, than the discipline to maintain a proper fifty-meter interval.

"Damn it!" Jaeger cursed out loud. They were moving too slow. Jaeger would never catch up with Alpha Company at this pace. The time was 0420.

Jaeger ordered his driver to increase speed. As the tank accelerated forward, the crew braced themselves for the rough cross-country ride across the broken desert terrain. Jaeger searched desperately for a visible landmark to orient himself.

Fear of failure drove Jaeger to increase his speed even more. The rest of 3d Platoon was left behind as Jaeger raced north. At last he observed what appeared to be Checkpoint One.

"Jones," Jaeger ordered over his tank intercom. "Move the tank to the high ground to our left and stop."

Jaeger looked behind for Sergeant Johnson's tank. He wasn't there! Jaeger realized that he was not only out of contact with the company, but now he was separated from his platoon. Jaeger looked at his watch again. The time was now 0436.

Karrummp! The sky lit up to the north with the splash of American artillery: 155mm howitzer shells and mortar bombs burst in orange-white explosions on suspected enemy positions. Flares shot into the air and hung high in the sky with an eerie glow, making the world a contrast of shadows and brightness.

The earphones of Jaeger's CVC helmet came alive.

"Romeo Four Seven, this is Delta Two Zero. Where the hell are you!" Jaeger could hear the unmistakable voice of Captain Russell.

"Delta Two Zero . . . this is Romeo Four Seven . . . I am at . . . ugh . . . Checkpoint One . . . providing overwatch," Jaeger replied, not too convincingly.

"Four Seven, I am holding my elements at Checkpoint Five," Russell said as calmly as possible. "Get a grip on the situation and move to my location ASAP! Out!"

Sergeant Riley's tank pulled up alongside Jaeger's M1. Jaeger could clearly see his platoon sergeant in the glow of the flares and artillery fire. With a violent jerk of his thumb, Riley motioned for Jaeger to step out of his hatch and jump over to Riley's tank.

"Lieutenant!" Riley roared. "What in the name of God is going on? Where in the hell do you think you are?"

Jaeger stood there, dazed, not saying a word.

"Johnson hit a ditch about six hundred meters back and broke a sprocket and two torsion bars. Nobody's hurt bad, but he is out of the fight. What the hell are we doing up here?" Riley pointed his blue-filtered flashlight at the map to a location southwest of Hill 766.

"I got disoriented," Jaeger said, defeated. "Are you sure we are here?" Jaeger pointed at the spot Riley was illuminating.

"Yes, and we are in one hell of a mess!" Riley said, looking at Jaeger as if he would tear out the lieutenant's throat. "Christ, Lieutenant. We are down to three tanks and we haven't even seen the enemy yet. The company is on the other side of the open area to our east and it will be daylight in less than forty minutes."

"All right," Jaeger said, gaining his composure. "I was up on that hill yesterday and that means that Checkpoint Five must be over there. Let's give this another try. You stay to my left and help me navigate. I'll keep Ramos to my right."

KARRUMMP! Incoming artillery screamed overhead and crashed into the top of Hill 766, just 400 meters from their position.

Jaeger ran back to his tank and plopped on his helmet. Within seconds, the platoon, now reduced to three tanks, was moving east to regain contact with Alpha Company. The time was now 0450.

KARRUMMP! KARRUMMP! KARRUMMP! Three 152mm artillery shells crashed into the ground only a hundred meters in front of Jaeger's moving tank. Without stopping the tank he pushed his turret hatch to the open protected position and screamed at his driver to increase speed. The sky was now completely illuminated by the nightmarish glow of enemy artillery flares.

KARRUMMP! KARRUMMP! KARRUMMP! The noise was deafening. Artillery exploded everywhere. The enemy had fire coming at Jaeger's platoon from every direction. Jaeger looked straight ahead as he tried to control the driver to avoid ditches and holes in the terrain.

KABOOM! There was a burst of light and sparks. A tremendous explosion occurred only fifty meters to Jaeger's right rear.

Jaeger's heart sank. A33 had been hit. An enemy missile hit the turret on the left side, at the left sponson box. Ramos's tank stopped abruptly. Smoke poured out of the turret. Illuminated by enemy artillery flares, Ramos's tank had been an easy mark for a Threat gunner.

Continuing to move, Jaeger glanced to his left rear and saw someone, probably Ramos, climb out and fall off the turret and onto the ground. Jaeger couldn't make out if the figure was alive or dead.

KARRUMMP! KARRUMMP! The artillery continued to fall.

I've lost him! By God, I've lost another crew . . . , Jaeger thought. Exposing his platoon's flank to the enemy's positions had just cost 3d Platoon a tank and crew.

BOOM! Riley, his turret pointing over his left side, returned fire immediately with his 105mm. Riley had not seen the missile launch, but he knew better than to do nothing.

Jaeger, filled with frustration at fighting an enemy he couldn't see, followed Riley's example and fired.

Karrummp! Karrummp! At the same moment, friendly mortar rounds fell between Jaeger's position and Eagle, billowing into clouds of whitish smoke. The smoke provided concealment for Jaeger and Riley as they raced east.

Jaeger didn't stop. Picking up speed, he moved toward Checkpoint 5.

"Romeo Four Seven, this is Delta Two Zero." Captain Russell reached out on the radio to save his embattled platoon leader. "I see you headed my way. I have smoke being laid to cover your move. What is your situation?"

"Two Zero, this is Four Seven," Jaeger said in a fast, nervous voice. "I have two down . . . two down. Request instructions. Over."

There was a long pause on the other end of the radio. Finally, Captain Russell radioed to Jaeger to continue to Checkpoint 5 and be prepared to follow him when he made the assault. Russell announced that he would move 1st Platoon to Checkpoint 3 and then maneuver the entire 2d and 3d Platoons around to the north and continue the assault of the enemy on Eagle from east to west.

The two surviving tanks of 3d Platoon covered the ground quickly, protected by the smoke screen. In a few minutes, Jaeger found 2d Platoon and linked up with them at Checkpoint 5.

Casualties occur quickly in modern war. Mistakes, even seemingly insignificant ones, are often paid for in blood. Jaeger thought about Ramos and hoped he was all right.

Jaeger reported his location to the company commander. Captain Russell ordered 2d Platoon to remain in overwatch positions at Checkpoint 5 and 1st Platoon to move to Checkpoint 3.

KARRUMMP! KARRUMMP! KARRUMMP! Enemy artillery now smashed into Checkpoint 5. Riley pulled into a hasty defensive position to Jaeger's left. Jaeger, confined and buttoned up in his tank, watched Riley's move through his vision blocks.

Standing in his turret, cramped, scared, and angry, Jaeger observed the enemy artillery falling. Its impact was almost overpowering. The ground shook and the shells seemed to suck the air right out of Jaeger's lungs. For a minute Jaeger thought that the enemy was using chemical weapons, and reached for his mask.

KARRUMMP! KARRUMMP! Jaeger was sick. He felt guilty and responsible for Ramos and Johnson. The constant sound of artillery, the scream of the radios, the smoke, and the dust drove Jaeger into a state of nausea. Focusing his remaining strength, he directed his attention to the mission at hand. He listened to his radio and tried to determine what was happening.

First Platoon radioed to Captain Russell. They had secured Checkpoint 3 and were scanning for targets. One of 2d Platoon's tanks was knocked out by the intense enemy artillery fire on Checkpoint 5. The company was now down to eleven tanks.

"Delta elements, this is Delta Two Zero," Russell ordered over his radio. "Let's go. Charlie, execute support fire. Romeo and Quebec, follow me."

The assault force, seven tanks strong, raced off to attack. Captain Russell was in the lead. Madsen's tanks started firing support fire, pumping 105mm rounds at enemy positions on Objective Eagle as fast as they could fire.

As Jaeger moved forward he observed Madsen's gunners firing from Checkpoint 3. A moving BMP became their first kill of the day, the glow from the burning BMP clearly distinguishing Objective Eagle for the assault force.

The sky began to get brighter with the approach of dawn.

Jaeger followed Russell's tank. Russell, leading the way around the wadi, suddenly drove into a concentrated hail of enemy machine gun fire. Fighting for its life against enemy infantry, Russell's tank took a hit from an RPG but continued to move and fire. Swinging his turret back and forth, Russell shattered the area with a flurry of .50-caliber machine gun fire.

Jaeger fired his machine guns to support his endangered commander. Undaunted, Russell's tank continued, firing all weapons at the Threat infantry that was now withdrawing to subsequent firing positions.

The company command frequency was quiet. Jaeger attempted to call the commander. No response. Jaeger could see that Russell's tank was still fighting. The RPG hit must have knocked out Russell's communications, Jaeger thought.

After a few moments, the XO, Lieutenant Shields, took command of the radio net and called for artillery to suppress the infantry. At that same moment, a brave enemy RPG-16 gunner jumped up from a trench and hit one of 2d Platoon's tanks in the rear grill doors. Jaeger passed by the stricken tank as its engine compartment burst into flames. The crew of the damaged tank, stunned but still functioning, traversed their turret and nailed the enemy soldier with machine gun fire. Several more RPG rounds, fired from another trench, again hit the damaged tank. After three hits the tank showed no sign of life and the engine fuel ignited in billowing clouds of black smoke.

"GUNNER, COAX, FIRE, AND ADJUST," Jaeger yelled into his intercom in an attempt to get the fleeing enemy RPG gunners. Jaeger's turret swung wildly back and forth as Colwell directed 7.62mm machine gun fire into a berm 400 meters to their front.

"Jones," Jaeger ordered his driver, "move right. We don't want to get too close to those RPGs."

Colwell fired another burst at the area with 7.62mm machine gun fire.

"Can you see them?" Jaeger asked over his intercom.

"Negative," Colwell announced as he continued to fire.

The battlefield was soon covered in dense smoke. Jaeger was still moving fast and was positioned off to Riley's left. Daylight was breaking and the smoke hung low, ten to fifteen feet over the battlefield. This inhibited the enemy more than it did the Americans. Jaeger could see through the smoke with his thermal sights, while the enemy, not so equipped, was effectively blind. Thus the M1 crews had a decisive advantage.

BOOM! BOOM! Jaeger watched as a BMP was forcibly torn apart by the strike of the two U.S. tank rounds. The BMP, about 900 meters to his front, broke apart in a cloud of black smoke and flying debris. Jaeger heard Madsen declare another kill over the radio.

Jaeger stopped trying to figure out what was happening. Bouncing across the rear of Objective Eagle, he concerned himself only with looking for targets. He concerned himself with living through this hell by killing the enemy before the enemy killed him.

KARRUMMP! KARRUMMP! Artillery fell all over Eagle, stripping the infantry out of their exposed firing positions. Jaeger watched as enemy infantrymen were caught on the run and slaughtered by the combined force of American artillery and charging tanks.

Section 12

The battle on Eagle now turned into a mad melee of charging tanks, smoke, dust, infantry, and artillery. Control was impossible. In the confusion, Jaeger lost sight of Captain Russell's tank. Driving west, Jaeger moved fast across a series of small ridges that dotted the terrain. The ridges reduced his field of fire to less than 300 meters. Riley, right behind him, fired his machine guns furiously at suspected enemy infantry positions.

"Romeo Four Seven, this is Red Four," Riley called to his platoon leader, switching back to his platoon radio net. "We are in the lead now. Stay with me; there has got to be another BMP in here somewhere!"

"Roger that, Red Four. . . . Wait!" Jaeger screamed as a BMP popped up directly to his front. "GUNNER, PC . . . FIRE!"

BOOM! Jaeger fired his 105mm cannon at the BMP. Jaeger's shell tore a gaping hole in the side of the BMP, exploding the vehicle in a bright orange fireball of death and twisted steel. The puny 30mm gun turret, sheared off by the force of the explosion, soared 200 feet into the air.

Jaeger didn't have time to celebrate. He passed by the burning, wrecked BMP and accelerated. He raced forward another 100 meters when an enemy T-72 tank, dug in all the way to the turret, reacted to Jaeger's sudden arrival. Jaeger and the Threat tank commander saw each other in almost the same instant.

Roll the dice.

If the total of the two dice is nine or less, go to Section 16.

If the total of the two dice is ten or greater, go to Section 18.

Section 13

Jaeger walked back to his platoon, moving as quickly as possible in the black, moonless desert night. He arrived at 0351. The company would move out in less than fifteen minutes. He didn't have much time, but he felt confident that his men could accomplish the mission.

Everyone was up, manning their tanks and ready to go. Riley had seen to everything. Jaeger ran over to Riley's tank and motioned for him to come down from the turret and meet with him on the ground. Riley, sensing the need for all tank commanders to gather for last-minute orders, sent his loader to go from tank to tank and fetch Ramos and Johnson to A34.

"We execute the operation as planned," Jaeger said triumphantly. "We will move behind 2d Platoon and attack Eagle from the east. The battalion has identified the following enemy vehicles on Objective Eagle, so write these down on your maps." Jaeger paused for every tank commander to copy the important information.

"Scouts have identified one tank on Eagle, near the high ground in the vicinity of grid LK928537, and two BMPs at grid LK932540. The enemy also appears to have a reserve tank company somewhere within range to counterattack us.

"The enemy is on Eagle with at least a reinforced BMP platoon. Their main strength is on our left, on the western side of Eagle. We know where two BMPs and one tank are. We will have to find the other BMP.

"We are the company main effort. We will follow behind 2d Platoon. First Platoon will provide suppressive fire from Checkpoint Five, while our platoon and 2d Platoon move forward to Checkpoint Three. Second Platoon will then drop off at Checkpoint Three and provide suppressive fire on Objective Eagle, as we swing around from the northeast and clear Eagle from east to west. We probably will have to dig them out one by one. The company commander will provide smoke and artillery fire for us on Eagle before we cross the LD.

"The enemy may try to counterattack once we get involved on Eagle," Jaeger continued, his tank commanders keenly listening to every word.

"If he counterattacks, battalion has a FASCAM artillery mine field available, and we may get a chance to use it if we have a good target. Brief your men and make sure you are ready. The time is now 0405. Any questions?"

"The ground is pretty deceptive between here and the start point. I had Johnson recon the route." Riley announced. "He coordinated with the platoon sergeant of 2d Platoon to make sure that we don't have any problems leaving the assembly area. They will wave a red-filtered flashlight in our direction to signify that their last vehicle has reached the start point. Johnson has already moved his tank to a position where he can see the signal. We are ready to do it!"

"Good job, Sergeant Riley!" Jaeger replied, seeing the value of parallel planning first hand. "Johnson, I'll let you lead up to Checkpoint Three. Everything else will be as previously planned. Anything else?"

Before anyone else could answer, the sound of 1st Platoon's M1 tanks told everyone that 2d Platoon was already on the move. First Platoon was moving out of the assembly area, headed toward Phase Line August, the line of departure!

Jaeger motioned for everyone to mount up. The tank commanders scrambled back to their vehicles. Johnson raced back to his tank, which was located at a vantage point that observed the company start point. Each tank started simultaneously on Sergeant Riley's order.

Jaeger peered through the blackness of the moonless night with night-vision goggles as he waited for the signal from Johnson. It won't be long now, he thought to himself.

In a few minutes Jaeger saw the signal from Johnson and moved his tank out to the start point. Ramos, in A33, followed fifty meters behind Jaeger. Sergeant Riley, in A34, followed fifty meters behind Ramos.

The night was the blackest night Jaeger could remember. In spite of the darkness, the tank drivers could see about seventy meters to their front, using their passive night driving viewers. The tanks of 3d Platoon advanced toward the enemy without a single visible light.

Jaeger followed Johnson's steady advance. The platoon was now 200 meters short of Phase Line August. The enemy had not yet identified the company's movement.

At 0425, right on schedule, the sky lit up to the north with the splash of American artillery and mortar shells. The shells crashed into suspected Threat positions on Eagle, exploding in bright orange-white bursts.

The earphones of Jaeger's CVC helmet came alive as radio listening silence was lifted and Captain Russell started issuing instructions.

"Romeo Four Seven, this is Delta Two Zero," Captain Russell radioed to his assault platoon leader. "I have initiated artillery on Eagle. What is your situation?"

"Two Zero, this is Four Seven," Jaeger said calmly. "Crossing August now, continuing to move, no problems. Over."

There was a short pause on the other end of the radio. Captain Russell ordered 1st Platoon to occupy overwatch positions on Checkpoint 5 and 2d Platoon to move to Checkpoint 3. First Platoon reported to Captain Russell that they had secured Checkpoint 5 and were scanning for targets.

Karrummp! Artillery fell in the empty center of the company zone, just east of Checkpoint 4. Since no one was there it caused no casualties. The enemy must be firing artillery at the place they think we are coming from, Jaeger thought. He must not know where we are.

At 0515, 2d Platoon reported set on Checkpoint 3 but was soon under fire from a Threat 30mm cannon and light machine gun fire. Captain Russell ordered 1st and 2d Platoons to start support fire on Eagle. With the roar of 2d Platoon's guns in the background, Russell told Jaeger to follow him around the right flank.

"Romeo Four Seven, this is Delta Two Zero," Captain Russell radioed to his assault platoon leader. "Execute assault. Follow me!"

"Two Zero, this is Four Seven," Jaeger said a bit excited. "Roger, we are right with you!"

Jaeger looked out his hatch, which was locked in the open protected position, and surveyed the scene. His tank hurried forward to the north, the rest of the platoon following in a "V" formation behind him. The early minutes of morning, and the glare from distant enemy flares, gave Jaeger just enough light to see the shapes of his tanks with the unaided eye. He was pleased with his platoon's quick reaction to orders. He felt a great sense of pride in his men and in the power of his tanks.

Jaeger observed the dark silhouette of Hill 798 to his left and knew from his study of the terrain that he must now maneuver to the east. Looking through his night vision goggles he clearly saw the wadi to his left front.

CRACK! Enemy machine gun fire flashed in his direction. Jaeger's tank was struck by a few insignificant hits from a light enemy machine gun.

TUNGKT. TUNGKT. A 30mm cannon projectile fired by a BMP

bounced off the flank of Ramos's tank. The strike caused no casualties but scared the crew, who fired back in the enemy's general direction with a 105mm cannon round. Ramos's shot missed, not really aimed at any specific target.

BOOM! BOOM! Both Ramos and Riley fired in the BMP's direction. Their fire was returned by a hail of enemy machine gun fire.

The wadi was directly to Jaeger's front. The approach into the wadi looked clear and wide. If Jaeger used the wadi he could sneak his platoon behind the Threat and hit them from the rear. Should he risk it?

TUNGKT! TUNGKT! Another volley of 30mm shells landed close to Jaeger's tank, missing him by inches. Although 30mm and machine gun fire wouldn't stop his assault, what if the enemy had RPGs or AT-4 antitank missiles? The opening to the wadi was now forty meters to his front. Should he use the wadi or not? Jaeger must decide!

If Jaeger decides to take his platoon down into the wadi, go to Section 26.

If Jaeger decides to continue as planned and disregard the wadi, go to Section 27.

Section 14

Jaeger arrived back at his platoon at 0351. The quiet of the early morning was interrupted by the muffled sounds of his men preparing for combat. Jaeger was confident that his men would perform as planned. He knew that his men were as ready as they would ever be.

Efficient as ever, Platoon Sergeant Riley had everyone up, manning their tanks and ready to go. Jaeger met Riley in front of Riley's tank, A34. Riley, sensing the need for all tank commanders to gather for last-minute orders, had already sent his loader to go from tank to tank and fetch each tank commander to A34.

The tank commanders huddled around their platoon leader. Jaeger opened his map on the front slope of Sergeant Riley's tank.

"Everything is on track," Jaeger said triumphantly. "We will move behind 2d Platoon, as planned, and attack the enemy on Eagle from the east. Battalion has identified the enemy on Eagle, at the following locations, so write these down on your maps." Jaeger paused for every tank commander to copy the important information.

"Battalion has observed two BMPs near grid LK932540," Jaeger said, pointing to his map with a blue-filtered flashlight. "They found one tank near the high-ground vicinity of Objective Eagle at LK928537.

"We are the company main effort. We can expect to find at least a reinforced BMP platoon on Eagle. The main enemy strength is on our left, on the western portion of Eagle. We know where two BMPs and one tank are. We will have to find the other BMP and any other tanks that the enemy might have.

"The enemy also appears to have a reserve tank company somewhere to the northeast. He may try to counterattack us with this force once we bust the bastards up on Eagle," Jaeger continued, his tank commanders listening intently to every word.

"If he counterattacks, we could be attacked with as many as thirteen tanks. Battalion has a FASCAM artillery mine field available, and we may get a chance to use it if we have a good target. If you see any dust trails coming at us from the north, call me ASAP! Brief your men and make sure you are ready. The time is now 0405. Are there any questions?"

"I had Johnson check out the route from here to the start point [SP]. He can get us to our SP where we will follow 2d Platoon," Riley announced.

"I also coordinated with their platoon sergeant for signals," Johnson interjected. "They will wave a red-filtered flashlight as their last vehicle crosses the SP. I moved my tank to a position where I can see the signal."

"OK, Sergeant Riley. Good job. We are ready!" Jaeger replied, seeing firsthand the value of parallel planning. "Johnson, I'll let you lead up to Checkpoint Three. Everything else will be as previously planned. Anything else?"

Before anyone could answer, the sound of 1st Platoon's M1 tanks could be heard nearby. First Platoon was moving out of the assembly area as the lead element of Alpha Company. They were headed toward Phase Line August, the line of departure.

Section 14

Jaeger motioned for everyone to mount up and watch for the signal to move out. The tank commanders scrambled back to their vehicles. Sergeant Riley waved his blue-filtered flashlight in a circle and each tank started its engine at the same moment.

Jaeger ran over to his tank and climbed up the left front slope to the TC's hatch. He took off his Kevlar helmet and stowed his gear in the side sponson box. Placing the CVC helmet on his head, he stood in the turret, ready to move.

"Crew Check!" Jaeger announced, peering out through the blackness, sweat covering his palms.

"We are all up and ready," Colwell said enthusiastically. "Fuel topped off, fifty-five rounds available, and main gun boresighted. I also set your frequencies on the VRC-12 radio. Sir, you are good to go."

"I love it when a plan falls together," Jaeger said, smiling to himself.

Everyone waited anxiously for the signal from Johnson. Finally his blue-filtered flashlight waved wildly back and forth. Jaeger observed the signal and ordered Jones to move the tank out to the start point.

The platoon moved in close column, with Johnson, Jaeger, Ramos, and Riley in order. Without a moon, the night was as black as coal. In spite of the darkness, the tank drivers could see about seventy meters to their front almost as clearly as in daylight, using their passive night driving viewers. The tanks of 3d Platoon advanced toward the enemy without a single visible light. Even the radio lights and the instrument panel lights in each M1 driver's compartment were taped over to provide the least signature possible.

Third Platoon moved steadily toward the line of departure at eighteen kilometers per hour. The column kicked up dust as it moved along. The darkness concealed their move.

The radio was silent. Jaeger listened to the whine of the engines and scanned the horizon for any source of light. Using his PVS-7 night vision goggles, Jaeger looked out his turret for any signs of the enemy. The bad guys must not have identified our movement yet, Jaeger thought.

The platoon was now about 500 meters short of Phase Line August. At 0425, right on schedule, the sky erupted to the north with the splash of artillery and mortar shells.

Jaeger could see the artillery smash into Eagle in bright, billowing flashes of light. The earphones of Jaeger's CVC helmet came alive as radio listening silence was lifted and Captain Russell began issuing instructions.

"Romeo Four Seven, this is Delta Two Zero," Captain Russell radioed to his assault platoon leader. "I have initiated artillery on Eagle. What is your situation?"

"Two Zero, this is Four Seven," Jaeger said calmly. "Crossing August now. Continuing to move. No problems. Over."

There was a short pause on the other end of the radio. Captain Russell ordered 1st Platoon to occupy overwatch positions on Checkpoint 5. He directed 2d Platoon to move to Checkpoint 3. A few moments later, 1st Platoon reported to Captain Russell that they were set on Checkpoint 5 and were scanning for targets.

KARRUMMP! KARRUMMP! Off to his left Jaeger observed artillery crashing into the empty center of the company zone, just east of Checkpoint 4. The enemy must be firing blindly, hoping to catch the Americans on the move.

At 0515, 2d Platoon reported over the radio that they were set on Checkpoint 3. Captain Russell ordered 1st and 2d Platoons to open fire on Eagle. Over the roar of 2d Platoon's guns, Russell radioed Jaeger to follow him around the right flank.

"Romeo Four Seven, this is Delta Two Zero," Captain Russell called to his assault platoon leader. "Execute assault. Follow me!"

"Two Zero, this is Four Seven," Jaeger said, a bit too fast. "Roger, we are right with you!"

Jaeger looked out of his hatch, which he had locked in the open protected position. The early-morning twilight and the glare from distant enemy flares gave him just enough light to see the shapes of his tanks. Jaeger was impressed with his platoon's quick reaction to his orders. He felt a great sense of pride in his men and his tanks. They were going to make it!

He observed the dark mass of Hill 798 to his left and realized that he must now maneuver to the east. Ordering his platoon into combat wedge formation, Jaeger began the assault. Captain Russell and his XO were advancing on the left and slightly forward of Jaeger's 3d Platoon.

"Sir, I think I have a target," Colwell announced over the intercom. "Yes . . . identified, BM—"

BOOM! BOOM! An enemy BMP was blown to pieces by the strike of two sabot rounds before Colwell could finish his statement. First Platoon's support fire must have killed the BMP. The full force of Madsen's support fire—four tank cannons and four .50-caliber machine guns plastering Eagle—reinforced Jaeger's confidence.

As Madsen's tanks were firing on Eagle, Jaeger observed Captain Russell drive ahead of the assault force and suddenly open up with his machine guns. Rockets flew through the air, burning past Russell's tank and exploding nearby. Enemy infantry popped up, firing machine guns and hurling antitank grenades.

"GUNNER, COAX, TROOPS . . . FIRE AND ADJUST," Jaeger shouted as he pointed the tank's turret at Russell's attackers.

KABOOM! A rocket-propelled grenade hit the side of Russell's M1 tank. Fighting for its life against enemy infantry, Russell's tank slowed after the RPG hit, but continued moving.

Colwell raked the area with machine gun fire, dropping several enemy with the first burst. Jaeger fired a burst from his .50-caliber machine gun.

Jaeger attempted to radio Russell but was unsuccessful. Russell's radio must have been knocked out when the RPG hit his tank. Following standard procedures, Lieutenant Shields, just to Russell's left rear, took command of the company radio net and called for artillery to suppress the infantry.

Sergeant Ramos in A33 and Sergeant Riley in A34 also concentrated their machine gun fire on the darting Threat infantry. The tanks continued their assault as the enemy quickly withdrew under the pressure of so much firepower.

After several tense minutes, the American artillery exploded above the assault force in deadly airbursts of screaming fléchettes. The remaining Threat infantry was pulverized by this artillery. Scores of variable-time–fuze high-explosive shells, now falling across most of Eagle, killed anything not under armor protection.

With Jaeger's platoon moving fast behind Eagle, the enemy's defenses were now turned. The remaining Threat armored vehicles had no other choice but to run or die in place.

The battlefield was covered in smoke. Daylight was breaking and the smoke clung low, ten to fifteen feet over Objective Eagle. Unable to see through the smoke, the enemy fire was inaccurate. The M1s, equipped with thermal sights, saw through the smoke and gained a decisive advantage. Using their thermal sights, Madsen's 1st Platoon and Williams's 2d Platoon continued to pour deadly suppressive fire across Eagle.

Moving out of his prepared position on the western side of Eagle, a BMP darted into the open. The BMP was attempting to reposition to an alternate position to engage the American threat from the east.

BOOM! BOOM! Jaeger watched as the BMP took two direct hits and burst into flames only 400 meters to his left front.

Jaeger lost sight of Captain Russell's tank but he couldn't stop to worry about that now. Jaeger continued the assault, moving at high speed across the broken terrain behind Objective Eagle. Colwell swung the turret back and forth, scanning for targets and firing his machine guns at suspicious locations. Johnson, Riley, and Ramos were following to the right rear, echeloned behind Jaeger.

"Romeo Four Seven, this is Red Four," Riley called to his platoon leader over the platoon radio net. "We are in the lead now; stay with me. Let's not get too far ahead. There has got to be another BMP and a T-72 out here somewhere!"

"Romeo Four Seven, this is Red Two," Sergeant Johnson interrupted. "I saw some movement to your left front; stay alert!"

"Roger that, Red Two . . . wait!" Jaeger screamed. "GUNNER, SABOT, PC!"

"Identified," Colwell announced.

"UP," Curn shouted as he rammed a HEAT round into the gun and set the firing safety to the fire position.

"FIRE!" Jaeger ordered.

BOOM! Colwell fired at a BMP that was backing up not thirty-five feet in front of A31. The round hit the BMP just below the turret. The shell tore a gaping hole into the side of the BMP and it exploded in a terrific orange-red fireball. The puny 30mm gun turret sheared off and soared 200 feet into the air.

Jaeger didn't have time to celebrate. As he passed by the burning, wrecked BMP, he saw a target off to his left. A T-72 tank, dug into the ground all the way to the turret, swung its gun over, aiming at Jaeger.

Roll the dice.

If the total of the two dice is four or less, go to Section 16.

If the total of the two dice is five or greater, go to Section 25.

Section 15

KARRUMMP! KARRUMMP! A33 took a direct hit from an enemy 152mm artillery shell. The shell smashed through the top rear of the turret and into the ammunition storage compartment. In a blinding flash, the ammunition exploded on the burning M1, sending a searing orange-blue flame fifty feet into the air.

Somehow, Ramos and his gunner survived the initial hit. They fell off their burning tank, only to be killed by enemy artillery as they scrambled to find protective cover. With so much artillery falling, they never had a chance outside their tank. Jaeger's heart sank as he watched the flames.

"Lieutenant, I see a column of vehicles heading south, just northeast of Checkpoint Thirteen," Colwell announced over the tank intercom.

BOOM! BOOM! Just then, as if to prove the accuracy of Colwell's sighting, both Riley's and Johnson's tanks opened up with main gun fire. Although the enemy tanks were almost 2,500 meters away, Riley hit one of them after firing his second round.

"GUNNER! SABOT, TANK," Jaeger shouted. Jaeger's loader fed another sabot round into the cannon.

"Identified!" Colwell cried.

"Fire and adjust!" Jaeger screamed.

BOOM! The 105mm gun leapt back, shaking the tank with the energy of the exit of another round. The air inside the tank was acrid; the smoke and the powder smell filled the crew's nostrils and left their throats parched and burning.

The actions inside the turret were automatic. The tired loader and excited gunner worked as fast as possible to pump rounds downrange and destroy targets. The tank recoiled with each shot.

The Threat column was now less than 2,000 meters away. Jaeger appeared to be getting no effective support from the rest of Alpha Company.

Jaeger, Riley, and Johnson continued to fire. They raced back and forth to alternate firing positions to avoid the enemy's return fire. With the Threat column closing quickly, Jaeger knew that he had to make a decision. Unable to contact his commander, he knew that he must decide to run, or to stay and fight an entire company with only three tanks. He was sure that Riley and Johnson would follow him no matter what he decided.

The enemy was getting closer. Time was short. Jaeger must decide!

If Jaeger decides to withdraw to live to fight another day, go to Section 20.

If Jaeger decides to stay and take on a Threat tank company with three M1 tanks, go to Section 19.

Section 16

Jaeger was too slow. The T-72 tank slammed a 125mm HVAPFSDS round into Jaeger's turret. The shock from the impact of the round was tremendous. Luckily, Jaeger didn't even have time to feel the pain.

Sometimes the best warrior is struck down by an unlucky situation. Sometimes the best plans fail. But often, the reason that luck turns sour is that the deck has been stacked against the player. To win, you must stack the deck in your favor. This can be done by preparing flexible and timely plans, understanding the enemy, and using reconnaissance to hit the enemy where he is weak.

General George S. Patton, Jr., once said that untutored courage is useless in the face of educated bullets. Modern war cannot be waged by amateurs. Leaders must be well versed in the art of leading men, planning their time, issuing orders, assigning tasks, and setting priorities. The techniques described below are offered as aids to assist you in your tactical planning.

Section 16

Friction

War is the realm of uncertainty and chance. A thousand distracters and mistakes attack the plan and make it unworkable. Little mistakes multiply their effect, causing each mistake to add to the other, until all the courage and luck in the world won't make the difference.

These factors collectively have been called friction. Clausewitz, the great nineteenth-century German military philosopher, defined friction as the force that makes the apparently easy so difficult. Friction has a psychological as well as physical impact. Friction is the inherent condition of war. It can be reduced but never eliminated. Self-induced friction must be minimized and the commander must learn to expect it and fight through the medium of friction. Only through iron willpower, strong leadership, and expert training can the friction of war be reduced. Friction must be overcome by focused, energetic leadership.

Time Planning

The first battle that any tactical commander must win is the battle to control his most precious resource—time. The leader must make a time plan his first priority. The leader must allocate time for his subordinates to prepare and plan. He must allow his subordinates adequate time to thoroughly brief and prepare their soldiers. Remember, time planning is an aid to execution, not a rigid guide that dictates how events will happen. In the worst case the leader must rely on the standard order to "follow me and do as I do."

Not all time is equal. On the battlefield, one hour of daylight is worth three hours of darkness. It does little good to use one-third of the available planning and preparation time in daylight for your planning, only to give your subordinates two-thirds of the remaining time in total darkness. Plan your time to maximize daylight. Squeeze out the value of each moment of daylight for reconnaissance, rehearsal, and observation. This time saved can grow into a combat advantage, such as better preparation, maintenance, and sleep. These things can make the difference.

Techniques such as parallel planning (where several elements of a unit are planning together and sharing the burden of the work), planning for several different courses of action, oral operations orders, visual reconnaissance from vantage points overlooking the battle area, and sand tables are time savers. Learn these techniques and save your men time to prepare, maintain, and rest. Get everyone working to assist your planning.

Agility

One of the major tenets of the U.S. Army's AirLand Battle doctrine is the concept of agility. Agility is the capability to act and think faster than your opponent. It is the first prerequisite for seizing and holding the initiative. Agility is created by rapidly concentrating friendly strength against enemy weakness. If this is done repeatedly, so that by the time the enemy reacts to an initial move, you have already executed another, the enemy can be disrupted to the point that his plans lead to uncoordinated, piecemeal responses.

Agility is as much a mental as a physical quality. Agility must be increased by having well-trained units, well-rehearsed standing operating procedures, and thorough, flexible planning. Leaders must build into their tactical plans the ability to shift the main effort with minimum delay. Plans must be oriented on the enemy by hitting the enemy where he is weak and driving that weakness home until he is defeated. Remember, the best course of action is usually the one that offers you the greatest amount of options during the execution.

Jaeger paid the ultimate sacrifice. He fought and lost. For whatever reasons, friction, luck, or just slow reflexes, Jaeger's war is over.

If you have what it takes to lead American soldiers to victory, go back to Section 1, learning from your mistakes, and fight again. Victory or Death!

Section 17

Jaeger and his men had won their first victory. But there was no time to relax and let down their guard. Jaeger knew that he must consolidate his defenses at Checkpoint 13, reallocate ammunition, select positions, and check out the ground. If the enemy counterattacked, he would be ready.

Jaeger radioed Riley on the platoon frequency and ordered him to get a quick status on fuel and ammunition. The M1 tank was a thirsty monster and had to be refueled after every ten hours of operation. Jaeger knew that the platoon would have to be resupplied before they could make another move.

He then surveyed the battlefield to his north and jotted down some locations that he would call to the company FIST to plot as artillery targets. Over the radio he designated two easily recognizable rock formations as target reference points, or TRPs. These TRPs would help him to direct his tank fires. By using easily visible reference points, he could designate targets for his gunners to engage.

The troops of Alpha Company were exhausted but triumphant. They had met the enemy and beaten him. The only U.S. casualties were two tanks—one from 1st Platoon, which blew a track on an enemy mine, without suffering any serious casualties, and one tank from 2d Platoon, which received a direct hit from a Threat AT-4 on Checkpoint 3. Two tankers had been wounded and one killed by the AT-4. In spite of these losses, Alpha Company's attack had been a great success.

Jaeger's platoon had carried the day. Jaeger acted first, when the situation called for action, without waiting for orders from his commander. The acid test of understanding the commander's intent is to be able to act, without orders, when the situation changes and it is impossible or too late to ask for instructions. Jaeger was able to act correctly because he understood his commander's intent and had briefed his men to understand that intent. He knew what Captain Russell wanted to do to the enemy, and he fought his platoon with that end in mind. This was a critical element of command for a mobile unit conducting maneuver warfare.

War is disorder, not precision. Tactics must be based on the enemy. To shape the battle, the tactical commander must think forward in terms of time and space. A leader must never become a slave to his own plans! Tactics must never conform to the control measures. If Jaeger had let his mind be hindered with the concept of defending Objective Eagle, rather than destroying the enemy, the coordinated counterattack of the Threat reserve tank company would surely have had greater success.

Jaeger's platoon was consolidating their defense when the brigade pushed a fresh battalion north to continue the attack. Because of Jaeger's platoon and Alpha Company, the brigade's attack soon became a pursuit. The Threat defense fell back under the pressure of the relentless American drive.

"You did a great job, Jaeger!" Captain Russell exclaimed as he arrived at Checkpoint 13 to praise his platoon leader.

"You beat an entire Threat tank company! Jaeger, I am going to recommend both you and Riley for the Silver Star," Russell said solemnly. "If it hadn't been for your efforts, we could have been wiped out on Eagle. Your actions saved the battalion."

"Thanks, but the credit really belongs to the men of 3d Platoon, sir," Jaeger said, waving his arm toward the men who had fought so well under his command. "I'd trade all this applause for a few days of rest and relaxation!"

"Fat chance!" Russell laughed. "Mount up your men and move to the southwest side of Checkpoint Eleven. That's our new assembly area. I have to go to battalion to receive the next operations order. I'll be back in an hour or so. Get your men ready for tomorrow's mission!"

"No rest for the weary!" Jaeger grimaced. "I'll see you at the new assembly area." Jaeger saluted Captain Russell smartly and ambled over to his tank commanders. Johnson and Ramos were proudly grouped around Sergeant Riley, waiting for their lieutenant to return with information on their next mission.

Go to Section 34.

Section 18

The T-72 was dug into the ground, hull down. This position offered Jaeger only a narrow turret shot. But the sun was low in the eastern sky and glared down directly in the eyes of the defenders. The enemy position was designed to face the south, not the north. To add to their problems, the crew of the T-72 could not see over the dirt mound that was piled to their left rear. Jaeger's visibility was better.

Jaeger's reactions were lightning fast. The T-72 tank swung its 125mm gun around quickly, but Jaeger beat him to the draw.

BOOM! There wasn't time for a formal fire command, and at less than 100 meters, the tank was hard to miss. The 105mm sabot round hit the T-72 just to the right of the main gun. It seared through the enemy tank, setting off the reactive armor in a blinding flash. The ammunition ignited inside, blowing off the turret in a terrific explosion. The explosion shook the ground near A31 and momentarily blinded Jaeger as he looked out from his hatch.

"Good shot, sir!" Sergeant Colwell shouted over the tank's intercom. "You really blew that bastard to pieces!"

"That one's for Ramos!" Jaeger cried vengefully. Jaeger pushed his CVC switch forward, to radio, and called Sergeant Riley.

"Red Four, this is Romeo Two Seven. See any more targets? Over."

"Negative, Four Seven," Riley replied. "Good shooting. I am moving to that small ridge to your left front to get a look. Cover my move."

"Roger, Red Four. I'll report to higher." Jaeger switched to the company command net and called Captain Russell. Russell had switched tanks with the XO because of his damaged radio. It was now 0628.

"Delta Two Zero, this is Romeo Four Seven. Spot report. Over." Jaeger called his commander with a sense of renewed determination in his voice.

"Romeo Four Seven, this is Delta Two Zero. Send it. Over," Russell answered.

"I have destroyed one BMP and one Tango Seven Two at grid LK934539. Continuing mission. Will call you if we see any more enemy in zone. Over."

"Roger, Romeo Four Seven. There shouldn't be any vehicles left on Eagle. Look out for their infantry; some may have survived the artillery. Once you get to the western edge of Eagle, take up hasty defensive positions and orient north. Call me once you are established on the west side of Eagle. I am moving 1st Platoon forward. Out." Russell's instructions were calm and deliberate. Russell understood that the higher in rank a leader was, the more calm he must appear.

KARRUMMP! KARRUMMP! Hundreds of artillery shells suddenly fell on Eagle in a huge storm of fire and flying steel. The crash of artillery was tremendous, overpowering the senses with flash, noise, and smoke. Jaeger buttoned up and began to navigate by looking through his vision blocks. He could hear the strike of metal on metal as his tank absorbed the fragments from high-explosive shells.

KARRUMMP! Hundreds of little bomblets fell all over his position. Several exploded on the top of his tank but did not penetrate the armor. He tried to call Sergeant Riley, but his radio produced only static. Looking back through his rear vision blocks, Jaeger observed that his radio antenna and matching unit had been completely blown away!

KARRUMMP! KARRUMMP! As the artillery fell, Jaeger realized that the enemy must have preplanned their fires to cover the positions on Objective Eagle. The enemy was pulverizing Eagle with artillery fire that was too accurate to mean anything else. If Jaeger stayed in these positions, all of his tanks would be damaged or destroyed.

KARRUMMP! KARRUMMP! KARRUMMP! The shelling increased. Jaeger moved past Sergeant Riley's tank, hoping Riley would follow. Riley, recognizing that his platoon leader was out of commo, instinctively moved along to Jaeger's right. They reached the western edge of Eagle, in spite of the shelling, and took up hasty defensive positions facing north. At least, Jaeger thought, if there were any enemy infantry out there, they were killed by their own artillery. Nothing dismounted could live through this.

Out of communication, Jaeger didn't know if the rest of the company had moved to Eagle. The radios were silent. Sergeant Riley was here, but that's all Jaeger knew.

"Lieutenant, I see a column of vehicles heading south, northeast of Checkpoint Thirteen," Colwell announced over the tank intercom.

BOOM! Just then, as if to prove the accuracy of Colwell's sighting, Riley's tank opened up with main gun fire. Riley's first round struck short of the lead vehicle of the enemy column. Although the

95

Threat tanks were approximately 2,500 meters away, Riley finally hit one of them after his third round.

"GUNNER! SABOT, TANK!" Jaeger shouted. Jaeger's loader fed another sabot round into the tank cannon.

"Identified!" Colwell cried.

"FIRE AND ADJUST!" Jaeger screamed.

BOOM! The 105mm gun jumped back, making the tank shake with the exit of the round. The air inside the tank was acrid, the smoke and the powder smell filling the crew's nostrils and leaving their throats parched and burning.

The actions inside the turret were automatic, with the tired loader and excited gunner working as fast as possible to pump rounds downrange. Steel shell casings littered the turret floor. The tank lurched back and forth with each shot, the gun spitting out an empty casing after each round was fired.

The Threat column was now less than 2,000 meters away.

Jaeger and Riley continued to fire and move back and forth to alternate firing positions to avoid the enemy's return fire. With the Threat column only minutes away, Jaeger knew that he had to make a decision. Unable to contact his commander, he hoped that Riley would follow him if he decided either to stay and fight or make a run for it.

The enemy column was closing the distance quickly. Time was slipping away. The artillery continued to hammer down on Jaeger's position. Jaeger had to decide now!

If Jaeger decides to withdraw to live to fight another day, go to Section 20.

If Jaeger decides to stay and take on a Threat tank company with two M1 tanks, go to Section 21.

Section 19

Wars are often won by a few brave men who refuse to submit to the enemy. In war, it is usually suicide to run in the face of the enemy. Jaeger knew that his options were limited. But he was a professional soldier. He was prepared to die if need be, but he wouldn't run!

The enemy tank column headed full force against the western edge of Objective Eagle. Jaeger could see at least seven T-72 tanks and a few BMPs. Several enemy tanks fired in Jaeger's direction.

BANG! Jaeger's tank shuddered from a hit from a Threat T-72 that miraculously glanced off the frontal armor.

"Thank God for the guys in Detroit!" Jaeger said out loud, praising the anonymous designers of the M1 tank over the tank intercom. "Anybody hurt? Crew check!"

"We are OK, Lieutenant!" Colwell replied shakily. "Alert! Two tanks, near Checkpoint Thirteen!"

"FIRE!" Jaeger yelled, his heart beating so fast that he was afraid it might burst out of his chest. The tank recoiled again with the firing of another round. Another steel 105mm casing clanged to the turret floor.

"TARGET! LEFT TANK!"

BOOM! Colwell fired automatically, not waiting for a command. Colwell hit the second enemy tank in the track, forcing it to spin around and come to a grinding halt.

Jaeger's crew was fighting desperately against the onrush of too many targets. Jaeger could hear Sergeant Riley and Sergeant Johnson continuing to fire, but he could not see them from his present position. Jaeger watched as the enemy pulled out of column formation and moved into line formation to make the final assault. There appeared to be five T-72 tanks and three BMPs left.

Jaeger opened his hatch to the open protected position to get a better picture of the battlefield. The open protected position covered the top of his head, protecting him from fragments. It also permitted an unrestricted view that was invaluable in close-in tank battles. The tank commander who could identify his enemy first was usually the winner.

The fresh air rushed into the tank and filled his lungs. Jaeger looked to the west and saw a series of flashes firing directly at the advancing enemy column. Madsen's 1st Platoon was hitting the enemy advance hard!

KABOOM! Suddenly A31 was hit by a powerful blow that threw Jaeger back against his hatch and down onto the turret floor. He hit the floor hard.

The tank had been hit in the flank, near the driver's compartment. The enemy round burned into the hull, spewing fire up and into the turret, reducing Specialist Curn to a bloody mass. Curn's limp body fell beneath the gun. Sergeant Colwell, still seated in the gunner's seat, was bleeding and unconscious. Jones, Jaeger's driver, was gone. His driver's compartment was a black, charred mess that showed only the strike of the enemy round. The inside of the turret filled with smoke and the exhaust of the Halon automatic fire extinguishers. Jaeger, straining to avoid blacking out, rushed to open the hatch.

Jaeger forced himself out of the hatch and fell on the top of the turret, vomiting. Smoke and Halon gas rushed out of the open TC's hatch. Jaeger struggled to regain his senses.

"I must get Colwell," Jaeger shouted out loud as he went back inside the turret to help his crew. With great effort, he yanked Colwell up and out onto the top of the turret. Colwell, delirious but alive, coughed and groaned.

Firing continued all around them as the enemy attempted a final assault on Eagle. Jaeger returned to the turret of the tank and searched Curn for a pulse. He didn't find one . . . Curn was dead. Angry, Jaeger reached back to check his tank commander's controls. The gun was still operative and loaded. He scanned the horizon for targets.

A Threat BMP moved out from the cover of a small rise and headed to the right. Jaeger tracked him for two seconds and fired the 105mm cannon from his tank commander's position. At 700 meters it was not a difficult shot.

Jaeger hit the BMP in the rear side, right in the troop compartment. The BMP swung around with the force of the impact and burst into flames. The back door to the BMP opened and a dazed infantryman fell to the ground. In the next moment, the BMP's ammunition ignited, incinerating the infantryman and the remainder of his squad in a bright ball of flame. BMPs burn brightly when the on-board ammunition lights up.

Unable to load another round, Jaeger climbed out of the turret. Colwell, one hand on the tank's wind sensor and the other holding his chest, screamed in pain. He was in bad shape. Mustering all of his remaining strength, Jaeger manhandled Colwell off the tank.

Out of nowhere, Sergeant Johnson and A33 arrived near Jaeger's smoking tank. Firing to protect his downed platoon leader, Johnson opened his hatch and waved for Jaeger and Colwell to jump aboard. Colwell, still dazed, couldn't move. Jaeger pulled Colwell over his shoulder in a fireman's carry and ran toward Johnson's tank.

Another BMP pulled out through the smoke and spotted Jaeger and Colwell. The BMP fired three long bursts from its coaxial machine gun before Johnson sent a sabot round into its hull, turning it into a mangled wreck.

Jaeger and Colwell went down. Jaeger was hit in the leg. Colwell wasn't so lucky, and took a round right through the head. Jaeger tried to run, not recognizing his wound, but his tangled leg refused to cooperate.

BOOM! BOOM! Riley showed up just to the left of Johnson's tank and provided additional covering fire. After the second round, Riley's loader leapt out of his hatch and ran over to his wounded platoon leader. Panting hard from the quick run, he checked Colwell and determined that he was beyond saving. He grabbed Jaeger and carried him back to A34, ignoring Jaeger's screams as he slung the wounded lieutenant over his shoulder. With Johnson now firing as fast as he could, Riley and his loader dragged Jaeger into the tank.

"Thanks, Riley," Jaeger cried in pain. "Aghh! God this hurts! Get the commander on the radio and call in some artillery on this position ASAP!"

"Roger, Lieutenant!" Riley shouted, as he watched Specialist Fourth Class Harrison try to bandage Jaeger's mutilated leg. Jaeger screamed out in pain as the tank lurched forward, driving his wounded knee into the side of the tank.

"Delta Two Zero, this is Romeo Four Four," Riley yelled urgently. "Request fire for effect, DPICM, LK930540, danger close. Five T-72s. Out!"

Two more T-72s came out of the smoke and immediately engaged Sergeant Johnson's tank. Johnson disabled one, hitting it in the lower left skirt. The T-72 broke to a jolting stop and spun to the left in a violent half circle. The enemy opened their tank hatches and the crew began to bail out of their damaged vehicle.

KABOOM! The other T-72 fired a 125mm round at Johnson's tank. The distance between them was less than 300 meters. Johnson's tank was hit right at the turret ring. The turret lurched backward, as if snapped in two, with tremendous velocity. The turret moved several feet to the rear of the tank, and the tank burst into flames. Black smoke billowed from the loader's and tank commander's hatches. There was no sign of life.

BOOM! Riley traversed and fired on the T-72 that had just killed Johnson. Riley's sabot round punctured the enemy tank's turret, forcing it to a sudden, mangled stop.

"Aghh!" Jaeger screamed as the spent 105mm casing struck him in his good leg. The turret of the M1 tank was crowded without adding an additional passenger. Riley's loader pushed Jaeger back against the wall and, working around his screaming platoon leader, attempted to load another round into the main gun.

Having lost all of his platoon but his own tank, Riley, incensed to fury and listening to the screams of his wounded platoon leader, fired another round at the burning hulk of the T-72. This second round ignited the T-72's ammunition, and the Threat tank turret shattered into red-hot, burning chunks of metal.

The last thing that Jaeger remembered was the sound of incoming artillery. The noise consumed him, as if artillery was landing everywhere around them. The pain was now too much. Jaeger passed out. . . .

Jaeger opened his eyes. He could make out the figure of Sergeant Riley and Captain Russell. He couldn't move.

"Don't try to move, Lieutenant," Riley said quietly, looking down at Jaeger as the medics attended to him on a stretcher.

"Who . . . who won?" Jaeger asked feebly.

"We did. You did a hell of a job, Lieutenant. Because we were able to stop them here, brigade was able to push a fresh battalion through Alpha Company's zone. They are driving north right now."

"You beat an entire Threat tank company, Jaeger. I am going to recommend both you and Riley for the Silver Star," Russell said solemnly. "If it hadn't been for your sacrifice, we could have been wiped out on Eagle. You saved the battalion. We will get you back to an aid station as fast as this M113 can go. Medics, take good care of him!"

Jaeger tried to reply but the world started to spin. Jaeger blacked out again.

The medics said that he had a good chance of making it.

Go to Section 22.

Section 20

The enemy tanks headed directly for Jaeger, firing in platoon volleys as they moved. Jaeger knew that they wouldn't stand a chance if they stood and fought it out. He could see at least nine T-72 tanks and several BMPs charging right for his position.

KABOOM! Jaeger's tank shuddered. Blinded momentarily by a great flash of light, Jaeger ducked down inside the turret. An enemy tank round had just hit and glanced off his turret.

"Thank God for the guys in Detroit!" Jaeger said out loud, praising the anonymous designers of the M1 tank over his intercom. "Anybody hurt?"

"We're all right, Lieutenant!" Colwell replied. "Alert! Identified four tanks, near Checkpoint Thirteen!"

"Let's get out of here!" Jaeger yelled, his heart beating so fast that he thought it would burst out of his chest.

Private First Class Jones, Jaeger's driver, threw the tank into reverse and pulled the tank behind a mound of dirt. Orienting the tank south, Jaeger looked behind for Sergeant Riley. Riley continued to fight the enemy. Near misses ricocheted all around his tank. Finally, Riley's tank took a direct hit right in the turret.

There was a terrible explosion. Fire and smoke billowed from Riley's tank commander's hatch. Two more enemy rounds hit the burning hulk. The enemy had overrun the position. Riley was dead.

"Riley's had it!" Jaeger cried hysterically. "Jones, let's get the hell out of here! Get moving!"

Jaeger watched through his rear vision blocks as the enemy, unopposed, rolled onto the western edge of Eagle and began to place accurate fire on the disorganized remnants of Alpha Company. Several Threat tanks headed south and then east to roll up Alpha Company's position. With the western edge of Eagle undefended, the rest of Alpha Company didn't stand a chance.

Jaeger stopped looking behind, tears filling his eyes. His tank raced south. He wanted to put as much distance as possible between his tank and the death occurring on Eagle.

"Jones, hit the smoke generator," Jaeger ordered. White billows of smoke spewed from the rear of the tank's engine compartment.

More T-72 tanks pulled onto Eagle. Looking south, the enemy tanks on Eagle observed the lone American M1 tank, trailing smoke, racing to the rear. A31 offered an easy mark for the enemy tank gunners.

BOOM! BOOM!

Jaeger was retreating fast, but not fast enough.

Go to Section 16.

Section 21

Jaeger figured the odds. If he tried to run away he stood a better than even chance of getting shot in the back. From Eagle he would be an easy mark for an enemy tank gunner. If he stayed and fought, he could at least take a few of the bastards with him. He couldn't run. He was made of sterner stuff than that. He couldn't abandon Riley. He owed that much to his men and to his unit. They were depending on him to do his part. He wasn't about to let them down.

Jaeger could see a column of at least nine T-72 tanks and a few BMPs moving south. They were headed full force against the western edge of Objective Eagle.

"GUNNER. SABOT, TWO TANKS!" Jaeger screamed into his intercom, laying the gun on the lead T-72 tank.

"Identified," Colwell answered coolly, knowing from Jaeger's tone of voice that they were committed to fighting from this position.

"FIRE AND ADJUST!" Jaeger ordered.

BOOM! The sabot round shot through the air like a bolt of white light and hit the lead T-72. The enemy tank stopped abruptly, a portion of its reactive armor exploding in a bright flash. The dead tank, lifeless, just sat there, its gun tube pointing skyward.

KABOOM! Lurching backward, Jaeger's tank shuddered from a hit from a T-72. The enemy shell miraculously glanced off A31's frontal armor.

"Thank God for the guys in Detroit!" Jaeger said out loud, praising the anonymous designers of the M1 tank over the intercom. "Crew report!"

"We are OK, Lieutenant!" Colwell replied. "IDENTIFIED! TWO MORE TANKS . . . ON THE WAY!"

BOOM! Colwell fired immediately. Jaeger braced himself; his heart was beating so fast he thought it would burst out of his chest. The tank recoiled again with the firing of another round. Another steel casing shot to the floor as the gun ejected the spent shell.

"TARGET! LEFT TANK!" Jaeger yelled.

BOOM! The gunner fired automatically, not waiting for a command. Colwell hit the second enemy tank in its tracks, making it spin around and come to a grinding halt.

BOOM! BOOM! Sergeant Riley continued to fire. Jaeger could see Riley's tank through his vision blocks, firing against the advancing enemy.

The enemy pulled out of column formation and quickly formed a firing line for the final assault. The enemy was firing from the short halt as they rushed forward.

It was now difficult to tell how many tanks the enemy had left. The dust from the charging vehicles and the smoke from burning vehicles obscured normal vision. Moving quickly, the enemy closed in for the kill.

KABOOM! Sergeant Riley's tank erupted in a ball of flame and sparks, the victim of a T-72's 125mm shell.

Jaeger opened his hatch to the open protected position in order to determine where the enemy was. Riley's tank, wrecked and smoking, showed no signs of life.

"Damn it. Those bastards!" Jaeger screamed. White-hot hatred and grief flowed through Jaeger's soul. "Jones, move forward, right front. Colwell, action left!" Jaeger swung the gun around to his left. Two T-72 tanks and a BMP were just 800 meters away, racing right for A31.

BOOM! Colwell fired and hit the lead T-72. The 105mm cannon recoiled with the shot of the sabot round. The steel casing from the round ejected with a clang onto a pile of other spent casings.

Section 21

"UP!" Curn yelled as he quickly loaded another round. Colwell, not wasting a second, adjusted the gun onto the second tank.

BOOM! This round hit the turret of the second enemy tank.

"Target!" Colwell yelled, his eyed glued to his gunner's primary sight (GPS). "But I got more targets on—"

KABOOM! Suddenly A31 was hit by a powerful blow that threw Jaeger back against his hatch and down onto the turret floor. He hit the floor hard. Blinding light and noise surrounded him. Everything went black for a moment.

Jaeger came to his senses and looked around. Specialist Curn, bloody and lifeless, had been thrown beneath the gun. Sergeant Colwell, still seated in his gunner's seat, was bleeding and unconscious. Jones, Jaeger's driver, didn't move. The tank had taken a direct flank hit in the driver's compartment.

The turret started to fill with smoke and the exhaust of the automatic fire extinguishers. Jaeger, gasping for breath, jumped up and tried to pull Colwell out of the tank. With great effort, he yanked Colwell up and out onto the top of the turret. The fresh air seemed to revive Colwell, but then he began to moan from the pain caused by his wounds.

Firing was continuing all around them as the enemy made their final assault on Eagle. Jaeger returned to the turret of the tank and searched Curn for a pulse. He didn't find one. Jones was dead, too.

Jaeger reached back to check his tank commander's controls. The turret didn't respond. He forced himself down into the gunner's seat. He checked the manual traversing handle and manually moved the turret. The gun was still operative and loaded. With his left hand on the manual firing device, he scanned for targets.

A BMP rushed out from a small rise and headed to the right. Jaeger tracked him for two seconds and violently cranked the manual blaster.

Nothing! The little magneto whirled in its casing. He cranked again.

BOOM! Jaeger hit the BMP in the rear side in the troop compartment. The BMP swung around with the force of the impact and burst into flames, its fuel supply igniting.

Unable to load another round, Jaeger climbed out of the turret. With all the strength he could muster, he struggled to pull Colwell off the tank. Painfully, Jaeger managed to drag Colwell to the safety of a small rock formation.

A T-72 tank rolled by and sent another 125mm fin-stabilized sabot round into Jaeger's dead vehicle. The T-72 then fired its machine guns at Jaeger before racing past him and heading east.

Jaeger didn't get far. Two BMPs dismounted their infantry to clear the objective area and police up any surviving American soldiers. The enemy had spent their energy against Jaeger's defenses. They didn't have enough force to take on the rest of Alpha Company, but they intended to hold the ground on the western edge of Eagle.

Before he could make good his escape, Jaeger and Colwell were captured. Overcome by the speed of events, Jaeger did not have time to resist. The enemy infantry forced him to abandon Colwell and move toward their BMP.

Jaeger was thrown to the ground and his hands were tied behind his back. Fifty meters away he saw an enemy soldier fire his AK-74 into the limp body of his gunner.

"You bastards!" Jaeger screamed as he tried to get up.

His guard responded by kicking him in the side several times. The last thing that Jaeger remembered was the distinctive sound of incoming artillery shells.

"They did a hell of a job," Madsen said sadly, surveying the battlefield and looking down at the mangled bodies of Jaeger and Colwell.

"They beat an entire enemy tank company. I am going to recommend both Jaeger and Riley for the Silver Star," Russell said solemnly. "If it hadn't been for their efforts, we would have been wiped out on Eagle. The sacrifice of 3d Platoon saved the battalion. They died like soldiers."

Go to Section 24.

Section 22

Jaeger's war is over. Learn from his mistakes! The following advice will assist you in future battles.

Section 22

Initiative

A leader must know when it is necessary to disobey orders. Often in war, the situation will move so quickly that junior leaders will have to make decisions on the spot. Time is the critical element. Subordinate commanders must make decisions on their own initiative, based upon a clear understanding of their commander's intent, rather than just passively passing information and waiting for orders. There would not be enough time to confirm every action with higher headquarters.

In AirLand Battle terms, *initiative* means setting or changing the terms of battle by action. This involves taking prudent risks. In the attack it implies never allowing the enemy to recover from the initial shock of the attack. Applied to individual soldiers and their leaders, it requires a willingness and an ability to act independently within the framework of the higher commander's intent.

When a decision is guided by the higher commander's intent, it is called initiative. Only in this way can a force act in concert with itself in the rapidly changing, ever chaotic environment of the battlefield. When a junior leader makes a decision that does not coincide with the commander's intent, or may be contrary to that intent, it is called a reckless gamble. Only experience and trust can grow leaders who can understand the difference and learn to act accordingly.

A professional soldier is always at work. As soon as one battle is finished, he prepares for the next. A pragmatist to the end, he knows that there will always be another. He learns from his mistakes and vows never to make the same error again.

Good warriors learn from their mistakes. Are you good enough to try again?

If you have what it takes to lead American soldiers to victory, go back to Section 1, learning from your mistakes, and fight again. Victory or Death!

Section 23

KARRUMMP! KARRUMMP! The artillery fire was increasing.

Jaeger knew that he didn't have a second to lose. How was he going to signal his platoon to follow him without a radio?

Moving back out of his hole, he maneuvered close enough to Sergeant Riley's tank to get his attention, then raced forward to Checkpoint 13. He held his breath as he waited for his platoon's reaction. Would they follow? Did they understand? Would he end up out there all alone?

After what seemed to be an eternity, Jaeger was relieved to see his three M1 tanks speeding north behind him. The artillery continued to fall on Eagle, but his platoon had now gained relative safety by moving out of the artillery impact area.

"Jones, move to that small scrub bush on the right side of the ridge to our front," Jaeger said to his driver over the tank intercom. Jaeger carefully directed Jones into a hasty firing position.

Two minutes later Jaeger had his entire platoon on Checkpoint 13. His wingman, Johnson, pulled up thirty meters to the left of Jaeger's tank and opened his hatch. Jaeger, realizing that he must leave his tank and take over a tank with good communications, informed his crew that he was going to leave A31 and take over A32.

Jaeger jumped out of his hatch and onto the ground, then sprinted the thirty meters in record time. Johnson, a true professional soldier, understood the platoon leader's dilemma and quickly made the transfer.

"Delta Two Zero, this is Romeo Four Seven. Over." Jaeger called his commander from his new tank.

"Romeo Four Seven, this is Delta Two Zero. What is your situation? Over," Russell answered impatiently.

"I am set on Checkpoint Thirteen with four tanks, observing north. Negative contact. I can observe for FASCAM at LK940570 if needed. Over."

"Roger, Romeo," Russell replied. "Good job! I am moving the rest of Delta forward to positions on the east of Eagle. Do you see any enemy headed your way? Over."

"Not yet," Jaeger said. "Wait. . . . Out."

"Lieutenant, I see some dust trails heading south, just northwest of Checkpoint Eleven," Specialist Fourth Class Hyatt, A32's gunner, announced over the tank intercom.

Jaeger jumped down to his commander's sight and verified the report. "Roger that," Jaeger grinned. "Good eyes, Hyatt! That must be the enemy counterattack force.

"Delta Two Zero, this is Romeo Four Seven," Jaeger radioed his commander. "I got dust trails headed south near Checkpoint Eleven. Over."

"Roger, Romeo," Russell replied. "Get me a good grid and I'll coordinate FASCAM."

"Roger, I estimate that they will be at . . . ," Jaeger paused to check his map. At standard battle speed of twenty kilometers per hour, or three minutes a kilometer, it should take the enemy fifteen minutes. ". . . at LK940560 in one five minutes. Over."

"I understand, Romeo." Russell's voice was calm and sincere. "I'll get you some help as soon as I can. Hang on. Out."

Jaeger was on his own. He switched his radio to the platoon radio frequency.

"Red elements, this is Romeo Four Seven," Jaeger said, trying to sound calm. "We got bad guys coming our way. Right now the enemy is behind Checkpoint Eleven. We have to stop them. They will be here in about fifteen minutes. Find yourself a good fighting position. Hold your fire until you hear my command. Acknowledge!"

"Romeo, this is Red Three. Roger," Ramos answered.

"Romeo, this is Red Four. Roger. Nice to have you back on the air," Riley replied, relieved that his platoon leader was now able to communicate again.

Jaeger switched his radio frequency back to the company command frequency and updated Captain Russell. Russell informed him that the FASCAM was approved and that the guns were ready and would fire as soon as he heard 3d Platoon open fire. In addition, Captain Russell informed Jaeger that he would eavesdrop on his net to make it easier for the lieutenant to fight the battle without switching frequencies.

Jaeger could see Staff Sergeant Johnson in the hatch of A31, Jaeger's old tank. Unable to communicate with him over the roar of the engines, Jaeger sent his loader out to A31 to inform Johnson not to fire until he saw the rest of the platoon engage. Johnson nodded, and waved a thumbs-up gesture to his platoon leader. The loader raced back to his tank.

Jaeger waited, watching the dust trails get closer with each passing second.

"Lieutenant!" Jaeger's new gunner cried. "IDENTIFIED . . . TANKS . . . RANGE TWO NINE HUNDRED!"

"Steady, Hyatt. Wait for the command." Jaeger's calm voice had a reassuring effect on his new crew. He jumped down to his sight, set at high power, to determine the makeup of the enemy force. He waited for the enemy to close within 2,500 meters.

"Red, this is Romeo Four Seven," Jaeger confidently called over the radio. "SABOT . . . TEN TANKS, THREE BMPS . . . DIRECT FRONT . . . DEPTH . . . FIRE AND ADJUST!"

BOOM! BOOM! BOOM! BOOM! The platoon fired almost at once, four fin-stabilized uranium-depleted sabot rounds moving faster than the speed of sound. Two T-72s burst into flames, their crews scattered to pieces across the hot desert floor.

"GUNNER! SABOT, LEAD TANK," Jaeger shouted. Jaeger's loader loaded another sabot round.

"IDENTIFIED!" his gunner cried.

"FIRE!" Jaeger screamed.

BOOM! The 105mm gun leapt back, making the tank shake with the exit of the round. Jaeger's round struck close to an enemy tank, missing it by inches.

"Doubtful right!" Jaeger yelled into his intercom. "Load sabot!"

"UP!" the loader answered after ramming another 105mm sabot round into the cannon.

"FIRE AND ADJUST!" Jaeger ordered, his eye glued to his tank commander's sight.

BOOM! Hyatt's second round hit its target dead center. The enemy tank froze in place.

The actions inside the turret were now automatic, with the anxious loader and excited gunner working as fast as possible to pump rounds downrange. The air inside the tank was acrid with the smell of smoke and powder. The tank recoiled back and forth. With each shot, empty steel shell casings ejected onto the turret floor.

The enemy advance continued. They were now less than 1,800 meters away. Riley's tank scored a direct hit on another BMP.

BOOM! BOOM! BOOM!

"Delta Two Zero, this is Romeo Four Seven," Jaeger pleaded into his microphone. "I need that FASCAM now! Over."

Before Captain Russell could answer the plea of his hard-pressed platoon leader, the artillery began to fall. As the artillery projectiles dispersed their loads, the ground became strewn with deadly antitank mines. Little wires sprang out from each mine as the mines hit the ground. Running over these sensitive wires triggered a tremendous explosion. If the mine exploded under a tank, the tank would be destroyed at its weakest point, the thinly armored belly.

The artillery landed 300 meters in front of the enemy column. The rounds kept falling, laying a FASCAM mine field 400 meters in diameter. You couldn't ask for better shooting from the artillerymen.

Jaeger's tanks continued to fire at the advancing enemy. The mines disabled one tank and one BMP immediately. The rest of the enemy detoured around the mine field by heading east and then south. This maneuver exposed their flank to 3d Platoon's guns.

BOOM! BOOM! BOOM! BOOM! Three more enemy tanks were hit by Jaeger's 105mm guns.

At last, the enemy had enough. Turning on their smoke generators, the remaining enemy vehicles raced north to the safety of their own lines. Jaeger used the burning hulks of the enemy tanks as reference points to direct the platoon's fire. Johnson, with a lucky shot, picked off another BMP before the enemy moved behind the cover of Checkpoint 11.

Go to Section 17.

Section 24

Sun Tzu, the famous Chinese military philosopher of 500 B.C., said that the skillful commander wins his victories before seeking battle; a commander destined to defeat fights in hope of winning. Jaeger squandered his time, attempted to do everything himself, and put his troops at a disadvantage. He fought in hope of winning rather than establishing the basis for victory before the battle.

Each action in war is the fleeting result of a unique combination of circumstances, requiring an original solution. No action can be viewed in total isolation. The tempo of modern war will push man and machine to the limit. Little mistakes multiply their effect, causing each mistake to add to the other until all the courage and luck in the world won't make the difference. Lost opportunities may never be regained. Success depends on your ability to deal with rapidly changing situations, adjusting for errors and capitalizing on the enemy's mistakes.

The essence of life is struggle and its goal is domination over your opponent. There are loftier goals with more profound meanings, but they exist only in the human mind. The reality of life is war. Sometimes the act of life boils down to seeing how many of your enemies you can take with you to the grave.

Often the best course of action is to hold tight and fight. Jaeger had the courage to know that other men were counting on his ability to stand and fight. He knew that the lives of the men in his company and in his battalion depended on his actions. Sometimes there is no safe way out. Sometimes you must die. Jaeger died fighting! Do you have what it takes to try again?

If you have what it takes to lead American soldiers to victory, go back to Section 1, learning from your mistakes, and fight again.

Section 25

The commander of the T-72 tank swung his 125mm gun around as fast as he could. Jaeger moved his turret quickly to meet this new threat.

Section 25

The T-72 was dug into the ground, hull down, and offered only a narrow turret shot. The sun was glaring down at an angle directly into the eyes of the defender, and the enemy tank commander must have had trouble seeing over the dirt mound that was piled to their left rear. Jaeger's visibility was better. Sometimes, that's all the edge that's needed.

Excited, Jaeger aimed at the T-72's turret and fired the M68 cannon from his tank commander's override controls. There wasn't time for a formal fire command.

BOOM! Jaeger missed the T-72 by inches, the high-velocity round hitting the dirt in front of the dug-in tank.

BOOM! A second round broke through the T-72's formidable armor protection and ignited the ammunition inside the tank. The turret blew off in a terrific explosion, shaking the ground all around and momentarily blinding Jaeger as he peered out from his hatch.

"You owe me one, Romeo," Johnson called over the radio to his platoon leader.

"Good shot, Red Two," Jaeger called over the radio, breathing a sigh of relief. "That was a close one!"

"That's what wingmen are for, Romeo!" Johnson cried. Johnson called Sergeant Riley. "Red Four, this is Red Two. See any more targets? Over."

"Negative, Red Two. Good shooting!" Riley replied. "Romeo . . . Red Three and I are going to move to that small ridge to your left front to see what is up ahead. You and Red Two cover our move."

"Roger, Red Four. I'll report to higher." Jaeger switched to the company command net and called Captain Russell. It was now 0628.

"Delta Two Zero, this is Romeo Four Seven. Spot report. Over." Jaeger called his commander with a sense of renewed determination in his voice.

"Romeo Four Seven, this is Delta Two Zero. Send it. Over," Russell answered.

"I have destroyed one BMP and one Tango Seven Two at grid LK934539. I have four tanks. Continuing mission. I will call you if we see any more enemy in zone. Over."

"Roger, Romeo Four Seven. Good job!" Russell said gleefully. "I lost commo in my tank and had to switch tanks with the XO. From what I gather, there shouldn't be many enemy left on Eagle.

"Once you get to the western edge of Eagle, take up hasty defensive positions and orient north. Call me once you are established on the west side of Eagle. I am moving 1st Platoon forward. Out." Russell's instructions were calm and deliberate. Jaeger sensed that Russell understood that the higher in rank a leader was, the more calm he must appear.

KARRUMMP! KARRUMMP! Hundreds of artillery shells fell on Eagle. The crash of the artillery was tremendous. Jaeger buttoned up and navigated by looking through his vision blocks. The field of view through the vision blocks was narrow but he was now totally protected by heavy armor. Jaeger could hear the side of his tank absorb the fragments from the high-explosive projectiles.

KARRUMMP! KARRUMMP! Scores of little bomblets fell over his position. One exploded on the top of his tank, with no apparent effect.

KARRUMMP! KARRUMMP! Jaeger tried to call Sergeant Riley, but his radio emitted only static. Looking back through his rear vision blocks, Jaeger could see that the radio antennas and radio matching unit had been completely blown away! As the artillery continued to fall, Jaeger realized that the enemy must have registered their old positions with their own artillery.

Unable to communicate by radio, Jaeger moved past Sergeant Riley's tank, hoping Riley would follow. Riley understood that his platoon leader was out of commo and instinctively moved along to Jaeger's right. Johnson and Ramos followed, keeping their positions in the platoon wedge formation. They reached the western edge of Eagle, in spite of the shelling, and took up hasty defensive positions facing north. At least, Jaeger thought, if there are any enemy infantry out here, they will be killed by their own artillery. Nothing could live through this!

KARRUMMP! KARRUMMP! Out of communication, Jaeger didn't know where the rest of Alpha Company was or who was winning the battle. From what he could observe from his vision blocks, his platoon of tanks appeared to be alone and totally engulfed in enemy artillery fire.

The sound of the enemy artillery was deafening. Riley pulled into an old enemy defensive position, just to the left of Jaeger. The artillery continued to fall. Jaeger and his tanks sat there, weathering the fire storm of 152mm shells. The crash of artillery on his platoon was demoralizing.

KARRUMMP! KARRUMMP! Jaeger looked to his front and saw a small ridge, about 1,000 meters due north. Through his vision blocks he struggled to observe the ridge and identified it as Checkpoint 13. No artillery was falling there.

KARRUMMP! Smoke shells now began falling on his position, diminishing visibility even more.

Jaeger knew that a crisis had been reached in the battle. He could not communicate with his commander or his platoon. The commander told him to hold the western side of Eagle! He was certain to lose someone if he just stayed on Eagle. No matter what happened, his ability to fight from these positions was greatly reduced. Should he stay put or move out? He had to decide what to do!

If Jaeger obeys orders and defends the western edge of Eagle, go to Section 15.

If Jaeger decides to seize Checkpoint 13, go to Section 23.

If Jaeger decides to pull out of Eagle and head south, go to Section 20.

Section 26

Jaeger could see the hail of fire coming from Objective Eagle and knew that there must be a better way to flank the enemy. As he raced forward he observed a slight dip in the ground off to his left front. Realizing that this depression was a natural path that led into the wadi, Jaeger decided to take a gamble and use the wadi as a covered route to get behind the enemy. Calling on the platoon radio net, Jaeger ordered his platoon to follow him.

"Delta Two Zero, this is Romeo Four Seven. I am entering the wadi to avoid enemy fire," Jaeger called over the company radio net to his commander as his platoon entered the wadi.

Russell answered. "Damn it, Romeo! I don't want you down there! Can you back up?"

"Negative, Delta Two Zero," Jaeger exclaimed. "But I am sure that I can get to the right flank of Eagle this way. We are receiving no fire down here."

"Roger, Romeo. Press on," Russell replied angrily, knowing that the platoon was already committed. "But if you try any more cowboy tricks on me, I will personally skin your hide! Out!"

Tracers flew high over their heads as 3d Platoon navigated along the winding wadi. The battle raged, but here with the protection of steep hills to both sides, 3d Platoon moved unhindered. The wadi was wide enough for two tanks in most locations and appeared to be totally unguarded.

"Red Three," Jaeger radioed his wingman, Staff Sergeant Johnson, "this is Romeo. Take the lead. Over."

"Roger, Romeo, watch my dust!" Johnson exclaimed excitedly as he raced his M1 past his platoon leader's tank and took the point.

Johnson raced about 200 meters ahead of Jaeger. The platoon was now strung out in column, four tanks barely able to see each other in the choking dust. They rushed along the serpentine track of the wadi toward Objective Eagle.

KABOOM!

"AMBUSH!" Johnson screamed over the platoon radio net. His tank was hit in the track by an enemy RPG-16. The tank, out of control, swerved left and hit the wadi bank. The right tank track rolled off the support roller and fell in front of the stopped M1.

Another RPG-16 team fired a deadly high-explosive projectile at Johnson's crippled tank. Rotating his turret quickly to the right, Johnson instinctively fired his main gun in the direction of the incoming fire.

KABOOM! The RPG struck first and hit the wounded M1 on top of the front slope, at the driver's compartment.

BOOM! Johnson's round, a sabot, loaded previously due to the armor threat, hit the bank of the wadi just below the RPG team. It showered the enemy soldiers with dirt and rocks but didn't kill anyone.

Jaeger watched in horror as Johnson fought for his life only fifty meters to his front. Because of the winding path of the wadi, he could see Johnson's tank but not all the enemy RPG teams. Unsure where the fire was coming from, Jaeger was reluctant to charge straight ahead. Firing his .50-caliber machine gun, Jaeger attempted to support Johnson.

Johnson fired his .50-caliber machine gun at the RPG team. He raked the top of the wadi with heavy fire and yelled to his loader to come up and man the 7.62mm machine gun on the top of the loader's station. Johnson killed three infantrymen and fired at any enemy "hero" who was crazy enough to raise his head above the berm.

Expending the last round of .50-caliber ammunition, Johnson leaned over to grab the loader's machine gun. An enemy RPG gunner stood up and fired another rocket-propelled grenade. The high-explosive warhead hit the top of Johnson's turret, just forward of the TC's hatch.

KABOOM! The force of the blast cut Johnson in two, leaving his bisected torso hanging off the side of the turret bustle rack.

BOOM! Jaeger fired a HEAT round in the direction of the enemy infantry, but the round flew high and missed.

The loader's hatch to A32 opened and a dazed figure jumped off the right side of the tank to the ground. The young American ran only a few yards before an enemy rifleman dropped him with a burst of AK-74 rifle fire.

A32 was destroyed and the entire crew was dead.

Jaeger had to do something!

If Jaeger charges the ambush and attempts to fight through the Threat infantry guarding the wadi, go to Section 28.

If Jaeger decides to withdraw and come back the way he came, go to Section 29.

Section 27

Jaeger knew that the risks of using a narrow defile, where the striking power of his platoon would be reduced to only one tank, were justified only if the route was clear and unguarded. He didn't have any idea what was in the wadi, and he wasn't about to risk his men on the gamble that the enemy would be stupid enough to leave it unguarded.

Ordering his platoon into platoon combat wedge, Jaeger began the assault. Captain Russell and his XO were on the left and slightly forward of 3d Platoon.

As Jaeger moved forward he observed Madsen's gunners firing from Checkpoint 3. A moving BMP became their first kill of the day. The glow from the burning BMP clearly distinguished Objective Eagle for the assault force.

The sky brightened with the approaching dawn.

Jaeger followed Russell's tank. Russell, leading the way around the wadi, suddenly drove into a concentrated wall of enemy machine gun and RPG fire. Fighting for its life against enemy infantry, Russell's tank took one RPG hit but continued moving. Swinging his turret back and forth, Russell shattered the area where the RPGs had been fired from with a flurry of machine gun fire.

Jaeger fired his machine guns to support his endangered commander. Undaunted, Russell's tank continued, firing all weapons at the Threat infantry, which was now hiding or moving to subsequent positions.

The company command frequency was quiet. Jaeger attempted to call the commander. No response. Jaeger could see that Russell's tank was still fighting, but the RPG hit must have knocked out the company commander's communications. After a few moments, the XO, Lieutenant Shields, took command of the radio net and called for artillery to suppress the infantry.

"GUNNER, COAX, FIRE and ADJUST," Jaeger yelled into his intercom in an attempt to kill the fleeing enemy RPG gunners. Jaeger's turret swung wildly back and forth as Colwell directed 7.62mm machine gun fire into a berm 400 meters to their front.

"Jones," Jaeger ordered his driver, "move right. We don't want to get too close to those RPGs."

Colwell fired another burst of 7.62mm machine gun fire.

"Can you see them?" Jaeger asked over his intercom.

"Negative," Colwell announced as he continued to fire.

The battlefield was now covered in dense smoke. Jaeger was still moving fast. Riley was off to his left. Daylight was breaking and the smoke clung low, ten to fifteen feet over the battlefield, making accurate gunnery for nonthermal sights very difficult. Seeing through the smoke with their thermal sights, the M1s had an advantage over the enemy.

BOOM! BOOM! Jaeger watched as a BMP was forcibly torn apart by the strike of the two U.S. tank rounds. The BMP, about 900 meters to his front, broke apart in a cloud of black smoke and flying debris. Jaeger heard Madsen declare another kill over the radio.

Sergeant Ramos, in A33, and Sergeant Riley, in A34, attacked the enemy infantry with machine guns. American artillery exploded overhead in deadly airbursts of screaming shrapnel. Barrages of variable-time fuze, now falling across the eastern tip of Eagle, eliminated the infantry threat.

With Jaeger's platoon moving fast behind Eagle's defenses, the remaining enemy armored vehicles had no other choice but to try to reposition or die in place. The enemy began to move to alternate positions.

"Romeo Four Seven, this is Red Four," Riley called to his platoon leader over the platoon radio net. "We are in the lead now. Stay with me; there has got to be another BMP and a T-72 in here somewhere!"

"Romeo Four Seven, this is Red Two," Sergeant Johnson interrupted. "I saw some movement to your left front. Stay alert!"

"Roger that, Red Two . . . wait!" Jaeger screamed. "GUNNER, SABOT, PC . . . FIRE!"

BOOM! Jaeger's 105mm cannon fired at a BMP that was backing up not thirty-five feet to his front. Jaeger's round hit the BMP just below the turret and tore a gaping hole in the side of the infantry fighting vehicle. In a horrific shredding of steel and fire, the BMP exploded, scattering fuel and flames in a wide circle around the burning hull. The puny 30mm gun turret soared a hundred feet into the air.

Jaeger didn't have time to celebrate. As he passed by the burning remains of the BMP, a Threat T-72, dug in all the way to the turret but facing the wrong way, swung its gun over its back deck.

Jaeger saw the T-72 almost at the same time.

Roll the dice.

If the total of the two dice is six or less, go to Section 16.

If the total of the two dice is seven or greater, go to Section 25.

Section 28

"Jones," Jaeger ordered his driver over the tank intercom, "move out fast, toward A32!" Overcome with rage, Jaeger decided to charge the enemy.

"GUNNER, COAX, TROOPS, RIGHT BANK OF THE WADI, FIRE AND ADJUST!" Snapping open his hatch, Jaeger fired his .50-caliber machine gun, adding his fires to that of the 7.62mm coax machine gun that was already raking the top of the wadi as they raced along. Unable to stop the determined tank rush, the few wounded and dazed enemy soldiers, now short of antitank rockets, withdrew to the east.

Squeezing past Johnson's charred tank, 3d Platoon broke out of the wadi and found itself behind Eagle. Jaeger ordered his three tanks to assault west and clear Eagle. Captain Russell and his XO appeared on the left and slightly forward of 3d Platoon.

Lieutenant Madsen reported knocking out another BMP on the west side of Eagle. Russell, leading the way around the wadi, called for artillery when he saw the withdrawing enemy infantry.

Moments later, American artillery exploded in deadly airbursts of screaming metal southwest of Jaeger's position. Barrages of variable-time fuze fell across Eagle and eliminated the enemy infantry.

Jaeger's three tanks moved fast behind Eagle's defenses. The battlefield was covered in smoke. Daylight was breaking and the smoke clung low, ten to fifteen feet over the battlefield, making accurate gunnery very difficult for the enemy. Seeing through the smoke with their thermal sights, the M1 tanks had the advantage.

Jaeger watched as another BMP popped out of his prepared position on the western side of Eagle. Before Jaeger could aim his tank cannon and fire, the BMP was incinerated by Madsen's gunners. Jaeger continued his assault, moving at high speed across the broken terrain behind Objective Eagle.

"Romeo Four Seven, this is Red Four," Riley called to his platoon leader over the platoon radio net. "We are in the lead now. Stay with me; there has got to be another BMP and a T-72 in here somewhere!"

"Romeo Four Seven, this is Red Three," Sergeant Ramos interrupted. "I saw some movement to your left front, sir. Stay alert! I'll act as your wingman."

"Roger that, Red Three . . . wait!" Jaeger screamed. "GUNNER, SABOT, PC . . . FIRE!"

BOOM! Jaeger's 105mm cannon fired at a BMP that was backing up not thirty feet to his front. Jaeger's round hit the BMP just below the turret. The shell burned into the turret ring of the BMP, exploding it in a bright red-orange fireball. The puny 30mm gun turret soared 200 feet into the air and fell, upside down, among the dirt and rocks of the desert floor.

Jaeger didn't have time to celebrate. As he passed by the burning wrecked BMP, a T-72, facing in the opposite direction and dug in all the way to the turret, swung its gun over its back deck. The T-72 aimed the big 125mm gun at Jaeger's tank. Jaeger saw the T-72 in the exact same instant.

Roll the dice.

If the total of the two dice is four or less, go to Section 16.

If the total of the two dice is five or greater, go to Section 30.

Section 29

Jaeger fought back the rage that was tearing him apart. Johnson was dead. It is my fault, he thought. I should have never come down this wadi! The way was blocked . . . what now? Artillery fell somewhere on the high ground east of his position.

"Red Four, this is Romeo Four Seven." Jaeger was angry. The light of battle filled his eyes. His words came quickly.

"Romeo, this is Red Four. I can't see what is going on at your position," Riley answered. "Everyone OK?"

"Negative! A32 is dead! Back up quick. I've got RPGs all over the place!" Jaeger scanned the sides of the wadi for enemy infantry. He fired several bursts of his .50-caliber machine gun. "Let's go, Red Four! I can't move until you back up!"

"Roger. Executing now!" Riley screamed over the platoon radio net. His tank lurched backward, moving as fast as possible in the winding, narrow defile.

Suddenly Jaeger was showered with machine gun and small arms fire from his right front. His right shoulder burned excruciatingly. He slumped down into the tank. A thick, greasy red fluid stained the upper right side of his chemical MOPP shirt.

"Damn it! I'm hit!" Jaeger cried out loud. Colwell immediately returned fire at the enemy with his 7.62mm coaxial machine gun. Curn leaned over to his wounded platoon leader and stared at the wound.

"Jones! Get us the hell out of here! BACK UP!" Jaeger yelled into his intercom at his driver. At the same moment Jaeger hit the tank's smoke grenade launchers by smashing at the grenade button with his good left arm.

The tank jerked backward and hit forcefully against the side of the wadi. The crew was thrown about inside like BB's in a can. Jaeger winced with pain as his wounded shoulder crashed forward into the laser range finder. Curn, coming to his senses first, jumped up to open his loader's hatch and man his 7.62mm machine gun.

Two enemy RPG gunners crawled along the edge of the wadi to get a better shot at their new prey. Shouting for machine gun fire to cover them, they both stood up and fired simultaneously at Jaeger's stalled tank.

KABOOM! KABOOM! Both rounds hit the top of A31's turret in a tremendous blinding flash of fire.

"Sir, are you OK?" Colwell said coughing, as he tried to revive his dazed commander. The turret was a mess. Curn, not moving, lay to the left of the gun, his face a mass of red burned flesh. The impact of the enemy grenades blew him right through his half-opened loader's hatch.

"Lieutenant!" Colwell screamed in panic as he shook his platoon leader. "We've got to get out of here!"

Jaeger couldn't seem to talk. Everything hurt. Colwell opened the TC's hatch and tried to see if there was a way off the tank. He reached for the handle and unlocked the TC's hatch. A hand from outside grabbed the hatch and flung it open. The last thing that Colwell saw was an enemy grenade bouncing to the turret floor.

In war, he who hesitates is lost, especially when you are in the kill zone of an enemy ambush. Once you commit a force down a narrow defile, there is no turning back. The wadi, a narrow, easily defended natural choke point, was heavily guarded by enemy infantry. Jaeger's mistake was to use an avenue of approach that had not been checked out or secured.

Jaeger paid the ultimate sacrifice. He fought and lost.

If you have what it takes to lead American soldiers to victory, go back to Section 1, learning from your mistakes, and fight again. Victory or Death!

Section 30

The Threat commander of the T-72 tank swung his 125mm gun around as fast as he could. Jaeger traversed his turret to meet the new threat. The T-72, dug into the ground and hull down, offered only a narrow turret shot. But the sun was glaring down at an angle directly into the eyes of the defenders, and they had trouble seeing over the dirt mound that was piled to their left rear. Jaeger's visibility was better.

BOOM! Jaeger fired first. There wasn't time for a formal fire command.

He missed the T-72 by inches, the high-velocity round hitting the mound next to the dug-in tank, causing a shower of rocks and dirt.

BOOM! A second round suddenly blasted into the T-72. The sabot round burned through the formidable armor protection and ignited the ammunition inside the tank. The turret blew off in a terrific explosion, momentarily blinding Jaeger as he peered out from his hatch.

Jaeger looked to his left and saw A33, the source of his deliverance.

"Good shot, Red Three," Jaeger called over the radio to Sergeant Ramos, his new wingman. "I owe you one!"

"That's what wingmen are for, Romeo!" Ramos cried. Ramos called Sergeant Riley. "Red Four, this is Red Three. See any more targets? Over."

"Negative, Red Three. Good shooting!" Riley replied. "Romeo, Red Three and I are going to move to that small ridge to your left front to get a look. Cover our move."

"Roger, Red Four. I'll report to higher." Jaeger switched to the company command net and called Captain Russell. It was now 0628.

"Delta Two Zero, this is Romeo Four Seven. Spot report. Over." Jaeger called his commander with a sense of renewed determination in his voice.

"Romeo Four Seven, this is Delta Two Zero. Send it. Over," Russell answered.

"I have destroyed one BMP and one Tango Seven Two at grid LK934539. I have three tanks left. Continuing mission. I'll inform you if we see any more enemy in our zone. Over."

"Roger, Romeo Four Seven! I lost radio communications and had to switch tanks with the XO. There shouldn't be much left on Eagle," Russell said without emotion. "Once you get to the western edge of Eagle, take up hasty defensive positions and orient north. Call me once you are established. I am moving 1st Platoon forward. Out."

KARRUMMP! KARRUMMP! Hundreds of artillery shells fell on Eagle. The crash of the artillery was sudden and tremendous. Jaeger buttoned up and tried to navigate by looking through the narrow vision blocks of his TC's station. He could hear the side of his tank absorb the fragments from the high-explosive projectiles. Thousands of little bomblets fell all over his position. One bomblet exploded on the top of his tank, with no apparent lethal effect.

KARRUMMP! KARRUMMP! Jaeger tried to call Sergeant Riley, but his radio didn't function. Looking back through his rear vision blocks he saw a tangled mess of metal where his radio antenna and radio matching unit had been! The enemy must have these positions registered with their artillery, Jaeger thought. They are hitting us hard!

KARRUMMP! KARRUMMP! Jaeger moved past Sergeant Riley's tank. Riley instinctively followed to Jaeger's right. Ramos also followed, keeping his position in the platoon wedge formation. They reached the western edge of Eagle, in spite of the shelling, and took up hasty defensive positions facing north. At least, Jaeger thought, if there are any enemy infantry out here, they will be killed by their own artillery. Nothing in the open could live through this!

Out of communication, Jaeger didn't know what was happening with Alpha Company. From what he could observe from his vision blocks, his platoon's tanks were completely alone, except for the enemy artillery fire. The enemy must be getting ready to counterattack, Jaeger thought.

KARRUMMP! KARRUMMP! Ramos pulled over to Jaeger's left into an unoccupied enemy tank position.

KABOOM! A huge explosion and the sound of shrapnel hitting the side of his tank dropped Jaeger to the turret floor. Stunned momentarily, he was helped back to the tank commander's position by Specialist Curn.

Looking out of his vision blocks, Jaeger scanned Ramos's tank. The side was charred and the track had rolled off to the rear of the tank. Jaeger breathed a sigh of relief when he saw that the turret was still moving, indicating that Ramos was scanning for targets. At least Ramos is alive, Jaeger thought. But now I am down to only two fully operational tanks.

KARRUMMP! KARRUMMP! KARRUMMP! KARRUMMP! Jaeger looked about a thousand meters to his front and saw a small ridge. The crash of the enemy artillery on his platoon was demoralizing. From his narrow vision blocks he studied the ridge and identified it as Checkpoint 13. No artillery was falling there.

KARRUMMP! KARRUMMP! Smoke shells were now falling in front of his position, reducing visibility even more. Checkpoint 13 looked like a good place to move to. From there he could still cover the western side of Eagle and get out of the artillery impact area in the bargain. But he had only three tanks, and one couldn't move! He couldn't afford to move to Checkpoint 13 with only two tanks. What if the enemy counterattacked with that reserve tank company!

Jaeger knew that a crisis had been reached in the battle. He could feel the moment and he knew that he must act. He could not communicate with his commander or his platoon. He was pretty sure that Riley would follow him if he moved out. But what about Ramos? Could he just leave Ramos behind? Besides, the commander had told him to hold the western side of Eagle. Russell didn't tell him to go forward and take Checkpoint 13.

KARRUMMP! KARRUMMP! If Jaeger didn't lose anyone else in this barrage, it would be a miracle. No matter what happened, his ability to fight from these positions had been greatly reduced. He had to decide!

If Jaeger obeys orders and defends the western edge of Eagle, go to Section 31.

If Jaeger decides to rush for Checkpoint 13 with only two tanks, go to Section 33.

If Jaeger decides to pull out of Eagle and head south, go to Section 20.

Section 31

Occupying the enemy's old fighting positions proved to be a big mistake, for the enemy had registered preplanned artillery concentrations on them.

KARRUMMP! KARRUMMP! A33 took another direct hit from the Threat artillery. In a blinding flash, the ammunition exploded on the burning M1, sending a searing orange-yellow flame fifty feet into the air. Ramos and his crew never had a chance. Jaeger's heart sank as he watched the burning tank.

Minutes passed. Jaeger did the best he could to get control of himself. Without communications and with the smashing of enemy artillery, it was almost impossible to think.

"Lieutenant, I see a column of vehicles heading south, just northeast of Checkpoint Thirteen," Colwell announced over the tank intercom.

BOOM! Just then, as if to prove the accuracy of Colwell's sighting, Riley's tank opened up with main gun fire on the front of the column. Although the enemy tanks were approximately 2,900 meters away, Riley hit one of them after his third round.

"GUNNER! SABOT, LEAD TANK!" Jaeger shouted, the chance for action jerking him out of his lethargy. Jaeger's loader fed a sabot round into the cannon.

"IDENTIFIED!" Colwell cried.

"FIRE!" Jaeger screamed. The 105mm gun recoiled back, making the tank shake with the exit of the fired round. "TARGET, LEFT TANK!"

The actions inside the turret turned automatic, with the tired loader and excited gunner working as fast as possible to pump rounds downrange. The tank gun recoiled with each shot, ejecting a hot steel casing onto the turret floor. The air inside the turret was acrid with the smoke of expended shells.

Jaeger stopped giving fire commands. Neither side was shooting well, but the artillery was greatly hampering Jaeger's and Riley's accuracy. There were plenty of targets but not enough time. The enemy was closing the distance quickly; he was now less than 2,400 meters away.

Jaeger and Riley continued to fire as fast as the tired loaders could feed rounds into their cannons. They didn't even attempt to move to alternate firing positions. There just wasn't time for that.

The battlefield was now a confusing swirl of dust and smoke. Burning vehicles displayed the path of the tank column. Relentlessly the enemy raced toward Jaeger's tanks.

With the Threat column only 1,500 meters away, Jaeger knew that he had to make a decision. Unable to contact his commander, he knew that he must decide to run or stay. Riley would follow him no matter what he decided. He had to decide now!

If Jaeger decides to withdraw to live to fight another day, go to Section 20.

If Jaeger decides to stay and take on a Threat tank company with two M1 tanks, go to Section 32.

Section 32

Sometimes a few men decide the fate of nations. Wars are often won by brave men who refuse to submit to the enemy. In war, it is usually suicide to run, and Jaeger knew that his options were limited. He was a professional soldier, and he was prepared to die if need be . . . but he wouldn't run!

The enemy column headed full force against the western edge of Objective Eagle. Jaeger could see eight T-72 tanks and a few BMPs.

KABOOM! Jerking backward, Jaeger's tank shuddered from a hit from a T-72 projectile. The enemy shell miraculously glanced off A31's frontal armor.

"God . . . that was close!" Jaeger said out loud over the tank's intercom. "Crew report. Anybody hurt?"

"We are OK, Lieutenant!" Colwell replied, a bit shaken. "Alert! Identified two tanks near Checkpoint Thirteen!"

"FIRE!" Jaeger yelled, his heart beating so fast that he thought it would burst out of his chest. The tank lurched again with the firing of another round.

"TARGET! LEFT TANK!"

BOOM! The gunner fired automatically, not waiting for a command. Colwell hit the second enemy tank in the road wheels, making it spin around and come to a grinding halt.

Jaeger's crew continued to fight desperately against the awesome rush of too many targets. The enemy pulled out of column formation and moved to line formation to make their final assault. There were six T-72 tanks and three BMPs left.

The artillery fire slackened. Jaeger opened his hatch to the open protected position to get a better view of the battlefield. This position covered the top of his head, protecting him from fragments, and allowed him to see the battlefield. The fresh air rushed into the tank and filled his lungs.

He looked to the west and saw a series of flashes. That must be Madsen's 1st Platoon, firing at the enemy, Jaeger thought. But the T-72s were now 800 meters away.

Section 32

KABOOM! Suddenly A31 was hit by a powerful blow that threw Jaeger back against his hatch and down onto the turret floor. Specialist Curn lay underneath the gun, his lifeless body bloody with fragment wounds. Sergeant Colwell was slumped against his gunner's seat, unconscious. Jones, Jaeger's driver, was gone; a charred scar was all that remained of his driver's station. The tank had taken a direct hit in the driver's compartment.

Jaeger blacked out. The tank filled with the smoke and the exhaust of the automatic fire extinguishers.

Struggling to gain consciousness, Jaeger finally came to his senses. He had to get everyone out. He tried to pull Colwell out of the tank. With great effort, he yanked him up and onto the top of the turret.

The fresh air seemed to revive Colwell, who moaned and cried out in pain. Firing was continuing all around them as the enemy attempted a final assault on Eagle.

Jaeger returned to the turret and searched Curn for a pulse. He didn't find one. He reached back to check his tank commander's controls. The gun was still operative and loaded. He scanned the horizon for targets.

A Threat BMP moved out from the cover of a small rise and headed to the right, directly into Jaeger's field of view. Jaeger tracked the BMP for two seconds, then fired from his tank commander's position.

BOOM! At 700 meters it was not a difficult shot. Jaeger hit the BMP in the rear side. The BMP swung around with the force of the impact and burst into flame, its fuel supply igniting as seven enemy infantrymen desperately tried to exit their burning carrier. Unable to load another round, Jaeger reached up to his .50-caliber machine gun, charged the bolt, and shot down the wounded survivors. He continued firing the machine gun until it ran out of ammunition.

Out of nowhere, Sergeant Riley arrived and moved his tank near Jaeger's smoking M1. Firing to protect his downed platoon leader, Riley opened his hatch and waved at Jaeger and Colwell to jump aboard.

Colwell, still dazed, couldn't move. Exhausted, Jaeger grabbed Colwell and manhandled the wounded man off the tank. He pulled Colwell over his shoulder in a fireman's carry, and the two of them moved toward Riley's tank.

A T-72 pulled out through the smoke and spotted Jaeger and Colwell. The T-72 fired three long bursts of its coaxial machine gun before Riley sent a sabot round into its hull and turned it into a flaming wreck.

Jaeger and Colwell went down. Jaeger was hit in the leg. Colwell wasn't so lucky; he took a round right through the head.

Jaeger tried to run, not recognizing his wound, but his tangled leg refused to cooperate. Riley's loader leapt out of his hatch, ran out to the stricken platoon leader, and carried him back to A34. With Riley's gunner firing as fast as he could, Riley and his loader dragged Jaeger into the tank.

"Thanks, Riley," Jaeger cried in pain. "God this hurts! Get the commander on the radio and call in some artillery on this position ASAP!"

"Roger, Lieutenant!" Riley shouted as he watched Private First Class Berry try to bandage Jaeger's mutilated leg. Jaeger screamed out in pain as the tank lurched forward, driving his wounded knee into the side of the turret.

"Delta Two Zero, this is Romeo Four Four," Riley yelled urgently. Request fire for effect, DPICM, LK930540, danger close. Five T-72s. Out!"

More T-72s came out of the smoke and immediately engaged Sergeant Riley's tank. Riley disabled one, hitting it in the lower left flank. The T-72 broke to a jolting stop and spun to the left in a violent half circle. The hatches opened and the crew quickly abandoned their smoking vehicle.

Desperately fighting for his life, Riley used all his skill to fight back the overwhelming force opposing him . . . but it was not enough.

A T-72 fired directly at A34 at less than 300 meters. Riley's tank was hit right at the turret ring. A34 lurched backward as if snapped in two, its turret moving several feet to the rear of the hull. Black smoke billowed from the loader's and tank commander's hatches. There was no sign of life.

Go to Section 24.

Section 33

Jaeger knew that he didn't have a second to lose. Moving back out of his hole, he maneuvered close enough to Sergeant Riley's tank to get his attention, then raced forward to Checkpoint 13. He held his breath as he waited for his platoon sergeant's reaction. Would he follow? Did he understand?

After what seemed to be an eternity, Jaeger saw Riley's M1 speeding north behind him. The artillery continued to fall on Eagle, but he and Riley had gained relative safety by moving out of the artillery impact area.

"Jones, move to that small scrub bush on the right side of the ridge to our front," Jaeger said to his driver over the tank intercom.

"Roger, sir," Jones replied as he skillfully maneuvered A31 to a hasty firing position on the southeast side of the small ridge designated as Checkpoint 13.

Two minutes later, Jaeger and Riley were established on Checkpoint 13. Riley pulled up thirty meters to Jaeger's left and opened his hatch. Jaeger informed his crew that he was going to leave A31 and take over A34, which still had communications. Jaeger jumped out of his hatch and onto the ground, then traversed the thirty meters in record time. Riley, a true professional soldier, understood the platoon leader's dilemma and quickly made the transfer.

"Delta Two Zero, this is Romeo Four Seven. Over," Jaeger radioed.

"Romeo Four Seven, this is Delta Two Zero. What is your situation? Over," Russell answered impatiently.

"I am set at Checkpoint Thirteen, with two tanks, looking north. Negative contact. I can observe for FASCAM if needed. Over."

"Roger, Romeo," Russell replied. "I hope that you can hold by yourself! I am moving the rest of Delta forward to the east of Eagle. I'll coordinate FASCAM right now at grid LK940560. That will put it just north of you. You have got to gain us some time. Hold on!"

"Lieutenant, I see a column of vehicles heading south, just northwest of Checkpoint Eleven," Specialist Fourth Class Harrison, A34's gunner, announced.

130

"Roger that, Harrison." Jaeger frowned. "Damn! That must be the enemy counterattack force." Jaeger reported the situation to Captain Russell, who informed him that the FASCAM was approved and on the way.

"Lieutenant!" Jaeger's gunner cried. "TANKS . . . RANGE, TWO FIVE HUNDRED!"

"Steady, Harrison. Wait for the command." Jaeger's calm voice had a reassuring effect on his new crew.

BOOM! BOOM! Jaeger and Riley fired almost at once, two uranium-depleted sabot rounds moving faster than the speed of sound. Riley hit the lead tank with his first round. The T-72 burst into flames in the hot, desolate desert south of Checkpoint 11.

Jaeger's round struck short.

"GUNNER! SABOT, TANK!" Jaeger shouted. The loader shoved another sabot round into the breech and swung out the spent case ejection guard to arm the cannon.

"IDENTIFIED!" Harrison cried.

"FIRE!" Jaeger screamed.

BOOM! The 105mm gun recoiled, shaking the tank with the exit of the round. This time Jaeger's round hit, killing the T-72 in a blinding flash of fire.

Another hot steel casing clanged to the turret floor. The air inside the tank was acrid, the smoke and the powder filling the crew's nostrils and leaving their throats parched and burning. Their actions inside the turret became automatic. The anxious loader and excited gunner worked as fast as demons to hurl more death at the enemy.

The column of T-72s closed on Jaeger's position. They were now less than 2,000 meters away.

"Delta Two Zero, this is Romeo Four Seven," Jaeger screamed into the microphone. "I need that FASCAM now! Over."

Before Captain Russell could answer the plea of his hard-pressed platoon leader, the artillery began to fall. The shells burst above the ground, dispersing their loads across a wide area. The target area was soon covered with deadly antitank mines. Little wires sprung out from each mine as it hit the ground. Merely touching the wires would set off a tremendous explosion.

The FASCAM artillery-delivered mine field landed 200 meters in front of the enemy column. The mine field was 400 meters in diameter and blocked the Threat's route of advance. You couldn't ask for better shooting!

Jaeger and Riley increased their fire. The mines disabled two tanks and one BMP almost immediately. The enemy tanks then tried to detour around the mine field. This maneuver exposed the flanks of the T-72s to Jaeger's guns. One more enemy tank was pulverized by the American M1s.

But the T-72s kept coming. Fast. Determined. Down to five tanks and two BMPs, they wanted revenge against the little band of defenders at Checkpoint 13.

Firing in massed salvos, the enemy engaged Sergeant Riley's tank. Desperately trying to evade getting hit, Riley tried to back up into a ditch. Two 125mm sabot rounds struck the front of his turret.

KABOOM! KABOOM! Riley was gone. Jaeger was all alone. Now it was his turn to bear the full wrath of the advancing enemy tanks.

BOOM! With white-hot anger, Jaeger fired and destroyed another enemy tank. Out of the corner of his eye he saw T-72s, moving fast, to the left of his position.

KABOOM! Clearly identified by his continued firing from the same position, Jaeger's tank took a direct hit in the left front hull.

Stunned with the dramatic impact of the collision with the enemy tank round, Jaeger tried to regain his senses. He yelled for a crew report, but no one answered. The tank filled with smoke and the exhaust of the automatic fire extinguishers. Unable to breathe, he forced open the hatch and rolled onto the top of the turret.

Getting his second wind, Jaeger attempted to go back into the tank and help Sergeant Riley's crew. The loader, Specialist Fourth Class Nelson, stumbled out from the loader's hatch.

A BMP rolled onto their position and sprayed the tank with machine gun fire. Nelson went down, wounded from the 7.62mm rounds.

Jaeger didn't have time to think. He moved instinctively back into the tank and grabbed the tank commander's override controls to fire his 105mm cannon at the advancing Threat armored vehicle. Luckily, the controls still functioned. The turret moved.

BOOM! Firing at point-blank range, Jaeger hit the BMP. The concussion from the exploding BMP forced Jaeger back into A34's turret. Choking for air in the bottom of the disabled tank, Jaeger pulled himself out and crawled onto the back deck of the tank.

Jaeger moved over to Nelson, who was bleeding badly from the left shoulder. Semiconscious, he groaned in pain as Jaeger applied a quick battle dressing to his wound. Jaeger stopped the bleeding and went back inside the tank to check out the rest of the crew. Specialist Fourth Class Harrison was dead. So was the driver.

Jaeger climbed back out of the turret and was greeted by an AK-74 muzzle pointing directly into his face.

An enemy infantry squad had appeared out of nowhere and surrounded the smoldering tank. Before Jaeger could react, the enemy squad took him prisoner. Overcome by the speed of events, Jaeger and Nelson did not have time to resist.

They were thrown to the ground and searched. The enemy squad seemed impressed with themselves for capturing an American officer. They tied Jaeger's hands with some type of fastening cord, stood him up, and pushed him in the direction of their BMP. Two enemy soldiers forced Nelson up and yelled at him to move to their BMP. Nelson stumbled along, his hands tied behind his back, unable to keep up because of his wounds.

Before Jaeger could reach the BMP, he heard the distinctive sound of 155mm artillery. He ran to get under cover, but he wasn't quick enough. The last thing he felt was the instantaneous pain of shrapnel; it came from the incoming American artillery and it exploded directly on top of him and his captors.

"They did a hell of a job," Madsen said sadly, surveying the battlefield and looking down at the mangled bodies of Jaeger and Nelson.

"They beat almost an entire Threat tank company. By their stand here, we were able to bring up the rest of the company and finish off the Threat reserve tank company. I don't know why Jaeger didn't listen to me about the wadi. But it really doesn't matter now.

"I am going to recommend both Jaeger and Riley for the Silver Star," Russell said solemnly. "If it hadn't been for their efforts, we could have been wiped out on Eagle. Their sacrifice saved the battalion. They died like soldiers."

Go to Section 22.

Section 34

Jaeger's platoon had been in an assembly area for the past two days. Everything had been unnaturally quiet, except for the almost steady overhead pyrotechnic display, provided by the air forces of both sides. Jaeger's men had used the time to clean weapons, fix damaged equipment, send letters home, and get some well-deserved rest.

Sleep. Most of all they wanted to sleep. Sergeant Riley made sure that everyone got as much rest as possible.

Sergeant Riley had made the most of the available time. He proved to be a great provider. He even made sure that everyone in the platoon took a shower. The shower wasn't much, but the men appreciated it all the same.

Third Platoon's shower consisted of an "Australian shower" water bag. This ingenious canvas device, reportedly developed in the country it was named for, was hung over a tank gun tube and trickled water out of several tiny holes. One soldier could wash while another stood on the back deck of the tank and poured water into the canvas bag from a plastic five-gallon water can.

Jaeger was taking care of "personal hygiene," as the army called it, and had just finished shaving. He brushed himself off in a vain attempt to remove some of the powder-fine dust that had permeated his Nomex tank crew uniform. It was impossible to get away from the dust.

The Nomex uniform, specially designed to protect tank crewmen, was much like the kind worn by helicopter pilots. It protected the wearer from the flashburn that often occurred when a tank was hit and caught fire. Many crewmen had been saved by wearing these uniforms.

But the Nomex suits were hot. It was already 95 degrees Fahrenheit and the morning was still young! Add to this the discomfort of eating, breathing, living, and fighting in a dustbowl, and things were downright miserable.

Jaeger's mind wandered back to home and more pleasant times. If he was back in Minnesota right now, he would probably be fishing, lying on the bank of a cool lake. . . . The rest of his daydream was too good to be true. Jaeger knew it couldn't last. He poured himself a cup of coffee from his trusty metal thermos.

Shhhhhhreeeeakkk! BOOOOM! The crashing sound of an enemy attack aircraft split the air above Jaeger's head. He instinctively hit the ground, spilling his coffee as he jumped for cover. Another ear-shattering shriek occurred as Jaeger lay nose down in the dust of the desert floor.

Jaeger looked up just in time to see a U.S. Air Force F-16 fire an air-to-air missile at the fleeing enemy aircraft. The missile seemed to stop in midair for a second; then it turned the enemy aircraft into a bright orange fireball, hurtling toward earth in an agonizing, uncontrolled dive.

Jaeger's men cheered, happy that a foe had been killed and feeling lucky that the aircraft had not been on an attack mission against them. There had been no warning of the enemy aircraft's approach. If it had been on a strike run against them, they would have been caught with their pants down.

Jaeger got up from the ground and uselessly tried to dust himself off again. His tank commanders, Sergeant First Class Riley, Staff Sergeant Johnson, Sergeant Ramos, and his gunner, Sergeant Colwell, also recovered and sat down again. (See Diagram 3 for vehicle numbers and radio call signs.) Jaeger picked up his empty canteen cup.

"There sure have been a lot of aviators buzzing around here these past few days," Staff Sergeant Riley said, directing his comment to his platoon leader.

"Right. Something must be up." Jaeger paused, searching for his words. Riley poured the lieutenant another cup of lukewarm coffee. "Now where was I?"

"You were just saying, Lieutenant," Johnson said with a wide smile, "that we were the best tankers in the army and that we are all going to be sent back to the rear for a few days of rest and relaxation!"

Everyone in the group laughed. The platoon had been through a lot together. They shared the camaraderie of a close-knit family.

"Yeah, now I remember," Jaeger replied, ignoring Johnson's quip. "First the big picture. There's a rumor at battalion about negotiations to end the fighting. It seems that the United Nations is having an important meeting this Friday. But it's still just a rumor right now. Even if peace

2ND MISSION

Vehicle Type	Vehicle Number	Commander	RADIO CALL SIGN
M1 TANK	A31	2d Lieutenant Sam Jaeger	Z11
M1 TANK	A32	Staff Sergeant Jerry Johnson	Z47
M1 TANK	A33	Sergeant Joseph Ramos	Z28
M1 TANK	A34	Platoon Sergeant William Riley	Z14
Other Important Characters			
M3 CFV	HQ 14	Platoon Sergeant Young	C14
M3 CFVs	HQ 11,12, 13 and 15.	Scout Platoon CFV Crews	C28, C42, C47 & C80
FIST-V	A 111	2d Lieutenant Don Rogers	V12
M1 TANK	HQ 66	Lieutenant Colonel Brown	V20

Diagram 3

talks start, they may not affect us for quite a while. Don't get your hopes up too high that we will all be going home soon."

The men sat up, interested now more than ever.

"Now, back to our little world," Jaeger said, pointing to his map. "Battalion is planning to move us, sometime tonight, to new defensive positions to the northeast. Intelligence reports that the enemy is on its way to drive us out of here."

"So much for negotiations," Riley said sarcastically.

"We could be in for a major fight," Jaeger continued. "I haven't been issued our new mission yet, but I'm sure to get the word soon. Battalion thinks that the enemy is getting ready for something big."

"I will inspect each tank and crew at 1000 today," Riley said seriously. "Take advantage of this slack time to complete your prep-to-combat checks and resupply. We were damn lucky in our last fight. The lieutenant pulled us through some tough times. But the fun days are over. Those bastards may not be so easy to beat this time."

Just as Riley finished speaking, Jaeger caught sight of a HUMVEE (a quarter-ton utility truck that took the place of the old army jeep, designated as HMMWV by the U.S. Army) heading their way. The HUMVEE moved up to them and stopped. Sergeant Bill Brock, the company first sergeant, was at the wheel.

"The old man needs to speak to you right away, Lieutenant." Brock reached over the side of his HUMVEE and spat a huge wad of tobacco on the ground. "You are to come with me, ASAP. Sergeant Riley, I've got some MREs, eight five-gallon water cans, and some POL package products in the back for you. Oh, and I almost forgot, I got some mail!"

"Mail! Brock, that's a word I had almost given up on," Riley said, grinning. "Lieutenant, you had better take off. I will get everything ready here."

"OK, Sergeant Riley, I'm on my way," Jaeger replied calmly. "This is probably about our new mission. It's 0705 right now. Be prepared to move by 1200, just in case. I'll get back to you as soon as I can."

"Yes, sir!" Riley replied respectfully. "Johnson, Ramos, give me a hand unloading this. Colwell, pass the word. I want all the loaders here in two minutes. Tell them we got letters from the States!"

Alpha Company, 3-69 Armor, was deployed in a large assembly area, with its platoons dispersed in several desert wadis to avoid providing a tempting target for enemy aircraft. The HUMVEE maneuvered well in the rocky desert terrain, but Jaeger still felt as though he had been bounced around in a cement mixer. The accumulation of several days of violent action was taking its toll on everyone. Jaeger felt the pain of minor bruises from head to foot. The last two days of rest had helped, but he wished it could be five days more.

Jaeger arrived at Alpha Company after a short but dusty ride with First Sergeant Brock. Jaeger climbed out of the HUMVEE and ambled over to the company command post. He was surprised to see the battalion commander, Lt. Col. Paul Brown, leaning over the hood of

Section 34

his own HUMVEE, talking with Captain Russell. Jaeger approached Colonel Brown and saluted.

"Lieutenant Jaeger," Colonel Brown said, very businesslike, "I don't have to tell you how tight things are right now. The task force is on the defensive because we don't have the supplies, primarily fuel, to launch a major drive north. The ports along the coast are clogged with supplies and more stuff is coming in each day. But our guys can't get it to us fast enough over this god-awful road net. We must defend this line for a few more days while we build up sufficient reserves of fuel to push forward.

"Jaeger," the colonel continued, looking down at his map, "I am putting you in command of the battalion's counterreconnaissance battle. I must get our counterreconnaissance screen established quickly. There isn't much time, so listen up and save your questions for later."

Jaeger looked at Russell—a controlled look but one that failed to hide his apprehension. The counterreconnaissance mission would put Jaeger and his men in front of the battalion's defense, on their own. They would be the first line against the enemy attack. It was a very dangerous mission. He had never done this kind of thing before. But then again, less than three days ago, he had never been in combat.

"Lieutenant Meyer, the battalion scout platoon leader, was wounded in action yesterday by enemy artillery," Brown said, looking at Jaeger as if he read his thoughts. "Normally, the scout platoon leader does this business. But Captain Russell and I agree that you can handle the responsibility. I saw what you can do in combat, and you have a good platoon. So you get the job."

Jaeger nervously shuffled his stance. Why do I always get so lucky, he thought.

"I am going to give you command of the scout platoon and a two-gun mortar section. The scout platoon sergeant, Sergeant Young, and the mortar section sergeant, Sergeant Martin, are moving their units to your assembly area right now." Brown paused to see Jaeger's reaction. Jaeger, trying to take all this in quickly, looked down at the colonel's map and pretended to be calm.

"Division says that three enemy divisions are on the march now and, at their present rate of advance, should make contact with our division tomorrow. Brigade intelligence expects a regiment-sized force of tanks and BMPs to attack through our sector at dawn tomorrow morning." Brown pointed to the map.

"I will hold two lanes open through our obstacle belt, one in the northeast and one in the northwest, to allow you and your men to get back to our positions. You can leave the scouts forward, if necessary. They can exfiltrate back later.

"Your mission is to defeat the enemy regimental recon units and dismounted infantry that may attempt to infiltrate our sector tonight. You will deploy your combined force forward of Phase Line Denmark and no farther forward than Phase Line Poland. I want you to be in position by 1400 today. How you set up is your business." Brown used a map pen to trace Jaeger's area of responsibility on his map.

"You will withdraw once you have determined the enemy's main effort and after you have radioed that information back to me. I must know where the enemy is going to hit us.

"Once you withdraw, you will move back to A Company, to position A12. I am holding A Company back as my battalion counterattack force. This overlay has the location of all of our planned positions and obstacles. It has all the information you will need for this mission." (See Map 8.) "What are your questions?"

"What about the enemy's division recon elements, sir?" Jaeger asked. "What activity has been observed in our sector?"

"None in our sector, but TF 1-69 fought a quick battle with a couple of tanks and BRDMs, probably a division recon team, this morning," Brown said, again pointing to the map sprawled out on the hood of his Hummer.

"Division and brigade intelligence believe that the enemy main effort will hit TF 1-69 to our east. The only roads are in their sector. Or it may be that the enemy division reconnaissance units are just damn good and have not yet been discovered by our guys. In any case, we have nothing to report on enemy activity in our sector. You are going to have to get in there, get in position, and find out.

"I will be able to support you with 155mm artillery from our direct support battalion," Brown continued. "You will have priority of fires during the counterreconnaissance battle. I may be able to get you even more artillery if you identify a high payoff target. I won't be able to give you any helicopter or air support. That's about it. Any more questions?"

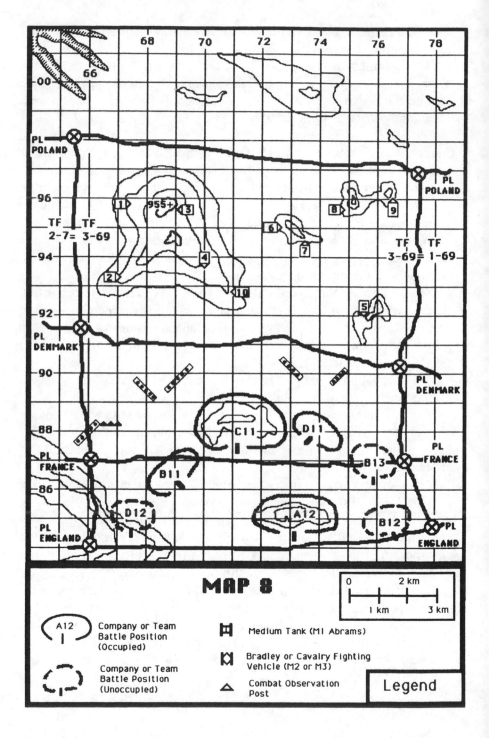

MAP 8

0   2 km
1 km   3 km

Legend

A12 — Company or Team Battle Position (Occupied)

— Company or Team Battle Position (Unoccupied)

⊞ Medium Tank (M1 Abrams)

◫ Bradley or Cavalry Fighting Vehicle (M2 or M3)

△ Combat Observation Post

"Sam," Captain Russell asked, "is there anything else you think you will need?"

"Yes, sir," Jaeger said, turning to his company commander. "I need a FIST [artillery fire support team]. Any FIST will do, but I would prefer to have Lieutenant Rogers. Don and I have worked together before, and he could make all the difference in the world."

"OK," Russell said admiringly. Jaeger wasn't missing a step. Russell seemed very proud of his young lieutenant. "But I won't be able to give him to you until 1200 today. He has some fire planning to do for me first."

"Thanks. . . . Colonel Brown, one last thing," Jaeger hesitated as he looked at the battalion commander. "The area is pretty large. I need to see as much of it as possible to deploy properly. Could I steal a few hours of helicopter time to see the area?"

"Jaeger, you must have read my mind," Brown said with a smile. "I've got the loan of the brigade commander's OH-58 for the next forty-five minutes. You can have twenty minutes. Will that be enough?"

"Yes, sir, that will be a great help," Jaeger said with a grin, happy for the chance to see the battlefield.

"Lieutenant Jaeger," Brown said as he clasped the younger officer on the shoulder, "you are going to do fine. Just blind them for me. Kill off their recon screen so they can't find our main defenses. Use the thermal sights of the M1 tank and scout's cavalry fighting vehicle to your advantage. Above all, find out the direction of the Threat main effort and get the word back to me ASAP!"

Jaeger contemplated his new mission on the bumpy ride back to his assembly area. The helicopter ride had given him a good appreciation of the terrain and scope of his mission. The pilot of the tiny OH-58 had flown close to the ground, buzzing by the terrain so fast that Jaeger had almost lost his breakfast. Nevertheless, he had seen the major terrain features and had gotten a pretty good idea of the possible enemy avenues of approach.

How he would deploy his small force was another question. Lost in his thoughts, he sat silently and stared at his map.

Jaeger knew that the Threat regimental reconnaissance company consisted of a headquarters section (one BMP), a BMP recon platoon (three BMP-2s), one BRDM recon platoon (three or four BRDM wheeled armored reconnaissance vehicles), and one motorcycle section (three Ural-3 motorcycles). The company, therefore, had a total of eight or nine armored vehicles and three motorcycles to conduct reconnaissance for the regiment.

Jaeger knew from his study of the enemy's doctrine that a Threat reconnaissance company commander normally divided his reconnaissance zone into two platoon reconnaissance sectors. One sector was often assigned to the BMP-equipped platoon and one to the BRDM platoon. Because the platoon equipped with the BRDMs had more vehicles, it often received the largest sector. Motorcycles were used primarily to carry messages between elements to reduce the need for radio communications.

The enemy's reconnaissance soldiers were trained to avoid combat and seek information. They were trained to prepare the advance of the regiment by breaching obstacles that were left unguarded. They would also report the location of any American tanks and antitank weapons for later destruction by artillery.

In addition, the enemy could employ dismounted infantry for reconnaissance, obstacle breaching, and infiltration attack. A favorite Threat tactic was to infiltrate an American position in the night, dig in, and then destroy the Americans with RPGs and grenades once the main attack began.

Jaeger's mission, of course, was to prevent this.

Jaeger mentally listed his force's strengths. The Americans possessed the best night fighting equipment in the world. Both the M1 tank and the cavalry fighting vehicle had thermal sighting devices. Thermal sights effectively turned night into day. No illumination was required. The sights, which were passive and couldn't be detected by the enemy, worked by determining the difference in temperature between the target and the target's surroundings. The more this difference in temperature, the easier it was to distinguish the target. Hot objects, such as tanks, armored personnel carriers, and people, gave off a lot of heat. On the thermal viewer, against the "cold" background of the desert terrain, these objects stuck out dramatically.

Some battalion scout platoons in the division had changed equipment and exchanged their cavalry fighting vehicles (CFVs) for HUMVEEs. Jaeger's battalion had not yet made this transition and maintained the old organization of six CFVs per scout platoon. With the scout platoon leader wounded and his CFV damaged, Jaeger would have a total of five CFVs.

The cavalry fighting vehicles would give the scouts an excellent capability to conduct a counterreconnaissance screen. In a fight, their 25mm chain gun could knock out everything short of a tank. The rapid-fire 25mm was devastating against dismounted infantry.

In addition, the CFVs had a two-shot TOW antitank wire-guided missile launcher that could destroy targets with great accuracy out to 3,000 meters. The TOW couldn't penetrate the special reactive armor of a T-72, but it would easily destroy a BRDM or a BMP at long range. The problem with the TOW, however, was in getting the long-range shot. Even in the desert, which many people think of as flat and featureless, gullies and wadis often reduced engagement ranges to less than 1,000 meters.

The biggest advantage, however, was always the caliber of the men who used the equipment. The scouts, or 19Ds, as their military occupational speciality (MOS) was numbered, were some of the best soldiers in the battalion. The scouts were trained in the business of reconnaissance and counterreconnaissance. They were all veterans now, cocky and confident.

The HUMVEE kicked up dust as First Sergeant Brock tried to miss the many rocks and boulders that dotted the desert floor. As the HUMVEE approached 3d Platoon, Jaeger could see that five CFVs, in various stages of being camouflaged, had joined his assembly area. Two M106 mortar carriers stood ominously in the open, near Jaeger's camouflaged tank. Jaeger got out of the HUMVEE, just in time to hear the bellowing voice of Platoon Sergeant Riley fry a young mortar sergeant who had failed to seek a covered and concealed position for his mortar carriers.

"Do you understand me, Sergeant!" Riley shouted at the singed mortarman.

"Yeah, Sarge, but look. . . ." Sergeant Martin complained, but he was cut short by the expression on Riley's face. "OK . . . OK, we are moving now. I'll be back in a few minutes to get your instructions." The mortar sergeant jumped into his M106. His two vehicles moved to find a place to hide.

"Lieutenant," Riley said, stern faced, "I have had more traffic in this area for the past twenty minutes than a New York street during rush hour! If the enemy doesn't know we are here now, they just don't have anyone watching. What is all this I hear from the scout platoon sergeant about the counterrecon battle?"

"I see you already know our mission," Jaeger replied, not surprised. Riley had a knack of keeping ahead of his platoon leader, and Jaeger had come to expect it. "Here it is. We are up against the recon elements of at least an enemy motorized rifle regiment. Our mission is to fight the counterreconnaissance battle, destroy the enemy's recon elements, and determine the location of the main enemy attack.

"We have to be in position by 1400 today," Jaeger said, pointing to his map overlaid with the battalion's battle graphics. "The sector is not far from here. We need to depart at 1245. Get everybody ready for combat. Pass the word. I want you, our tank commanders, the scout platoon sergeant, the scout vehicle commanders, and the mortar section sergeant here at 1020 for the operations order."

"Roger, Lieutenant," Riley replied, admiring the way his officer was able to take charge of the situation without wasting time. "I'll have SP4 Harrison construct another terrain model of the sector. Let me have that overlay and I will copy your graphics."

Jaeger knew that Riley would get everything ready for the mission. As platoon leader, Jaeger now had to focus his energy on developing a plan.

Jaeger's force now consisted of four M1 tanks, five cavalry fighting vehicles, and two M106 mortar carriers. Rogers's FIST-V armored personnel carrier would join him later. Jaeger's small force was expected to screen an area twelve kilometers wide and six kilometers deep. How was he going to accomplish this mission on such an extended front with so little force?

Jaeger analyzed his new tactical problem using the troop leading procedures (see Appendix C) that he had been trained to use in the Armor Officer's Basic Course at Fort Knox, Kentucky. He knew that he must develop a tentative plan based on the factors of mission, enemy, terrain, troops available, and time. Like most concepts in the army, someone had developed a handy memory aid to help planners remember these critical planning factors. The acronym, derived from the first letter of each factor, is METT-T.

Jaeger, from his previous combat experience, knew that time was one of his most important resources. He was determined not to waste a single minute. He immediately wrote up a simple time plan and issued it to Sergeant Riley.

Jaeger determined that there were basically three ways he could organize to accomplish the counterreconnaissance mission. (A) He could deploy the M1s and CFVs in separate observation posts. This would give him nine positions and a good chance of finding the enemy reconnaissance as it tried to penetrate his screen line. (B) He could deploy in depth with the scout platoon forward and his tank platoon, centrally located, in position to react to enemy actions. This would make the scouts responsible for the screen line and have Jaeger act as an attack force. (C) He could deploy the M1s and CFVs in pairs to take advantage of the capabilities of both weapon systems. This would reduce his observation posts to only five (four with a CFV/M1 pair and one CFV alone), but would give him the capability to kill anything the enemy sent at him.

Time was critical. His initial deployment would be difficult, if not impossible, to change once he sent the troops on their missions. Jaeger had to quickly determine his plan!

If Jaeger chooses Option A, to deploy both the scouts and tanks in separate positions, go to Section 35.

If Jaeger chooses Option B, to deploy the scouts forward and the tank platoon as a unit in a central location, go to Section 36.

If Jaeger chooses Option C, to deploy the scouts and tanks in pairs, go to Section 37.

Section 35

"This is going to be a night battle," Jaeger said out loud, staring at the map. Sitting in the shade of his tank, he studied the geography of his map closely. The first problem was to figure out the means of finding the enemy reconnaissance—in the dark.

The helicopter reconnaissance that Jaeger had conducted had proved to him that he could not cover the entire sector without dispersing his force. He figured that if he occupied key observation posts on the high ground, he would be able to get the early warning that he needed to find the enemy reconnaissance as it entered the task force sector. With nine observation posts, using thermal sights, Jaeger's force should be able to view the entire area.

The next problem was to figure out how to kill the enemy recon forces. If his observation posts could find the enemy, the mortars and artillery could kill them. If Jaeger could direct the battalion's supporting artillery on the enemy's recon elements as they approached his lines, he might cause them to abandon their mission or be destroyed. With priority of battalion artillery fires, Jaeger would be able to put a lethal amount of artillery on the enemy in a short period of time.

His last task was to determine the enemy's main avenue of attack. The solution to this seemed to be positioning his observation posts on high ground that overlooked the most possible enemy avenues of approach. Jaeger positioned his observation posts at Checkpoints 1 through 9 to overlook these avenues. He planned to position himself at Checkpoint 4. He labeled the avenues of approach alpha, bravo, charlie, and delta (see Map 9).

Jaeger worked purposefully on his operations order. He realized that detecting the enemy in time was the key. Accurate and timely reporting, therefore, was essential. Each observation post would have to be alert, ready to report, and, if need be, fight.

To accomplish this, control was essential. Jaeger would control the action along the entire front from his command post. Each observation post must detect the enemy in time for Jaeger to react with mortars and artillery. After the enemy recon had been destroyed or dispersed

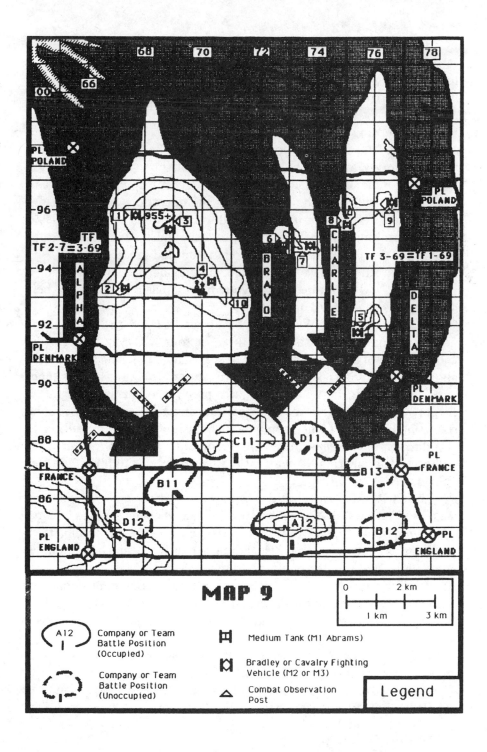

MAP 9

		0	2 km
		1 km	3 km

Legend

```
A12    Company or Team
 |     Battle Position
       (Occupied)

       Company or Team
       Battle Position
       (Unoccupied)
```

⊟ Medium Tank (M1 Abrams)

⋈ Bradley or Cavalry Fighting
   Vehicle (M2 or M3)

△ Combat Observation
   Post

by artillery, Jaeger would order the withdrawal of each outpost in stages. In this fashion he could control the movement of each member of his force as they withdrew to the protection of friendly lines. Jaeger completed his plan at 1015.

As Jaeger finished, he realized that the shade that had protected him from the burning rays of the hot desert sun had slowly receded. The effect of the heat and his efforts at concentration had physically drained him. Mustering his strength, Jaeger walked over to Sergeant Riley's tank and got under the shaded lean-to that was constructed from a tank tarp. This shade would be the sight for the operations order briefing.

The leaders of Jaeger's newly formed force sat in the shade of Riley's lean-to, drinking water from their canteens and studying the terrain model that Specialist Fourth Class Harrison had created.

"Sergeant Riley, are we ready?" Jaeger announced, sounding serious.

"Yes, sir," Riley replied. "Everyone has the basic graphics on their maps and is ready for your order."

"Situation. Enemy: We should be up against a regimental reconnaissance company consisting of three or four BRDMs, four BMPs, and a number of dismounted patrols." Jaeger paused to let this information about the enemy's task organization register in the minds of his men.

"The Threat recon units are usually pretty good at what they do," Jaeger said. "They choose their best men from the regiment for the regimental reconnaissance company. They should avoid us and try to slip through our screen. The enemy recon units focus on information-gathering and clearing the way for the regiment, not fighting," Jaeger emphasized.

"Their BRDM-2 scout vehicles, four-wheel drive armored carriers, are quiet. The BRDM-2s were designed for reconnaissance, not as infantry fighting vehicles. Each BRDM-2 carries a crew of four: a commander, gunner, driver, and co-driver. The armor is relatively thin—14mm thick at the hull—and can be easily penetrated by a .50-caliber machine gun. Armed with a heavy 14.5mm machine gun and a 7.62mm machine gun in the conically shaped turret, the BRDM-2 is no match for a Bradley or a tank. But with speed and stealth, it makes a pretty good reconnaissance vehicle.

"The BMP-2s are more dangerous. Their 30mm cannon won't kill an M1, but they also carry a mounted AT-4 or AT-5 missile launcher. The AT-4 or AT-5 can stop a tank. We should have the advantage over the BMPs with our thermal sights, but they can be dangerous." Jaeger paused to catch his breath.

148

"Our greatest worry will be their dismounted troops. The enemy has been known to put as many as two companies of dismounted infantry forward of the regiment to help their reconnaissance units find and destroy our positions. They will attempt to infiltrate our positions during the night and take us out with RPGs and grenades.

"Friendly Situation: We have TF 2-7 to our left and TF 1-69 to our right. Our battalion commander's intent is to determine the enemy's main attack early, fight him deep with artillery to disrupt the tempo of his advance, and reposition forces to catch the threat in a prearranged kill zone.

"Mission: Team Jaeger," the platoon leader announced, "will conduct counterreconnaissance operations to destroy enemy recon forces and determine the direction of the enemy's main attack in sector. We must be in position not later than 1400 today. Upon completion of the counterreconnaissance mission, Team Jaeger will revert to Alpha Company control.

"Execution: Concept of the Operation," Jaeger continued. "My intent is for our nine observation posts to find the enemy. Artillery will kill him. Accurate reporting and quick communications are essential."

Jaeger cited off the essentials of his operations order, pointing out key terrain and enemy avenues of approach as he talked. Jaeger's confidence and professional manner were contagious, and the scouts and mortarmen gained respect for their new commander.

"I am going to position you in nine different observation posts. Tankers and scouts will both have the same mission. Your job is primarily to see the enemy, and report his location to me. I will kill him with artillery. Calls for fire will go directly to Lieutenant Rogers, our FIST. The FIST and the mortar section will be located with me at Checkpoint Four." Jaeger paused, pointing at the terrain model with a long stick.

"When we withdraw, you will move on my order . . . get this straight, ON ORDER. No one . . . and I mean NO ONE, is to leave his position unless I tell him to. I can't afford a hole in our screen line." Jaeger emphasized his words. Everyone knew that he meant business.

"Sergeant Riley, you will occupy Checkpoint Six," Jaeger said as he pointed to the corresponding spot on the terrain model. "Sergeant Young, I want you at Checkpoint Nine. Johnson and Ramos at Checkpoints Two and Eight, respectively. I want scouts at Checkpoints One, Three, Five, and Seven."

Jaeger briefed the details of the plan, assigned each crew a position, described the routes of withdrawal, and explained the coordinating

149

instructions. He used the terrain model to great benefit, pointing to each position and telling the soldiers the information about the ground that he had learned from his helicopter reconnaissance. Jaeger went into considerable detail concerning communications and radio frequencies. Finally, he asked for questions.

"What," asked Scout Platoon Sergeant Young, pausing slightly, "if we can't reach you on the radio?"

"Fight through any commo problems. If all else fails, shoot a star cluster. We will use red star clusters to signify an enemy sighting," Jaeger said. "Anyone who sees a red star cluster, report it to me, with an approximate location, and I will direct the artillery fire based upon your sighting. Sergeant Riley will issue you each four red star clusters before you depart this meeting.

"Any other questions?" Jaeger asked, eager to get on with the mission. "The time is now 1046. Brief your crews. I will conduct a briefback of all vehicle commanders right after this briefing. We will conduct a rehearsal, over the terrain model, here at 1200. We will move out at 1245. Let's go!"

Go to Section 38.

Section 36

Sitting in the shade of his tank, Lieutenant Jaeger studied his map closely. His first problem was to figure out how to command his forces, in the pitch-black night, spread out over twelve kilometers of rough desert. The helicopter reconnaissance had made this job a little easier. A reconnaissance was worth a hundred maps. He had seen the critical importance of Hill 955 with his own eyes. He knew that his forces would be stretched thin. He could not observe such a large area without dispersing his force. Jaeger was sure, however, that if he dispersed *all* of his forces, he would lose all flexibility.

If I was the Threat reconnaissance company commander, what would I do? Jaeger thought, as he contemplated the map. I have too many options to cover. If I guess wrong, the enemy could slip behind me. and, when the main force strikes, slice right through the American lines. The best course of action is always the one that permits the greatest number of options during the execution. How can I build flexibility into my plan?

If I try to command and control a series of small outposts, spread out over this great a distance, I am bound to fail. I have to solve this problem based upon my strengths and exploiting the enemy's weaknesses.

A strong mobile reserve was his solution. A well-placed screen line, backed up by a hard-hitting "killing" force, made the most sense. The M1 tank platoon could move fast enough to take advantage of the enemy's moves. Most importantly, the entire counterrecon battle could take place at night, Jaeger thought. The night fighting capability of the M1 tank could be a decisive advantage.

I will use the scouts to find the enemy, Jaeger thought, mentally listing his force's advantages over the enemy. The scouts are trained in the business of finding the enemy and I can count on them to act independently, without a lot of instructions. They know how to operate a screen and how to survive behind enemy lines. I can position the scouts forward, as a screen of observation posts under the command of their platoon sergeant.

The next problem is to figure out how to kill the enemy reconnaissance forces. If the scouts find the enemy, the tank platoon could act as the killing force. With the aid of the mortar section and the battalion's direct support artillery, we should be able to make short work of a Threat BRDM or BMP platoon.

The last and most important task is to determine the enemy's main direction of attack. The success of the Threat reconnaissance will determine this. Once their reconnaissance discovers a weak spot, the motorized rifle regiment commander could drive for this location with all his power.

Exploit success; attack enemy weakness. That was the enemy's doctrine. There will be precious little time to react as the regiment, with more than 170 combat vehicles, supported by heavy concentrations of artillery, races to break through the American defenses. And they always attack where their reconnaissance proves that their enemy is the weakest.

Jaeger, therefore, decided to locate his tank platoon as a "flying wing" that would move rapidly to counterattack enemy reconnaissance elements as they were discovered. In this way, Jaeger could command a decisive portion of his force and act to destroy the enemy. He would command his force against the enemy, not merely try to control a series of outposts that might be overrun one at a time.

The mortars and Lieutenant Rogers would stay with Jaeger. Rogers's job was to direct the fires of the mortars and battalion direct support artillery. Jaeger expected to use the mortars as his own hip-pocket artillery, just in case he couldn't get in touch with battalion artillery in time. Although the artillery was very important, Jaeger could not trust the destruction of the enemy to artillery fires alone.

Jaeger felt that any plan that required too much active control was prone to fail. The chaos of battle demanded decentralized execution. Battle was too complex for one man to try to control the action. His previous combat experience had taught him that too many little things went wrong and worked against the plan. Jaeger wanted the chaos to work for him, not against him.

Jaeger determined the most likely avenues of enemy approach based on his knowledge of the enemy and a careful study of the terrain. He identified four primary avenues and marked them with red arrows on his map. He gave each arrow a code name, labeling them California, Utah, Ohio, and New York, from west to east (see Map 10).

Lastly, he positioned 3d Platoon in a horseshoe-shaped position at Checkpoint 4. From there, Jaeger could personally overlook both the California and Utah avenues. He also determined the movement times for his tank platoon attack force from Checkpoint 4 to the other checkpoints, and drew the times directly onto his acetate map.

Jaeger concentrated on completing his operations order. He realized that the early detection of the enemy was vital. To increase his reaction time to enemy sightings, the scouts would call for artillery fires directly to the FIST.

The success of the battle depended to a great extent on Team Jaeger's ability to communicate. Accurate reporting would be the only means to make the artillery kill the enemy. But Jaeger was not going to rest the failure or success of his plan on active communications alone. Each observation post would have to know what to do even if communications were lost. Each soldier would have to know the commander's intent and act as required by the situation.

Jaeger sat in the shade of his tank, completing his order. As he worked on his plan, the sun moved higher and higher in the sky and his comfortable

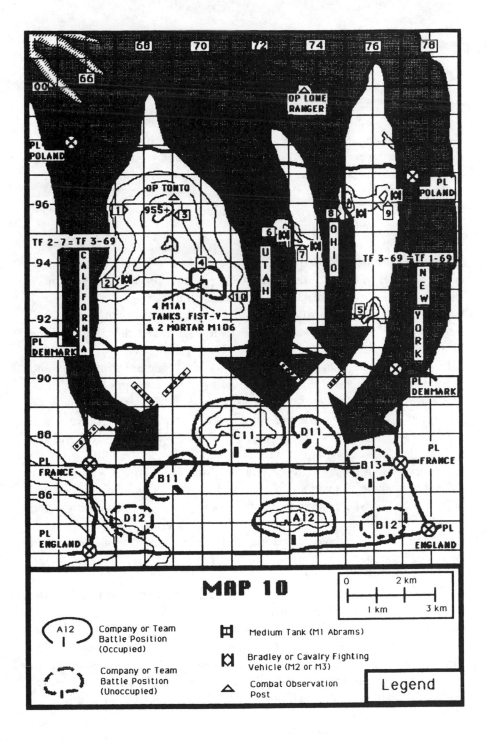

shade receded, then finally vanished. The early-morning breeze that had graced the desert was replaced by the stifling heat of midday. The combined effect of the temperature and his effort at concentration filled him with a sudden tiredness. Mustering his strength, Jaeger walked over to Sergeant Riley's shaded lean-to.

His NCOs were seated under the tarp, drinking water from their canteens and studying the terrain model that Specialist Fourth Class Harrison had created. The air was still and quiet. Everyone was waiting for the word.

"Sergeant Riley, are we ready?" Jaeger announced purposefully, breaking the silence.

"Yes, sir," Riley replied. "Everyone has the basic graphics on their maps and is ready for your order."

"Situation. Enemy: We should be up against a regimental reconnaissance company consisting of three or four BRDMs, four BMPs, and a number of dismounted patrols." Jaeger paused to let the enemy's composition register in the minds of his men.

"The Threat recon units are usually pretty good at what they do," Jaeger said. "They choose their best men from the regiment for the regimental reconnaissance company. They should avoid us and try to slip behind our screen. The enemy wants intelligence information and they want to dismantle our obstacles, not fight us," Jaeger emphasized.

"Their BRDM-2 scout vehicles, four-wheel drive armored carriers, are quiet. They were designed for reconnaissance, not fighting. Each BRDM-2 carries a crew of four: a commander, gunner, driver, and co-driver. The armor is relatively thin—14mm thick at the hull—and can be easily penetrated by a .50-caliber machine gun. Armed with a heavy 14.5mm machine gun and a 7.62mm machine gun in the conically shaped turret, the BRDM-2 is no match for a Bradley or a tank. But with speed and stealth, it makes a pretty good reconnaissance vehicle.

"Their BMPs are more dangerous, with their 30mm cannon. We should have the advantage over them with our thermal sights." Jaeger paused to catch his breath.

"The real worry will be their BMPs and their dismounted troops. The enemy has been known to put as many as two companies of dismounted antitank missile–equipped infantry forward of the regiment. The infantry's mission is to help their reconnaissance units find us and to take out our critical positions that block the regiment's approach.

"Friendly Situation: We have TF 2-7 to our left and TF 1-69 to our right. The battalion commander's intent is to determine the enemy's main attack early, fight him deep with artillery to disrupt the tempo of his advance, and reposition forces to catch the threat in a prearranged kill zone. We are a vital part of his plan. Our most important task is to determine the location of the enemy's main attack.

"Mission: Team Jaeger," the platoon leader announced, "will conduct counterreconnaissance operations to destroy enemy recon forces and determine the direction of the enemy's main attack in our sector. We must be in position no later than 1400 today. Upon completion of the counterrecon mission, Team Jaeger will revert to Alpha Company control.

"Execution: Concept of the Operation," Jaeger continued. "My intent is to have the scouts find the enemy. Fight only as a last resort, or if you have an easy target. The tanks, under my command, will move as a unit to attack specific enemy penetrations. Reporting the direction of the enemy main attack is *the* essential mission. Every effort must be made to get the information about the enemy's direction of attack to the battalion commander. If communications fail, the direction of the enemy main attack will be indicated by firing two red and one green star cluster."

Jaeger explained the essentials of his plan and issued mission-type instructions to Sergeant Young. The men gained more confidence in their tasks as Jaeger continued the briefing. His professional and confident manner reinforced their own confidence. As always in war, leadership makes the big difference.

"The scouts will form a forward screen line under the command of Platoon Sergeant Young," Jaeger said, looking at the eager scout platoon sergeant. "Sergeant Young, I want you to position your men to observe the four primary avenues of approach. I want you to weight your effort in the east. I expect you to pick your own positions based on your best estimate of the enemy's capabilities and the terrain.

"Your job is to see the enemy, not fight," Jaeger emphasized. "Tell me where he is and use your direct fire as a last resort. Scouts will primarily use artillery to kill enemy recon. Shoot only if you have to, or if you get an easy target of opportunity. You have permission to move anywhere within Phase Line Poland and Phase Line Denmark to accomplish your mission.

"When the enemy attack begins, don't worry if you get bypassed. Accurate reporting will save your hide by allowing the battalion to win the battle. If battalion loses, then none of us will be safe. If you get bypassed, stay in position, snipe at the enemy as he passes you, and exfiltrate back to our lines *after* the battle is over. Again, your essential task is to report the direction of the enemy's main attack." Jaeger paused.

"The tanks, mortars, and the FIST will be located at Checkpoint Four." Jaeger emphasized his words so that everyone could clearly understand his concept. "If we don't destroy the enemy recon elements with artillery fires, I will maneuver my tanks against the enemy and destroy him. I will then withdraw the tanks and mortars back through friendly lines. I intend to move to position A12 prior to sunrise."

Jaeger explained the details of his order, the organization of the march to the counterrecon sector, the positioning on Checkpoint 4, and the routes of withdrawal through the friendly obstacle system. He explained the coordinating instructions and went into considerable detail concerning communications and radio frequencies. He then explained the chain of command succession if he became a casualty. Finally, he asked for questions.

"What," asked the scout platoon sergeant, pausing slightly, "if we can't reach you on the radio?"

"Work through any communications problems," Jaeger exclaimed, slapping his thigh with his hand for emphasis. "I will set up my command post on the best ground available for radio communications. Relay messages from vehicle to vehicle if necessary. Move to better ground to transmit important messages. If the enemy tries to jam us, transmit from behind a hill. Jamming is line-of-sight restrictive, so you may be able to force your transmission through. Always fight through the jamming. Make sure you have all of our alternate frequencies. In a worst case situation, fight like hell. The noise will direct us to your position.

"Any other questions?" Jaeger asked, eager to get on with the mission. "The time is now 1046. Sergeant Riley will issue each scout commander four red star clusters, and two green, before you depart this meeting. Brief your crews. I will conduct a briefback with the scout and mortar leaders right after this briefing. I will conduct a rehearsal with the scout platoon sergeant and the mortar section sergeant, using the terrain model, here at 1200. We will move out at 1245. Sergeant Young, submit any areas where you want preplanned artillery targets at that time. Let's go!"

Go to Section 39.

Section 37

Lieutenant Jaeger, drenched in sweat, sat in the shade of his tank. He studied his map closely, following the contour intervals of the 1:50,000 scale military map with precision, looking for the slightest advantage offered by the terrain. The helicopter reconnaissance proved that he would be spread very thin. After his first experience with combat, Jaeger had learned the value of using the ground. He was determined to make geography work in his favor.

His first problem was to figure out how he was going to command his forces, dispersed over twelve kilometers of rugged desert, on a dark, moonless night. Jaeger knew that his men would have to observe an extremely large area. Commanding this decentralized force was going to be quite a challenge.

I must use the advantages of the scout cavalry fighting vehicle and the firepower of the M1 tank, Jaeger thought, mentally listing his force's strengths and weaknesses. I will organize into tank-CFV teams that can detect and kill the enemy on their own. The scouts are trained in the business of finding the enemy. I can count on them to act independently, without a lot of instructions. They know how to operate an observation post. The tanks know how to destroy targets. By combining these capabilities into four counterreconnaissance teams, I can fight the battle without a lot of active control.

The last task, and the most crucial, was to determine the enemy's main direction of attack. This couldn't be discerned until early in the morning, when Jaeger's men actually would face the awesome force of an entire motorized rifle regiment, with more than 170 combat vehicles, racing to break through the American defenses. Exploit success; attack enemy weakness. Attack where their reconnaissance proved that their enemy was weak. That was the enemy's doctrine.

Jaeger, therefore, decided to locate his tank-CFV teams on decisive terrain features from where he could both detect and kill the enemy. As the enemy main attack began, his teams would detect the attack, stay in position, and continue to report. The teams that were not in the area of the enemy's main attack would rush back to friendly lines.

With a little luck, and the superior speed of the M1 and Bradley vehicles, Jaeger could have the majority of his force back in Alpha Company's position before the enemy reached Phase Line Denmark.

Jaeger planned to place a tank-CFV team at Checkpoints 2, 6, and 8. He would have a team of two scout CFVs at Checkpoint 3. Jaeger would position his tank, the mortars, and the FIST (Lieutenant Rogers) at Checkpoint 10. Rogers could direct the fires of the mortars and battalion direct support artillery. Jaeger expected the fires of artillery and mortars to supplement the direct fire capability of his counterrecon teams.

Jaeger knew that the tanks and CFVs would do the majority of the killing with their direct fires. He wanted each team to kill the enemy reconnaissance elements before they reached Phase Line Denmark. He didn't believe that artillery alone could do the killing. He knew that it would be difficult to control indirect fires against fleeting, moving enemy targets at night.

Jaeger felt that any plan that rested too much on active control was prone to fail. Modern war was too chaotic to attempt to control every move of even a tank platoon, let alone a composite force spread out twelve kilometers apart.

His previous experience in combat had taught him that too many little things went wrong and worked against the plan. Jaeger wanted the chaos to work for him, not against him. His design was to make each team self-sufficient, strong enough to fight and report on their own. The battle could then be fought without active control.

Jaeger planned his positions in two vehicle pairs as follows: Checkpoint 2, Sergeant Johnson in A32 and a scout CFV; Checkpoint 3, Sergeant Young in his CFV and another scout CFV; Checkpoint 6, Sergeant Riley in A34 and a scout CFV; Checkpoint 9, Sergeant Ramos in A33 and a scout CFV; and finally Checkpoint 10, Jaeger himself in A31, the mortar carriers, and Lieutenant Rogers's FIST-V. He identified four primary enemy avenues of approach. He gave each area a code name, labeling them brown, orange, pink, and red, from west to east (see Map 11).

Jaeger focused all his energy on completing his operations order. He realized that it was crucial to find the enemy early and fast. Each team would call in artillery fires directly to the FIST. Accurate reporting was also very important, but he was not going to rest the failure or success of his plan on communications alone. Each observation post

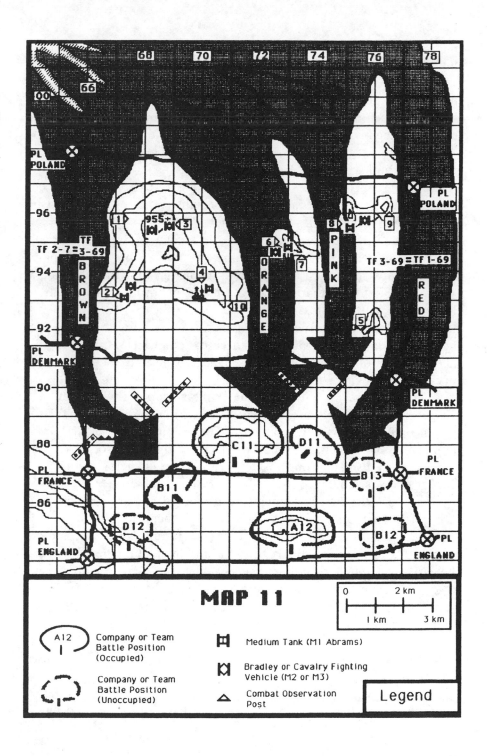

MAP 11

Legend

A12	Company or Team Battle Position (Occupied)
(dashed)	Company or Team Battle Position (Unoccupied)

Medium Tank (M1 Abrams)

Bradley or Cavalry Fighting Vehicle (M2 or M3)

Combat Observation Post

must know what to do even if communications were lost. Jaeger completed his plan at 1025.

As he finished, he realized that the shade protecting him from the hot sun had slowly slipped away. The effect of the heat and his efforts at concentration had drained him of his energy. The sun burned down, making his brain feel as though it were in a Kevlar oven. Mustering his strength, Jaeger walked over to the shaded lean-to that Sergeant Riley had built for the operations order briefing.

The men sat in this makeshift shade, drinking water from their canteens and studying the terrain model that Specialist Fourth Class Harrison had created. Jaeger took off his helmet.

"Sergeant Riley, let's get started," Jaeger announced, sounding serious.

"Yes, sir," Riley replied. "Everyone already has the basic graphics on their maps and I have briefed them on the terrain with the model."

"Good. First the situation." Jaeger began his order, not needing to look at his written notes.

"Situation. Enemy: We should be up against a regimental reconnaissance company consisting of three or four BRDMs, four BMPs, and a number of dismounted patrols." Jaeger paused to let the enemy's organization register in the minds of his men.

"The Threat recon units are usually pretty good at what they do," Jaeger said. "They choose their best men from the regiment for the regimental reconnaissance company. They should avoid us and try to slip behind our screen. The enemy wants intelligence information and they want to dismantle our obstacles, not fight our tanks and CFVs," Jaeger emphasized.

"Their BRDM-2 scout vehicles, four-wheel-drive armored carriers, are quiet. They are designed for reconnaissance, not fighting. Each BRDM-2 carries a crew of four: commander, gunner, driver, and co-driver. The armor is relatively thin—14mm thick at the hull—and can be easily penetrated by a .50-caliber machine gun. Armed with a heavy 14.5mm machine gun and a 7.62mm machine gun in the conically shaped turret, the BRDM-2 is no match for a Bradley or a tank. But with speed and stealth it makes a pretty good reconnaissance vehicle.

"Their BMPs are more dangerous, with their 30mm cannon. We should have the advantage over them with our thermal sights." Jaeger paused to catch his breath.

"The real worry will be their BMPs and their dismounted infantry armed with antitank missiles. The enemy has been known to put as many as two companies of dismounts forward to help their reconnaissance units find and knock out our positions.

"Friendly Situation: We have TF 2-7 to our left and TF 1-69 to our right. The battalion commander's intent is to determine the enemy's main attack early, fight him deep with artillery to disrupt the tempo of his advance, and reposition forces to catch the threat in a prearranged kill zone. We are a vital part of his ability to determine where the main attack is and in calling for long-range artillery fires.

"Mission: Team Jaeger will conduct counterreconnaissance operations to destroy enemy recon forces and determine the direction of the enemy's main attack in sector. We must be in position no later than 1400 today. Upon completion of the counterrecon mission, Team Jaeger will revert to Alpha Company control.

"Execution: Concept of the Operation," Jaeger continued. "My intent is to destroy the enemy as soon as they are identified. Reporting the direction of the enemy main attack is *the* essential mission. The team that identifies the enemy main effort will stay in contact. If communications fail, the direction of the enemy main attack will be indicated by firing two red and one green star cluster.

"We will form five counterrecon teams. Three of these, the ones located at Checkpoints Two, Six, and Nine, will each consist of an M1 tank and a CFV. The fourth team will be under Sergeant Young's command. Sergeant Young," Jaeger said, looking at the eager scout platoon sergeant, "will be at Checkpoint Three and will consist of two CFVs."

Jaeger continued explaining the details of the order, assigning the exact positions of each vehicle, the organization of the march to the counterrecon sector, and the routes of withdrawal through the friendly obstacle system. He then explained the coordinating instructions and issued detailed information concerning communications and radio frequencies. Finally, he asked for questions.

"What," asked the scout platoon sergeant, pausing slightly, "if we can't reach you on the radio?"

"Work through any communications problems," Jaeger exclaimed, slapping his thigh with his hand for emphasis. "I will set up my command post at Checkpoint Ten. This looks like the best ground for radio communications and it puts the mortars in a central position to support everyone.

"If communication becomes a problem," Jaeger continued, "relay messages from vehicle to vehicle. Move to better ground to transmit important messages. If the enemy tries to jam us, get on the south side of a hill and try to transmit. The terrain can mask some of the effects of his jamming. Whatever happens, don't just give up trying to talk on the radio. Fight through the jamming. Make sure you have all of our alternate frequencies. In a worst case situation, fight like hell. The noise will direct us to your position.

"Any other questions?" Jaeger asked, looking at his men. They sat quietly, each in his own thoughts. "OK, then . . . the time is now 1046. Sergeant Riley will issue each team leader three red and one green star cluster before you depart this meeting. Brief your crews. I will conduct a briefback with the ranking NCOs of each team, here, right after this briefing. I will conduct a rehearsal, using the terrain model, with all team commanders. We will move out at 1255. I will issue a list of preplanned targets to each team at that time. Let's go!"

Go to Section 40.

Section 38

At 1200, just as Captain Russell had promised, Lieutenant Rogers arrived at Jaeger's assembly area. Jaeger was happy to see Rogers. He had worked with the young artillery lieutenant before, and they had a deep mutual respect for each other.

There was another reason that Jaeger was happy to see Lieutenant Rogers. The killing firepower of the battalion's artillery was essential to Jaeger's plan. Without the artillery, Jaeger's forces might be too scattered to stop the enemy.

Jaeger was running late with his briefbacks and had to rush to fill Rogers in on the concept of the operation.

At 1230 the battalion commander, Lieutenant Colonel Brown, called Jaeger on the radio to check on his preparations. Jaeger told him that he had to delay his departure until 1330, and that he would not be able to occupy the counterreconnaissance area by 1400. The task force commander was not pleased.

Moving as fast as possible, Jaeger finally arrived at Checkpoint 4 at 1430. By 1500 Sergeant Riley reported that he had occupied Checkpoint 6. At 1520 Sergeant Young reported that he was set at Checkpoint 9 and relayed that Checkpoints 5 and 8 were also in position. It wasn't until 1540 that all of Jaeger's positions were finally occupied. So far, no one had seen any sign of the enemy.

Jaeger, with his tank on the high ground at Checkpoint 4, dismounted and walked over to the crest of the hill. Sergeant Colwell moved up to the tank commander's position as his lieutenant climbed off the big M1 tank. Jaeger waved at Lieutenant Rogers's FIST-V vehicle, signaling for his friend to dismount and meet him.

Jaeger lay down on his belly, leaned on both elbows as he held his German-made binoculars to his eyes, and carefully scanned the horizon in search of movement.

"See anything?" Rogers asked, crawling next to Jaeger.

"Negative," Jaeger replied. "But I didn't expect the bastards to come barreling in here in broad daylight. You can bet that the enemy has scouts out, probably already in position, just waiting for dark to come and have a look at us."

"The old man seemed a bit pissed that we didn't get here on time," Rogers said matter-of-factly.

"Well," Jaeger replied, shrugging off the implication that he was tardy, "I can do only so much. He didn't give me enough time to prepare."

"Do you think we can stop them?" Rogers questioned nervously, changing the subject.

"We don't have much of a choice. It depends a lot on your artillery, Don, and on the reports we get," Jaeger replied, nodding thoughtfully. "We will just have to hope we see them before they see us."

"OK, Sam. Let's go over the artillery plan again," Rogers said, returning back to business. "I need some more information."

The hours passed with no enemy contact. Sunset came at 2130. All checkpoints reported on the situation in their areas every half hour. Jaeger began to worry around 2330, when he could no longer contact Checkpoint 9.

"Zulu One One, this is Zulu Two Eight. Spot report. Over," Ramos whispered to Jaeger over the radio.

"Zulu Two Eight, this is Zulu One One. Send it. Over!" Jaeger replied, thankful that a contact had finally broken the tension of waiting.

"Observing vehicle movement." Ramos paused, checking his map with a small, blue-filtered flashlight. "Possibly two BRDMs at grid 752988. Over."

"Can you get a fix for artillery? Over," Jaeger replied.

"Negative, Zulu One One. I can't see them now. I didn't get a chance to laze them and determine their range," Ramos said, referring to the ability of his laser range finder to determine the range to a target with great accuracy. "I'll keep my eyes peeled. Over."

"Roger, Zulu Two Eight. . . . All stations, this is Zulu One One. Keep alert. Enemy has been sighted north of Checkpoint Eight," Jaeger announced. "Zulu One One. Out."

Time went by and the radios were ominously quiet. Jaeger, standing in the tank commander's station, waited nervously. The night was passing by slowly . . . tediously. If his plan was going to work, he must have advance warning of the enemy's approach. His biggest fear was that the enemy would somehow slip by his outposts without being seen.

"Zulu One One, this is Zulu One Four!" Jaeger's radio crackled to life. Sergeant Riley was trying to reach him. "My dismounted observation post reports firing off to my right. Sounds like 25mm. Over."

"Roger Zulu One Four, I can see the flashes now," Jaeger replied, turning his head quickly to his left. The shooting was taking place almost seven kilometers away from Jaeger's position. From his location on high ground on the southeast side of Hill 955 (Checkpoint 4), he determined that the firing was taking place near Checkpoint 9. He looked at his watch. The luminous hands read 2340. "Any contact with Checkpoint Eight or Nine? Over."

"Negative, Zulu One One," Riley answered.

"Zulu One One, this is Zulu Two Eight!" Ramos said, screaming over his radio. "I am at Checkpoint Eight. There's a fight going on at Checkpoint Nine. I can't reach Checkpoint Nine on the radio. Over."

"Roger, Zulu Two Eight. Stay calm," Jaeger ordered, his voice reaching out to Ramos, trying to assure him that everything would work out. "Any idea what's coming your way?"

"I can't tell, Zulu One One," Ramos reported. I see green tracers and 25mm cannonfire. . . . Now it's stopped. Over."

"Roger, Zulu Two Eight," Jaeger answered. "Stay alert. Call for artillery if you positively identify a target. Zulu One One. Out."

"Charlie One Four, this is Zulu One One," Jaeger radioed to Sergeant Young at Checkpoint 9. "What is your situation? Over."

There was no answer.

Jaeger jumped down to his tank commander's sight. He scanned the area around Checkpoint 9, trying to get a feel for what was happening. His sight was set for wide angle and he soon was able to observe the tracer ammunition firing through the air. He followed the tracers to their source with his sights. Suddenly, an explosion, spouting hot flames above the ground, illuminated the area around Checkpoint 9 for one brief instant.

"Zulu One One, this is Charlie One Four. Spot report. Over." Young sounded very tired as he slowly spoke into the microphone.

"Send it, Charlie One Four," Jaeger replied, relieved to hear Sergeant Young's voice.

"Engaged four BRDMs at grid LK766962. Destroyed one. The rest headed south. I lost one man . . . KIA. . . . Over."

"Roger, Charlie One Four," Jaeger said. "Wait. Break. . . . Charlie Four Two, this is Zulu One One."

Damn! Jaeger thought. The enemy has already penetrated my screen! Maybe if I can alert the scout at Checkpoint 5, he could pick them up and hit the enemy with artillery.

"Zulu One One, this is Charlie Four Two," the young scout sergeant at Checkpoint 5 replied.

"Charlie Four Two, there are three BRDMs headed your way. Stay alert. As soon as you identify them, call me for artillery support. Over."

"Wilco, Zulu One One," the scout reported confidently. "We are ready. Out."

Jaeger radioed the battalion commander and reported the contact and the loss of one scout soldier.

The night passed slowly. It was now midnight. The cloudless desert sky was bright with starlight. Jaeger waited in anticipation for the call from Checkpoint 5, reporting the BRDMs that had raced by Checkpoint 9. Lieutenant Rogers was ready to call for artillery at the first positive sighting. Nothing happened. Checkpoint 5 reported no enemy movement. Jaeger was worried.

Section 38

The dead silence of the battlefield was suddenly replaced by the muffled staccato of distant machine guns. Flares shot up in the air near Checkpoint 1. From his position, Jaeger could not see what was happening, but he could make out the arch of a red star cluster, high over the northwest side of Hill 955.

"Zulu One One, this is Zulu Four Seven. Spot report. Over," Sergeant Johnson, at Checkpoint 2, reported. "I've got firing in the vicinity of Checkpoint One, but I can't make out if it is enemy or friendly."

"Roger. Break. . . . Charlie Two Eight, this is Zulu One One. Report!" Jaeger demanded, trying to reach Checkpoint 1 on the radio. Jaeger waited thirty seconds for a reply. There was no response.

"Break. . . . Charlie Four Seven . . . Charlie Four Seven. . . . What is your situation?"

Again, silence. Jaeger heard only the rushing sound of his radios. Checkpoint 3 did not answer.

Jaeger quickly analyzed the situation. Three BRDMs had already broken through and were headed south. God only knows where they were now. He couldn't reach Checkpoint 1 or Checkpoint 3 by radio. Maybe they were dead. . . .

There was a battle going on at Checkpoint 1 and he couldn't find out what was happening there either. If Checkpoint 1 was lost, he could have a major penetration in the west as well.

Jaeger's counterrecon battle seemed to be falling apart piece by piece! He had to do something to take charge of the situation. He needed to support Checkpoint 1. But how? Jaeger must decide.

If Jaeger decides to call for artillery to fire on Checkpoint 1, go to Section 41.

If Jaeger decides to wait for more information, go to Section 42.

If Jaeger decides to order Sergeant Johnson to attack from Checkpoint 2 to Checkpoint 1, go to Section 43.

Section 39

At 1200, Jaeger's ten-vehicle force was joined by Lieutenant Rogers. Jaeger was happy to see Rogers. A good artilleryman was worth his weight in gold, and Rogers was one of the best. Jaeger appreciated how important artillery was to the success of his plan. Every member of Team Jaeger would depend on Rogers to deliver lethal and accurate concentrations of mortar and 155mm artillery fire.

Sergeant Young and Rogers met for the first time and quickly started working together. Young introduced Rogers to his vehicle commanders and, together, they discussed the artillery plan. Young took extra care to show Rogers the patrol plans and the locations of each position that he intended to occupy. Young wanted to make sure that friendly artillery didn't hit his men.

Jaeger was impressed with Young's take-charge attitude. There was no doubt that the scout platoon sergeant knew his trade. Given the right amount of freedom of action, Sergeant Young came forward with natural aggressiveness. His leadership and initiative could be an important combat multiplier.

At 1230 the battalion commander, Lieutenant Colonel Brown, called Jaeger on the radio and asked about his progress. Jaeger reported that everything was on track. The battalion commander wished him luck and reemphasized the importance of determining the location of the enemy's main attack.

At 1245 Jaeger ordered his column to move out. By 1330, Jaeger was in position at Checkpoint 4, and Sergeant Young reported that his patrols were active and that he had negative contact with the enemy.

Jaeger, with his tank positioned on the high ground at Checkpoint 4, climbed down from his big M1 and walked over to the crest of the hill to get a better look. Sergeant Colwell instinctively moved up to the tank commander's station and put on Jaeger's CVC helmet to monitor the radio. Jaeger waved at Lieutenant Rogers's FIST-V vehicle, signaling for Rogers to dismount and meet with him on the ground.

Lying belly down at the crest of the hill, Jaeger carefully observed the battlefield with his seven-power German-made binoculars. Rogers crawled up to join him.

"See anything?" Rogers asked, bringing his binoculars to his eyes.

"Negative," Jaeger replied. "But I didn't expect to see much activity now . . . not in broad daylight. The enemy isn't that sloppy. I'll bet that he has scouts out, though . . . probably already in position, just waiting for dark to come and have a look at us."

"Do you think we can stop them?" Rogers questioned, looking over at Jaeger very seriously.

"Well, that depends a lot on your artillery, and on the men," Jaeger replied confidently. "From the looks of our team—you and the mortars, Sergeant Young's scouts, and my guys—I'd say we have a damn good chance of kicking their ass!"

The hours passed by with no enemy contact. Sunset came at 2130.

Sergeant Young, after consulting with Jaeger over the radio, established two additional dismounted observation posts forward of the original counterreconnaissance screen. One was located just north of Checkpoint 3. True to the colors of a good scout, Young broke the rules and positioned the second dismounted observation post out of bounds. The position was just too good to deny. He put two of his best men, SP4 Jim Bodrie and PFC Cliff Parry, on the high ground at LK735996. Bodrie and Parry quietly occupied this position just before dark.

Armed only with M-16s, passive night vision goggles (PVS-7s), a PRC-77 FM radio, and two days of water, both teams dug into the desert soil and occupied an observation post that gave them a remarkable view of the area forward of Phase Line Poland.

Young had trained these men thoroughly and both teams constructed their positions with overhead cover—enough to withstand anything but a direct hit from an artillery shell. This involved using sheet metal strips and prefilled sandbags that they carried on their CFVs to provide overhead cover. With prefilled sandbags, these positions could be constructed in very little time.

Young called the position at LK735996 Lone Ranger, and the one north of Checkpoint 3 Tonto. Both positions had good observation of the critical enemy avenues of approach. These positions multiplied the effectiveness of the counterreconnaissance screen by providing additional depth to the battlefield.

Young radioed the locations of each position to Jaeger to ensure that artillery no-fire areas were planned around each scout position. He coordinated with Lieutenant Rogers to ensure that artillery no-fire areas were established around each dismounted scout observation post. A no-fire area is a graphic control measure that helps to identify friendly positions to friendly artillery units. This would decrease the chances of killing his own men with friendly fire.

"Zulu One One, this is Charlie One Four. Spot report. Over," Sergeant Young reported to Jaeger over the radio.

"Charlie One Four, this is Zulu One One. Send it. Over," Jaeger replied, thankful that something had finally broken the tension of waiting.

"Lone Ranger reports observing vehicle movement." Young paused, checking his map with a small, blue-filtered flashlight. "Possibly two BRDMs at grid LK732018. Over."

"Roger," Jaeger replied. "Request artillery. Over."

"Negative, Zulu One One. I want to let them get closer," Young said eagerly. "I want to make sure that they don't get away."

"Roger, Four Seven. It's your show. Break. . . . All stations, this is Zulu One One. Keep alert. Enemy sighted at LK732018," Jaeger announced. "Zulu One One. Out."

It was a little past midnight. Time was going by slowly. The radios were ominously quiet. Jaeger, standing in the tank commander's station in his tank, nervously watched for signs of activity to the northeast.

Tungkt, Tungkt, Tungkt, Tungkt. The unmistakable sound of a Bradley 25mm cannon could be heard in the vicinity of Checkpoint 9. A white-hot explosion lit up the northeastern sky.

"Charlie One Four, this is Zulu One One," Jaeger radioed to Sergeant Young at Checkpoint 9. "What is your situation? Over."

Tungkt, Tungkt, Tungkt. There was no answer.

Jaeger waited, wishing he could do something.

"Zulu One One, this is Charlie One Four!" Jaeger's radio crackled to life. "Destroyed two motorcycle scouts," Sergeant Young reported jubilantly. "Two BRDMs . . . no, make that four . . . heading south. Request artillery, I'll adjust. Over."

"Roger, Charlie One Four, I can see the flashes now," Jaeger replied, turning his head quickly to his left. The fighting was taking place almost eight kilometers away from Jaeger's position. From his location on high ground on the southeast side of Hill 955 (Checkpoint 4), he could see a bright fire burning in the vicinity of Checkpoint 9. He looked at his watch. The luminous hands read 0037.

"Be careful," Jaeger said, a bit worried that his scout platoon sergeant might get too aggressive. "I can't afford to lose you. Over."

"Roger, Zulu One One," Young answered, the concentration of battle clearly in his voice. "We'll be OK. We just can't pass this one up. I am going to engage with TOW missiles as soon as the artillery lands. I'll call you back when we are finished. Out!"

The sound of U.S. 155mm artillery screaming toward the enemy south of Checkpoint 9 gave Jaeger a sense of power and pride. Young was doing a great job. Hopefully, he would bag all the BRDMs.

Karrummp! After several tense minutes, white flash-bursts of artillery crashed into the ground where Sergeant Young had called for artillery fire. The artillery landed short and Sergeant Young relayed his corrections to Lieutenant Rogers.

Jaeger could see the backblast of a TOW missile launched from Sergeant Young's position. After a few seconds, the missile, looking like a flying beam of light, erupted in a fiery explosion.

Karrummp! Karrummp! More artillery landed on the distant targets. Another TOW missile launched and exploded in the blackness of the desert.

"Zulu One One, this is Charlie One Four. Spot report. Over." Young sounded victorious as he slowly spoke into the microphone. "Two confirmed kills. Two with the TOW. One possible artillery hit on a third BRDM. One may have gotten away and headed south. Over."

"Roger, Charlie One Four," Jaeger said. "Can you get the one that is heading south?" Jaeger's tone was serious.

"Negative, Zulu One One," Young said a bit reluctantly. "I know I killed two . . . they are burning. I lost the trail of two BRDMs. They probably ran in the direction of Checkpoint 5. I don't have anyone back there to pick him up. But he won't be quite as brave now. My guess is that he will slow down rather than fall into another ambush. You could easily stop him with one of your tanks."

Jaeger needed to decide what to do. One good enemy BRDM recon crew could gather a lot of information. If two broke through, it might be all that the Threat needed to determine where to launch their attack.

Jaeger decided that he had three options: Move his platoon against the BRDMs and intercept them before they reach Phase Line Denmark; send Sergeant Riley and Ramos to hunt for the BRDMs before they reach Phase Line Denmark; or let the BRDMs go and stay put at Checkpoint 4.

If Jaeger decides to move his platoon against the BRDMs, go to Section 45.

If Jaeger decides to send Sergeant Riley and Ramos against the BRDMs, go to Section 46.

If Jaeger decides to wait at Checkpoint 4 and develop the situation further, go to Section 47.

Section 40

At noon Lieutenant Rogers joined Jaeger's small group of four M1 tanks, five cavalry fighting vehicles, and two M106 mortar tracks. Jaeger was happy to see Rogers. A good artilleryman was worth his weight in gold, and Rogers was one of the best. Jaeger knew that he would depend on his friend to keep them all alive.

Jaeger briefed Rogers on the mission and took extra care to show him each friendly position and each suspected enemy avenue of approach. Rogers immediately worked with Jaeger to complete the artillery plan to support Jaeger's concept of the operation. A skilled artillery fire support planner, Rogers completed the artillery plan in record time.

At 1230 the battalion commander, Lieutenant Colonel Brown, called Jaeger on the radio and demanded a status report. Jaeger responded positively, telling the commander that the team would move out on time. The battalion commander wished Jaeger luck and reemphasized the importance of locating the enemy's main attack.

At 1245 Jaeger ordered his column to move out. By 1330 he was in position at Checkpoint 4, and the other elements of Team Jaeger were still getting set. By 1400, everyone was in place. All reported no enemy contact.

Jaeger, with his tank facing northeast on the southern slope of the high ground at Checkpoint 4, dismounted and walked up to the crest of the hill to get a better look. Sergeant Colwell moved up to the tank commander's position as his lieutenant climbed off the big M1 tank. Jaeger waved at Lieutenant Rogers, signaling for him to dismount and meet with him on the ground.

"See anything?" Rogers asked, crawling next to Jaeger and bringing his own pair of binoculars to his eyes. Jaeger was lying down in a prone position, carefully scanning the horizon with his binoculars.

"Nothing," Jaeger replied. "Not even a dust cloud. But I didn't expect the enemy to come barreling in here in broad daylight. You can bet that he has scouts out, probably already in position, just waiting for dark to come so they can have a look at us."

"Do you think that we can stop them?" said Rogers, hardly believing that he had asked such a question.

"Well, that depends a lot on your artillery and on the men," Jaeger replied quietly. "If we can observe them first, we have a good chance of knocking them out. I just hope that they don't sneak by us through this rugged terrain. This area is a lot rougher than it appears on the map."

Jaeger waited. The hours passed with no enemy contact. Sunset occurred at 2130. He received reports every thirty minutes. Not a single enemy was observed.

Around midnight, Sergeant Ramos at Checkpoint 8 thought he saw movement to the north but couldn't verify any targets. Rogers called for 155mm artillery illumination, based on Ramos's spot report, but no enemy was discovered.

Jaeger began to get a bad feeling. He hoped that the enemy wouldn't come this way after all.

Time went by, and the radios were ominously quiet. Jaeger, standing in the tank commander's station of his tank, nervously watched to the northeast for signs of activity.

"Zulu One One, this is Zulu One Four. Spot report. Over," Riley yelled into the radio. "I got a large group of infantry, dismounts, at grid LK700962. Request artillery. Over!"

"Roger, Zulu One Four. I'll get it," Jaeger shouted. Lieutenant Rogers acknowledged that he heard the request and immediately called for a deadly volley of 155mm artillery.

The mortars at Checkpoint 4 rushed into action. Sergeant Martin shouted out commands. His two mortar crews went through their actions at the guns with drilled perfection. The steady *thuunk* of the mortar rounds leaving the mortar tubes at Checkpoint 4 filled the air with electricity.

Located on the ridge at Checkpoint 4, Jaeger felt better now that things were happening. He listened to the radio and thought about his next move. He looked through his tank commander's sight, observing the distant target area and waiting for the mortars and artillery to land.

Karrummp! The mortars hit the target area first. The first two rounds hit to the left of the target, but Sergeant Riley quickly called in corrections to Lieutenant Rogers. Luckily for Riley, the enemy infantry had taken a short halt, possibly to check their direction of movement. The subsequent artillery fire hit the enemy infantry right on target, forcing them to hit the dirt and seek cover.

Karrummp! Karrummp!

Looking through his thermal sights, Riley reported that the artillery had blown down the little figures like toy soldiers being brushed away by a gigantic broom. The explosions lit up the night.

After ten minutes of firing, the artillery and the mortars stopped. Riley reported to Jaeger that a scan of the area with his thermal sight showed no movement. It appeared that this enemy infantry unit had been neutralized.

A flare ignited high over the northern slope of Hill 955. It burned brightly, fluttering as the parachute swayed back and forth in the wind, and floated slowly to the ground.

"Zulu One One," Young said calmly into his radio microphone. "I have dismounted movement at grid LK685968. Request artillery. Over."

"Charlie One Four," Rogers replied before Jaeger could answer. "This is Victor One Two. I understand. We saw your flare. You adjust. Mortars on the way!"

"Charlie One Four, this is Zulu One One," Jaeger added. "Can you handle it?"

"Roger One One, I think so," Young replied, very businesslike. "I don't have a real fix on what is out there. There are so many wadis and erosion ditches in this area that you could move a battalion of grunts to Hill 955 without being seen. I'll get back to you as soon as I get some definite targets. Out."

Jaeger peered out his hatch to observe the actions of the mortarmen. The mortar crews quickly reacted to this new call for fire. With trained precision they adjusted their sights, prepared the proper mortar charges, and dropped their lethal bombs into the mortar tubes. Within minutes mortar rounds fell just north of Checkpoint 3. The explosions erupted in quick bursts of light and flame. If there was any enemy infantry crawling up Hill 955, they were in for a rough time.

Jaeger was very glad to have the mortars with him to deal with this infantry threat. The 4.2-inch mortar won't do much against an armored vehicle, but it was an excellent weapon against unprotected, dismounted infantry. With a maximum effective range of 6,800 meters, the mortars provided an excellent combination of extended range and lethality to the counterreconnaissance force.

Another lull set in. Jaeger continued to receive negative reports from his four teams. No one had confirmed any more enemy movement. *Maybe we got them all,* Jaeger thought. *Maybe we've scared them off.*

He jumped out of his tank and walked over to Lieutenant Rogers's FIST-V.

"Hello, Sam," Rogers said with a sleepy smile. "Things seem to be going pretty good so far."

"Yeah," Jaeger replied. "I'm worried. We don't—" Jaeger was interrupted in the middle of his sentence by the sound of battle several kilometers off to his west.

Boom! Tungkt, Tungkt, Tungkt, Tungkt. Jaeger heard the muffled sound of tank fire and a Bradley 25mm cannon.

Both officers stopped what they were doing and ran back to their radios. Jaeger raced back to his tank and hopped up on the hull, banging his knee. Pain surged through his body as he struggled to squirm into the tank commander's position and grab his CVC helmet. Thrusting the helmet on his head, he listened for a report from one of his outposts. He looked at his watch . . . it was 0310.

"Zulu One One, this is Zulu Four Seven!" It was Johnson, at Checkpoint 2, speaking a lot faster than normal. "Spot report. Over."

"Zulu Four Seven, this is One One," Jaeger replied quickly, anxious for information. "Send it."

"Engaged three BMPs at grid LK650950," Johnson said, now slowing down his speech enough to make it intelligible. "I say again, engaged three BMPs at grid LK650950. Destroyed one. Over."

"Roger, Zulu Four Seven," Jaeger replied. "Which way did the other two go? Over."

"Unknown. We lost them," Johnson answered dejectedly. "They must have withdrawn to the north. We will continue to observe. I'll call you as soon as we get another contact. Over."

"Roger, Four Seven," Jaeger said. "Good shooting. Keep scanning. We will get some artillery on your last grid."

"It's already on the way," Lieutenant Rogers announced over the radio.

Karrummp! Karrummp! Jaeger could hear the sound of artillery landing near Johnson's position.

Jaeger gathered his thoughts and reported to battalion tactical operations center (TOC). So far he had discovered, and possibly destroyed, an enemy infantry patrol and now these BMPs. He hadn't lost anyone, but he was worried that the enemy was somehow slipping by his widely dispersed outposts.

It was now 0345. It would be light at 0500, with sunrise at 0540. If he was going move back to battle position A12 safely, he must move everyone no later than 0430. But which way would the regiment attack? Jaeger wasn't sure.

Jaeger had two options. The first was to wait in his positions, to the very last minute, until he could positively determine the direction of the enemy's main attack. This could prove tricky and he might not be able to disengage his forces in time. The other option was to move at 0430 and get back to battle position A12 before 0500. Which option should he choose? Jaeger must decide!

If Jaeger decides to wait, go to Section 48.

If Jaeger decides to pull back to battle position A12, go to Section 49.

Section 41

Jaeger heard the faint crack of machine guns and the mean snap of grenades to the northwest. This sound was soon replaced by that of artillery shells swooshing overhead and the dull, terrible thud of artillery striking the ground.

The U.S. artillery smashed into Checkpoint 1. Jaeger ordered Rogers to request variable-time–fuze rounds, in order to air-burst the artillery over the heads of the enemy infantry. If his men were alive on Checkpoint 1, they could button up in their CFV and wait out the storm of fire. If they were already dead . . . well, then maybe Jaeger could wreak vengeance on their attackers.

Not knowing if the artillery had any effect, Jaeger ordered Rogers to repeat the strike. The sound of the shells continued as Jaeger eagerly waited to hear a call on the radio from Checkpoint 1.

Checkpoint 1 remained silent.

Go to Section 52.

Section 42

Jaeger could hear the faint crack of machine gun fire and the muffled explosions of grenades off to the northwest. What was happening at Checkpoint 1?

"Charlie Two Eight, this is Zulu One One." Jaeger waited for a reply, hoping that Checkpoint 1 would respond.

Silence.

Suddenly Jaeger's radio came alive with a report, not from Checkpoint 1 but from Sergeant Riley.

"Zulu One One, this is Zulu One Four. Spot report. Over," Riley yelled into the radio. "I got a large group of infantry, dismounts, at grid LK700962. Request artillery. Over!"

"Roger Zulu One Four. I'll get it," Jaeger shouted. Lieutenant Rogers acknowledged with the wave of his hand that he too had heard the request for fire and would immediately call in a deadly volley of 155mm artillery.

The wait for the artillery seemed to last forever. Sergeant Martin's mortars joined in, with Sergeant Riley calling in the corrections. After ten minutes of firing, the artillery stopped.

Riley scanned the area with his thermal sights, looking for movement.

"Zulu One One, this is Zulu One Four," Riley reported over the radio. "The artillery hit them like a huge rock squashing a bug. If anyone has survived the bombardment, they are not moving."

"Roger One Four," Jaeger replied. "Good job. Try to reach Charlie Two Eight for me. I can't reach them and I'm afraid they may have run into trouble."

"Wilco, Zulu One One," Riley responded. "I'll try."

Riley didn't get a response either. The men at Checkpoint 1 must have been killed in action.

Jaeger watched as a white parachute flare ignited high over the northern slope of Hill 955. The flare burned brightly, fluttering as its parachute swayed back and forth, and floated slowly to the ground. Something must be happening near Checkpoint 3.

Jaeger radioed the scout on Checkpoint 3. No response. Jaeger tried again.

A lump formed in the pit of his stomach. There was still no answer from Checkpoint 3. What was happening?

Boom! Jaeger heard the distant sound of tank fire. Looking to his left Jaeger could see a flurry of green tracers and explosions. Although he was at least 1,000 meters away from the battle, he could see the flash of a 105mm cannon. He knew that Johnson was in trouble.

"Zulu One One, this is Zulu Four Seven. Over." Johnson screamed for his platoon leader. "Zulu One One. Spot report. CONTACT!"

"Zulu Four Seven, this is Zulu One One," Jaeger answered over the radio. "Send it. What is your situation?"

Boom! The only response was the firing of Johnson's 105mm cannon and the sound of machine gun fire.

Jaeger yelled to the mortars to lay down a protective barrage of high explosive, danger close, to Johnson's position on Checkpoint 2. Rogers acknowledged the request. Sergeant Martin barked out some quick commands.

Thuunk . . . Thuunk . . . The mortars began their barrage. High-explosive shells were on their way to kill Johnson's attackers. More orders were issued. The mortarmen executed their drill to adjust the mortars. With precision and care the mortar bombs were rapidly prepared. Sights were quickly set. The command was given to fire.

Thuunk . . . Thuunk . . . Death was on the way. The rounds left the tubes and the hungry mortars were refed.

KABOOM! The air ripped apart with a shattering explosion as one of the mortar carriers disintegrated in a ball of flame. The "cheese charges," precut explosive charges used to propel the mortar rounds, burned white hot as the mortar ammunition cooked off in a fiery, terrible explosion.

Enemy infantry! Jaeger saw men running everywhere. The enemy was attacking Checkpoint 4!

Jaeger immediately buttoned up and began spraying the area with .50-caliber machine gun fire.

"Jones! Move out!" Jaeger shouted to his driver over the intercom. "Forward!" The big tank lurched forward, moving up the narrow dirt trail to their front. Colwell fired the coaxial 7.62mm machine gun at everything that moved. The turret swung around wildly.

KABOOM! Another huge explosion tore through the remaining M106 mortar carrier.

Sergeant Martin, on his feet with his M-16 in hand, fired at the advancing enemy infantry. The blast from the explosion of his track, only twenty feet away, blew him to the ground. Struggling to get up, he was cut down by a stream of enemy machine gun fire.

In the confusion, Jones drove the tank into a ditch. A31 violently pitched forward, throwing Jaeger hard against his .50-caliber machine gun.

"Back up!" Jaeger cried, his ammunition expended.

Roll the dice.

If the total of the two dice is four or less, go to Section 53.

If the total of the two dice is five or more, go to Section 55.

Section 43

"Zulu Four Seven, this is Zulu One One," Jaeger said into his radio microphone mouthpiece. "Do you have contact with Charlie Four Seven? Over."

"Negative, Zulu. I saw a lot of firing a few moments ago. It looks quiet now," Johnson reported.

Jaeger knew that he had to do something. Firing artillery blindly, without anyone to direct the fire, would probably be ineffective. Besides, he had a scout crew there. What if their radio wasn't working? Checkpoint 3 was the closest to Checkpoint 1, but now he couldn't reach them either! Had Checkpoints 1 and 3 fallen to the enemy?

"Zulu Four Seven, move to Checkpoint One as carefully as possible. Find out what is happening." Jaeger paused to gather his thoughts. "Keep in radio contact with me at all times. I will get you mortar and artillery support if you need it. Over."

There was a long period of silence.

"Roger, Zulu," Johnson replied, not sounding too confident. "Are you sure that you want me to move from here? The ground is pretty rough and I have a great view of avenue of approach alpha from my present location."

"Affirmative, Zulu Four Seven," Jaeger replied sternly. "Move out ASAP. Over!"

Johnson didn't even reply. He just clicked his transmitter switch twice, sending two short bursts of static to Jaeger to acknowledge his obedience and his anger.

Jaeger waited impatiently. Another fifteen minutes passed with no enemy contact. Finally the silence was broken as Johnson called over the radio.

"Zulu One One, this is Zulu Four Seven." Johnson's tone was hot enough to melt steel.

"I've busted up on this crazy move you gave me. I slid down a steep slope on the west side of Hill 955. The tank is listing to the left side. I'm in a ditch. My left track is off and the road wheels on the right side are dug into a three-foot erosion ditch. I'm not going anywhere;

179

not unless you can get another tank to pull me out. There is no way that I will be able to free her without a tow. What do you want me to do now?"

"Shit!" Jaeger said out loud. "That's all I need. Now what do I do?" Jaeger had to decide!

If Jaeger goes to help Johnson, go to Section 69.

If Jaeger tells Johnson to stay put, and Jaeger continues his mission at Checkpoint 4, go to Section 70.

Section 44

Therefore I say: Know your enemy and know yourself; in a hundred battles you will never be in peril. When you are ignorant of the enemy but know yourself, your chances of winning or losing are equal. If ignorant both of your enemy and of yourself, you are certain in every battle to be in peril.

Sun Tzu, 500 B.C.

As Sun Tzu recommended almost 2,500 years ago, you must know your own capabilities and the enemy's to be sure of victory. The following advice may help you in future battles.

Threat Reconnaissance Doctrine

The Threat's doctrine demands extensive reconnaissance. The Threat style of centralized command and control requires that each commander have detailed information on the enemy's location and capabilities. At the tactical level, the success of the motorized rifle regiment depends on the accuracy and timeliness of the information gained by their regimental reconnaissance company. If you can disrupt this reconnaissance, if you can blind the Threat commander by killing his reconnaissance, you have gained a significant advantage over the enemy.

Threat reconnaissance follows a simple philosophy of surfaces and gaps. Surfaces are the hard places, defended by units prepared to fight. Gaps are the weak spots, undefended or improperly guarded. Threat reconnaissance units seek the gaps. The axis of advance for the regiment is determined by the results of the reconnaissance and is shifted in response to what the reconnaissance finds. The enemy wants to get into their enemy's rear area as swiftly as possible. By reporting the vital information of where the defender is *not*, the regiment decides where it will attack. Finding an avenue of approach unguarded or poorly defended, they will secure this approach, clear the obstacles, and wait for the regiment's attack.

Depth

In terms of the United States Army's AirLand Battle doctrine, the reconnaissance battle involves the concept of depth. Depth is the extension of operations in space, time, and resources. This includes obtaining the necessary maneuver space and the necessary time to plan, arrange, and execute operations. Momentum in the attack and elasticity in the defense are derived from depth. In both the offense and defense, therefore, winning the reconnaissance battle is the first step in gaining the depth necessary to defeat the enemy.

Traditionally, Americans have lost the reconnaissance battle, often out of default, simply because American forces failed to conduct aggressive patrolling on their own. To win the reconnaissance battle you must throw the enemy off balance early with raids, spoiling attacks, reconnaissance by fire, and the bold use of supporting artillery.

Spreading the tanks and scouts out over a twelve-kilometer counterreconnaissance battle area made the area one huge gap. Jaeger was unable to react to a major penetration of his screen; his plan lacked the depth necessary to give him an extension of his operations in space, time, or resources.

The Threat reconnaissance units took Jaeger's plan apart one piece at a time. The enemy got into the battalion area and reported to their commander where the Americans were strong and where they were weak. With this information they hit the American defenses in the least defended areas. Using fast movement as their weapon, the enemy disrupted the American defense.

Successful reconnaissance was the reason for their success. Lack of depth was a major factor in Jaeger's defeat.

Return to Section 34 and try again!

Section 45

Jaeger climbed out of the tank commander's station of his M1 tank and ran over to Riley's tank. He waved to Sergeant Riley, signaling for him to dismount and meet him on the ground. Riley got out of A34 and walked along the side of his tank to talk to Jaeger.

"One, possibly two, BRDMs have broken through the screen line near Checkpoint Nine. They are headed in the direction of Checkpoint Five. We are going to go get them."

"OK, Lieutenant," Riley said with a grin. "I monitored Young's radio transmission. We can move out in five minutes."

"Look, Riley." Jaeger grabbed his platoon sergeant by the arm. "You brief Ramos and Johnson. I will brief Lieutenant Rogers. I am going to leave Rogers here, with the mortars, while we are gone. He will be in a better situation to maintain communications from here."

"Good," Riley said with a wink. "Besides, trying to hit two runaway BRDMs with artillery can be near impossible. But, let's tell the mortars to fire some mortar illumination between Checkpoint Nine and Checkpoint Five. Maybe it will slow them down a bit. You know they hate to move fast when they think someone's watching."

"Right." Jaeger looked at his watch. "I'll tell the mortars what to do. It's 0115 now. We move out at 0125. Let's go."

Jaeger and Riley moved off to their tasks. Riley ran over to Ramos's tank and together they moved to Johnson's tank. Under the cloudless sky Riley briefed both men on the situation. Jaeger made it over to the FIST-V and briefed Lieutenant Rogers and Sergeant Martin.

Jaeger moved out at 0125, followed by Johnson, Riley, and then Ramos. He radioed Lieutenant Colonel Brown and issued him a complete report. Then Jaeger switched back to his counterrecon frequency as his tanks slowly moved across the desert, on the lookout for the enemy BRDMs. It was now 0200.

"Zulu One One, this is Charlie One Four. Spot report," Sergeant Young radioed.

"This is Zulu One One. Send it. Over," Jaeger replied.

"I've lost contact with the men at OP Tonto," Young said with a worried tone that reinforced the seriousness of the problem. "They started to have trouble with their radio, and then they went off the air. I don't think that they have enemy contact. Over."

"Great . . . just great," Jaeger replied. "Can you get someone else to observe their sector who has a good radio?"

"Not any time soon," Young replied. "I'll work on it. Over."

"Negative," Jaeger answered. "Just stay in position and continue the mission. Call me if you get any new word from them. Out."

"Zulu One One," the scout sergeant at Checkpoint 2 radioed. "This is Charlie Eight Zero. FLASH SPOT REPORT! Observing dismounted infantry at grid LK676942. Request artillery. Over!" Silhouetted against the "cold" side of Hill 955, the scout CFV at Checkpoint 2 was able to pick up the image of dismounted enemy soldiers in their thermal sights.

"Charlie Eight Zero," Rogers replied before Jaeger could answer. "This is Victor One Two. Dismounted infantry . . . grid LK676942. You adjust. Mortars on the way!"

Jaeger looked back, out of his tank, in the direction of Checkpoint 4. He was about a kilometer and a half away now, but he could see the faint light from the mortars as the mortar bombs left the tubes. Rogers was doing a good job. Everything was under control.

Jaeger looked back in horror as Checkpoint 4 began to glow with the fire of battle. There was one big explosion as a vehicle blew up. The white-hot flash of mortar "cheese charges," precut explosive charges that were used to propel the mortar rounds, burned brightly in the night air.

"Victor One Two, this is Zulu One One." Jaeger frantically tried to reach Rogers. "Victor One Two, this is Zulu One One!"

No reply. Tracers arched into the sky in all directions from Checkpoint 4.

"Zulu One Four, turn around," Jaeger ordered savagely, choking back his anger as best he could. "Blitz back to Checkpoint Four. Follow me!"

Was Checkpoint 4 now in enemy hands?

Go to Section 58.

Section 46

Jaeger hopped out of the tank commander's station of his M1 tank and ran over to Riley's tank. He waved at Riley to meet him on the ground. Riley got out of A34 and walked along the side of his tank to talk to Jaeger.

"Two BRDMs may have broken through the screen line near Checkpoint Nine. They are headed in the direction of Checkpoint Five. I want you and Ramos to go get them."

"OK, Lieutenant," Riley said with a grin. "I monitored Young's radio transmission. I think that you are making the right decision."

"Look, Riley." Jaeger grabbed the older man by the arm. "Don't take any big chances. I need you and Ramos too much. Find those BRDMs, eliminate them, and get back here as soon as you can."

"Don't worry about us, Jaeger," Riley said with a wink. "We'll be all right. With your permission, I will fire some mortar illumination to keep those BRDMs honest . . . you know, slow them down a bit. They won't move so fast if they think we are watching them."

"Right." Jaeger looked at his watch. "It's 0115 now. Be back before 0330 if you don't find them."

Jaeger and Riley shook hands and went back to their tanks. Riley ran over to Ramos's tank and briefed him on the situation. Riley moved out three minutes later, with Ramos in A33 trailing fifty meters behind.

Jaeger radioed battalion and gave the battalion commander a complete report, then he waited.

"Zulu One One, this is Charlie One Four. Spot report," Sergeant Young radioed.

"This is Zulu One One. Send it. Over," Jaeger replied.

"I've lost contact with the men at OP Tonto," Young said with a worried tone that reinforced the seriousness of the problem. "They started to have trouble with their radio, and then they went off the air. I don't think that they have enemy contact. Over."

"Great . . . just great," Jaeger replied. "Can you get someone else to observe their sector who has a good radio?"

"Not any time soon," Young replied. "I'll work on it. Over."

"Negative," Jaeger answered. "Just stay in position and continue the mission. Call me if you get any new word from them. Out."

Jaeger contemplated his next move, but the radio again interrupted his thoughts.

"Zulu One One," the scout sergeant at Checkpoint 2 radioed. "This is Charlie Eight Zero. FLASH SPOT REPORT. Observing dismounted infantry at grid LK676942. Request artillery. Over!"

"Charlie Eight Zero," Jaeger replied. "This is Zulu One One. I understand. You adjust. Mortars on the way!"

Thuunk . . . Thuunk . . . The mortars began their barrage. High-explosive shells were on their way to kill the enemy at Checkpoint 2. More orders were issued. The mortarmen executed their drill to adjust the mortars. With precision and care the mortar bombs were rapidly prepared. Sights were quickly set. The command was given to fire.

Thuunk . . . Thuunk . . . Death was on the way. The rounds left the tubes and the hungry mortars were refed.

Craaaackk! Suddenly, Sergeant Johnson, about one hundred meters off to Jaeger's left, fired his machine guns.

"Zulu One One," Johnson shouted over the radio. "I got dismounts coming at me, a hundred meters to my front!"

"Roger Four Seven!" Jaeger said excitedly. Jaeger's tank was positioned on Checkpoint 4, looking to the northeast. He would have to turn and orient northwest to help Johnson.

"I'm on my way." In the same breath Jaeger yelled through his intercom to tell Jones to start the tank and back up.

Johnson continued firing, not waiting to hear Jaeger's reply. His machine gun fire tore into the advancing enemy infantry, who immediately returned automatic rifle fire, machine gun fire, and RPG antitank rockets. The air was soon filled with the eerie glow of illumination flares and tracer bullets.

The enemy infantry fired their RPGs wildly, unable to see clearly in the dark. To add to the confusion, the darkness was interrupted by the blinding flash of weapons and the superbright illumination of explosions.

Johnson's tank put out a tremendous amount of firepower, which took a terrible toll on the advancing enemy. The enemy infantrymen were stunned by the surprise encounter with Johnson's tank, and reeled back in shock from the firepower that tore at them.

The enemy infantrymen darted back and forth quickly in small teams of three or four men, rushing forward.

Jones slammed the tank into reverse and it charged backward. Jaeger swung the turret in the direction of the firing. Jones pivoted the tank, changing direction and moving the sixty-ton steel monster forward. Colwell scanned for targets using his thermal sight, swinging the turret back and forth.

As Jaeger arrived close enough to support Johnson, the air ripped apart with a shattering explosion as one of the mortar carriers absorbed a direct hit from an RPG. The "cheese charges" used to propel the mortar rounds ignited, burning brightly as the mortar ammunition erupted in a fiery, terrible explosion. Jaeger saw men running everywhere.

"GUNNER! HEAT. TROOPS," Jaeger shouted at the top of his lungs with a combination of excitement and fear.

Colwell identified the largest group of hot spots he could find and yelled, "Identified!"

"FIRE!" Jaeger ordered.

BOOM! The 105mm projectile screamed through the black night, hitting in front of a group of enemy infantry 300 meters from the tank. The projectile exploded with tremendous force, sending pieces of the enemy through the air.

But they kept coming. The enemy infantry increased their rate of machine gun fire and continued to assault Checkpoint 4 in short, quick rushes.

They want this hill, Jaeger thought to himself, and they are deter-mined to kill us.

The enemy was so close now that Colwell could make out their faces in his thermal sight. A31's machine guns stuttered their deadly chorus.

The bastards seemed to be everywhere!

Roll the dice.

If the total of the two dice is five or more, go to Section 56.

If the total of the two dice is four or less, go to Section 57.

Section 47

Jaeger radioed battalion and told the battalion S3 (operations officer) the situation. Jaeger wasn't about to split his forces on a wild goose chase in the dark. The two BRDMs that got past Sergeant Young could be anywhere. He was just as likely to get killed by friendly tanks or Bradleys if he started hunting BRDMs so close to Phase Line Den-mark. He knew that it was better to warn the battalion and let them take care of the intruders as they tried to breach Phase Line Denmark.

Jaeger's most important mission was to determine the direction of the enemy's main attack. He had to keep that in mind at all times. He had analyzed the terrain well, posted his men in the most effective way possible, and left a large amount of freedom of action to the scouts. But he had to remind himself that his primary mission was to inform the battalion of the direction of the enemy's main attack. Anything else was secondary.

The night passed slowly. Jaeger checked his watch and waited. The hardest part of battle was the waiting.

Jaeger began to question himself. Could he stop the enemy infiltration into his sector? He hoped that he could destroy the majority of the enemy's recon units before they reached Phase Line Denmark. Had he done everything he could possibly do? Shouldn't he be doing something more?

Jaeger remembered George S. Patton's famous dictum: "Never take counsel of your fears."

It was now 0200. Time passed. Jaeger waited.

"Zulu One One, this is Charlie One Four. Spot report," Sergeant Young radioed.

"This is Zulu One One. Send it. Over," Jaeger replied.

"I've lost contact with the men at OP Tonto," Young said with a worried tone that reinforced the seriousness of the problem. "They started to have trouble with their radio, and then they went off the air. I don't think that they have enemy contact. Over."

"Great . . . just great," Jaeger replied. "Can you get someone else to observe their sector who has a good radio?"

"Not any time soon," Young replied. "I'll work on it. Over."

"Negative," Jaeger answered. "Just stay in position and continue the mission. Call me if you get any new word from them. Out."

Jaeger contemplated his next move, but the radio again interrupted his thoughts.

"Zulu One One," the scout sergeant at Checkpoint 2 radioed. "This is Charlie Eight Zero observing dismounted infantry at grid LK676942. Request artillery. Over!"

"Charlie Eight Zero," Jaeger replied. "Roger, artillery on the way!"

Thuunk . . . Thuunk . . . The mortars began their barrage. High-explosive shells were on their way to kill the enemy at Checkpoint 2. More orders were issued. The mortarmen executed their drill to adjust the mortar sights. With precision and care the mortar bombs were rapidly prepared. Sights were quickly set. The command was given to fire.

Thuunk . . . Thuunk . . . Death was on the way. The rounds left the tubes and the hungry mortars were refed.

The mortars struck the enemy first. The explosions lit up the night. The sounds of the explosions overpowered the feeble screams of the men caught in the impact area.

The scout at Checkpoint 2 ordered a repeat of the artillery, this time with variable-time–fuze ammunition that would burst in the air over the heads of the enemy. Soon the sky above the target area was popping with bursts of orange and red.

After several minutes of firing, the artillery stopped. The scout scanned the area with his thermal sights, looking for the enemy. Nothing moved. It was now 0230.

"Zulu One One, this is Charlie Two Eight. Spot report. Over," the scout at Checkpoint 6 yelled into the radio. "I got a group of infantry, dismounts, at grid LK700962. Request artillery. Over!"

"Roger, Zulu One Four. I'll get it," Jaeger shouted. Lieutenant Rogers acknowledged the request and immediately called in a deadly volley of 155mm artillery.

The artillery took only a few minutes to land on target. Sergeant Martin's mortars joined in with the Checkpoint 6 scout calling in the corrections. After ten minutes of firing, the artillery stopped.

The scout scanned the area with his thermal sights. He reported to Jaeger that he saw no movement. The artillery had done its job well.

CRRAACK! . . . CRRAACK! . . . CRRAACK! Several rounds ricocheted harmlessly off Jaeger's tank. Checkpoint 4 suddenly burst with light and fire.

Sergeant Riley and Sergeant Ramos, about 100 meters off to Jaeger's and Johnson's left, fired their tank's machine guns. Tracers streamed through the night sky, bouncing off rocks and hitting moving shadows that were jumping from one piece of cover to the next.

Flares arched into the air, casting a ghostly glow over Checkpoint 4.

"Zulu One One," Riley shouted over the sound of his machine guns firing. "I got dismounts coming at me, 300 meters to my front!"

"Roger, Four Seven!" Jaeger said excitedly. Jaeger's tank was positioned on the northeast portion of Checkpoint 4. Johnson's tank, A32, was just sixty meters to Jaeger's right, slightly downhill. Jaeger would have to turn and orient northwest to help Riley.

"I'm on my way," Jaeger shouted over his radio. Johnson, like the good wingman he was, followed the lieutenant's lead and maneuvered to the sound of the guns. In the same breath, Jaeger yelled through his intercom for Jones to start the tank and back up.

KABOOM! A huge explosion burst just to the right of Riley's tank. An RPG rocket missed his tank by only a few meters.

BOOM! Riley responded with a 105mm HEAT round. The muzzle blast from A34 was blinding. The concussion from the muzzle blast sent dirt, dust, and rocks flying in the direction of travel on the round.

The high-explosive round shot straight, like a line of light, and erupted against the desert hillside in a shower of rocks, steel, and death.

Riley and Ramos continued firing, their overwhelming firepower making the enemy's return fire slacken. Their fire broke up the advancing enemy infantry, who were now crawling to avoid the hot metal searing through the air.

The intensity of the fire stunned the enemy infantry and drove them to seek cover. With all machine guns blazing, Riley and Ramos stopped the attack cold.

KABOOM! Another wild RPG shot flew ineffectually past Riley's tank. The sky was now bright with the eerie glow of illumination flares and green and red tracer bullets.

Jones slammed the tank into reverse and it jerked backward. Jaeger swung the turret in the direction of the firing. Jones pivoted the tank to the left and moved the tank forward. Colwell scanned for targets, firing his machine guns without command as soon as a target appeared.

Jaeger directed the tank to a position close enough to support Riley.

"GUNNER! HEAT. TROOPS," Jaeger shouted at the top of his lungs.

Colwell identified the largest group of hot spots he could find and yelled, "Identified!"

"FIRE!" Jaeger ordered.

BOOM! The 105mm projectile screamed through the black night, hitting in front of a group of enemy infantry not more than 700 meters from the tank.

The projectile exploded with tremendous force, sending human pieces in all directions. Johnson fired round after round from his main gun at the infantry. The enemy didn't stand a chance.

The enemy had gotten a lot more than they had bargained for. Within minutes, Lieutenant Rogers had effective artillery strikes falling near Checkpoint 4 to ensure the enemy's annihilation.

After several minutes of earth-shattering noise and flame, the fighting stopped. The firepower of the four tanks ended the battle quickly. Except for the cries of wounded enemy soldiers, the night was quiet. Unwilling to lose any of his own men searching for the enemy in the dark, Jaeger ordered all of his men in Checkpoint 4 to stay inside their perimeter and prepare to move to Checkpoint 10.

Within a few minutes, Jaeger received a status report from everyone at Checkpoint 4. They had been extremely lucky. Not a single American had been killed, although one of Sergeant Martin's men had been hit by a stray bullet in the left hand. Jaeger thought to himself . . . we took out an entire enemy infantry company.

It was now 0300, and only two more hours remained until BMNT (before morning nautical twilight—the twilight time right before sunrise). With all the action Jaeger had seen tonight, BMNT appeared to be the most likely time for the enemy to attack. The enemy, however, still had a substantial regimental recon force that had not been accounted for. Jaeger radioed battalion and gave the battalion commander a complete report.

"Zulu One One," an excited voice cried out over the radio. "Spot report. I have three BMPs at grid LK650950, moving southeast. Over."

"Roger, Charlie Eight Zero." Jaeger recognized the voice of the scout at Checkpoint 2. "Keep them under observation. I'll get back to you. Out."

Jaeger thought about his mission. Above all, he had to determine the direction of the enemy's main attack. Jaeger realized that he had to make a quick decision about those BMPs. Should he attack them, or should he let them go? Jaeger must decide!

If Jaeger decides to attack the BMPs, go to Section 64.

If Jaeger decides not to engage the BMPs, go to Section 73.

Section 48

"Victor Two Zero, this is Zulu One One. Over," Jaeger reported.

"Zulu One One, this is Victor Two Zero," Lieutenant Colonel Brown replied.

"I have completed the counterreconnaissance mission," Jaeger said confidently. "I suspect that the enemy will attack down the orange or pink avenue of approach. I say again, orange or pink avenue of approach. I want your permission to stay in position to verify this. I have good positions here where we can fight from as the enemy approaches. Over."

"Roger, Zulu One One," Brown replied quickly. "I concur. I will alert all elements that you are not moving to A12. Keep on this frequency and alert me as soon as you discover the direction of the attack. Over."

"Wilco," Jaeger answered. "You can count on us. Over."

"Just remember, the direction of their attack is your primary mission. I won't have to move anyone if they attack down orange or pink avenues of approach. I must know if the situation changes. I must have that information as early as you get it," Colonel Brown reiterated. "Out."

At 0450 the radios went totally dead, transmitting only white noise—the nothing sound that is transmitted over an FM frequency that is being blocked out by a high-power jamming radio. Jaeger quickly disconnected his antenna inside the tank to determine if he was being jammed.

When he received the normal rush sound from his radio, he knew that it was enemy electronic jamming. Jumping the dials to alternate frequencies produced the same result. The enemy must be barrage jamming every frequency, Jaeger thought. The attack must be on!

KARRUMMP!

As if to confirm Jaeger's suspicions, the earth suddenly erupted in a flash of fire and steel. The shock of a tremendous volume of artillery crushed in all around Checkpoint 4. Jaeger and his crew immediately put on their NBC protective masks. The amount of fire was tremendous. Anyone caught out in the open would be instantly killed.

KARRUMMP! KARRUMMP! The noise was unbearable. The artillery kept falling. Tired, claustrophobic from the closed hatch and being forced to wear the chemical mask, Jaeger struggled uncomfortably to see the battlefield. Colwell was scanning for targets.

Jaeger hadn't slept a wink all night, but he wasn't tired. The instinct for survival had his senses at their highest pitch.

KARRUMMP! Jaeger watched in horror as Rogers's FIST-V was hit by an enemy 152mm artillery shell. Rogers didn't have a chance. The artillery tore his track apart as if it were made of cardboard. The debris—twisted metal and flesh—burst upon the desert floor, scattering in all directions.

KARRUMMP! KARRUMMP! The impact from each artillery round made Jaeger's tank shudder. Suddenly the fire slackened, shifting farther south.

"Thank God," Jaeger said over the tank's intercom, his voice muffled by his protective mask. "Everyone OK?"

KABOOM! Suddenly there was a blinding flash. Not artillery this time, but RPGs. The air ripped apart with a shattering explosion as one of the mortar carriers was hit by an RPG. The M106 mortar carrier took the impact squarely on the left side. The round blew out the entire right side wall, showing the guts of the vehicle; the track looked like a ruptured sardine can. It smoldered and then ignited in a terrible ball of flame.

The on-board mortar ammunition exploded. Metal and half-exploded mortar shells flew through the air. The debris of the M106 mortar carrier burned and emitted a cloud of billowing black smoke. Jaeger saw men running everywhere.

"Colwell. Enemy infantry! Where in the hell did they come from?" Jaeger shouted.

Colwell swung the tank turret around.

"GUNNER, COAX! TROOPS!" Jaeger screamed. "FIRE AND ADJUST!" At the same time, Jaeger fired his .50-caliber machine gun from inside the turret, spraying the area with bullets.

KABOOM! An RPG exploded just inches away from Jaeger's tank.

"Jones! Back up!" Jaeger shouted to his driver over the intercom. "Hold your right track!" The big M1 lurched backward, pivoting to face left. With the tank pointing uphill now, Colwell continued to fire his coax machine gun.

"Jones, MOVE FORWARD!" Jaeger yelled. "Up the hill . . . move . . . move. . . . MOVE!" The A31 raced up the narrow dirt trail to their front. Colwell continued shooting, flattening the area to both sides of the tank with accurate and deadly machine gun fire. Moving the turret from the gunner's position, he slung it back and forth, cutting down every enemy infantryman he could see.

Another rocket ripped through the air and hit Jaeger's tank on the left side. Jones, losing control momentarily, spun the damaged tank into a ditch. The tank forcefully pitched forward, throwing the crew against the turret walls.

"Back up!" Jaeger cried, his .50-caliber ammunition expended.

Roll the dice.

If the total of the two dice is three or less, go to Section 53.

If the total of the two dice is four through nine, go to Section 54.

If the total of the two dice is ten through twelve, go to Section 61.

Section 49

Jaeger didn't have a moment to lose. Making a net radio call, he ordered all of his outposts to prepare to move back to battle position A12. Jaeger then called Lieutenant Colonel Brown.

"Victor Two Zero, this is Zulu One One. Over."

"Zulu One One, this is Victor Two Zero," Lieutenant Colonel Brown replied.

"I have done all that I can do out here. The enemy is active in the brown and orange avenues of approach. I suspect that he will attack down one of those axes. If I stay here any longer I will not make it back to A12. I can leave the scout elements at Checkpoint Three to observe. Request permission to move my heavy elements to battle position A12. Over."

There was a long pause.

"Roger, Zulu One One," Brown finally replied. "Move your elements back to A12. Leave the scouts at Checkpoint Three in position. I will alert all units to hold fire until you report set in A12. Over."

"Wilco," Jaeger answered. "Moving now. Out."

Jaeger ordered Sergeant Young to stay in position with his scouts and observe. It was Young's job to radio battalion and confirm the enemy's direction of attack. Young had been a "stay behind" before. He never had liked the mission, but he understood its necessity.

Jaeger ordered his team to move back to battle position A12 over individual infiltration routes. Checkpoints 2 and 10 would enter friendly lines from the west and Checkpoints 6 and 8 from the east.

Jaeger crossed Phase Line France with the two mortar tracks and Lieutenant Rogers's FIST-V vehicle at 0450.

Just as he crossed Phase Line France, the radios went totally dead with white noise—the nothing sound that is transmitted over an FM frequency that is being jammed. Jaeger quickly disconnected his antenna cable to determine if he was being jammed. He knew he was when he received the normal rush sound from his radio. Switching to alternate frequencies produced the same result. The enemy was barrage jamming every frequency. The attack must be on!

As if to confirm Jaeger's suspicions, the earth behind his column suddenly exploded in a flash of fire and steel. Artillery engulfed Checkpoints 4 and 10. It also landed on the forward positions of Team Charlie in battle position C11.

Anyone caught out in the open was killed instantly. Armored vehicles, dug into the hard desert ground by bulldozers, survived fairly well. Those infantrymen who did not prepare adequate overhead cover for their foxholes and fighting positions did not live to regret their error.

Jaeger and his crew immediately put on their NBC protective masks. The enemy hadn't used gas weapons yet, but there was always a first time. Team Jaeger, minus Sergeant Young's two CFVs, arrived on battle position A12 at 0520. The artillery fell there just as they arrived.

KARRUMMP! One of the mortars moving into a hasty position was hit by an enemy 152mm projectile. The vehicle stopped abruptly, jumped into the air slightly, and shuddered to a tortured halt. The inside of the aluminum M106 mortar carrier echoed with the strike of the round. The rear ramp blew open and the guts of the vehicle were scattered everywhere. There were no survivors.

Unable to talk to his unit by radio, and buttoned up by the power of the enemy's artillery, Jaeger prayed that his tanks would operate without his direction.

Taking a position on the western side of battle position A12, Jaeger's platoon was the right side of the U-shaped company position. Jaeger moved into a hasty, hull-down position, using a small rise to his front to mask a portion of his vehicle. Looking through his vision blocks, he saw another tank, probably Johnson, to his left.

KARRUMMP! KARRUMMP! KARRUMMP! The noise was unbearable. The artillery kept falling. Tired, claustrophobic from the closed hatch and from being forced to wear the uncomfortable chemical protective mask, Jaeger struggled and strained to see the battlefield. Colwell searched for targets.

Although Jaeger hadn't slept a wink all night, he wasn't tired now. The instinct for survival had his senses at their highest pitch.

KARRUMMP! The impact from each artillery round made the tank shudder. Pieces of metal clanked and scraped against the sides of Jaeger's M1 tank.

Suddenly vehicles appeared in Colwell's tank sights.

"Are they enemy or friendly?" Jaeger questioned, trying to scream above the roar of the shells blasting outside.

"I can't tell!" Colwell said, his voice muffled by the microphone of his protective mask. "Identified! T-72s."

"GUNNER, SABOT, THREE TANKS," Jaeger yelled through the tank's intercom system.

The enemy was coming from the east! The battalion moved to stop the attack along axis brown or orange. But the enemy was attacking down red! It's all my fault, Jaeger thought.

"Identified," Colwell announced, waiting for Jaeger's command to fire.

"Sir, IDENTIFIED!" Colwell shouted again.

"FIRE!" Jaeger cried, shocked out of his thoughts by Colwell.

BOOM! Jaeger's tank cannon recoiled from the shot. The shell, screaming through the air, hit its mark. A T-72, 1,700 meters away from Jaeger's position, jerked to a halt, its turret blown off in a terrific explosion.

Other T-72s turned their turrets in Jaeger's direction and fired a platoon volley. The enemy sped south, seemingly unstoppable.

Shells burst all around Jaeger's tank. Third Platoon was firing madly . . . independently . . . putting up a terrific fight.

The enemy artillery slackened. Tanks and BMPs were racing south as fast as they could travel over the rough terrain. Explosions and thick black smoke covered the area. Firing in volleys at the defenders, the moving Threat tanks had poor accuracy. Another T-72 burst into flames from a direct hit.

Jaeger saw a group of enemy tanks break off from the main column and head directly for battle position A12. He couldn't see all of his own tanks, but he could tell by the sound that his platoon's fires had slowed. Had he lost some tanks? There was no time to find out.

"Jones," Jaeger yelled into his intercom. "Back up. Find a position to our left."

Jones backed up the M1 and darted to the left front, searching for a position to fire from.

"IDENTIFIED! THREE TANKS," Colwell screamed.

Roll the dice.

If the total of the two dice is four or less, go to Section 51.

If the total of the two dice is five or more, go to Section 63.

Section 50

Thus, what is of supreme importance in war is to attack the enemy's strategy. . . . Therefore, determine the enemy's plans and you will know which strategy will be successful and which will not. . . . Thus, one able to gain victory by modifying his tactics in accordance with the enemy situation may be said to be divine.

Sun Tzu, 500 B.C.

Future battlefields will be more intense, chaotic, and destructive than ever before. The increased lethality of modern weapons has forced units to disperse to survive. With greater dispersal of units, the quality and effectiveness of junior leaders have a proportionately greater impact.

AirLand Battle is the tactical and operational doctrine of the United States Army. AirLand Battle doctrine recognizes this lethal and confusing environment by proposing decentralized control and emphasizing independent action. Implicit versus explicit understanding is expected. To accomplish this takes the kind of tactical planning that will enhance initiative, agility, depth, and synchronization. The planning function of the leader is vital. Through his plan the leader transmits his intent to accomplish the unit's mission. AirLand Battle doctrine recognizes that the "most essential element of combat power is competent and confident leadership." The leader establishes the dynamics of combat power through maneuver, firepower, protection, and leadership. He unleashes this potential through his tactical plan.

AirLand Battle doctrine seeks to employ maneuver to focus on the defeat of the enemy's plan. It is America's answer to modern ground combat. AirLand Battle recognizes maneuver as the dynamic element of combat. Maneuver enables smaller forces to defeat larger ones. A key element of maneuver warfare is to think and act faster than your opponent. It is based on securing or retaining the initiative and exercising it aggressively to accomplish the mission. The end result of the application of maneuver warfare is the enemy's loss of cohesion to the point where he can no longer operate as an effective fighting force.

Initiative

Initiative is defined as the ability to set or change the terms of battle by action. Initiative requires a constant effort to force the enemy to conform to your designs of operational purpose and tempo while maintaining your own freedom of action. At the individual level, initiative requires a willingness by soldiers and subordinate commanders to act independently within the framework of the higher commander's intent. Initiative emphasizes the decentralization of decision-making authority "to the lowest practical level because overcentralization slows action and leads to inertia."

In the attack, initiative implies that the attacker maintain the tempo of the attack to ensure that the enemy never recovers from the initial blow. "It requires surprise in selecting the time and place of the attack; concentration, speed, audacity and violence in execution; the seeking of soft spots; flexible shifting of the main effort; and prompt transition to exploitation. The goal is the creation of a fluid situation in which the enemy steadily loses track of events and thus coherence." Retaining the initiative over time requires foresight, planning beyond the initial contact, and the anticipation of key battlefield events.

In the defense, initiative implies rapidly gaining control of the situation from your opponent. The defender must quickly negate the attacker's initial advantage of choice of time and place of the attack. Intelligence and reconnaissance operations provide the defender with early warning in order to accomplish this task. Planning must anticipate likely enemy courses of action and provide contingency moves to counter the enemy actions.

Agility

Agility is the ability to act faster than the enemy. It is the first requirement for gaining the initiative. Rapid thinking and rapid action permit the fast concentration of friendly strength against enemy vulnerabilities. It is the successive concentration of strength against weakness that produces tactical victory and permits smaller forces to disorient, fragment, and eventually defeat much larger opposing formations.

In the end, agility is as much a mental as a physical quality. Agility is created in tactical plans that prepare for more than one course of action. The best tactical plan is always that which offers the greatest number of options during the execution of the plan. By focusing on the enemy, and realizing that the enemy will never react according to *your* plan, the tactical planner can develop alternate courses of action that can be executed in minimum time once the enemy's moves are discovered.

Depth

Depth is the "extension of operations in space, time and resources." Through the use of depth, a commander obtains the necessary space to maneuver effectively; the necessary time to plan, arrange, and execute operations; and the necessary resources to win. Operations must be conducted in depth to degrade the enemy's freedom of action and inhibit his flexibility. Depth emphasizes the ability of friendly forces to conduct planning in time to degrade the enemy's freedom of action. This is often achieved by upsetting the enemy's plan.

Synchronization

Synchronization is the arrangement of battlefield activities in time, space, and purpose to produce maximum relative combat power at the decisive point. Synchronization involves the visualization of the battle, anticipation, and unity of purpose. It involves the coordinated action of many independent parts all focused to achieve one aim. Synchronization requires planning but need not rely solely on explicit coordination. Implicit understanding can result in synchronized action if the commander's intent is clearly understood and the procedures and techniques of battle are well drilled and rehearsed.

Jaeger won through a combination of skill, boldness, good tactics, and luck. His mission was to destroy the enemy's reconnaissance elements and determine the direction of the enemy's main attack. His success was made possible, in large measure, by his ability to analyze the factors of the battlefield as they pertained to his platoon.

The planning function of the small unit tactical leader is vital. The leader transmits his intent and accomplishes the unit's mission through his plan. Plans must focus on the enemy and recognize the critical value of time. They should be precise enough to preserve synchronization throughout the battle and yet flexible enough to respond to changes or to capitalize on fleeting opportunities. With everyone working in parallel to accomplish Jaeger's intent, Team Jaeger was able to act faster than the enemy could react. This agility was essential to Jaeger's success.

Effective counterreconnaissance demands aggressive planning that aims at destroying the enemy reconnaissance elements before they can be used effectively. If the enemy cannot be destroyed he must be blinded. If he cannot be blinded he must be deceived. The counterreconnaissance battle must be won. It is the first step to victory on the defensive.

Jaeger organized his counterreconnaissance forces into an acquisition force and a killing force. The acquisition force was deployed as a screen line. Its mission was to find the enemy. They fought the enemy only as a last resort or if they had a particularly easy target of opportunity. The screen line aggressively used artillery fires to kill and blind the enemy reconnaissance elements.

The acquisition force was deployed in depth. Their observation posts were both mounted and dismounted. Sergeant First Class Young, the scout platoon sergeant, employed two stay-behind observation posts to provide greater depth to his screen. Stay-behind forces gave the acquisition force an enhanced capability to detect enemy actions and add greater reaction time.

The killing force, on the other hand, was designed to do most of the fighting against the enemy reconnaissance elements. The screen line detected the approach of main enemy reconnaissance units, and the killing force destroyed them. The killing force should be located along the most likely enemy avenue of approach. The M1 tank, combining firepower, mobility, and protection, was particularly well suited for this role.

Jaeger conducted an effective counterreconnaissance battle. He established the dynamics of combat power—maneuver, firepower, and protection—through his leadership. He made the difference between victory and defeat.

Go to Section 88.

Section 51

"FIRE!" Jaeger commanded.

The tank jerked from the gun's recoil. The round screamed forward, hitting the enemy tank in the front at the driver's compartment and stopping it in its tracks. Several other T-72s raced toward Jaeger's position.

Section 51

They were only 900 meters away now, and there were just too many of them.

BOOM! BOOM! Jaeger heard the sound of tank fire to his left. Looking through his vision blocks he saw Sergeant Riley's tank, firing repeatedly at the enemy tank formation.

"Sabot. Left tank," Jaeger yelled, encouraged by the arrival of Riley.

BOOM! Without waiting for the command, Colwell fired the main gun as soon as he heard an "Up" from Curn. Curn was loading as fast as he could. The turret floor was filled with steel 105mm shell casings, ejected by the gun.

Colwell's round hit another T-72 but glanced off the side of the armor due to the angle of the strike. The enemy kept coming. Colwell could now see more BMPs behind the tanks.

Three enemy tanks appeared within 700 meters of Jaeger's tank.

"IDENTIFIED, THREE TANKS," Colwell screamed, ready to fire.

"LEFT TANK, FIRE!" Jaeger ordered. "Jones, move back after the second round."

BOOM! Colwell fired before Jaeger could complete his sentence to Jones. The hypervelocity round hit the T-72 this time, exploding its turret six feet into the air. Colwell instinctively moved his sights to the center tank, moving the turret quickly and firing as soon as his sights were set.

"TARGET, CENTER TANK," Jaeger yelled. "Jones, move out . . . BACK UP!"

Jones raced the M1 engine and lurched the big tank backward thirty feet.

KABOOM! Jaeger looked to his left and watched in horror as Riley's tank smoldered from a direct hit from an enemy tank gun. The round struck the right front of the turret, right behind the tank commander and gunner station. The tank sat motionless. There was no sign of life from A34.

"Damn it!" Jaeger cried out loud, anger overcoming him. "Jones! Move forward. Let's get those sons of bitches. Colwell. ACTION, RIGHT FRONT."

A31 popped back up to the small ridge.

BOOM! Colwell immediately fired at the advancing enemy armored vehicles. There were plenty of targets to shoot at. Colwell hit a BMP and then turned the turret quickly to fire at another.

Jaeger, looking to his left, saw a more dangerous target. Taking control of the gun, he swung the turret hard left.

Roll the dice.

If the total of the two dice is ten or less, go to Section 63.

If the total of the two dice is eleven or more, go to Section 79.

Section 52

"Zulu Four Seven, this is Zulu One One," Jaeger said through his radio microphone. "What is your situation?"

"Zulu One One, this is Zulu Four Seven," Johnson replied. "Negative contact, but it is too quiet out here. I would like to fire some illumination and see if I flush anything out. Over."

"Roger, Four Seven," Jaeger replied, thinking that Johnson had a good idea. "You call it from your position over the mortar frequency. Out."

The mortars began firing illumination shells. Johnson asked for a repeat, and then for high explosive. Jaeger could tell that Johnson had contact when he heard short bursts from a .50-caliber machine gun.

"Zulu Four Seven, what are you firing at?" Jaeger questioned, trying to calm his tank commander at Checkpoint 2. "Do you have contact? Over."

"Uh . . . Zulu . . . I thought I saw something moving," Johnson answered hesitatingly. "Roger. I have definite contact on a BMP. Grid . . . uh . . . LK650958. Over."

"Roger, hang in there," Jaeger said. "Switch to the FIST frequency. You adjust. Get fires on them right away. I'll stay on this net."

The radios inside the FIST's APC came to life. The mortars began dropping HE rounds into their tubes. The steady *thuunnk* sound caused by the exit of the mortar rocket as it left the tube added to the noise.

Jaeger looked around his small perimeter at Checkpoint 4. Positioned in the tank commander's station of his M1, overlooking the low ground between Checkpoint 4 and Checkpoint 6, he scanned the terrain through his tank's thermal sight. Not observing any hot spots, he stood up in his hatch and watched the mortars as they carried on their deadly work.

KABOOM! Suddenly there was a blinding flash. The air ripped apart with a shattering explosion as one of the mortar carriers took a direct hit from an RPG. The "cheese charges," used to propel the mortar rounds, burned brightly as the mortar ammunition cooked off in a terrible ball of flame.

Jaeger saw men running everywhere. Enemy infantry! Where the hell did those bastards come from! Checkpoint 4 was under attack by enemy infantry. He immediately buttoned up and swung the turret around.

"GUNNER, COAX! TROOPS!" Jaeger screamed. "FIRE AND ADJUST!"

At the same time, Jaeger fired his .50-caliber machine gun from inside his turret, spraying the area with bullets.

"Jones! Back up!" Jaeger shouted to his driver over the intercom. "Hold your right track!" The big tank lurched backward, moving out of the camouflage netting and pivoting to face left. Their tank, pointing uphill now, continued to fire.

KABOOM! An RPG rocket hit the ground just to the right of Jaeger's tank.

"Jones, MOVE FORWARD!" Jaeger yelled. "Up the hill . . . move . . . move . . . MOVE!"

A31 raced up the narrow dirt trail to their front. Colwell continued shooting his 7.62mm coax machine gun. Moving the turret from the gunner's position, Colwell jerked the turret around back and forth, firing at targets.

Another huge explosion ripped through the remaining M106 mortar carrier. Sergeant Martin, out in the open and kneeling on the ground with his M-16 in hand, fired at the advancing enemy infiltrators. He killed two attackers just as the blast from the explosion of his track, only twenty feet away, blew him to the ground. Struggling to get up, he was cut down by a stream of enemy machine gun fire.

Another RPG barely missed Jaeger's tank. Jaeger swung his .50 caliber in the direction of the RPG gunner and fired a continuous burst.

Jones turned A31 violently to the left, in a last-second attempt to avoid a big rock. Missing the rock, Jones crashed the tank into a ditch. The tank forcefully pitched forward, throwing the crew against the turret walls.

"Back up!" Jaeger cried, his .50-caliber ammunition expended.

Roll the dice.

If the total of the two dice is five or less, go to Section 54.

If the total of the two dice is six or more, go to Section 55.

Section 53

Reacting quickly, Jones slammed the tank into reverse. The tank jumped backward just as two enemy RPG gunners were about to launch their rockets. The powerful engines of the M1 tank threw the tank straight into them, pulverizing the two enemy soldiers before they could get their shots off. Jaeger, out of machine gun ammunition, swung the turret around, ready to fire the main gun.

"GUNNER! HEAT. MACHINE GUN NEST," Jaeger shouted at the top of his lungs, laying the tank gun in the general direction of a bursting flash of light, 600 meters to their right front. "FIRE!"

The 105mm projectile screamed through the smoke, hitting an enemy machine gun position not more than 600 meters from the tank. The projectile exploded with tremendous force, sending pieces of enemy soldiers all over.

But the enemy kept coming. They wanted this hill, and they seemed determined to kill Jaeger's tank. Infantrymen popped up, firing at Jaeger's tank, and rushing to get within hand grenade range.

"Jones," Jaeger ordered. "Hard right turn. Turn completely around.

Let's get off this hill! GRENADES!" Jaeger fired the smoke grenade projectors on both sides of the turret and braced himself as the tank made a violent pivoting movement. The grenades shot off in a frontal arc in front of the tank, landing in the midst of the enemy infantry.

KABOOM! Suddenly, a loud explosion occurred on the loader's side of the turret. The tank took a direct hit from an RPG!

Jaeger looked at Curn, the loader, who had been thrown over toward the main gun. "Are you OK?" Jaeger shouted.

"Huh . . . yes, sir," Curn replied, picking himself up and bracing to get his balance. "I'm fine . . . what happened?"

"Jones, move out fast, straight down the hill," Jaeger ordered. "Hit your smoke generator! Let's get the hell out of here!"

The tank raced down the dirt trail, spewing billowing clouds of white smoke. Jaeger called battalion to give them a situation report and call for artillery.

Within minutes artillery fell on Checkpoint 4. The enemy infantry on the hill were devastated. Jaeger watched without remorse as air-bursting shells exploded over Checkpoint 4 and sliced into the remaining enemy.

Jaeger ordered Jones to stop the tank at the bottom of the hill.

"Crew report," Jaeger announced feebly over the intercom. He felt sick. Sergeant Martin and the entire mortar section had been wiped out. Jaeger didn't know what had happened to Lieutenant Rogers.

"We are all right, sir," Colwell reported. "I'll get the coax reloaded. Do you want me to pop out and check for damage?"

"Negative!" Jaeger answered, not willing to lose another man to enemy infantry. "Load the coax . . . Jones, keep a lookout through your vision blocks."

"Zulu One Four, this is Zulu One One. Over," Jaeger radioed, trying to reach his platoon sergeant.

"Zulu One One, this is Zulu One Four. Is everything all right? Over," Riley replied.

"Negative. The enemy has Checkpoint Four. We were attacked by dismounts. I have lost the other elements that were with me at Checkpoint Four," Jaeger said, very defeated. "I have lost contact with Checkpoints One and Two. They are presumed dead. I have negative contact with Checkpoint Three. I am now at Checkpoint Ten. What is your situation? Over."

There was a long pause.

"No enemy contact," Riley replied. "Checkpoints Seven, Eight, and Nine report negative contact. I cannot reach any other checkpoints. Over."

"Roger." Jaeger felt as if he was going to pass out. Think! How can I save this situation? Jaeger had to decide!

If Jaeger decides to link up with Sergeant Riley, go to Section 55.

If Jaeger decides to fight his way back up the hill and reoccupy Checkpoint 4, go to Section 68.

If Jaeger decides to move to Checkpoint 2 to cover the western approach, go to Section 78.

Section 54

Jones forced the tank into reverse. Just as two enemy RPG gunners were about to launch their rockets, the powerful engines of the M1 pushed the tank backward, smashing the two enemy soldiers before they could get their shots off.

Jaeger, out of machine gun ammunition, closed his hatch and grabbed the commander's override control.

"GUNNER . . . HEAT. ENEMY MACHINE GUN," Jaeger ordered as he swung the turret in the direction of the target.

"IDENTIFIED!" Colwell shouted, clearly making out the enemy machine gunner in his thermal sight.

The loader shouted "UP."

"FIRE!" Jaeger commanded.

The 105mm projectile screamed through the black night, hitting the enemy position not more than 600 meters from Jaeger's tank. The high-explosive antitank round went off in a blinding flash of flame and steel. When the smoke cleared, the enemy machine gun team was gone.

Section 54

But the determined rush of the infiltrators continued. The enemy moved forward in groups of three or four, firing RPGs and hurling grenades, fanatically trying to drive the Americans off Checkpoint 4.

More enemy infantrymen popped up near Jaeger's position.

KABOOM! KABOOM! Jaeger's tank stopped instantly, like a toy grabbed by some giant hand. Two RPG rockets hit Jaeger's tank on the left side. The track, busted in half by the explosion, rolled off the support rollers. Jones, not knowing the extent of the damage, frantically tried to make the tank move.

"She won't budge, sir," Jones exclaimed.

"GRENADES!" Jaeger yelled as he triggered all banks of his external smoke grenades. "Jones! Start the smoke generator. Curn, man your loader's machine gun!"

Curn, ammo can in hand, opened his hatch and quickly loaded the 7.62mm machine gun on top of the turret. Jaeger radioed for artillery while Curn fired a steady stream of 7.62mm tracers at the darting black silhouettes of moving enemy soldiers.

The noise was deafening. Smoke billowed from the M1 tank's engine. Tracers flew wildly everywhere, ricocheting off metal and striking flesh. Curn stopped firing; he was out of ammunition.

Jaeger's tank was raked by enemy machine gun fire. Curn fell inside the turret, bleeding from the face. Jaeger pushed open his hatch, reached over for Curn's machine gun, and awkwardly tried to reload from his position.

Colwell stopped firing the coaxial machine gun, also out of 7.62mm ammunition.

Jaeger desperately searched for Curn's extra ammunition. More bullets ricocheted off the top of the tank. Driven down into the turret by the enemy fire, Jaeger slammed the hatch shut and waited for the artillery to hit.

Jaeger could sense that someone—the enemy—had jumped onto the back deck of his tank. He quickly reached for the loader's hatch release, pulled hard, and closed the hatch. Then he pulled his .45-caliber automatic pistol from his shoulder holster, pulled back the slide, and chambered a round.

KARRUMMP! KARRUMMP! The artillery fell on Checkpoint 4.

KARRUMMP! A tremendous explosion landed close to the tank. Suddenly, there wasn't anyone on top of A31.

KARRUMMP! Colwell began to move the turret and scan for targets. Shards of flying steel smashed against the sides of Jaeger's battered M1 tank. Colwell closed the shield over his thermal sight to protect it from artillery shrapnel.

KARRUMMP! KARRUMMP! Jaeger repeated the artillery three times. The big 155mm shells made the earth quiver with each explosion. The barrage seemed to last forever. Fragments of steel tore at the top of his tank, making a terrible mess of his radio antennae. Finally the rain of explosive shells stopped.

Colwell squirmed out of his seat and began placing a bandage on Curn.

"How is he?" Jaeger asked, his ears ringing from the crash of the artillery.

"He's in pretty bad shape, Lieutenant . . . unconscious," Colwell said grimly. "He took some metal splinters in the mouth and neck. I've stopped the bleeding."

Jaeger looked around at the scene at Checkpoint 4. The mortars and the FIST-V were burning hulks. Dead enemy soldiers lay all over the ground. No one in the open had survived the artillery barrage . . . no one could have survived. Jaeger and his crew were alone on Checkpoint 4.

Jaeger must think fast. Curn won't survive much longer without medical attention. Jaeger can't expect any help. He and his crew are totally alone and on their own. Jaeger must decide what to do!

If Jaeger decides to stay at Checkpoint 4, go to Section 75.

If Jaeger decides to try to make it back to friendly lines, go to Section 87.

Section 55

"Jones, we can't stay here. Move it!" Jaeger ordered.

The tank would not respond.

"Damn it. She won't budge!" Jones cursed out loud over the intercom.

Jaeger tried to swing the turret around, over the back deck, but there wasn't enough time.

KABOOM! KABOOM! Two rocket-propelled grenades hit the rear of the tank. One hit the rear grill doors, ruining the engine. Smoke billowed out from the cavity formed by the RPG blast. The engine fuel ignited, engulfing the area in thick black smoke. The other grenade hit the bustle rack, burning a hole through the crew's personal equipment in the bustle rack and striking the rear of the turret. The tank jerked forward with the force of the two blasts.

"Everyone OK?" Jaeger yelled, his intercom no longer working. Jaeger could see Colwell and Curn, both shaken but alive. "Jones, are you all right?"

"He's OK, sir," Colwell shouted back, hearing Curn yell from the driver's compartment.

"Grab your gear and your weapons," Jaeger said. "We will try to make a break for it. I'm firing grenades now."

Jaeger pushed the grenade firing button. Only the right bank of red phosphorous grenades fired. The left side launchers must have been damaged in the explosion. Jaeger pushed open his hatch, his .45-caliber pistol cocked and ready to fire.

An enemy rifleman stood on the ground in front of the tank. Jones opened his hatch, not knowing that the enemy was there. Totally surprised, Jones sat there exposed, looking up at the enemy soldier. The enemy infantryman hesitated for a second, then fired his weapon.

The AK-74 bullets ripped into Jones before he had a chance to close the hatch again.

Jaeger jumped up and fired his .45 three times at the enemy rifleman. The soldier took all three slugs, the shock from the rounds knocking him off his feet. He fell down next to the track, a huge circle of blood marking where Jaeger's bullets impacted against his chest.

Another enemy rifleman rushed out from the smoke, one arm reaching for a handhold to climb up on the turret, the other hand holding a grenade. Jaeger pivoted and fired again, hitting this attacker in the forehead. Jaeger's victim toppled over, falling back into the smoke. Jaeger ducked down, back into the turret.

"Colwell!" Jaeger said with a hard, stern voice. "Get over at the loader's hatch. When I say go, we will both drop a grenade out the hatch and make a run for it. Curn, you take the M-16 rifle and follow us out."

Jaeger and Colwell looked at each other, weapons ready.

"Sir, I just want to say—" Colwell said, looking sadly at Jaeger.

"Save it," Jaeger replied with a grin. "You just buy the beer when we get back to friendly lines. OK . . . NOW!"

Jaeger and Colwell simultaneously opened their hatches and dropped out their grenades. They waited several seconds for the blast. The explosions threw dirt and debris up into the loader's hatch. Both Jaeger and Colwell jumped up with their pistols ready and struggled out of the hatches onto the top of the M1.

Jaeger hit the ground on his side of the tank. Colwell went the other way. A machine gun started to fire. The bullets bounced off Colwell's side of the tank.

"I'm hit . . . God . . . I'm hit," Colwell yelled.

"Colwell!" Jaeger shouted. He crawled on his belly to the front of the tank, passing the two enemy soldiers he had gunned down. Searching for a heavier weapon, Jaeger picked up the AK-74 from the man who had killed Jones.

"I'm over here, sir," Colwell screamed as he tried to crawl from the other side of the tank toward the front.

An enemy rifleman ran off to his left. Jaeger fired but missed. Another soldier rushed at them, tossing a grenade. It landed between Jaeger and Colwell. For one awful second the two men stared at each other and the grenade.

Jaeger pulled the grenade to his chest and took the full force of the blast.

Go to Section 44.

Section 56

BOOM! Jaeger's tank fired again . . . and again. After five rounds he opened his TC's hatch and began firing his .50-caliber machine gun. Colwell was pumping machine gun fire at the enemy in controlled twelve-round bursts. With his thermal sight, the attacking infantry were easy marks. Jaeger yelled to Curn to jump up and man the 7.62mm loader's machine gun.

Curn, ammo can in hand, opened his hatch and quickly loaded the machine gun on top of the turret. Jaeger radioed for artillery while Curn was firing.

The noise, smoke, fire, and confusion consumed the crew of A31. They fought like crazy men. Smoke billowed from the burning M106. Jaeger's tank was raked by machine gun fire, bullets madly pinging off the metal sides. Tracers flew wildly everywhere, ricocheting off metal and striking flesh.

Three enemy grenadiers fired a volley of RPGs at Johnson's tank. Several missed, exploding harmlessly to the right and left sides of A32. One finally hit its mark, blasting the compensating idler wheel to pieces. The explosion blew rocks and metal up in a fiery shower, but Johnson kept firing and firing.

Another RPG exploded next to the surviving M106 mortar carrier, missing it by inches. Sergeant Martin, on the ground with his M-16 in hand, fired at the advancing enemy infantry. He rallied his mortarmen in a valiant defense of the guns. Throwing hand grenades and firing with their M-16 rifles, they kept up a steady fire on the enemy.

Lieutenant Rogers, the fire support officer, was pinned down by a hail of enemy rifle fire. Closing the hatches on his FIST-V, Rogers rushed to get his track out of the killing zone before his vehicle became the next RPG target.

An RPG gunner bravely stood up to fire his grenade at Rogers's withdrawing APC. Colwell, just in the nick of time, cut him down with his coax machine gun.

KARRUMMP! KARRUMMP! American artillery fire crashed into Checkpoint 4. Martin and his men rushed for cover in their vehicles and closed the hatches.

212

KARRUMMP! The screams of dying enemy infantry could be heard in between the roar of the artillery.

KARRUMMP! KARRUMMP! The U.S. shells burst high overhead. Their M582 time fuzes caused detonation eighteen feet above the ground, sending a deadly array of white-hot metal fragments down on the infantry below. The rounds landed right on target. The enemy could not hide. The shelling lasted for six minutes—it seemed like a lifetime—and then there was silence.

"Zulu Four Seven," Jaeger radioed his wingman in the tank not more than fifty meters to his left. "Everybody OK?"

"Roger, Zulu One One," Johnson replied tiredly. "Thanks. You got here just in time. My tank took an RPG on the left side. I can't tell yet, but I may have lost my track. Everyone's pretty shook up, but we're all right."

Jaeger opened his hatch and dismounted, his .45 pistol cocked and ready. He jumped off his tank and walked over to Sergeant Martin, who was holding one of his young gunners in his arms. Lieutenant Rogers was also there.

Everyone was very quiet.

"He's dead," Martin said sobbing, trying to hold in his grief. "I lost four men and the mortar, Lieutenant."

Jaeger didn't reply immediately. He was totally exhausted—drained from the exertion and the emotion of the fight, tired of having to make the decisions of life and death. He looked around at the scene of the battle. The smell of gunpowder and death mingled with the smoke. He was really beginning to hate this madness.

"Sergeant Martin," Jaeger said softly. "You have four other men who are counting on you. The entire team is depending on your mortar fires. We can't let down now," Jaeger gestured toward the dead mortarmen. "Especially for their sake."

"OK, Lieutenant, OK. You're right." Martin forced himself out of his trance and gently placed the fallen soldier on the ground. He stood up, grabbed his rifle, and walked over to his one operational mortar. In control again, he issued instructions to his men and returned to the professional business of being a combat mortar section sergeant.

Johnson, cradling an AK-74 rifle that he had picked up off a dead enemy soldier, walked over to the lieutenant and reported.

"Sir, I think that we got all of the enemy infantry. The artillery really did a job on them. If any got away they must have fled to the northwest. We haven't see anything moving at all."

"How is A32?" Jaeger questioned, hoping that Johnson's tank would be in good enough shape to move.

"I lost my left track and an idler wheel," Johnson replied. "I may be able to short-track it."

"Good. Fix it," Jaeger ordered. "We can't stay here. I want to move to Checkpoint Ten as soon as possible."

It could have been worse . . . much worse, Jaeger thought. We still hold Checkpoint 4. We have destroyed almost an entire company of enemy infantry. The enemy must understand by now that Hill 955 is heavily occupied. Losing an entire infantry company has taught him this lesson the hard way. Knowing this, he will want to avoid Hill 955 and attack along axis Ohio or New York.

Jaeger radioed battalion and gave the battalion commander a complete report. Then he received a call from one of his scouts.

"Zulu One One." Jaeger recognized the voice of the scout at Checkpoint 2. "Spot report. I am observing three BMPs at grid LK650950, moving southeast. Over."

"Roger, Charlie Eight Zero," Jaeger replied. "I've got my FIST here to back you up. I want you to call for artillery and take them out as best you can. Let them close on you and use your 25mm. You have got to stop them. I've got nobody else in range. Over."

"No problem, Zulu," the scout answered confidently. "We got these bastards. Switching frequencies to fire support push now. I'll call you back later. Out."

Tungkt, Tungkt. Tracer rounds bounced high into the night sky near Checkpoint 2.

Tungkt, Tungkt, Tungkt, Tungkt. Jaeger heard the muffled sound of 25mm cannonfire. He looked at his watch. It was 0310.

"Zulu One One, this is Charlie Eight Zero!" It was the scout at Checkpoint 2, sounding triumphant. "Spot report. Over."

"Charlie Eight Zero, this is Zulu One One," Jaeger replied quickly, anxious for information. "Send it."

"Engaged three BMPs at grid LK650950," Checkpoint 2 answered. "I destroyed one, possibly two. Over."

"Roger, Charlie Eight Zero," Jaeger replied. "What about the third one? Over."

"Unknown. I lost him," the scout answered dejectedly. "He must be hiding in one of the wadis out there. I'll call you as soon as I get another contact. Over."

"Roger, Eight Zero," Jaeger said. "Super job. Good shooting! Out."

Jaeger radioed another situation report to battalion. It was now 0345. Johnson reported to Jaeger that his tank wouldn't be able to roll for another hour, at best. It would be getting light at 0500. If Jaeger was to move the team back to battle position A12 safely, he must move everyone no later than 0430. With Johnson's battle damage, he wouldn't be able to move until 0445 at the earliest. That would be cutting it very close.

Which way will the regiment attack? Jaeger thought, weighing the possibilities. One thing for sure, the enemy had been stopped cold on this side.

"Zulu One One." The familiar voice of Sergeant Riley filled Jaeger's CVC headset. "This is Zulu One Four. We got one BRDM. Can't find the other. I'm at Checkpoint Five. What are your orders?"

"Zulu One Four. Good to hear from you again," Jaeger replied, happy to hear that his platoon sergeant and Ramos were all right. "Wait. Out."

The killing portion of the counterrecon mission appeared to be over. No matter what Jaeger decided, he knew that he must now leave the scouts in position to determine the direction of the enemy's main attack.

As Jaeger saw it, he had two options. The first was to wait for Johnson to repair A32 and race like hell back to battle position A12. Riley could move there on his own and meet Jaeger on the battle position. This could prove tricky if Johnson took too long.

The other option was to tow A32 back to A12, put Johnson and his crew in a mortar track, and move at 0430. He could meet Riley at battle position A12. What should he do? Jaeger must decide!

If Jaeger decides to wait for Johnson's tank to be fixed, go to Section 59.

 If Jaeger decides to tow Johnson's tank and pull back to battle position A12, go to Section 60.

Section 57

"Colwell! TROOPS . . . FIRE!" Jaeger shouted into his intercom, his adrenaline pumping, as he swung the turret in the direction of the rifle fire and began firing his .50-caliber machine gun.

Colwell obediently pumped machine gun fire in the direction of the enemy. With his thermal sight, the attacking infantry were easy marks.

Jaeger yelled to Curn to jump up and man the 7.62mm loader's machine gun. Curn, ammo can in hand, opened his hatch and quickly loaded the machine gun on top of the turret. Jaeger radioed for artillery fire while Curn was firing.

Tracers flew wild in every direction, ricocheting off metal and zinging through the air. Smoke billowed from the burning M106 mortar carrier.

Three enemy grenadiers rushed out from the cover of a ditch and fired a volley of RPGs at Johnson's tank. One missed, exploding harmlessly to the right side of A32. Two hit their mark. One hit the left side of the tank at the base of the forwardmost road wheel. The other skimmed the top of the turret and exploded against the loader's machine gun pedestal.

The force of the explosion engulfed the tank with fire and debris. Johnson slumped down inside the turret, wounded and blinded from the blast.

The loader, who had been firing the 7.62mm machine gun on the turret roof, wasn't there anymore. He was just gone.

At the same time, Jaeger's tank was raked by machine gun fire.

"Jones! Back up!" Jaeger shouted to his driver over the intercom. "Hold your right track!" The big tank lurched backward, moving out of the camouflage netting and pivoting to face left. With their tank pointing uphill now, Jaeger's crew continued to fire.

KABOOM! An RPG rocket hit the ground just to the right of Jaeger's tank, exploding in a bright orange fireball.

"Jones, MOVE FORWARD!" Jaeger yelled. "Up the hill . . . move . . . move . . . MOVE!"

A31 raced up the narrow dirt trail to their front. Colwell continued shooting his coaxial 7.62mm machine gun. He moved the turret with

216

his gunner's controls, sliding the turret back and forth, firing at targets.

Another huge explosion ripped through the remaining M106 mortar carrier. Sergeant Martin, out in the open and kneeling on the ground with his M-16 in hand, fired at the dismounted attackers. The blast from the explosion of his track, only twenty feet away, flattened him to the ground. Struggling to get up, he was cut down by a stream of machine gun fire.

Lieutenant Rogers, the fire support officer, was pinned down by a hail of rifle fire. His FIST-V backed up quickly, then hit a large rock and stalled momentarily. An RPG gunner stood up to fire his grenade at the withdrawing APC.

Colwell, just in the nick of time, cut the RPG gunner in two with his coax machine gun.

KARRUMMP! KARRUMMP! Finally, the U.S. artillery exploded on Checkpoint 4. The screams of dying enemy infantry could be heard in between the roar of the artillery.

KARRUMMP! KARRUMMP! KARRUMMP! Jaeger buttoned up his hatch. Curn automatically did the same. Colwell continued to search for targets and sprayed 7.62mm machine gun fire on any enemy infantry stupid enough to appear in his sights.

KARRUMMP! KARRUMMP! Jaeger could feel the ground shaking with the impact of every round. Shrapnel impacted against his tank, reinforcing the lethality of the moment.

The artillery shelling lasted for six minutes, then there was silence.

Jaeger ordered Colwell to scan for targets and to shoot anything that moved. Colwell searched, fired a few bursts, but found that the enemy was gone. Apparently the artillery had done its job.

Jaeger dismounted, his .45-caliber pistol cocked and ready, and walked over to where Sergeant Martin was lying face down in the dirt. He found Lieutenant Rogers standing over the body.

"He's dead," Rogers said. "They are all dead, Sam, all the mortarmen. I've already checked them."

Jaeger didn't have a reply. What could he possibly say? He looked around at the scene of battle. This was my fault, he thought. I am responsible for these men. I let them down. Where the hell was Checkpoint 3! Why didn't we see them before they hit us? Jaeger felt exhausted.

"Sam," Rogers said calmly, looking at Jaeger as if reading his thoughts. "It's not your fault. We need you. The battalion is depending on you. The enemy could hit us any minute."

Section 57

Rogers touched Jaeger's shoulder and walked slowly back to his FIST-V. Realizing that the enemy might return, Rogers got his crew working on checking out the vehicle for damage and preparing to move.

Johnson walked over to the lieutenant, an enemy AK-74 rifle cradled in his arms. The left side of Johnson's face was bandaged with a hasty combat dressing.

"Sir, I think that we got all of the enemy infantry," Johnson said vengefully. "The artillery kicked the hell out of the sons of bitches. If any of the bastards got away, they must have run to the northwest. We haven't seen anything moving at all."

"How are you doing?" Jaeger asked, looking at Johnson's wound.

"I lost Jefferson. We can't even find his body," Johnson said sorrowfully. "It's not right. To come all this way and disappear. It's not right."

"How's your wound?" Jaeger repeated, feeling more fatigued with each passing question.

"I'll be OK. It's just a burn and a few metal splinters," Johnson said. "The explosion knocked the wind out of me. It's my tank that I am worried about. They hit my left track and a road wheel, but I think I can short-track it."

"Good. Get it fixed," Jaeger ordered. "I'll send Curn over to give you a hand. I want to move to Checkpoint Ten as soon as possible. I want to get the hell out of here." Jaeger paused, hesitating, searching for the right words. "Johnson, you did a super job just now."

Johnson walked back to his tank silently.

Jaeger still held Checkpoint 4. But he had lost nine men and both of his M106 mortar carriers. Although he had destroyed almost an entire company of enemy infantry, that was poor consolation for losing the men of the mortar section and Specialist Jefferson.

At least he knew where the enemy would attack the next morning. If the enemy thought that Hill 955 was heavily occupied, as the loss of their infantry assault should indicate, they would want to avoid this strong point and attack along axis Ohio or New York. Jaeger radioed battalion and gave the battalion commander a complete report.

Jaeger didn't have long to catch his breath. As soon as he had completed his report to battalion, his radio crackled with an urgent spot report from Checkpoint 2.

"Zulu One One." Jaeger recognized the voice of the scout at Checkpoint 2. "Spot report. I have three BMPs at grid LK650950, moving southeast. Over."

"Roger, Charlie Eight Zero," Jaeger replied. "Keep them under observation. I'll get back to you. Out."

Jaeger realized that he had to make a quick decision about those BMPs. Should he tell the scout to knock them out from Checkpoint 2? Should he try to get them himself? Or should he just let them go, banking on the idea that they would pull the rest of the regiment in their direction? Jaeger must decide!

If Jaeger decides to call for artillery and orders the scout at Checkpoint 2 to engage the BMPs, go to Section 64.

If Jaeger decides to use his tank, the artillery, and the scout at Checkpoint 2 to ambush the BMPs, go to Section 65.

If Jaeger decides to let them go in order to convince them that this avenue of approach is clear, go to Section 66.

Section 58

Jaeger maneuvered his platoon past Checkpoint 5 without any sight of the BRDMs. The four tanks of Jaeger's platoon were traveling in an extended "V" formation, with Jaeger in the lead followed by Johnson. To Jaeger's right was Ramos, followed by Sergeant Riley. Jaeger glanced at his watch. It was now 0200.

"Zulu One Four, this is Zulu One One," Jaeger called over the radio to Riley. "Can you reach Victor One Two?"

"Negative," Riley replied with disgust. "We should. . . ."

BOOM! Ramos fired his main gun at a target 800 meters to his right, interrupting Riley's transmission in mid sentence. A BRDM, traveling south, took the hypervelocity sabot round dead center. The BRDM fell apart as if it were made of cardboard, and then began to burn.

Just then Jaeger, monitoring the team radio net, heard Checkpoint 2 report sighting dismounted infantry.

Section 58

"Zulu One One, this is Zulu Two Eight," Ramos said triumphantly. "Scratch one BRDM."

"All stations clear the net!" Jaeger ordered. Charlie Eight Zero was trying to call him but he couldn't make out the message. (Note: Only platoon leaders and platoon sergeants have two radios in their tanks—one that transmits and receives and one that only receives. This capability enables leaders to fight their units and to monitor another frequency at the same time. Often, the simultaneous transmission of important messages over both frequencies can be confusing. In this situation, Riley stayed on the platoon net and the battalion command net while Jaeger was on the platoon net and the counterreconnaissance team net. In this way they worked as a team to keep communications open.)

"Charlie Eight Zero, this is Zulu One One," Jaeger said over the team frequency. "What is your situation? Over."

"I've got dismounts headed my way," the scout at Checkpoint 2 said, sounding scared. "Where is the mortar support? Hold it . . . I'll get back to you."

"Zulu One One," the scout sergeant at Checkpoint 2 radioed. "This is Charlie Eight Zero. FLASH spot report! Observing dismounted infantry at grid LK676942. Request artillery. Over!"

"Charlie Eight Zero," Rogers replied before Jaeger could answer. "This is Victor One Two. Dismounted infantry attacking. We need help."

Jaeger looked back in the direction of Checkpoint 4, which suddenly was bright with the light of explosions.

"Victor One Two, this is Zulu One One." Jaeger frantically tried to reach Rogers. "Victor One Two, this is Zulu One One!"

No reply. Checkpoint 4 glowed with the fire of battle. Tracers arched into the sky in all directions. Two white parachute flares dropped slowly in the air, lighting up the sky above the checkpoint.

"Zulu One Four, turn around," Jaeger ordered savagely, choking back his anger. "Blitz back to Checkpoint Four. Follow me!"

Jaeger's platoon approached Checkpoint 4 in traveling formation, his tanks tucked into a narrow "V" as they drove up the southern slope of Hill 955. They got within 900 meters of their old position when Jaeger became suspicious.

"Zulu One Four, I don't like the look of this," Jaeger said to his platoon sergeant.

"Roger, One One," Riley replied. "Let's move carefully. Move to bounding overwatch. You cover my move."

"Roger, One Four," Jaeger replied. "Let's go."

Riley and Ramos pushed their tanks ahead while Jaeger and Johnson scanned for targets. Riley advanced only 200 meters when suddenly both tanks fired their machine guns.

"This area is crawling with enemy," Riley screamed into his radio microphone.

BOOM! Everything was happening at once. Ramos fired his main gun at a group of enemy infantry. A shower of RPGs splattered against a rock near Ramos's tank. Jaeger and Johnson fired their machine guns to support the forward section.

"Zulu One Four," Jaeger ordered. "Get out of there!"

A bright, blinding explosion hit Johnson's tank. Although the RPG grenade hit directly in the turret, the tank kept on moving, apparently unaffected. Johnson fired wildly, violently swinging his turret left, searching out the RPG gunner with machine gun fire. Jaeger also swung his turret around. Threat infantry seemed to be everywhere.

"Damn it . . . Colwell . . . TROOPS!" Jaeger yelled into his intercom, forgetting his standard fire command. "FIRE AND ADJUST. Get the bastards!"

Roll the dice.

If the total of the two dice is four or less, go to Section 62.

If the total of the two dice is five or more, go to Section 72.

Section 59

Jaeger walked over to Johnson's tank. Both Jaeger's and Johnson's crews were working feverishly to fix the broken track. The enemy RPG round had completely destroyed the left idler wheel support arm. If they could short-track the tank—run the tank track over the next road wheel and ignore the damaged idler wheel—A32 might be able to limp off Checkpoint 4. It was now 0445.

"How much longer?" Jaeger asked, becoming brisk. "We have got to get out of here."

"Fifteen more minutes and we are finished, Lieutenant," Johnson replied without turning his head.

"Jaeger!" Rogers shouted from the open ramp of his darkened FIST-V. "Battalion is on the radio for you."

Jaeger ran back to his tank, hopped up to the TC's hatch, and reached for his CVC helmet.

"Victor Two Zero, this is Zulu One One. Over," Jaeger reported.

"Zulu One One, this is Victor Two Zero," Lieutenant Colonel Brown replied. "What is your situation?"

"I am still at Checkpoint Four. The rest of my heavy elements are moving to A12. The Charlie elements [scouts] will stay in position," Jaeger said confidently. "I suspect that the enemy will attack down the California or Utah avenue of approach. Over."

"Roger, Zulu One One," Brown replied quickly. "You better get out of there—" The colonel's radio transmission was replaced by an unusual mechanical silence.

At 0450 the radios went totally dead with white noise—the nothing sound that is transmitted over an FM frequency that is being blocked out by a high-power jamming radio. The enemy must be barrage jamming every frequency, Jaeger thought. The attack must be on!

Then, with a crash like the roar of a giant freight train, the earth around Jaeger suddenly erupted in a flash of fire and steel. Jaeger desperately reached for the handle to close his hatch and protect himself.

KARRUMMP! KARRUMMP! Jaeger could feel the ground shaking with the impact of every round. Shrapnel impacted against the sides of his tank, reinforcing the lethality of the moment.

The shock of a tremendous volume of artillery crushed in all around Checkpoint 4. The amount of fire was devastating. Jaeger was alone in his tank; the crew was outside helping Johnson! More metal smashed against the sides and roof of A31.

KARRUMMP! KARRUMMP! The noise was unbearable. The artillery kept falling. Tired, claustrophobic from the closed hatch, and worried about his crew, Jaeger struggled uncomfortably to see the battlefield. The radio was useless. Jaeger looked through his vision blocks in the direction of Johnson's tank.

KARRUMMP! KARRUMMP! Jaeger watched in horror as Rogers's FIST-V took a direct hit from a Threat 152mm artillery shell. Rogers didn't have a chance. The enemy shell tore Rogers's track apart as if it were made of cardboard. It burned brightly, illuminating the area around Johnson's tank.

KARRUMMP! Jaeger could not see anyone moving. The impact from the artillery rounds dropped Jaeger to the turret floor. He lay there, feeling the shock of each round, praying that he would survive.

Suddenly the shock waves slackened, then shifted relentlessly south.

Jaeger lifted open his hatch, trying to listen to make sure that the fire had shifted away from Checkpoint 4. His ears were ringing so badly that he couldn't hear a thing.

After a few moments, Jaeger pushed himself out of the hatch and rushed over to Johnson's tank. The crew was strewn about like so many broken dolls. Jaeger saw Colwell and Curn, bloody and lifeless, lying in a shallow ditch. He checked both soldiers and found no vital signs. He could not find Jones.

"Help me . . . help me," a voice from under the tank cried feebly.

It was Johnson. He must have crawled under the tank when the firing started, Jaeger thought. Tearing underneath A32, Jaeger dug at the earth and pulled Johnson out. Johnson screamed with pain. Blood was spurting out of the mangled limb that used to be his left leg. A piece of shrapnel had completely severed it.

Jaeger quickly tore off his belt and applied a tourniquet above Johnson's wound. Blood continued to shoot out from the smashed appendage as Jaeger forced the tourniquet down hard and twisted with all his might.

Section 59

Johnson screamed again—a sad, animal-like screech—grabbed Jaeger's shoulder with the intensity of ten men, then passed out.

Sergeant Martin ran over to Jaeger, panting from his quick sprint.

"Lieutenant! Rogers and his crew are dead," Martin said hysterically, clearly in shock. "I lost another man. We have got to get out of here. We have got to leave now!"

Jaeger grabbed Martin and shook him with both hands. "Damn it! Damn it!" Jaeger said furiously. "I give the orders around here. Get your men to carry Johnson into your APC. I will destroy the tanks. Then, WHEN I SAY SO, we will leave here. Do you have that straight?"

"Yes, sir," Martin said weakly. Jaeger released him and Martin ran back to his mortar track.

Jaeger wanted to quit. He felt nauseous. The death around him was overwhelming. He was responsible for the lives of so many men and now most of them were dead.

It's all my fault, he said to himself. We should have left right after the enemy infantry attack was repulsed.

Jaeger heard the rumble of artillery. It was 0530 and there was a battle being fought. He couldn't see very much of it, but from the location of the explosions, the battle was somewhere to the southeast. Was he wrong about the enemy's direction of attack? Had they attacked along the New York axis instead?

Jaeger, Johnson, and Martin raced south in their lone M106 mortar carrier. The bumpy ride mercilessly jostled them around inside the cramped APC. Johnson looked worse with each passing minute and remained unconscious. In the early-morning light, without any radio communications, Martin directed the M106 toward the openings in the friendly mine fields.

Jaeger had no way of knowing that the task force had closed the lanes in the mine fields. The driver of the M106, buttoned up and looking through vision blocks to drive, couldn't see the friendly mines in his path.

KABOOM! An antitank mine erupted right under the belly of the M106 mortar carrier. The searing flame caused by the mine's shaped charge burned through the thin aluminum plate and disintegrated the contents of the APC. Jaeger and Martin never knew what hit them. They had no time for pain. Friendly mines kill you just as dead as enemy mines.

*   *   *

Jaeger died and the enemy regiment broke through the American defenses. The Threat assault succeeded because Jaeger failed to win the counterreconnaissance battle. He failed to determine the direction of the Threat attack in time for the task force commander to reposition his forces. Most importantly, he underestimated the power of Threat artillery.

Skill and luck often determine the outcome of battle. Jaeger had done many things right, but a few bad decisions turned luck and the momentum of the situation against him. Protecting the force is often an important means of defeating the enemy. After the infantry battle on Checkpoint 4, Jaeger should have moved, recognizing the fact that the enemy knew he was there.

Surviving an enemy artillery barrage, even in an armored vehicle, depends largely on not being at ground zero. Whenever possible, positions should be sited that offer defilade from enemy artillery fires. As a last resort, armor protection and quick movement should be used to get out of artillery impact areas.

Leadership makes the difference in war. History is full of examples where one leader made the difference. Jaeger's mistakes are examples to learn from. Don't make the same mistake again.

Return to Section 34 and try again.

Section 60

"Johnson!" Jaeger shouted at his wingman. "We don't have time to waste. The enemy knows that we are here. Hook your tow cables to my tank and I'll tow you back to A12."

"Yes, sir!" Johnson said. "I don't want to stay here any longer than we need to. We will be ready in ten minutes."

Section 60

"Jaeger!" Rogers shouted from the open ramp of his darkened FIST-V. "Battalion is on the radio for you."

Jaeger ran back to his tank, hopped up to the TC's hatch, and reached for his CVC helmet.

"Victor Two Zero, this is Zulu One One. Over," Jaeger reported.

"Zulu One One, this is Victor Two Zero," Lieutenant Colonel Brown replied. "What is your situation?"

"I am preparing to move from Checkpoint Four to A12. The rest of my heavy elements are moving to A12 now. The Charlie elements [scouts] will stay in position," Jaeger said confidently. "I have had the most enemy activity down the California and Utah avenues of approach. We have stopped them here. Over."

"Roger, Zulu One One," Brown replied quickly. "Where do you feel that they will attack?"

"We stopped them in the west. If they want a quick victory, they won't be coming this way."

"Roger, I agree," commented Lieutenant Colonel Brown. "Get back to battle position A12 with your heavy elements as soon as possible. I'll alert the forward elements to be on the lookout for you. Report to me when you are in position. Out."

Jaeger's small column moved out for Checkpoint 10. Jaeger led, towing Johnson's tank, followed by the FIST-V and the remaining M106 mortar carrier. The going was rough and, because he was towing Johnson's tank, the progress was very slow.

Jaeger looked at his watch. It was 0430. It would take another hour at this speed before they would arrive at battle position A12.

"Zulu Four Seven," Jaeger said over the radio to Johnson. "This isn't going to work. It's taking too much time. Take out her firing pin, grab the machine guns, and hop into the mortar's track. We will leave her here."

"Oh, come on Zulu One One," Johnson pleaded. "We can make it!"

"NEGATIVE!" Jaeger said firmly. "Don't waste time. Move now and get those cables unhooked."

"Zulu One One, this is Charlie One Four," Sergeant Young called Jaeger on the counterrecon frequency. "Spot report. Observing three BMPs and one T-72 moving south along New York at LK778978."

"Roger, Charlie One Four," Jaeger replied. "Good job. Continue to observe. That's probably the combat reconnaissance patrol of the regiment. Do not . . . I repeat, do not engage. Let them pass by. Out."

This may be our chance, Jaeger thought. If we can let these BMPs go by unmolested, the enemy may be tricked into coming down the New York axis.

Jaeger knew that there was not a moment to lose. He quickly called Lieutenant Colonel Brown.

"Victor Two Zero, this is Zulu One One. Over," Jaeger radioed.

"Zulu One One, this is Victor Two Zero," Lieutenant Colonel Brown replied.

"Scouts report three BMPs and one T-72 near Checkpoint Nine moving south. That is probably a combat reconnaissance patrol from the regiment. I suspect that the enemy will attack down the Ohio or New York . . . I say again, Ohio or New York avenue of approach. I am at Checkpoint Ten. I will arrive in A12 by 0510. Over."

"Roger, Zulu One One," Brown replied quickly. "I concur. Get back to A12 ASAP. Over."

"Wilco," Jaeger answered. "Over."

"Good job." Brown hesitated, as if searching for additional words and not finding any. "Good luck, Zulu One One. Out."

Go to Section 80.

Section 61

"Jones!" Jaeger screamed. "Move back. NOW!"

Jones slammed the tank into reverse. The tank surged backward, just as an enemy RPG gunner was about to launch his rocket. The powerful engines of the M1 pushed the tank right through the enemy soldier, pulverizing him before he could fire. Jaeger, out of machine gun ammunition, swung the turret around, preparing to use the 105mm cannon.

"GUNNER! HEAT. TROOPS!" Jaeger shouted at the top of his lungs. "FIRE!"

Section 61

BOOM! The 105mm projectile screamed through the early-morning air, hitting near a clump of enemy soldiers not more than seventy meters in front of the tank. The projectile exploded with tremendous force, killing several enemy soldiers and sending several others running for cover.

The enemy kept coming. They seemed to want this hill, and they appeared determined to kill Jaeger's tank.

KABOOM! KABOOM! Jaeger's tank stopped instantly, like a toy being grabbed by some giant hand. Two RPG rockets hit the tank on the left side. The track rolled off the support rollers. Jones, not knowing the extent of the damage from the hit, continued to try to move the tank.

"Jones! Hit the smoke generator," Jaeger yelled as he fired all banks of his external smoke grenades. "Curn, man your loader's machine gun!"

Curn, ammo can in hand, opened his hatch and quickly loaded the machine gun on top of the turret. Jaeger tried to call for artillery from battalion, but the concussion from the RPG hit rendered his radio useless.

The noise was deafening. Smoke billowed from the M1 tank's engine. Tracers flew wildly everywhere, ricocheting off metal and striking flesh. Jaeger's tank was raked by machine gun fire. Jaeger was sure that they were done for.

Curn fell inside the turret, bleeding from the face. Jaeger reached over from the tank commander's hatch and awkwardly fired the loader's machine gun from his position. Colwell, firing until he ran out of 7.62mm ammunition, screamed to Jaeger to load a HEAT round into the main gun.

Jaeger buttoned up his hatch. Colwell continued to search for targets and sprayed 7.62mm machine gun fire on any enemy infantry stupid enough to appear in his sights. Then there was silence.

Jaeger ordered Colwell to scan for targets and to shoot anything that moved. Colwell searched, and fired a few bursts. Jones turned off the smoke generator.

Jaeger and Colwell scanned for targets and hoped beyond hope that they had killed all the enemy infantry. After a few more minutes without seeing anyone, Jaeger opened his hatch.

He pulled back the slide on his .45-caliber pistol and chambered a round. In one quick move he stood up in the turret, his pistol at the ready, and aimed out at the darkness. He surveyed the battlefield but found no targets. Nothing moved.

Colwell squirmed out of his seat and started to bandage Curn. Jaeger popped back down inside the turret.

"How is he?" Jaeger asked, his ears ringing from the sounds of the battle.

"He's in pretty bad shape, Lieutenant," Colwell said grimly. "He took some shrapnel splinters in the mouth and neck. I think I've stopped the bleeding."

Jaeger looked around at the scene at Checkpoint 4. The mortars and the FIST-V were burning, their hulks hardly resembling the effective armored vehicles they once were. Dead enemy soldiers lay all over the ground. The enemy had either all been killed or had withdrawn. Jaeger and his crew, immobilized and alone, were all that was left alive on Checkpoint 4.

Jaeger was out of machine gun ammunition. His tank could not be repaired without major assistance. From his position he could still fire on targets coming down the orange avenue of approach. He still had plenty of main gun ammunition, but he would be no better than a pillbox, since his tank was unable to move.

Curn was badly wounded and would not make it without medical support. Should he destroy his own tank and try to get back to friendly lines with his crew? Should he stay put and do what he could to fight from his immobilized tank? There wasn't any time to spare. Jaeger must decide!

If Jaeger decides to stay and fight, go to Section 75.

If Jaeger decides to escape and evade back to friendly lines, go to Section 87.

Section 62

Jaeger fired his .50-caliber machine gun while Colwell sprayed the area with 7.62mm bullets.

"One One, this is One Four," Riley screamed over his radio. "We are headed your way!"

"Roger, One Four!" Jaeger replied. "Any sight of the FIST and the mortars?"

"Sir," Colwell interrupted, yelling over the intercom. "I'm out of coax."

Just then Jaeger's .50 caliber jammed.

"Shit! Jones move forward and find me some cover!" Jaeger popped open his hatch and attempted to clear the .50-caliber machine gun while the tank darted to a new position. His fingers bled as he tore the skin on his right hand, working to free the jammed round in the breech of the heavy machine gun.

He had almost cleared the gun when Jones brought the tank to an abrupt halt.

Craaackk! Jaeger never saw the enemy machine gunner who killed him. The enemy soldier fired a full burst at the top of the turret with his PKM 7.62mm machine gun. Jaeger took the full effect of the fire in his right side, shoulder, and head. He fell inside the tank and a few moments later, he died.

Jaeger had done several things right. He had organized his forces to conduct the counterreconnaissance battle in an effective manner. The friction of battle, however, worked against him, as it works against everyone in war. And, in the end, he just got unlucky.

Jaeger made several errors, however, that caused his luck to turn into disaster. First, he split his command by leaving the mortars and fire support officer behind as he raced off to chase two enemy armored vehicles (the two BRDMs that got past Checkpoint 9). The composition of the enemy reconnaissance company is a motorcycle section, one platoon of three BMPs, one platoon of BRDMs, and a BMP headquarters vehicle. By committing his killing force, his only reserve, against two BRDMs, he did not secure his most important mission—to determine the direction of the enemy's main attack. The commander must command the entire counterreconnaissance battle.

Second, as the commander of the counterreconnaissance force he should have kept his fire support officer with him. The fire support officer is his source of artillery and mortar fires. If he loses him and the mortars, he loses half of his combat power.

Jaeger is dead. Learn from his mistakes and don't make the same mistakes again.

Go to Section 34 and start again.

Section 63

"FIRE!" Jaeger commanded.

The tank jerked from the recoil of the gun. The round screamed forward, hitting an enemy tank and stopping it in its tracks. Several other T-72s raced toward Jaeger's position. They were only 900 meters away now, and there were just too many of them.

KABOOM! A tremendous force hit Jaeger's tank. Thrown against the inside walls, the crew absorbed the wrath of the projectile. Jaeger hit the tank commander's sight hard.

The turret spun ten degrees to the right with the force of the impact, and pinned Curn under the gun. The automatic fire extinguishers went off, flooding the fighting compartment with smoke and extinguisher exhaust.

Jaeger couldn't breathe! He fumbled for his hatch release and used all his force to open it. Fresh air rushed in. He tore off his chemical protective mask and painfully muscled his way out of the turret. He lay on the top for a few seconds, dazed.

"Colwell, Curn!" Jaeger rolled over to his hatch and looked inside. The smoke was so thick he couldn't see. He crawled back into the hatch and reached down for Sergeant Colwell. Groping in the smoke, choking and teary eyed, he grabbed Colwell's uniform. Yanking with all his might, Jaeger tried to drag his gunner to the top of the tank.

Jaeger failed on his first attempt. Gasping for air, he stopped halfway and returned to the top to catch his breath.

He had to try again. He headed back inside and pulled the limp body of Sergeant Colwell out of the gunner's seat and onto the floor of the tank. Mustering all his strength, he manhandled Colwell to the top and forced him out of the turret. Colwell lay on the flat top of the M1 tank, struggling for air.

"Colwell, hang in there. I have to get Curn," Jaeger said to his dazed gunner.

As Jaeger climbed back into the TC's station, he saw a Threat tank to his right, fifty meters away. The T-72 fired a burst from its machine guns. Jaeger was hit in the shoulder and chest. Spinning backward, he fell down into the turret and hit hard against the tank commander's stand. He landed on his back, with his feet above him.

"I must get up," Jaeger said in a whisper as he died, his life blood oozing onto the turret floor. "I must. . . ."

The T-72 fired a 125mm projectile into A31, just in case. The tank crumpled with the blast, the turret taking the round in the right rear section. The ammunition ignited. The fire burned blue hot. The soul of the tank flickered in the desert wind.

The enemy continued its race to the south.

Go to Section 44.

Section 64

Jaeger radioed the scout at Checkpoint 2.

"Charlie Eight Zero," Jaeger ordered. "Hold your fire. Let the BMPs get as close as possible, and then kill as many as you can. Over."

"Wilco, Zulu One One," the scout at Checkpoint 2 replied. "Those BMPs are mine. I am switching over to the artillery frequency to call for fire. I'll get back with you later. Out."

Karrummp! Suddenly the sky above Checkpoint 2 burst with the explosions of American artillery.

Tungkt, Tungkt, Tungkt. Jaeger heard the muffled sound of 25mm fire from Checkpoint 2. He looked at his watch and waited nervously for the report. It was 0310.

"Zulu One One, this is Charlie Eight Zero!" It was the scout at Checkpoint 2, sounding triumphant. "Spot report. Over."

"Charlie Eight Zero, this is Zulu One One," Jaeger replied, eager for information. "Send it."

"Engaged three BMPs at grid LK650950," Checkpoint 2 answered. "I destroyed one, damaged another. Over."

"Roger, Charlie Eight Zero," Jaeger replied. "Which way did they go? Over."

"Unknown. I lost them," the scout answered dejectedly. "They turned around and ran away to the north. I'll call you as soon as I get another contact. Over."

"Roger, Eight Zero," Jaeger said. "Good shooting! Out."

Jaeger moved everyone at Checkpoint 4 to Checkpoint 10. It was now 0345. It would be getting light at 0500. If he was to move to battle position A12 safely, he must move everyone no later than 0430.

"Which way will the regiment attack?" Jaeger said out loud to himself. The killing portion of the counterrecon mission appeared to be over. He had stopped the enemy on the western side of the battalion's sector. His mission, however, was to identify the direction of the enemy's main attack. He knew that he must leave someone in position to verify the direction of that attack. Could the scouts do this alone?

Jaeger determined that he had two options: move to battle position A12 now, or stay put until the last possible minute, to make sure of the direction of the enemy attack. Jaeger must decide!

If Jaeger decides to move to battle position A12 now, go to Section 80.

If Jaeger decides to wait until he is sure of the direction of the enemy's main attack, go to Section 85.

Section 65

Jaeger decided to take his tank and destroy the three BMPs moving southeast from grid LK650950. He radioed the scout at Checkpoint 2 to wait, and not to engage them unless fired upon.

Before leaving Checkpoint 4, he ordered Johnson to try to fix his tank as fast as he could. Jaeger told Lieutenant Rogers to wait at Checkpoint 4 until he returned.

Jaeger departed Checkpoint 4 at 0300. He had a score to settle!

Jaeger's movement to Checkpoint 2 was slow but deliberate. He knew that he was out in the desert all alone and he didn't want to fall into an enemy tank or RPG ambush.

"Jones," Jaeger directed his driver. "Move to that rise to our front and stop while we check out what is ahead."

"Roger," Jones replied obediently.

The tank came to a gentle, rolling halt. Colwell and Jaeger scanned the horizon with their thermal sights.

Suddenly Jaeger was face to face with a BRDM not more than eighty meters to his front.

BOOM! Jaeger fired his 105mm cannon from the TC's override without issuing a fire command. Jaeger, surprised by the encounter as much as the enemy was, missed the lead BMP by inches.

Jaeger's crew sprung into action like a rattler ready to strike. The actions of the crew were automatically superfast. Curn loaded another HEAT round into the massive breech of the 105mm cannon. Colwell, now in control of the gun, aimed with a vengeance, determined to kill the enemy.

"ON THE WAY!" Colwell screamed.

BOOM! The second round was more accurate. The shot hit the BMP right in the center. The HEAT round burned into the vehicle with awesome intensity, blowing the BMP apart in a terrific explosion. The enemy vehicle disintegrated into a burning mass of metal and flesh.

"TARGET!" Jaeger announced, bent on revenge. He had a personal score to settle. "LEFT BMP. FIRE!"

"ON THE WAY!" Colwell aimed at the left BMP that was now trying to break for cover. At this range he couldn't miss.

BOOM! The shell hit the second BMP in the right front side. The energy from the projectile spun the vehicle sideways, flipping it upside down.

"Colwell!" Jaeger yelled. "Where did the third one go? GET HIM!"

Roll the dice.

If the total of the two dice is six or less, go to Section 67.

If the total of the two dice is seven or more, go to Section 86.

Section 66

Jaeger decided to make the enemy's doctrine work in his favor. If I let those BMPs get by, Jaeger thought, maybe I can pull the rest of the regiment behind them and fake them into attacking along an avenue that they think is lightly defended.

"Charlie Eight Zero, this is Zulu One One," Jaeger radioed, hoping that the scout at Checkpoint 2 was steady enough to handle what Jaeger had in mind. "Let the BMPs pass. I say again, let them pass. Keep them under observation as long as you can and report back to me. Over."

"Roger, Zulu One One," the scout said, sounding a bit puzzled.

Jaeger knew that there was not a moment to lose. He called Sergeant Riley on the radio and gave him an update on the situation. Jaeger ordered Riley to switch to the battalion command net and take command if he lost contact with Jaeger. Jaeger called Lieutenant Colonel Brown.

"Victor Two Zero, this is Zulu One One. Over," Jaeger reported.

"Zulu One One, this is Victor Two Zero," Lieutenant Colonel Brown answered.

Section 66

"We observed three BMPs moving southeast along axis California near Checkpoint Two," Jaeger continued. "These BMPs are heading toward Phase Line Denmark. Do not engage them. With any luck we can sucker the enemy into believing that he can make easy progress down California.

"I suspect that enemy will attack along California. I need to maintain my position to verify direction of enemy attack. I say again, request permission to stay in position. If I can get my tanks between Checkpoints Two and Ten, I can hit them in the flank as they drive down California. Over."

There was a long, tense pause on the radio. Lieutenant Colonel Brown was mentally war gaming Jaeger's suggestion.

"Roger, Zulu One One," Brown replied, pausing for a moment. "It's a bold move and just might work. I concur. Move to a reverse slope position south of Hill 955 as soon as possible with your tanks. I will alert all elements that you will stay in position. Out."

Jaeger radioed Riley to meet him at LK675933. He radioed Sergeant Young to have his scouts remain in position, report, and snipe at the enemy once the battle started. He ordered Johnson to disable his tank and double up with Lieutenant Rogers. Jaeger then moved to LK675933 as fast as possible.

Jaeger's plan was simple. He would take his remaining firepower (three tanks—the CFV at Checkpoint 2, the mortars, and the FIST), and fire into the flank of the enemy column that should attack down axis California. He was gambling that his reading of enemy doctrine was correct and that California offered the enemy the approach of least resistance. In a little over an hour, he would know if his guess had been correct.

Go to Section 71.

Section 67

Karrummp! Suddenly the sky above Checkpoint 2 burst with the explosions of American artillery.

Tungkt, Tungkt, Tungkt. Jaeger heard the muffled sound of 25mm fire near Checkpoint 2. He looked at his watch. It was 0310. He waited nervously for the report.

"Zulu One One, this is Charlie Eight Zero!" It was the scout at Checkpoint 2, sounding triumphant. "Spot report. Over."

"Charlie Eight Zero, this is Zulu One One," Jaeger replied, eager for information. "Send it."

"Destroyed one BMP at grid LK670923," Checkpoint 2 answered. "We got them all. Over."

"He got the sucker!" Colwell screamed with delight to Jaeger over the tank intercom.

"Good job, Charlie Eight Zero," Jaeger said, flushed with victory. "Good job!"

Jaeger reported to battalion. It was now 0345. It would be getting light at 0500. If he was to move the tanks back to battle position A12 safely, he must move them no later than 0430. Was Johnson ready? Jaeger raced back to Checkpoint 4 and arrived there at 0440.

Go to Section 59.

Section 68

"Jones!" Jaeger yelled, white hot with anger. "Move forward, we're going back to Checkpoint Four! Curn. Load HEAT. Colwell, I want you to fire as soon as you see the bastards!"

Jones slammed the tank into forward. He continued to accelerate as the tank raced north. The powerful engines of the M1 pushed the tank up the hill as if it were an unstoppable force. Jaeger opened his hatch, reloaded and charged his .50-caliber machine gun.

"IDENTIFIED," Colwell yelled as he saw a group of infantry 700 meters away at Checkpoint 4.

"Jones, stop," Jaeger shouted at the top of his lungs. The tank smoothly settled to a halt. "FIRE!"

The 105mm projectile screamed through the early-morning air, hitting near a group of enemy soldiers. The projectile exploded on target, sending metal and rocks everywhere in a deadly rain of death.

"Colwell, continue firing. FIRE and ADJUST," Jaeger yelled as he began firing his .50-caliber machine gun. Bullets smashed into the area around Checkpoint 4, drilling the ground with lead.

BOOM! BOOM! Colwell's fire was devastating. He fired 105mm rounds as fast as Curn could load.

"Sir," Colwell announced. "They are running. Let's go get them!"

"Jones," Jaeger ordered with bloodlust in his voice, "move out. Get them. Run over the bastards. Go . . . GO!"

A31 moved quickly up the hill. The enemy infantry was running uphill in small scattered groups. Colwell switched from the main gun to his coax and shot them down as they ran away.

A few brave RPG gunners stayed behind. Two enemy soldiers popped up with RPGs as Jaeger came within eighty meters of their position.

KABOOM! KABOOM! Jaeger's tank stopped, jerking to the left as if pushed by some giant hand. One of the RPG rockets hit A31's left side. The track rolled off the support rollers, grinding under the forward momentum of the heavy tank. Jones, not knowing the track was hit, continued to try to move the tank.

"Jones! Hit the smoke generator," Jaeger yelled as he fired all banks of his external smoke grenades. "Curn, man your loader's machine gun!"

Curn, ammo can in hand, opened his hatch and quickly loaded his machine gun on top of the turret. Jaeger cranked down his machine gun and fired a concentrated burst of .50-caliber slugs into an RPG gunner as he attempted to load another grenade into the launcher.

Smoke billowed from the tank's engine, filling the battlefield with a thick white smoke. Tracers flew wildly all around. Colwell turned the turret in a 180-degree arc back and forth, firing his coax.

An enemy machine gunner raked the top of Jaeger's turret with fire from his PKM. Curn, hit by the bullets, fell inside the turret, bleeding from the face and arm.

Jaeger reached over from the tank commander's hatch and awkwardly fired the machine gun in the enemy's direction. Colwell found the enemy machine gunner and dropped him with a burst of 7.62mm fire. Colwell and Jaeger kept firing until they both ran out of ammunition. Then everything got very quiet.

Colwell continued to scan for targets. Jones turned off the smoke generator. Jaeger and Colwell, glued to their positions, scanned the immediate battlefield, unsure that they had killed all the Threat infantry. After a few more minutes without seeing anyone, Jaeger figured that the enemy had been defeated on Checkpoint 4. Jaeger and his crew had won.

Colwell squirmed out of his seat, moved over to Curn's unconscious body, and started to bandage him.

"How is he?" Jaeger asked, his ears ringing from the sounds of the battle.

"Not good, Lieutenant," Colwell said grimly, Curn's blood splattered all over his Nomex uniform. "He took a bullet in the arm and neck. It's a wonder he is still alive. I think I've stopped the bleeding."

Jaeger looked around at the scene at Checkpoint 4. The mortars and the FIST-V were smoking hulks. Dead enemy soldiers lay all over the ground. No one else had survived . . . no one. Jaeger and his crew, immobilized and alone, were all that was left alive on Checkpoint 4.

Although Jaeger still had plenty of main gun ammunition, he was out of machine gun ammunition. He would not be able to fix his tank without help. From his position he may be able to fire on a few targets coming down the bravo avenue of approach. It was, however, not a good position to fight from. In addition, Curn was badly wounded and would die soon without medical support.

What should he do? Should he destroy his own tank and try to get back to friendly lines with his crew, or should he stay and fight? There wasn't any time to waste. Jaeger must decide!

If Jaeger decides to stay and fight, go to Section 75.

If Jaeger decides to escape and evade back to friendly lines, go to Section 87.

Section 69

Jaeger couldn't leave Johnson there to die. He ordered Lieutenant Rogers to stay at Checkpoint 4 while he rescued Johnson. With a little luck, he could get him out of there in an hour or so.

Jaeger attempted to contact the scouts at Checkpoint 3 but received no response. What if they had been taken out? Jaeger thought. There wasn't time to worry about it.

"Zulu Four Seven, this is Zulu One One. Over," Jaeger said, hoping to find Johnson at his radio.

"Go ahead, Zulu." Johnson's voice sounded disgusted and scared.

"I am moving to your position, Zulu Four Seven," Jaeger answered. "Get your tow cables hooked up. I should be at your location in twenty minutes. Over."

"Roger, Zulu One One," Johnson replied, sounding a bit reassured. "I knew that you wouldn't leave us out here. Thanks."

Jaeger moved out quickly to help Johnson. Bouncing around in the top of the turret, trying to hold on as Jones maneuvered the tank to the west, Jaeger had a difficult time seeing the terrain. Johnson's crew was still a good two kilometers away.

240

Looking to the northwest, Jaeger saw red and green tracer bullets flying high in the area where Johnson should be.

"Contact! Zulu One One, this is Zulu Four Seven. I've got enemy infantry. Request artillery. I need—"

Johnson's request ended in mid sentence.

Jaeger rushed to the sound of the fighting. He was now heading west about 1,200 meters away from Checkpoint 4.

Jaeger attempted to reach Johnson on the radio. No reply. He radioed back to Lieutenant Rogers but couldn't reach him either.

"Zulu One One . . . this . . . is . . ." The radio transmission was too weak to be heard. Jaeger strained his ears to pick up the message.

"Damn it!" Jaeger shouted over his intercom. "Jones, head north, up the hill. Take it easy. I need to get to high ground to get back in communications."

"Yes, sir." Jones dutifully pulled the tank to the right and began climbing the south side of Hill 955.

"Last calling station, this is Zulu One One," Jaeger pleaded. "Come in. Over." With his head and shoulders sticking out of the tank commander's hatch, Jaeger could see firing and explosions at Checkpoint 4.

"The mortars!" Jaeger screamed. "Damn it, they are hitting the mortars! Jones, turn right, head back to Checkpoint Four, quick!"

Jaeger's tank raced on the uneven slope of Hill 955. Jones did a great job missing the boulders and ditches that seemed to jump up at him out of the dark. The tank handled magnificently, but the going was still slow.

"Faster, Jones, we have got to get back to Checkpoint Four!"

Trying to oblige, Jones revved the engine. The tank's gas turbine whined in the night, sounding like a mad elephant on a rampage. But tanks were not made to race on uneven slopes in pitch darkness, in spite of the driver's excellent night driving viewer.

"Jones, STOP!" Jaeger yelled, too late.

The tank crashed into a deep wadi, lurching forward and smashing the crew against the front turret wall. The force of the impact was terrific.

"Are you OK, Lieutenant?" Jones asked, hoping beyond hope for an answer.

Jaeger opened his eyes. The bright morning sun blinded him. His shoulder burned. The sound of firing could be heard off in the distance. He couldn't feel his legs.

"What. . . . what happened?" Jaeger attempted to sit up but failed. "Where is Sergeant Colwell . . . the mortars?"

"SHHH! Sir, keep quiet," Jones whispered. "An enemy patrol just walked by here not more than ten minutes ago. Colwell is dead. Broken neck. I sent Curn for help over an hour ago, but I haven't heard from him since. How you feeling, Lieutenant?"

"Never mind that," Jaeger answered angrily. He tried to get up. Pain tore through his shoulder. Had he dislocated it? Why couldn't he sit up? He felt cold. "What happened to battalion?"

"There was one hell of a battle this morning, sir," Jones replied. "I don't know who won, but I have been watching enemy columns head south all morning. It doesn't look good. Neither do you. Sir, you have lost a lot of blood."

Jaeger wanted to die. He had let down the battalion. God only knew what happened to the rest of 3d Platoon. He felt very cold.

"Jones, we've got to get out of here," Jaeger said feebly. "We. . . ."

Jones held his platoon leader and began to cry.

Go to Section 44.

Section 70

"Zulu Four Seven, this is Zulu One One," Jaeger said with determination. "You are on your own. I can't leave here right now. Hunker down where you are and report any activity that you see."

There was another long silence. It cut like a cold wind.

"Roger, Zulu," Johnson said bitterly.

"Zulu Four Seven, I know your situation is tight," Jaeger replied just as angrily. "You can still help me beat these bastards! Set up a perimeter around your tank and stay put. I promise to get you in the morning.

"If you see anything," Jaeger continued, "call me. We can have mortar support to you in a few seconds. Out."

*   *   *

Jaeger reported to battalion and radioed his latest information. He called Johnson every ten minutes to reassure his stranded tank commander that he was not forgotten. Suddenly, Jaeger's earphones were filled with Sergeant Johnson's desperate appeal for help.

"Zulu One One, this is Zulu Four Seven. CONTACT!" Johnson reported excitedly, whispering into the radio microphone. "I've got dismounts at grid 677939, moving south. Over."

"Roger Four Seven," Jaeger replied nervously. "Don't engage them unless absolutely necessary. I have mortars coming your way. Hang in there!" Jaeger knew that Johnson was in deep trouble.

Looking to the northwest, Jaeger saw red and green tracer bullets bouncing high in the sky over the area where Johnson should be.

"Zulu One One, I've got enemy infantry everywhere. Request artillery. I am engaging now. I need—"

Johnson's request ended in mid sentence. Jaeger attempted to reach Johnson on the radio. No reply.

"Damn it!" Jaeger shouted over his intercom.

"Zulu Four Seven, this is Zulu One One. Come in. Over," Jaeger pleaded. As he attempted to radio Johnson, Jaeger could see the mortars begin their fire mission.

"Zulu Four Seven . . . Zulu Four Seven," Rogers said, trying to call Johnson and answer his call for support. "Mortars on the way! Danger close!"

Thuunk . . . Thuunk. The mortars fired their barrage. High-explosive shells were on their way. More orders were issued. The mortarmen executed their drill. With precision and care the mortar bombs were rapidly prepared. Sights were quickly set. The command was given to fire.

Thuunk . . . Thuunk. Death was on the way. The rounds left the tubes and the hungry mortars were refed. More rounds arched high overhead to hit near Johnson's position.

KABOOM! A blinding blue-white flash knocked Jaeger backward. One of the M106 mortar carriers exploded in a fiery, terrible explosion. Sparks flew high overhead as the mortar ammunition began to burn and explode.

Recovering from the initial shock of the blast, Jaeger slowly regained his night vision. He saw men running everywhere. Enemy infantry! Where the hell did they come from? He immediately buttoned up and began spraying the area with .50-caliber machine gun fire.

"Jones! Move out!" Jaeger shouted to his driver over the intercom. "Forward!" The big tank lurched forward, moving up the narrow dirt trail to their front. Colwell fired his coax 7.62mm machine gun, moving the turret left and right as he searched for targets.

KABOOM! Another huge explosion ripped through the remaining M106 mortar carrier.

Sergeant Martin, on the ground with his M-16 in hand, fired at the enemy infantry. He hit two infiltrators before the blast from the explosion of his track, only ten feet away, flattened him to the ground. Struggling to get up, he was shot dead by an AK-74 automatic rifle.

The enemy infantry moved quickly to occupy Checkpoint 4. They shot white parachute flares over Checkpoint 4 to illuminate the battlefield in an attempt to finish off the Americans with accurate machine gun and RPG fire.

Jaeger, protected in his turret, fired his .50-caliber machine gun at the darting enemy figures. His accuracy was poor, due to the rapid movement of the tank, but the effect kept the enemy ducking.

Racing uphill, Jones tried to avoid both enemy fire and the huge rocks that dotted the landscape. His night driving viewer washed out momentarily from the illumination from the flares. Turning sharply to avoid a large stone, Jones accidentally crashed the tank into a deep erosion ditch. The tank violently pitched forward.

Jaeger held onto the sides of the TC's station to steady himself. He tried to aim and fire his .50-caliber machine gun, but it failed to function. Angrily, he forced open the TC's hatch and attempted to charge the weapon again. Lifting open the feed cover, he realized that he was out of ammunition.

"Back up!" Jaeger cried.

Roll the dice.

If the total of the two dice is four or less, go to Section 53.

If the total of the two dice is five or more, go to Section 55.

Section 71

Jaeger moved with Rogers and Sergeant Martin's remaining mortar track to the new rendezvous point. Riley arrived shortly after Jaeger at 0440. Jaeger and Riley dismounted and met together on the ground.

"So, Lieutenant." Riley put both hands on his hips and stared at the lieutenant in the cloudless night. "We are going to take on the entire enemy regiment ourselves?"

"Yeah, something like that," Jaeger said, then briskly got to the point. "I am sure that the enemy will attack down California . . . over there." He pointed to the low ground to the southwest. "I let those BMPs get through to make them think that we are weak in the west," Jaeger said, looking at his watch. It was 0444. "We have Hill 955 to protect us from artillery fire and they shouldn't expect us to fire on them from their rear."

"You got a good idea there," Riley said with a grin.

"Jaeger!" Rogers shouted from the open ramp of his darkened FIST-V. "Battalion is on the radio for you."

Jaeger ran back to his tank, hopped up to the TC's hatch, and reached for his CVC helmet.

"Victor Two Zero, this is Zulu One One. Over," Jaeger reported.

"Zulu One One, this is Victor Two Zero," Lieutenant Colonel Brown replied. "What is your situation?"

"I am at LK675930 with three tanks and my FIST. The Charlie elements [scouts] will stay in position," Jaeger said confidently. "We are ready for them. Over."

"Roger, Zulu One One," Brown replied quickly. "If they come down California, kill as many as you can. If they come down Utah, move east and do the same. Good luck. Don't try—" The colonel's radio transmission was interrupted in mid sentence and replaced with silence.

At 0450 the radios began transmitting white noise. No communications were getting through. White noise is the nothing sound that is transmitted over an FM radio frequency that is being blocked out by a high-power jamming emitter. Jaeger tried the alternate frequencies but got the same result. The enemy must be barrage jamming every frequency, Jaeger thought. The attack must be on!

Karrummp! Karrummp! Then, with a crash like the roar of a distant freight train, enemy artillery began to fall on Checkpoint 4 and the battalion's forward positions. Jaeger's men buttoned up and watched the faraway flashes curiously. No artillery fell on Jaeger's men. The reverse slope of Hill 955 was protecting them nicely.

Karrummp! Karrummp! The noise was now continuous but more distant. The artillery was falling in a rolling series of concentrated barrages. Most of the U.S. positions seemed to have been targeted and took quite a beating.

Jaeger opened his hatch to the open protected position to get a better view of the battlefield. It was almost light now, and he could see without using his trusted night vision goggles. Ramos was to his right, Riley to his left. They also had their hatches in the open protected position and were glancing at Jaeger.

Riley gave Jaeger the thumbs-up sign. Jaeger felt as if he could take on an army with such men!

The radio was useless. Jaeger looked through his vision blocks in the direction of California. Riley and Ramos would just have to follow the standard SOP when radio contact was lost: "Follow me and do as I do."

"Colwell," Jaeger said calmly. "I don't want you to hit the lead tanks. Let them pass . . . let's say the first five or so. Then I want you to open up on the BMPs first. I want to strip away their infantry. But, if in doubt, shoot!"

"Roger, sir," Colwell said over the intercom. "Just bring on the targets."

Colwell didn't have long to wait.

At 0550 the first tanks streamed past Jaeger's position. The enemy attacked along California, just as Jaeger had predicted. The low ground filled with smoke as the enemy tried to cover their rapid advance. The enemy intended to blow through the American lines with their usual recipe of tempo and mass.

Jaeger's thermal sight saw right through the smoke. His tanks were ready. From this angle of fire they would be shooting at the enemy's flanks and grill doors.

"IDENTIFIED!" Colwell screamed, his palms sweaty and his trigger finger eager to send a sabot round into an enemy vehicle. The enemy was less than 1,300 meters away, racing south. They were in perfect column formation and obviously hadn't met any serious opposition so far. Each T-72 and BMP was about fifty meters apart, moving fast, maintaining their formation.

Colwell let the first four vehicles go by. The enemy didn't see Jaeger's tanks.

"FIRE," Jaeger yelled.

BOOM! BOOM! BOOM! The three well-trained M1 tank crews fired almost simultaneously. Three BMPs went up in flames, their wreckage thrown about in fantastic contortions of busted metal and burning rubber. More enemy vehicles kept racing south, looking to their front, unaware of the direction of the fire coming from Jaeger's tanks.

BOOM! BOOM! BOOM! Three more BMPs were hit. A T-72 tank appeared and turned its turret in Jaeger's direction.

"GUNNER, SABOT, TANK," Jaeger shouted, swinging the gun over in the direction of the enemy tank.

"IDENTIFIED!" Colwell replied.

"FIRE!" The round shot from Jaeger's gun tube and hit the enemy tank squarely on the left side of its turret. The T-72 shuddered from the strike and jerked quickly to a stop from the force of the explosion.

Riley and Ramos continued to kill BMPs. The valley was now littered with burning enemy vehicles. Sergeant Martin fired his mortars at the enemy, making his own corrections, forcing the enemy to button up.

"Colwell, they know that we are here now," Jaeger said over the intercom, his voice overcontrolled to hide the excitement. "Switch to hitting tanks as soon as they appear."

Before Jaeger could finish his words, three more T-72 tanks turned against Jaeger's position, on line, executing a perfect attack drill.

Roll the dice.

If the total of the two dice is six or less, go to Section 74.

If the total of the two dice is seven to ten, go to Section 76.

If the total of the two dice is eleven or more, go to Section 63.

Section 72

Jaeger fired his .50-caliber machine gun while Colwell sprayed the area with 7.62mm bullets. A31 moved quickly, first left, then right, as Jones tried to miss boulders and rough terrain.

"One One, this is One Four," Riley screamed over his radio. "We are headed your way!"

"Roger, One Four!" Jaeger replied. "We need you here!"

"I'm out of coax . . . I'm out of coax," Colwell interrupted, yelling over the intercom.

Jaeger's .50-caliber machine gun jammed and quit firing.

"Shit! Jones, move forward. Run them over!" Jaeger yelled as he fired all banks of his external smoke grenades. "Jones, start the smoke generator."

Jones jinked wildly, smashing enemy infantry into the dust. The red phosphorous grenades shot out from the tank in all directions. Smoke filled the area, spewing from the rear of Jaeger's tank and from the exploding grenades.

An RPG rocket swooshed by Jaeger's TC's hatch, missing the cover by inches. Racing downhill from the RPG ambush, Riley and Ramos continued the fight, firing machine guns and their cannons as fast as targets appeared.

KABOOM! An RPG hit Johnson's tank on the left track skirt. A32 ground to a jerking halt. The turret continued to rotate as Johnson's gunner riddled the area with 7.62mm machine gun fire. Several more enemy infantrymen fell prey to Johnson's lethal machine guns.

"Damn it. By God, that's enough!" Jaeger screamed over the intercom. "GUNNER. HEAT, TROOPS . . . FIRE!"

BOOM! Colwell fired at the closest group of enemy that he could find. The 105mm cannon blast illuminated the night. The high-explosive antitank (HEAT) round shot through the air at tremendous speed. It struck the hard desert floor with a blinding explosion, only sixty meters from the tank.

The enemy couldn't take any more. They were grossly overmatched by the combined firepower of Jaeger's M1 tank platoon. The survivors tried desperately to flee to the northwest, avoiding the tanks' deadly tracks and their searching machine guns. Dead enemy infantry were sprawled all over Checkpoint 4.

Soon it became quiet again. Checkpoint 4 was back in American hands.

Go to Section 77.

Section 73

It was time to take the initiative. So far, Jaeger had merely been reacting to the enemy's moves. Now, he had a golden opportunity to make the enemy's doctrine work in his favor.

If I let those BMPs get by, Jaeger thought, maybe I can pull the rest of the regiment to attack along an avenue that they think is lightly defended. Then I might be able to ambush them as they push south.

"Charlie Eight Zero, this is Zulu One One," Jaeger radioed, hoping that the scout at Checkpoint 2 was steady enough to handle what Jaeger had in mind. "Let the BMPs pass. I say again, let them pass. Don't let them see you. Keep them under observation as long as you can and report back to me. Over."

"Roger, Zulu One One," the scout said, sounding a bit puzzled.

Jaeger knew that there was not a moment to lose. He walked over to Sergeant Riley's tank. Jaeger pulled the slide forward on his .45-caliber pistol and chambered a round, just in case any enemy infantry were still about. Riley, already dismounted, met him at the side of his tank, A34.

"Riley," Jaeger yelled, the sound of the firing still ringing in his ears, "we got three BMPs moving south near Checkpoint Two."

"Let's go get the bastards," Riley said sternly. "We can be ready to move in five minutes."

"Negative. I have a better idea," Jaeger said, pulling out his map and illuminating it near Checkpoint 2.

"If we let them get by, they may report to their boss that the California axis is the path of least resistance. If we let them think they can bust through us there," Jaeger pointed to the map, "maybe we can sucker them into attacking us just where we want them to."

"And if our tanks are between Checkpoint Two and Checkpoint Ten as they come south," Riley said with a grin, "we could shoot them from the rear and they might not even figure out what's happening."

"That's the pitch!" Jaeger said. "What do you think?"

"Let's do it," Riley said confidently. "Hill 955 is the best protection we will get from the enemy's artillery. On the southern slope—" Riley looked at Jaeger's map, his finger tracing the contour lines under the blue glow of Jaeger's flashlight, "near LK675925, we will be well protected. Once the enemy starts pouring down California, we can ambush them as they go by."

"OK. I'll call Colonel Brown and tell him what we want to do. Tell Lieutenant Rogers to plan some artillery for me all along the length of California. Get everyone else ready to move. I want to get out of here as soon as possible."

Jaeger ran back to his tank to call Lieutenant Colonel Brown. Riley moved off to get the group organized. The black, cloudless desert night was quiet now. Jaeger knew that wouldn't last long.

"Victor Two Zero, this is Zulu One One. Over," Jaeger reported.

"Zulu One One, this is Victor Two Zero," Lieutenant Colonel Brown answered.

"We observed three BMPs moving southeast along axis California near Checkpoint Two. If we let them go, the bad guys may believe that we are weak in the west. If we can fool them, I'll bet a month's pay that they will attack along California. Over."

"Roger, Zulu One One," Lieutenant Colonel Brown said. "I'm with you so far."

"If I maintain a position between Checkpoint Two and Checkpoint Ten, I can hit them in the flank as they drive down California. Over."

There was a long pause on the radio. Lieutenant Colonel Brown was mentally war gaming Jaeger's suggestion.

"Roger, Zulu One One," Brown replied, pausing for a moment. "It's a bold move and it just might work. I concur. Move to a reverse slope position south of Hill 955 as soon as possible. I will alert all elements that you will not be moving back to battle position A12. I will move my elements to receive them on this end. I will alert Team Bravo about the BMPs and tell them to hold their fire. Over."

"I will fire two red and one green star cluster to designate their main attack down California," Jaeger added, "in case we lose radio contact."

"Good idea," Brown replied. "That will be my signal to move Team Delta to battle position D12. Don't try to be a hero, just weaken them for us without getting yourself overrun. Get moving and good luck. Out."

Jaeger found a good defensive position that faced south, at LK677930. All of his elements—the four tanks, two mortar carriers, and Lieutenant Rogers's FIST-V—took up positions by 0440. The scout at Checkpoint 2, in an excellent position, covered their back. Jaeger dismounted and checked the ground to his front.

"Jaeger!" Rogers shouted from the open ramp of his darkened FIST-V. "Battalion is on the radio for you."

Jaeger ran back to his tank, hopped up to the TC's hatch, and reached for his CVC helmet.

"Victor Two Zero, this is Zulu One One. Over," Jaeger reported.

"Zulu One One, this is Victor Two Zero," Lieutenant Colonel Brown replied. "What is your situation?"

"I am set in position. The Charlie elements [scouts] will stay in position and report as needed," Jaeger said confidently. "We will be ready if they attack down the California or the Utah avenue of approach. Over."

"Roger, Zulu One One," Brown replied quickly. "Give them hell. I've got a group of artillery targets along both approaches. If they—" The colonel's radio transmission was replaced by a strange mechanical silence. It was now 0450.

The radios went totally dead with white noise—the nothing sound that is transmitted over an FM frequency that is being blocked out by a high-power jamming radio.

The enemy was barrage jamming every frequency, Jaeger thought. The attack must be on!

Karrummp. Karrummp. With a crash like the roar of a distant freight train, enemy artillery began to fall like rain on Checkpoint 4, about

2,000 meters away to the northeast. Artillery also began landing on the battalion's forward positions at B11 and C11. Jaeger's men buttoned up their hatches and watched the faraway flashes curiously. No artillery fell on Jaeger's men. The reverse slope of Hill 955 was protecting them nicely.

Karrummp. Karrummp. The noise was continuous but getting more distant with each passing minute.

Jaeger opened his hatch to the open protected position to get a better view of the battlefield. It was almost light now, and he could see without using his trusty night vision goggles. Riley was to his right and Johnson to his left. Ramos was off to Riley's right. The mortars were behind them all, tucked neatly into a wadi.

Riley also had his hatch in the open protected position. He glanced at Jaeger, giving him the thumbs-up sign. With such men, a leader could do anything, thought Jaeger. His heart filled with pride as he looked at his thin line of tanks, ready to ambush a regiment!

The radio was useless. The Threat jamming was totally effective. Jaeger looked through his vision blocks in the direction of California. Riley, Ramos, and Johnson would just have to follow the standard SOP when radio contact was lost: "Follow me and do as I do."

"Colwell," Jaeger said calmly. "I don't want to hit the lead tanks. Let them pass . . . let's say the first five or so. Then I want you to open up. I don't want them to know where we are hitting them from. Aim for the BMPs first. I want to strip away their infantry. But, when in doubt, shoot!"

"Roger, sir," Colwell said over the intercom. "Just bring on the targets."

Colwell didn't have long to wait.

At 0530 the first tanks streamed past Jaeger's position on the south side of Hill 955. The enemy attacked along California, just as Jaeger had predicted. The low ground filled with smoke as the enemy tried to cover their advance. The smoke worked in Jaeger's favor. His thermal sights saw right through the smoke, whereas the enemy was reduced to very limited visibility.

"IDENTIFIED!" Colwell screamed, his palms sweaty and his trigger finger eager to send a sabot round into an enemy vehicle. The enemy armored vehicles were less than 1,300 meters away, racing south in perfect column formation. Each BMP and tank was about fifty meters apart, moving fast. They did not show any indication of being aware of Jaeger's tanks.

Colwell let the first four vehicles go by.

"Fire!" Jaeger yelled.

BOOM! BOOM! BOOM! BOOM! The four well-trained M1 tank crews fired almost simultaneously. Three BMPs went up in flames, their wreckage thrown about in a fantastic contortion of busted metal, smoke, and burning rubber. More Threat vehicles raced south, avoiding the wreckage but not noticing where their comrades were being hit from.

BOOM! BOOM! BOOM! BOOM! Four more BMPs were hit. Suddenly two T-72 tanks appeared and turned their turrets in Jaeger's direction.

"GUNNER, SABOT, TWO TANKS," Jaeger shouted, swinging the gun over in the direction of one of the enemy tanks.

"IDENTIFIED!" Colwell replied.

"FIRE!"

BOOM! The round shot from Jaeger's gun tube and hit the enemy tank squarely on the left side of its turret. There was a splash of sparks as the tank quickly jerked to a stop from the force of the explosion.

BOOM! BOOM! Johnson killed the second T-72 in almost the same instant. Riley and Ramos continued to kill BMPs.

The valley was now littered with burning enemy vehicles. The enemy seem confused and began to slow down. Sergeant Martin fired his mortars at the enemy hulks, making his own corrections, adding to the enemy's trouble.

"Colwell, they know that we are here now," Jaeger said over the intercom, his voice overcontrolled to hide the excitement. "Switch to hitting tanks as soon as they appear."

Before Jaeger could finish his words, three T-72 tanks turned against Jaeger's position, executing a perfect action-left battle drill. They all aimed at Jaeger.

Roll the dice.

If the total of the two dice is nine or less, go to Section 82.

If the total of the two dice is ten or more, go to Section 74.

Section 74

"Fire!" Jaeger commanded.

BOOM! The tank jerked from the gun's recoil. The round screamed forward, hitting an enemy tank in the front right support wheel, stopping it in its tracks. Several other T-72s raced toward Jaeger's position. They were only 900 meters away now, and there were just too many of them.

KABOOM! A tremendous force hit Jaeger's tank. Thrown against the inside walls, the crew absorbed the wrath of the projectile. Jaeger hit the tank commander's sight hard. The turret spun ten degrees to the right with the force of the impact, pinning Curn under the gun.

The automatic fire extinguishers discharged. Smoke and extinguisher exhaust flooded the fighting compartment. Jaeger couldn't breathe!

He fumbled for his hatch release and used all of his strength to open it. Fresh air rushed in. Jaeger tore off his chemical protective mask and painfully muscled his way out of the turret. He lay on the top for a few seconds, dazed.

"Colwell, Curn!" Jaeger rolled over to his hatch and looked inside. The smoke was so thick he couldn't see. He crawled back into the hatch and reached down for Sergeant Colwell. Jaeger, blinded by the smoke, his eyes watering and burning, found Colwell and yanked with all his might to drag his gunner to the top of the tank.

Gasping for air, he stopped halfway and returned to the top to catch his breath. Back down again, he pulled the limp body of his sergeant to the top and forced him out of the turret.

Jaeger saw that Colwell was still breathing. He left him on the flat top roof of the M1 and started to go back down into the turret to get Curn. Before he could climb into the TC's station, Jaeger saw a T-72 tank coming right for him, only 300 meters away.

BOOM! Sergeant Riley's tank, appearing out of nowhere, smashed the T-72 before it had a chance to finish Jaeger. The Threat tank flipped on its side, slid into a ditch, and exploded.

"I must get Curn," Jaeger said out loud.

But he didn't have time for that. His tank began to burn, the 105mm rounds igniting inside the ammunition storage area in the turret. The force blew Jaeger off the tank and onto the hard sand below.

* * *

Lieutenant Colonel Brown drove his HUMVEE up to the scene of Jaeger's last battle. The fighting had ended several hours ago. The enemy regiment had been crushed. More than 170 burned-out and destroyed Threat BMPs, tanks, and self-propelled artillery pieces lay scattered in clumps along axis California. The defeat of the enemy in Colonel Brown's sector had disrupted the enemy plan and allowed the division commander to slaughter the enemy's second echelon forces with rocket artillery and Apache attack helicopters. The Americans had won a great victory.

Brown found Jaeger and three other casualties laid out on the ground, covered with ponchos. Sergeant Riley sat silently next to the body of his fallen lieutenant.

"Sergeant Riley," Lieutenant Colonel Brown asked quietly, "are you OK?"

"Yes, sir," Riley said slowly, not bothering to rise but not meaning any disrespect. "But I didn't do very well for my lieutenant here."

"Sergeant Riley," Colonel Brown said firmly. "Jaeger was a soldier. One of the best I ever met. We all take our chances. His luck just ran out."

"He did a good job, Colonel," Riley said sadly, holding a handful of dog tags from the dead men. "I have never seen a better officer."

"He won this battle. He blinded the enemy and then faked him into attacking just where we wanted him to attack," Brown said with admiration. "A lot of Americans are alive today because of him."

"So what happens now?" Riley asked.

"We move out in five hours. Brigade has another mission for us," Brown said without emotion. "You had better get your men ready. There is still a war to fight."

Jaeger accomplished his mission. The price for the American victory was relatively cheap. Relatively. For Jaeger it was total. Jaeger paid the ultimate sacrifice leading his soldiers.

The little things often add up until the wave of luck and the momentum of the situation overcome even the best of soldiers. Jaeger knew the score. But because he accomplished his mission, the enemy was defeated. One man *can* make a difference.

The task force won, but you could do better. Go to Section 34 and try again.

Section 75

After the heavy fighting for Hill 955, Jaeger was surprised that his radio was still functioning. He warned the battalion commander that the enemy would take the brown or orange avenue of approach. The battalion commander may have already moved Delta Company to battle position D12, to reinforce the threatened area, Jaeger thought.

"We may be stuck here," Jaeger said to his crew over the tank intercom, "but we will sure take a lot of them with us. At least we accomplished our mission." Jaeger and his crew stoically prepared to meet the onslaught of the Threat motorized rifle regiment.

At 0450 Jaeger tried to reach the battalion commander on the radio but got no response. He turned off the squelch setting and discovered that his radio was receiving only white noise—the nothing sound that is transmitted over an FM frequency that is being jammed. Jaeger quickly disconnected his antenna hookup inside the tank to determine if it was Threat jamming. When he received the normal rush sound from his radio after disconnecting the antenna, he knew that he was being jammed. Jaeger switched frequencies but discovered that all channels were transmitting the same jamming signal. The enemy must be jamming every frequency. The attack must be on!

KARRUMMP! High-explosive 152mm shells hit all over Jaeger's position. Dirt and steel pulverized his tank. Metal struck the sides with furious strength, as if trying to get inside. The storm of fire damaged or destroyed his machine guns, wind sensor mast, and radio antenna, all of which were positioned on top of the tank, unprotected by armor.

The concussion from the rounds, the noise, and the fear of imminent death gripped Jaeger's stomach in knots. God! When will this end! Unable to talk to anyone by radio, and buttoned up by the power of the enemy's artillery, Jaeger prayed for the artillery to stop.

KARRUMMP! KARRUMMP! KARRUMMP! The noise was unbearable. Tired, confined, and scared, Jaeger struggled uncomfortably to see the battlefield. Colwell scanned for targets.

Jaeger hadn't slept a wink all night, but he wasn't tired now. The instinct for survival had his senses at their highest pitch.

KARRUMMP! Each artillery round made the tank shudder. How long could this go on?

CRRAAASSHHH! A tremendous explosion rocked the tank. Jaeger's tank took a direct hit from a 152mm artillery shell. The force of the impact pushed the tank into a ditch and over onto its left side. Thrown around inside, the crew took a beating from the sudden impact. Jaeger hit hard against the side of the tank. He felt numb all over and finally blacked out.

Taking the approach that reconnaissance proved to be lightly defended, the Threat commander drove his regiment relentlessly down the eastern axis and into the rear of the American defenses. Captain Russell's men at battle position A12 fought like demons. They destroyed almost an entire motorized rifle battalion. Clouds of smoke hung low over battle position A12. Burning Threat tanks and BMPs littered the area in front of Russell's tanks. But it wasn't enough. The second and third battalions of the regiment cut through Alpha Company like a hot knife through butter.

The enemy regiment overran Alpha Company and annihilated them before Lieutenant Colonel Brown could reposition his forces. By 0750 the battle was over. The rest of the battalion was picked apart piecemeal while the main Threat columns streamed south.

Following up on this success, the Threat division commander committed his second echelon regiments to the same axis. The situation for the Americans was disastrous. Brown's defense, ruptured and pierced, turned into a piecemeal battle of attrition. Unable to stop the Threat drive, the entire U.S. division was in jeopardy of being defeated.

Scores of Threat aircraft soared overhead, flying to strike targets deep behind American lines. There was a brief but futile fight between Threat MiGs and three U.S. Marine Corps Harrier jump jets. Outnumbered and outmatched, the Marines fought valiantly. Two were finally shot down by the MiGs. The third Harrier was chased away.

Then the HINDs, lethal antitank helicopters, appeared. These huge, heavily armed helicopters were built to act as flying tanks. Slow and ponderous by western helicopter standards, the HINDs were heavily armed and difficult to kill. They flew south, low off the ground, massive and unstoppable. They fired on the disorganized survivors of Jaeger's battalion, who were fleeing to the south, trying to reach American lines.

The enemy pursued the American force with a vengeance. The Americans took a tremendous beating. The flames of burning Bradleys and M1 Abrams tanks lit the road to the coast.

"Sir . . . sir. Are you all right?" Colwell said, looking down at his platoon leader.

"What . . . huh? Where is . . ." Jaeger struggled to regain consciousness. Pain surged all through his body. He couldn't feel his shoulder. He opened his eyes to see Colwell. Blood caked the left side of Colwell's face. The sounds of battle were distant.

A31, on its side and silent, lay broken, offering them some cover from the enemy.

"Sir. Don't die!" Colwell said. "Curn and Jones are dead. I don't know about the rest of the company. I haven't seen any friendlies lately. We got to get out of here. Can you walk?"

"I don't know. Help me up," Jaeger said, wincing at the effort to sit up.

As Colwell struggled with his wounded platoon leader, a squad of enemy soldiers appeared beside the rear of the overturned tank. The enemy soldier in charge screamed at them and gestured to put their hands up.

Colwell put up his hands. Jaeger, lying on his back, merely closed his eyes.

Both were taken prisoner.

Jaeger failed in his mission. Go to Section 34 and try again!

Section 76

"GUNNER, SABOT, THREE TANKS," Jaeger yelled through the tank's intercom system.

"IDENTIFIED," Colwell announced.

"UP!" Curn shouted as he pushed the gun's safety lever in the fire position.

"FIRE!" Jaeger ordered, bracing himself for firing.

BOOM! Jaeger's tank jerked backward from the recoil of the tank's 105mm cannon. The shell, screaming through the air, hit its mark in one terrible blinding flash of metal against metal. The T-72 tank, 100 meters away from Jaeger's position, crashed to a halt, its turret ripped off in a terrific explosion.

The rest of the platoon fired madly, furiously. Tanks and BMPs were racing south as fast as they could travel over the rough terrain. Firing in volleys at the defenders, the enemy's accuracy was poor.

Another T-72 tank, hit by a sabot round from Riley's tank, burst into flames.

KABOOM! Jaeger looked to his left and saw A33 take a direct hit from a T-72 tank. The round burned right into the turret, which stopped moving. Jaeger wondered if Ramos and his crew were still alive.

Amazingly, the enemy tanks and BMPs stopped moving and took up hasty firing positions. They aimed in all directions, returning fire against the cauldron of death that surrounded them from front and rear. Firing in volleys, they pounded Team Bravo, on battle position B11, with fire. Jaeger saw Team Bravo fighting desperately, taking hits but giving more than they received.

The enemy advance stalled and died in front of Team Bravo's battle position B11. Jaeger's accurate direct fire had a lot to do with the enemy defeat. As Team Bravo acted as the cork in the bottle, a flight of U.S. A-10 ground attack aircraft raced over the battlefield and added to the regiment's destruction. Several HIND-D helicopters that appeared on the scene in the final moments of the battle were destroyed by the A-10s.

Almost 170 Threat vehicles littered the landscape along avenue of approach California. It had all taken less than two hours.

The cost, however, was high. The battalion was now at 65 percent strength. Team Bravo took the greatest losses and was down to eight tanks and two Bradleys. Alpha Company had lost two tanks from 1st Platoon and one from 2d Platoon.

Jaeger lost A33. Ramos and his gunner and driver survived, but the loader was killed by the impact of the enemy round.

The enemy's second echelon was stopped cold by long-range artillery, close air support, and Apache attack helicopters. The enemy made a few penetrations elsewhere in the division's sector, but they were unable to exploit their success.

The enemy attack failed and the American line held.

Go to Section 81.

Section 77

Jaeger checked his watch. It was 0300. Jaeger's platoon occupied Checkpoint 4 with a tank pointing in each cardinal direction, to provide 360-degree security. Wrecked vehicles, dead soldiers, and the broken equipment of war littered the area at Checkpoint 4.

Jaeger called Sergeant Riley on the radio and asked him for an update on the ammunition and fuel situation. Riley reported that the platoon was short of machine gun ammunition but would have enough main gun ammunition after they redistributed ammo within the platoon. Fuel was low, but there was enough to last them until noon. The tank crews took no casualties in the firefight at Checkpoint 4, but Johnson's tank, hit by two RPGs, would have to be towed or repaired.

Jaeger felt sick. The mortars and Rogers were dead, their vehicles all destroyed and burning. It was his fault. He was in charge.

Jaeger called Lieutenant Colonel Brown.

"Victor Two Zero, this is Zulu One One. Over," Jaeger reported.

"Zulu One One, this is Victor Two Zero," Lieutenant Colonel Brown answered.

"I am down to six vehicles. The scouts stopped them in the east. We took out a dismounted infantry company at Checkpoint Four, but I've lost Checkpoint Two. I also lost Lieutenant Rogers and the mortar section at Checkpoint Four."

There was a short pause while this information registered with the battalion commander.

"I suspect this means that the enemy will attack along California or Utah," Jaeger continued. "I say again, California or Utah avenues of approach. Request permission to move to battle position A12. Over."

"Roger, Zulu One One. Wait." There was a longer pause now, as the battalion commander decided what to do with Jaeger.

"Zulu One One," Brown replied. He was short and to the point. "Move your tanks back to A12. Leave the scouts forward to continue the screen. I will alert all elements to hold fire until you report set in A12. Over."

"Wilco," Jaeger answered. "We will move in ten minutes. Over."

"Don't waste any time. Out," Brown ordered.

Johnson and Riley had done everything they could to get A32 fixed in time, but the job was impossible. Jaeger recommended towing the tank, but Riley suggested that, with only forty-five minutes of darkness left to reach battle position A12, they would never make it. Jaeger finally made the decision to disable A32 and leave it on Checkpoint 4.

Placing a thermite grenade on the breech, Johnson sadly completed the destruction of his tank. Johnson's crew split up and climbed aboard Ramos's and Riley's tanks.

Jaeger headed toward battle position A12. His three tanks crossed Phase Line France at 0450. Just as they did so, the radios went quiet with white noises.

White noise is the nothing sound that is transmitted over an FM frequency that is being jammed. The enemy uses this to jam FM radio transmission at critical times in battle. Often the person being jammed doesn't even know he has a problem until it's too late.

Jaeger quickly disconnected his antenna connection inside the tank to determine if it was in fact jamming. As soon as the disconnection was complete, the normal rush sound could be heard in his radio earphones. Now he was sure that he was being jammed. He quickly switched to his designated alternate frequencies, but these too were controlled by jamming.

The enemy must be barrage jamming every frequency, he thought. The attack must have started!

KARRUMMP! Jaeger was right.

Section 77

KARRUMMP! KARRUMMP! In a crash of fire and flying steel, the area behind Jaeger's column suddenly exploded with the impact of 152mm artillery. Artillery also smashed into Team Charlie on battle position C11. Jaeger and his crew immediately donned their NBC protective masks.

KARRUMMP! KARRUMMP! The amount of artillery fire was overpowering. Anyone caught out in the open would be instantly killed. Armored vehicles, dug into the hard desert ground by bulldozers, were surviving fairly well. Those infantrymen in Team Charlie's battle position who did not prepare adequate overhead cover for their foxholes and fighting positions did not live long enough to regret their error.

Jaeger's three tanks arrived on battle position A12 at 0520. The artillery fell there as they arrived. High-explosive 152mm shells hit the ground, tearing huge gaps in the earth and filling the battle position with dust and smoke. Flying metal struck the sides of the tanks with furious strength, as if trying to get inside.

The M1s weathered this storm of fire fairly well. The machine guns, crew equipment, wind sensor masts, and radio antennae on the top of the tanks took a beating. The concussion from the rounds, the noise, and the fear of imminent death gripped Jaeger's stomach in knots. God! When will this end!

Unable to talk to his unit by radio, and buttoned up by the power of the enemy's artillery, Jaeger prayed that his tanks would operate without active control.

Taking a position on the western side of battle position A12, Jaeger's platoon was to be the right side of the U-shaped company position. Jaeger moved into a hasty hull-down position, using a small rise to his front to mask a portion of his vehicle. The position protected him a bit from the crush of the artillery. Looking through his vision blocks, he could see another tank, probably Ramos's, to his left.

KARRUMMP! KARRUMMP! The noise was unbearable. Jaeger struggled uncomfortably to see the battlefield. Tired and afraid, Jaeger held onto his TC's station to weather the fire storm of artillery shells.

Jaeger hadn't slept a wink all night. He was operating on sheer nerve and fear, his senses at their highest pitch. Wearing his chemical mask as a precaution against enemy gas shells added to his misery.

Colwell continued to scan for targets.

KARRUMMP! The impact from each artillery round made the tank shudder. Suddenly dust trails appeared in Colwell's tank sights.

"Are they enemy or friendly?" Jaeger questioned, trying to scream above the roar of the shells blasting outside.

"I can't tell!" Colwell said, his voice muffled by the microphone of his protective mask. "IDENTIFIED! T-72s."

The enemy artillery fire began to roll off, away from Jaeger's position.

"GUNNER, SABOT, THREE TANKS," Jaeger yelled through the tank's intercom system. "FIRE!"

BOOM! Jaeger's tank recoiled from the firing of the tank's 105mm cannon. The sabot round tore through the air and impacted on the turret of a T-72. The tank, 1,900 meters away from Jaeger's position, jerked to a halt, its turret ripped off in a terrific explosion.

The rest of the platoon was firing independently, as rapidly as they could reload, aim, and fire again. White cloudlike smoke hung low in the morning air over the battlefield. Tanks and BMPs were racing south as fast as they could travel over the rough terrain, taking advantage of the poor visibility.

The M1 tank gunners, using their thermal sights, saw the enemy in spite of the smoke and opened fire with devastating accuracy. The enemy, firing in volleys at the defenders, returned fire with much less success. One enemy vehicle after another was destroyed. The pace of the drive south was hampered as BMPs and tanks slowed down and turned to avoid the wreckage that blocked the approaches to the south.

A platoon of T-72 tanks broke from the main direction of advance and pivoted in the direction of Jaeger's position. The enemy platoon made a paradelike turn and rapidly formed a firing line. Firing as they moved, the T-72s charged at Jaeger's M1s with their 125mm cannons, firing as fast as the automatic loaders could push another round into the breech.

Taking control of the turret override controls, Jaeger swung the main gun hard left.

Roll the dice.

If the total of the two dice is five or less, go to Section 63.

If the total of the two dice is six or more, go to Section 83.

Section 78

Time was slipping away. Jaeger called Sergeant Riley on the radio and gave him an update of the situation. Jaeger ordered Riley to switch to the battalion command net and take command if he lost contact with Jaeger. He then called Lieutenant Colonel Brown.

"Victor Two Zero, this is Zulu One One. Over," Jaeger reported.

"Zulu One One, this is Victor Two Zero," Lieutenant Colonel Brown answered.

"I am down to six vehicles. I suspect that the enemy will attack along the alpha or bravo . . . I say again . . . alpha or bravo avenue. I will move to Checkpoint Two to cover the main avenue of approach. I need to maintain my team in position to verify the direction of the enemy's attack. I say again, request permission to keep everyone in position. I recommend that you shoot at anything that moves south. Over."

"Roger, Zulu One One," Brown replied, pausing for a moment. "I concur. I will alert all elements that you will stay in position. Over."

"Wilco," Jaeger answered. "Moving now to Checkpoint Two. Out."

"All Zulu stations, this is Zulu One One," Jaeger said methodically over his radio. "Stay in position and continue the mission. I am moving to Checkpoint Two. Out."

Jaeger's movement to Checkpoint 2 was slow and deliberate. He knew that he was alone and he didn't want to fall into an enemy ambush. He directed Jones to move forward several hundred meters, halt, and then scan the area carefully.

Jones eased the tank to a slow stop in a good firing position overlooking the terrain to their front.

"Shit! There's a BMP . . . GUNNER . . . ," Jaeger exclaimed, seeing an enemy BMP moving at them not 200 meters ahead.

BOOM! Jaeger fired his 105mm cannon from the TC override control without completing a fire command. Jaeger, surprised by the encounter as much as the enemy was, missed the lead BMP by inches.

Jaeger's crew sprung into action like a rattlesnake ready to strike. The actions of the crew were automatic. Curn reloaded a HEAT round into the massive breech of the 105mm cannon. Colwell, now in control of the gun, aimed with a vengeance, determined to kill the enemy.

"ON THE WAY!" Colwell screamed.

BOOM! The second round was more accurate. The shot hit the BMP directly in its center of mass. The HEAT round burned into the vehicle with awesome intensity, blowing apart the BMP in a terrific explosion. The enemy vehicle disintegrated into a burning mass of metal and flesh.

"TARGET!" Jaeger announced, also bent on revenge. He had a personal score to settle. "LOAD SABOT. LEFT BMP. FIRE!"

"ON THE WAY!" Colwell aimed at the left BMP that was now trying to break for cover. At this range he could not miss.

BOOM! The hypervelocity shell hit the second BMP in the right front side. The energy from the projectile spun the vehicle sideways. It too began to burn.

"Colwell!" Jaeger yelled. "Where did the third one go? Get him!"

The third BMP fired its 30mm cannon at A31. The gun raked the side of the M1, hitting the left side track but not stopping the tank. Colwell fired again.

BOOM! The third BMP was destroyed, its small turret ripped off and thrown on the ground by the tremendous power of the 105mm sabot round.

"Got the sucker!" Colwell screamed with delight. The second BMP now exploded, its fuel igniting. The BMP's crew frantically tried to abandon their vehicle and avoid the flames. Colwell switched to the coax machine gun and finished them off.

And then it was quiet. No one said a word for a very long time. Jaeger and Colwell, subdued and tired, watched the fires created by their handiwork.

Jaeger's tank limped into a position near Checkpoint 2 at 0425. Apparently, A31 took several 30mm hits that damaged two road wheels on the left side. Unwilling to stop, Jaeger continued on to Checkpoint 2.

The move to Checkpoint 2 took another twenty minutes because of A31's damaged suspension. As soon as they arrived, Jaeger directed

Jones to occupy a hasty fighting position. Stoically, Jaeger's crew found a good position from which they could meet the enemy regiment.

The left track busted in two just as A31 pulled into position on Checkpoint 2. At least they had a great view of the alpha avenue of approach.

Go to Section 86.

Section 79

Jaeger didn't have time for a fire command. The enemy tank was less than 500 meters away. He fired the gun himself, from the TC's override. His aim was good. The T-72 absorbed the round right in the front, under the cannon. The tank, which had been racing at Jaeger at top speed, swung violently to its right and slammed into a ditch.

Jaeger observed to his left, swinging the turret over the right side of the hull. A blinding flash, an explosion not five feet to his front, threw him to the back of the TC's station.

"What the hell!" Colwell shouted angrily. "Curn, check the gun."

"Jones, back up!" Jaeger screamed as he hit all banks of his smoke grenade projectors. "Keep going."

The tank took a direct hit in the gun tube, cutting the barrel in two right above the driver's hatch. Another round whistled by A31, missing by inches, as the tank churned up the sand and powered rearward.

"The main gun is gone, Lieutenant," Curn reported over the intercom.

CRRAAASSHHH! A tremendous explosion rocked the tank. The force of the impact pushed the tank into a ditch and over onto its left side. Thrown around inside, the crew took a beating from the sudden stop.

Jaeger blacked out.

*   *   *

"Sir . . . sir. Are you all right?" Colwell said, looking down at his wounded platoon leader.

"What? Huh . . . Where is . . . ?" Jaeger struggled to regain consciousness. Pain surged all through his body. He couldn't feel his shoulder. He opened his eyes to see Colwell. Blood caked the left side of Colwell's face.

The sounds of battle were distant. A31, on its side and silent, lay broken and useless.

"Sir, hang in there," Colwell said. "Curn and Jones are dead. I don't know about the rest of the company. I haven't seen any friendlies lately. We are all that's left. We got to get out of here. Can you walk?"

"I don't know. Help me up," Jaeger said, wincing at the effort to sit up.

As Colwell struggled with his wounded platoon leader, a squad of enemy soldiers appeared beside the rear of the overturned tank.

The enemy soldier in charge screamed at Colwell and gestured with his AK-74 rifle.

Colwell instinctively put up his hands. Jaeger, unable to rise, simply closed his eyes. Jaeger and Colwell were both taken prisoner.

The Threat regiment drove relentlessly to the rear of the American defenses. Because of the success achieved in this zone, the Threat division commander committed his second echelon regiments to the same axis. The situation for the Americans was disastrous. Unable to stop the enemy drive, the entire American division was in jeopardy of being defeated.

Go to Section 44.

Section 80

Jaeger knew that time was critical. Calling Sergeant Young on the radio, he ordered him to switch to the battalion command net and talk directly to the battalion commander once he confirmed the direction of the enemy's main attack. Jaeger radioed Lieutenant Colonel Brown.

"Victor Two Zero, this is Zulu One One. Over," Jaeger reported.

"Zulu One One, this is Victor Two Zero," Lieutenant Colonel Brown replied.

"I have completed the counterreconnaissance mission. I suspect that the enemy will attack down the Ohio or New York avenue of approach. I say again, Ohio or New York. Charlie elements will stay in position to verify. I recommend that you make your displacements accordingly. Over."

"Roger, Zulu One One," Brown replied quickly. "I concur. Move your tanks back to A12. I will alert all elements to hold fire until you report set in A12. Over."

"Wilco," Jaeger answered. "Moving now. Out."

Jaeger crossed Phase Line France with his four tanks, the two mortar tracks, and Lieutenant Rogers's FIST vehicle at 0450. Just as he was crossing France, all radio transmissions ceased. He quickly switched to his designated alternate frequencies but found these too were controlled by jamming. The enemy must be barrage jamming every frequency, he thought to himself. The attack must be on!

KARRUMMP! As if to confirm Jaeger's suspicions, the earth behind Jaeger's column suddenly erupted in a flash of fire and flying steel. Artillery smashed into Team Charlie in battle position C11. Jaeger and his crew immediately donned their NBC protective masks.

KARRUMMP! KARRUMMP! The amount of artillery fire was overpowering. Anyone caught out in the open was instantly killed. Armored vehicles, dug into the hard desert ground by bulldozers, survived fairly well. Those infantrymen who did not prepare adequate overhead cover for their foxholes and fighting positions, however, did not live long enough to regret their error.

Team Jaeger, minus the scouts, arrived on battle position A12 at 0520. The artillery fell there as they arrived.

KABOOM! One of the mortars, moving into a hasty position, took a direct hit from an enemy 152mm artillery projectile. The inside of the aluminum M106 mortar carrier echoed with the strike of the round. The vehicle stopped abruptly, jumped into the air slightly, and shuddered to a complete halt. The rear ramp was blown open by the force of the explosion, throwing the insides of the vehicle—material and human—in all directions. There were no survivors of the shattered mortar track.

Unable to talk to his unit by radio, and buttoned up by the power of the enemy's artillery, Jaeger prayed that his tanks would operate without orders and do what was necessary.

Taking a position on the western side of battle position A12, Jaeger's platoon occupied the right side of the bow-shaped company position. Jaeger moved into a hasty hull-down position and used a small rise to mask the front of his vehicle. Looking through his vision blocks, he saw another tank, probably Ramos's, to his left.

KARRUMMP! KARRUMMP! The noise was unbearable. Jaeger struggled uncomfortably to see the battlefield. The smoke, the smell of burning diesel fuel, and the concussion from the artillery shells dominated the crew's senses. Jaeger's chest tightened; it was difficult to think, hard to breathe. He looked through his vision blocks in search of the enemy.

Colwell continued to move the turret back and forth and scan for targets with his thermal sight.

KARRUMMP! KARRUMMP! The impact from each artillery round made the tank shudder. The battlefield was now covered in white smoke.

Suddenly dust trails appeared in Colwell's tank sights.

"Are they enemy or friendly?" Jaeger questioned, trying to scream above the roar of the shells blasting outside. "I don't want to fire on any of our guys moving to subsequent positions."

"I can't tell!" Colwell said, his voice muffled by the microphone of his protective mask. "Wait. IDENTIFIED! T-72s."

"GUNNER, SABOT, THREE TANKS," Jaeger yelled through the tank's intercom system. "FIRE!"

BOOM! Jaeger's tank recoiled backward from the firing of the tank's 105mm cannon. The shell, screaming through the air, hit its mark. The T-72 tank, 900 meters away from Jaeger's position, jerked to a halt, its turret ripped off in a terrific explosion.

BOOM! BOOM! The rest of the platoon was firing madly, furiously. The enemy artillery fire slackened, rolling away from Jaeger's position. The T-72 tanks and BMPs were racing south as fast as they could travel over the rough terrain. Firing in volleys at the defenders, their accuracy was poor.

BOOM! Another T-72 was hit and burst into flames.

Amazingly, the enemy tanks and BMPs stopped moving and took up hasty firing positions. They aimed in all directions, returning fire against the cauldron of death that surrounded them on three sides. Firing in volleys, they pummeled Team Bravo on battle position B12 with their 125mm and 30mm cannonfire. In spite of the heavy smoke, Jaeger saw Team Bravo fighting desperately, taking hits but giving more than they received.

"The colonel must have moved Team Bravo to battle position B12," Jaeger said to Colwell over the intercom as Colwell fired another round, smashing another BMP with a sabot round.

"Good shot, Colwell," Jaeger said excitedly. "They must not see us in the smoke. Keep pounding the bastards. Bravo Company needs our help."

The Threat attack stalled and died in front of Team Bravo's battle position B12. Team Bravo acted as the cork in the bottle. A flight of U.S. Marine Harrier jump jets raced over the battlefield and added to the regiment's destruction. Several HIND-D helicopters that appeared on the scene in the final moments of the battle were destroyed by the Harriers.

Almost 170 Threat vehicles littered the landscape along avenue of approach New York. It had all taken less than two hours.

The cost, however, had been high. The battalion was now at 65 percent strength. Team Bravo took the greatest losses and was reduced to five tanks and two Bradleys. Alpha Company lost two tanks from 1st Platoon and one from 2d Platoon. Jaeger lost A33. Ramos took a direct hit in the side of his turret from two T-72s just as he had moved into position on A12. The rounds penetrated the side turret armor and killed Ramos and the loader instantly. The driver and gunner survived. No one even knew Ramos was hit until after the battle.

The enemy's second echelon was stopped cold by long-range artillery, close air support, and Apache attack helicopters. The enemy made a few penetrations in other brigade sectors but were unable to exploit their success.

The enemy attack failed and the American defenses held.

Go to Section 81.

Section 81

Enemy reconnaissance operations usually begin well before friendly forces enter an area of operations. The patrols are small, move with stealth, and focus on detecting our positions and obstacles. In general, the enemy reconnaissance avoids a fight unless they encounter a critical target, such as a nuclear weapon facility, a key command and control unit, or a very important objective that is critical to the advance of the main force.

The counterreconnaissance force must prevent the enemy from seeing the preparation of positions and obstacles if the task force is to gain surprise. The weaker one's own force, the more essential surprise becomes. If the defender can surprise the attacker with well-placed defenses, and channelize him with well-concealed obstacles, surprise can work for the defender.

Effective counterreconnaissance demands aggressive planning that aims at destroying the enemy reconnaissance elements before they can be used effectively. The counterreconnaissance battle must be planned so as to use all available assets to detect the enemy reconnaissance elements early. If the enemy cannot be destroyed, he must be blinded.

If he cannot be blinded, he must be deceived. The counterreconnaissance battle must be won. It is the first step in gaining victory in a defensive battle.

The doctrine of the United States Army, called AirLand Battle, emphasizes decentralized battle tactics conducted by aggressive, competent junior leaders. These small unit leaders are expected to take advantage of enemy mistakes and act within the framework of the commander's intent to secure the mission.

The planning function of these leaders is vital to the execution of decentralized tactics. The leader transmits his intent and accomplishes the unit's mission through his plan. Tactical planning must, therefore, be precise enough to preserve synchronization throughout the battle and flexible enough to respond to changes or to capitalize on fleeting opportunities.

A military decision must be determined by the burning desire to beat the enemy and not by the wish to avoid defeat. Any decision that just avoids defeat is not enough. Aggressive action is required to achieve victory. Jaeger succeeded in commanding the counterreconnaissance battle. Enemy reconnaissance was not able to develop a true picture of the task force's defenses. Blinded by Team Jaeger, the enemy regiment was committed without adequate reconnaissance preparation and was defeated in detail. Unable to achieve success in penetrating the American lines, the Threats did not commit their follow-on echelons.

But Jaeger and the battalion took excessive casualties in this battle. The reason was Jaeger's inability to transmit the direction of the enemy's main attack soon enough and his inability to take advantage of the enemy's weaknesses in time. If Team Bravo had been moved several minutes earlier, they could have occupied their prepared positions and inflicted enemy casualties with fewer friendly losses.

You won, but you could have done better. Armed with this insight, go back to Section 34 and try again.

Section 82

"FIRE," Jaeger yelled.

BOOM! BOOM! BOOM! BOOM! Jaeger's sabot round was followed immediately by three more from the tanks in his platoon. A flash of flame hit the lead T-72. It crashed to a stop, its turret motionless. A split-second later a second 105mm round hit the same tank directly at the union of the turret and the hull. The turret shifted backward four feet and a huge fireball erupted from inside. The T-72's ammunition had ignited.

BOOM! BOOM! The other two T-72s were hit by Sergeant Riley and Sergeant Ramos. Next, two BMPs went up in flames, their twisted hulls thrown about like toys. The enemy didn't sense where the firing was coming from until it was too late.

Lieutenant Rogers fired two red and one green star cluster into the air to warn the battalion of the enemy's main attack. Although the normal FM frequencies were jammed, Rogers repeatedly attempted to contact the battalion fire support officer on his TACFIRE digital radio system. He was not sure that the information would reach the guns through this jamming, but he felt that it was worth a try.

The mortars, using direct aiming, fired as fast as they could drop their rounds into the mortar tubes. Their rounds added to the enemy's confusion and death.

BOOM! BOOM! BOOM! BOOM! Four more BMPs were hit. The kill zone near the southwestern point of Hill 955 was now clogged with wrecked Threat vehicles. The enemy, still racing south in battalion column formation, did not know where the firing was coming from. Looking forward, darting in and out of the thick smoke, no one thought to look to their rear.

BOOM! BOOM! BOOM! BOOM! Jaeger's gunners continued to destroy the attacking Threat column. An entire company of BMPs now lay in ruins in Jaeger's kill zone. Finally, a T-72 tank observed Jaeger's fire and returned fire with his 125mm cannon.

"They found us," Jaeger shouted to Colwell over the tank intercom. "Kill the tanks!"

Suddenly four more T-72 tanks appeared and turned their turrets in Jaeger's direction.

"GUNNER, SABOT, TANK," Jaeger shouted, swinging the gun over in the direction of the nearest enemy tank.

"IDENTIFIED!" Colwell replied.

Roll the dice.

If the total of the two dice is three or less, go to Section 74.

If the total of the two dice is four or more, go to Section 84.

Section 83

"FIRE AND ADJUST!" Jaeger commanded, screaming with excitement and fear.

BOOM! The tank jerked backward from the gun's recoil. The round shrieked forward, hitting an enemy tank in the front at the driver's compartment, stopping it in its tracks. Several other T-72s raced toward Jaeger's position. They were only 900 meters away now, and there were just too many of them.

BOOM! BOOM! Jaeger heard the sound of tank fire to his left. Looking through his vision blocks he saw Sergeant Riley's tank, firing repeatedly at the enemy tank formation.

"SABOT. LEFT TANK," Jaeger yelled, encouraged by the arrival of Riley.

Without waiting for the command to fire, Colwell fired the main gun as soon as he heard an "Up" from Curn. Curn was loading as fast as he could. The turret floor was filled with steel 105mm shell casings expended by the gun.

BOOM! Jaeger's round hit another T-72 but glanced off its excellent side armor due to the angle of the strike.

The enemy kept coming. Colwell identified more BMPs behind the tanks.

Three Threat tanks appeared within 700 meters of Jaeger's tank.

"IDENTIFIED, THREE TANKS," Colwell screamed, ready to fire.

"LEFT TANK, FIRE," Jaeger ordered. "Jones, move back after the second round."

BOOM! Colwell fired before Jaeger could complete his sentence to Jones. The hypervelocity round dissected the T-72 this time, sending its turret six feet into the air. Colwell instinctively moved his sights to the center tank, moving the turret quickly and firing as soon as his sights were set.

"TARGET, CENTER TANK," Jaeger yelled. "Jones, move out."

Jones raced the M1 engine as the tank lurched backward thirty feet.

Jaeger looked to his left and watched in horror as he saw Riley's tank take a direct hit from a T-72 125mm tank gun. The round struck the right front of the turret, right behind the tank commander and gunner's station. The tank shuddered from the strike and then sat motionless.

"Damn it!" Jaeger cried out loud, anger overcoming him. "Jones! Move forward. Let's get those sons of bitches. Colwell, ACTION RIGHT FRONT."

A31 popped back up to the small ridge and Colwell fired at the advancing enemy. There were plenty of targets to shoot at. Colwell hit a BMP with his first round and relayed the gun for another shot.

CRRAAASSHHH! A tremendous explosion rocked the tank. The force of the impact pushed the tank into a ditch and over onto its left side. Thrown around inside, the crew took a beating from the sudden stop. Jaeger hit hard against the side of the tank. He felt numb all over and finally lost consciousness.

Taking the route that his reconnaissance had proved to be lightly defended, the Threat commander drove his regiment relentlessly down axis California and into the rear of the American defenses. Captain Russell's men at A12 fought like demons. They destroyed almost an entire motorized rifle battalion.

Clouds of smoke hung low over the battle position. Burning Threat tanks and BMPs littered the area in front of Russell's tanks. But it wasn't enough. The second and third battalions of the regiment cut through Alpha Company in battle position A12 like a hot knife through butter.

The enemy overran Alpha Company and annihilated them before Lieutenant Colonel Brown could effectively support his outnumbered right flank. By 0750 the battle was over. The rest of the battalion was picked apart piecemeal while the main Threat columns streamed south. Because of the success achieved in this zone, the Threat division commander committed his second echelon regiments to the same axis. The situation for the Americans was disastrous. Unable to stop the Threat drive, the entire division was in jeopardy of being defeated.

Scores of Threat aircraft soared overhead, flying to strike targets deep behind American lines. There was a brief but futile fight between Threat aircraft and three U.S. Marine Corps Harrier jump jets. Outnumbered and outmatched, the Marines fought valiantly. Two Marine aircraft were finally shot down by the MiGs. The third, low on fuel, was chased away.

Then the HINDs, enemy antitank helicopters, appeared. These huge, heavily armed helicopters were built to act as flying tanks. They flew south, close to the ground, massive and unstoppable. They fired on the disorganized survivors of Jaeger's battalion who were fleeing to the south, trying to reach American lines.

The Americans took a terrible beating.

"Sir, sir, are you all right?" Colwell said, looking down at his platoon leader.

"What? Huh . . . where is . . . ?" Jaeger struggled to regain consciousness. Pain surged through his body. He couldn't feel his shoulder or his arms. He opened his eyes to see Colwell. Blood caked the left side of Colwell's face.

The sounds of battle were distant. A31, on its side and silent, lay broken and defeated.

"Sir. For God's sake, don't die," Colwell pleaded. "Curn and Jones are dead. I don't know about the rest of the company. I think that we are the only ones left. We have got to get out of here. Can you walk?"

"I don't know. Help me up," Jaeger said, wincing in pain at the effort to sit up.

As Colwell struggled with his wounded platoon leader, a squad of enemy soldiers appeared beside the rear of the overturned tank. The enemy soldier in charge screamed at the Americans and fired his rifle in the dirt next to Colwell to show that he meant business.

Colwell instinctively put up his hands. Jaeger, lying on his back, merely closed his eyes. Both were taken prisoner. For Jaeger, the war was over.

Jaeger failed in his mission. Go to Section 34 and try again!

Section 84

"FIRE!" Jaeger commanded.

BOOM! The tank recoiled from the explosion of the 105mm round. The sabot shell screamed forward, hitting an enemy tank in the front, stopping it in its tracks. Two more T-72 tanks charged toward Jaeger's position. They fired their huge 125mm cannons as they raced at Jaeger. They were less than 900 meters away now, and there were just too many of them.

KARRUMMP! KARRUMMP! The area around axis California was obscured in fire, smoke, and dust. The sky was filled with explosions. Shells burst overhead and shot forth a scattering array of antitank bomblets on top of the enemy regiment.

KARRUMMP! KARRUMMP! Shell after shell exploded, perforating the Threat vehicles from above and stopping them in their tracks.

Lieutenant Colonel Brown worked through the jamming and directed the artillery to unleash its deadly effects at the exact right spot.

BOOM! BOOM! Jaeger and his platoon kept up the fire. Anything moving past the tip of Hill 955, southwest of Checkpoint 2, was devastated by their accurate tank gunnery. Soon, there were few vehicles left to shoot at.

Jaeger's action had disrupted the enemy's timetable. Stacked up behind the destroyed regiment, the enemy follow-on echelons were slaughtered by a combined assault of long-range rocket artillery, A-10 close air support aircraft, and Apache attack helicopters.

The enemy regiment had been crushed. More than 170 burned-out and destroyed BMPs, T-72 tanks, and self-propelled artillery pieces lay scattered in clumps along axis California. The Americans had won a great victory.

Go to Section 50.

Section 85

Jaeger knew the value of time and he didn't want to waste a second. He knew that he must move to a good position to determine the main avenue of the enemy's attack. He radioed Lieutenant Colonel Brown.

"Victor Two Zero, this is Zulu One One. Over," Jaeger reported.

"Zulu One One, this is Victor Two Zero," Lieutenant Colonel Brown replied.

"I have completed the counterreconnaissance mission. I suspect that the enemy will attack down the Ohio or New York avenue of approach. I say again, Ohio or New York. I want to stay in position with all elements to verify the avenue of approach. Over."

"Roger, Zulu One One," Brown replied quickly. "I concur. I will alert all elements that you will not be moving back to A12. Over."

"Wilco," Jaeger answered. "Over."

"I'll give you all the artillery fire that I can." Brown hesitated, as if searching for additional words and not finding any. "Good luck, Zulu One One. Out."

Jaeger formed his tanks into a horseshoe-shaped position at Checkpoint 10, with A31 and A32 looking northeast and A33 and A34 orienting west. All of his tanks were set in their positions by 0450.

Jaeger tried to call the battalion commander but received no reply.

Attempting another call to Sergeant Riley, he discovered that his radio could neither transmit nor receive. Checking his radio carefully, Jaeger determined that the enemy was jamming his FM frequency. Attempting to go to alternate frequencies was not effective. Jaeger received the same white noise sound. The enemy must be jamming every frequency, he thought. The attack must be on!

Karrummp! Karrummp! As if to confirm Jaeger's suspicions, the earth suddenly erupted in a flash of fire and steel four kilometers to the south of Jaeger's position. Artillery landed on the forward positions of Team Charlie in battle position C11. Unable to talk to his unit by radio, Jaeger prayed that his tanks would fight effectively without direction.

From his position on the eastern side of Checkpoint 10, Jaeger had a commanding view of the Utah and Ohio avenues of approach. Looking through his hatch, which he had adjusted to the open protected position, he could see Johnson to his right.

Suddenly dust trails appeared in Colwell's tank sights.

"Identified! T-72s," Colwell shouted.

"GUNNER, SABOT, THREE TANKS," Jaeger yelled through the tank's intercom system. Colwell aimed at the lead tank, almost 1,400 meters away.

"FIRE!"

BOOM! Jaeger's tank jumped backward from the recoil of the tank's 105mm cannon. The shell, screaming through the air, hit its mark. The enemy tank jerked to a halt, its turret blown off in a terrific explosion. Riley and Ramos heard the firing and moved to Jaeger's left, taking positions slightly uphill from their platoon leader.

The entire platoon was now firing independently as fast as they could fire. Still unable to control his fires by radio, Jaeger watched with pride as his platoon took apart the lead company of the enemy column.

Enemy T-72 tanks and BMPs were racing south as fast as they could travel over the rough desert terrain. Jaeger's gunners had excellent flank shots at them. Another T-72 burst into flames.

Firing in volleys at the Americans, the second enemy company attacked into Jaeger's position. The enemy armored vehicles fired as they moved, but their accuracy was poor. The enemy, 900 meters away, was now closing on Jaeger's position.

BOOM! BOOM! BOOM! Another group of enemy tanks lay burning to the east of Checkpoint 10. The lead T-72s were so close now that they were difficult to miss.

The enemy's main attack, with two reinforced motorized rifle battalions, came down avenue of approach Ohio. The supporting attack, with one battalion attacking along avenue of approach Utah, was dismembered by Jaeger's platoon. Smoke covered the battlefield. The enemy artillery concentrated on battle position B13, taking a serious toll on Team Bravo's tanks and Bradleys.

"The colonel must have moved Team Bravo to battle position B13," Jaeger said to Colwell over the intercom.

BOOM! Colwell fired another round at the enemy. "The smoke is working to our advantage. They can't see us but we can see them. Keep firing!"

Amazingly, the enemy tanks and BMPs stopped moving and took up hasty firing positions in front of battle position D11. They oriented south. Firing in volleys, they pummeled the position to the south with fire. But the American tanks and Bradleys on battle position D11 were well dug in and their return fire took a serious toll on the enemy.

Stalled along axis Ohio, the enemy switched his main effort to axis Utah. Tanks began streaming down axis Utah and soon impaled themselves against Jaeger's platoon. Firing in volleys, the enemy attempted to bust through the gauntlet of fire created by Jaeger's tanks at Checkpoint 10. With the enemy rushing Checkpoint 10 at maximum speed, Jaeger's tanks were close to being overrun.

Three T-72s fired at A33 from less than 400 meters. Two rounds missed. One hit Ramos's tank, sending hot molten steel into the turret and hitting the ammunition storage bins.

Jaeger and Riley returned fire and got all three of the T-72s. Johnson fired and killed a ZSU 23-4 self-propelled air defense weapon that was trying to move around a burning BMP. So far, 3d Platoon had destroyed fifteen Threat tanks, three BMPs, and a ZSU 23-4.

But Jaeger was taking casualties. A33 was ablaze. The ammunition compartment began to smoke and burn vigorously. Finally the ammunition ignited, sending a huge orange fireball forty feet into the air.

Fortunately for Ramos and his crew, the M1's ammunition compartment was designed to protect the crew. If the ammunition exploded, the force shot straight up, through the blast panels in the turret roof. Ramos, dazed and superficially wounded from the explosion, but alive, ordered his crew to evacuate the tank. They jumped out and ran over to an erosion ditch twenty-five meters away from their burning tank.

"FIRE!" Jaeger commanded.

BOOM! The tank recoiled from the explosion of the 105mm round. The sabot shell screamed forward, hitting an enemy tank in the front, stopping it in its tracks. Two more T-72 tanks charged toward Jaeger's position. They fired their huge 125mm cannons as they raced at Jaeger. They were right on top of him now, and there were just too many of them.

KARRUMMP! KARRUMMP! The area around axis Utah was obscured in fire, smoke, and dust. The sky was filled with explosions. Shells burst overhead and shot forth a scattering array of antitank bomblets on top of the enemy regiment.

"IDENTIFIED, THREE TANKS," Colwell screamed, ready to fire.

"LEFT TANK, FIRE," Jaeger ordered. "Jones, move back after the second round."

BOOM! Colwell fired before Jaeger could complete his sentence to Jones. The hypervelocity round dissected the T-72 this time, sending its turret six feet into the air. Colwell instinctively moved his sights to the center tank, moving the turret quickly and firing as soon as his sights were set.

"TARGET, CENTER TANK," Jaeger yelled. "Jones, move out."

Jones raced the M1 engine as the tank lurched backward thirty feet.

KARRUMMP! KARRUMMP! Shell after shell exploded, perforating the Threat vehicles from above and stopping them in their tracks.

Lieutenant Colonel Brown worked through the jamming and directed the artillery to unleash its deadly effects at the exact right spot.

The enemy drive was stalled in front of battle position B13 and defeated in front of battle position C11. The combined fires of three company teams, Bravo, Delta, and Charlie, devastated the enemy's advancing columns. A flight of U.S. Marine Harrier jump jets raced over the battlefield and added to the regiment's destruction. Several HIND-D helicopters appeared on the scene in the final moments of the battle and were destroyed by the Harriers with air-to-air missiles.

In less than two hours, the battle was over. More than 100 Threat vehicles littered the landscape along avenues of approach Ohio and Utah.

The enemy's first echelon regiment had been defeated. The regiment, with only seventy vehicles or so left, broke off the attack and withdrew to the north. The Threat second echelon was not committed because a breakthrough was not achieved.

This delay allowed the U.S division commander to launch a devastating spoiling attack on the second echelon with long-range rocket artillery, A-10 close air support aircraft, and Apache attack helicopters. Losing more of his force to this deep attack, the Threat division commander withdrew his remaining forces to the north. The enemy attack had failed and the American line held.

The cost was high but the enemy had been stopped. Lieutenant Colonel Brown's Task Force 3-69 was now at 80 percent strength and would need reinforcements in both personnel and equipment. Team Bravo took the greatest losses, including the deaths of the company commander and many of the officers. Bravo Company was reduced to seven tanks and two Bradleys. Delta Company lost two tanks and three Bradleys.

Go to Section 81.

Section 86

Jaeger was sure that the enemy would be coming down one of the western approaches. He radioed the battalion commander that the enemy would probably take one of the two western avenues of approach. Based on Jaeger's report, the battalion commander moved Delta Company to battle position D12 to reinforce the threatened area, in anticipation of the enemy attack.

"We may be stuck here," Jaeger said to his crew over the tank intercom, "but we sure can take a lot of them with us. At least we accomplished our mission."

Jaeger and his crew stoically prepared to meet the onslaught of an enemy regiment.

At 0450 Jaeger tried to reach the battalion commander on the radio but there was no response. Jaeger quickly disconnected his antenna cable and then tried switching frequencies. Nothing worked. The enemy must be jamming every frequency, he thought. The attack must be on!

Karrummp! Karrummp! Battle positions B12 and C11 suddenly

exploded in flashes of fire and white-hot steel. Hundreds of small but deadly bomblets, dispersed in the air by exploding enemy artillery shells, landed all over the forward positions of Team Charlie in battle position C11.

Poor bastards, Jaeger thought. They were really taking a beating. Unable to talk to anyone on the radio, he waited and watched.

Minutes passed. The artillery fell farther south. Something was wrong. No vehicles appeared in Colwell's sights. Jaeger, scanning the horizon with his binoculars, saw no movement down the expected avenue of approach. The regimental attack must be going down somewhere else, but where? He turned his binoculars to the southeast and watched in horror as a full motorized rifle regiment attacked in force along the eastern side of the battalion's sector. Three reinforced motorized rifle battalions—a total of more than 170 armored fighting vehicles—barreled south at top speed. Supported by an overwhelming amount of artillery fire, the Threat regiment headed straight for battle position A12.

Opposing an entire regiment with only two platoons of M1 tanks was Alpha Company. Captain Russell's tanks opened up on the enemy at maximum range. They fought like demons. The flashes from Russell's tank guns soon grew sporadic, but their deadly accuracy was taking its toll on the lead formation. Destroyed enemy vehicles began to pile up in front of the outnumbered Alpha Company position.

Clouds of smoke hung low over the battlefield. Looking through his binoculars, Jaeger could see burning Threat tanks and BMPs. But it wasn't enough. The enemy wasn't stopping. The second and third battalions of the regiment pushed forward through the wreckage of burning vehicles and overran Russell's position.

Jaeger sadly watched the battle from his position on Checkpoint 2. Bypassed and alone, he could do little to influence the battle. The firing on Alpha Company's battle position stopped. The fate of the company was clear. Alpha Company was gone.

By 0750 the battle was over. Threat columns streamed south. A steady stream of enemy tanks, BMPs, and antiaircraft vehicles raced in long, fast-moving columns. Occasionally an enemy tank or a BMP would fire its main gun or machine guns at a lone surviving American vehicle that had managed to escape the initial carnage of the breakthrough regiment. These futile battles were very one-sided and Jaeger watched in horror as one American vehicle after another went up in flames.

Section 86

Scores of Threat aircraft soared overhead, flying to strike targets deep behind American lines. There was a brief but futile fight between seven Threat aircraft and three U.S. Marine Corps Harrier jump jets. Outnumbered and outmatched, the Marines fought valiantly. Two Marine aircraft were finally shot down by the MiGs. The third Marine Harrier was chased away.

After the MiGs came the HINDs, large and powerful antitank helicopters. These huge, heavily armed helicopters were built to act as flying tanks. They sought out and fired on the few survivors of Jaeger's task force who were still alive and now fleeing to the south. With no air defense to oppose them, the HINDs had an easy time picking off their prey. The HINDs' precision guided missiles struck one American vehicle after another. More HINDs continued on, flying south, supporting the movement of the breakthrough forces.

Jaeger felt sick. He had failed in his mission. His tank was unable to move and he was now well behind the front lines. He and his crew were alive, but without support their chances for survival in the hot desert were slim. Rumor had it that the enemy didn't take prisoners. Was that true or just a rumor? Jaeger wasn't sure.

Jaeger failed in his mission. Go to Section 34 and try again!

Section 87

Jaeger knew that Curn didn't stand a chance unless he could get him to medical care soon. He checked his radio and found that the antenna matching unit had been shot away. Jaeger tried several times to make radio contact with any other station, but had no luck.

"Great. That's all we need," Jaeger said, taking off his CVC helmet and slamming it down on the turret floor. "We won't do anyone any good here. Colwell, grab your gear. Make a litter for Curn and let's get the hell out of here."

"Yes, sir," Colwell replied quietly, looking at Curn, whom he held in his arms. Placing Curn down gently on the turret floor, he climbed out of the hatch.

In several minutes they had constructed a litter out of ponchos and gun tube rammer staffs. The crew worked together to get Curn out of the tank as carefully as possible. Try as they could, the job of lifting the injured man out of the tank turret without causing him more pain was impossible. Curn screamed in agony as one of his wounded arms hit the roof of the turret. Finally, Jaeger, Colwell, and Jones manhandled their wounded comrade to the desert floor, placing him as gently as possible on the poncho litter.

"You two take Curn behind those rocks over there," Jaeger said, pointing to a place 200 meters away, "while I destroy the tank."

Jaeger climbed into the turret and loaded a HEAT round. He then climbed out of the turret and carefully walked over onto the back deck. He opened an engine access plate on the back deck of the tank, pulled the pin on a thermite grenade, and placed the grenade next to the engine. Then he jumped off and dove for cover.

Five seconds later, the grenade went off, exploding in a bright silvery white fountain of melting steel. The grenade burned through the tank's turbine engine, destroying the tank's power plant. While the tank engine was burning, Jaeger ran to the front of the tank and threw a grenade down the gun tube to finish off the job. The HEAT round, chambered in the gun's breech, exploded, destroying the gun and the inside of the turret.

From the protection of their ditch, the crew of A31 sadly watched the tank burn.

"OK, saddle up," Jaeger said to his crew. "Colwell, you and Jones carry the stretcher while I get us headed in the right direction."

They began the long walk back to friendly lines. Jaeger took turns with Jones and Colwell carrying Curn. Moaning at first, Curn grew quieter as the soldiers continued to walk south toward the U.S. positions. The blackness of the night was giving way to an eerie twilight. Jaeger looked at his watch . . . 0500.

TATATATASHRESHESHEAK. The sound of incoming artillery engulfed them.

KARRUMMP! The earth shook from the terrific explosion of an artillery round, 200 meters from Jaeger and his men. Everyone hit the ground immediately, startled by the near miss and dropping the litter. Curn hit the ground hard but didn't utter a sound.

KARRUMMP! KARRUMMP! Artillery was landing everywhere—big 152mm shells. The ground shuddered with each impact. The high explosives burst on the hard, rocky desert, sending their lethal shards in every direction. The air whistled with steel and the crash of the explosions.

"I've got to get out of here! We are all going to die!" Jones screamed, out of control. He stood up as if to run, and a burst of shrapnel cut him in half. His limp remains fell to the ground.

KARRUMMP! Jaeger and Colwell clawed at the ground in horror and tried to get lower into the safety of the earth. They could barely breathe from the concussion caused by the explosions. Noise, dust, and dirt overwhelmed their senses. There was nothing they could do. There was no place to hide, no cover to crawl to. The shelling did not stop.

They had walked into an enemy artillery strike. It was their final act. A 152mm shell landed right between Jaeger and Colwell. For them the war was over. Forever.

Go to Section 44.

Section 88

"You did one hell of a job, Jaeger," Lieutenant Colonel Brown said, patting Sam on the back. "You are a natural soldier and I am very proud of you. But I've got some bad news."

"That's right, Sam," Captain Russell said, looking solemn and serious.

Second Lieutenant Sam Jaeger looked nervously around at his platoon. The men of 3d Platoon stood around him in a semicircle as Captain Russell and Lieutenant Colonel Brown addressed him. Sergeant Riley stood there grinning, acting like an expecting father.

"Sir, I don't understand," Jaeger said. "What do you mean, bad news?"

"Well, *Captain* Jaeger, for one thing," the colonel said with a grin, "you are out of uniform." The colonel reached over with his right hand, magically produced a small pocket knife, and cut off Jaeger's cloth second lieutenant's bar.

"Put this on," Captain Russell said with a wide smile. "It fits you better." Russell pinned the shiny silver captain's bars on Jaeger's collar.

"But now for the bad news," Brown continued. "As you know, Captain Bergnar, the Bravo Company commander, was killed yesterday. There is only one officer left in his company—Lieutenant Phillips. You will take command, effective immediately."

"Command? Sir . . ." Jaeger hesitated. The thought of leaving his platoon raced through his mind. "Sir, I'm not qualified . . . I . . ."

"Bull!" Brown interrupted. "The United States is at war. We don't have a large supply of qualified captains. I need you in Bravo Company, now, and I can't wait two months to get a replacement. The rank goes with the job. Besides, you don't have a choice. Those men need a commander. Report to Bravo Company by 1700 today."

"But, sir," Jaeger continued, "what about my platoon?" Jaeger was stunned. Riley was grinning so hard that his face hurt.

"Sam has got a good point, sir. It may be a long time before we get replacement officers," Russell said to Colonel Brown. "I can't wait forever for a new lieutenant. What about a replacement for Jaeger?"

"I've got a solution for that, too," Lieutenant Colonel Brown said. "Second Lieutenant Riley, front and center!"

Section 88

"Now wait a minute, sir," Riley protested, his grin totally absent now.

"That's the ticket," Jaeger said, laughing. "It's about time this platoon got itself some real leadership!"

Captain Jaeger reported to Bravo Company at 1700 as ordered. He knew that there was plenty of work to do before he was ready to command effectively. It wasn't easy taking over a tank company, especially after most of the officers had been killed or wounded. He also knew that it wouldn't be long before his company would be back in the fight. Replacements were coming in every day. There was training to organize and tanks to inspect. The war wouldn't slow down for Jaeger. Tomorrow's mission might decide the entire war.

But that is another story.

Appendix A

Weapons Data

QUICK REFERENCE TO WEAPON RANGES

THREAT	
Weapon	**Max Effective Range** (in meters)
T-80 Tank 125mm gun	2,100 m
T-72 Tank 125mm gun	2,100 m
BMP-2 30 mm cannon	2-4,000 m
AT-4 Spigot ATGM	2,000 m
AT-5 Spandrel ATGM	4,000 m
AT-8 Songster ATGM	4,000 m

UNITED STATES	
Weapon	**Max Effective Range** (in meters)
M1A1 Tank 120 mm gun	2,500 m
M1 Tank 105 mm gun	2,500 m
M3 CFV 25 mm cannon	
High Explosive ammo	3,000 m
Anti vehicle (APDS)	1,700 m
TOW ATGM	3,750 m
M106 Mortar Carrier	6,800 m HIGH EXPLOSIVE
107 mm mortar	5.490 m ILLUMINATION

Soviet

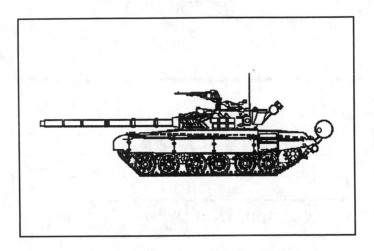

T-80 Main Battle Tank

Armament - 125mm smoothbore hypervelocity cannon.

Main Gun Maximum Effective Range - 2,500 meters.

AT-8 Songster Tank-Launched Antitank Guided Missile (ATGM) -
Maximum effective range is approximately 4,000 meters. The Songster is a radio frequency–guided ATGM designed to destroy enemy antitank missile launchers.

Combat Weight - 42 metric tons.

Engine - Turbine, 900–980 horsepower.

Armor - Enhanced reactive armor over special laminated base armor. The T-80 has more effective armor protection than the T-72 tank.

Crew - 3: commander, driver, and gunner. (Both the T-80 and T-72 Soviet tanks use an automatic mechanical loading device.)

Basic Load of Ammunition - 40 125mm rounds.

Secondary Armament - 12.7mm turret-mounted machine gun and one 7.62mm machine gun mounted coaxially with the main gun.

Fire Control System - Laser range finder and image intensification sights.

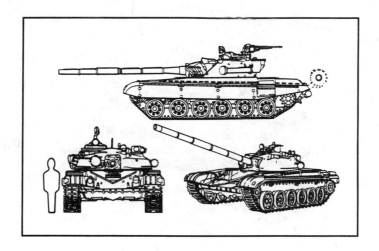

T-72 Main Battle Tank

Armament - 125mm smoothbore hypervelocity cannon.
Main Gun Maximum Effective Range - 2,500 meters.
Combat Weight - 41 metric tons.
Engine - V-12, 780-horsepower diesel.
Armor - Very effective enhanced armor, with reactive armor boxes attached that defeat infantry ATGM and HEAT missiles.
Crew - 3: commander, driver, and gunner. (This tank uses an automatic mechanical loading device.)
Basic Load of Ammunition - 40 125mm rounds.
Secondary Armament - 12.7mm turret-mounted machine gun and one 7.62mm machine gun mounted coaxially with the main gun.
Fire Control System - Laser range finder and active infrared night sights.

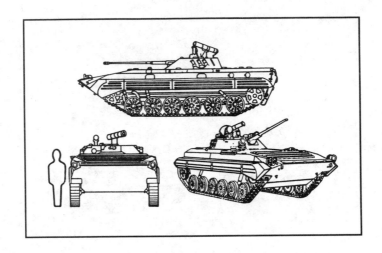

BMP-2

Armament - 30mm automatic cannon.

30mm Gun Maximum Effective Range - 1,500 meters.

Tube-Launched Antitank Guided Missile (ATGM) Maximum Effective Range - Two types can be mounted: AT-4 = 2,000 meters; AT-5 = 4,000 meters.

Combat Weight - 13.5 metric tons.

Engine - V-6, 290-horsepower diesel.

Armor - 19 inches of magnesium steel alloy in the hull, 23 inches in the turret.

Crew - 3: commander, gunner, and driver. Carries a 9-man infantry squad.

Basic Load of Ammunition - 700 30mm rounds.

Secondary Armament - AT-4 Spigot or AT-5 Spandrel tubed-launched ATGM mounted on the turret.

Fire Control System - Optical range finder and image intensification sights.

RPG-16

Soviet Antitank Guided Missile (ATGM) and Rocket-Propelled Grenade (RPG) Effects

	RANGE	CREW	WARHEAD	EFFECT AGAINST US M1A1 TANK
AT-5 Spandrel	4,000 meters	2	HEAT	KILL
AT-4 Spigot	2,000 meters	1	HEAT	KILL
RPG-16	800 meters	1	HEAT	MOBILITY KILL
RPG-18	300 meters	1	HEAT	MOBILITY KILL

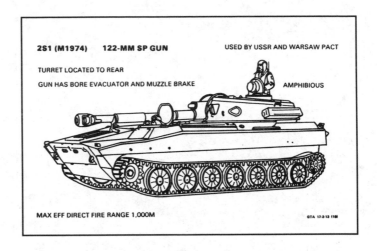

2S1 122mm Self-propelled Howitzer

Armament - 122mm howitzer.
Maximum Effective Range - 15,300 meters.
Combat Weight - 16 metric tons.
Engine - V-8, 300 horsepower diesel.
Armor - 15mm hull, 20mm turret.
Crew - 4 on board plus 2 in separate ammunition-carrying vehicle.
Basic Load of Ammunition - 40 122mm howitzer rounds.
Secondary Armament - None.
Fire Control System - Direct fire sight and panoramic telescope.
Armor-Piercing Capability in Direct Fire - 460mm of armor.
Rate of Fire - 8 rounds per minute.

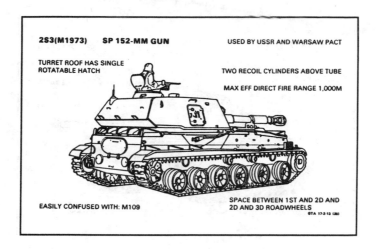

2S3 152mm Self-propelled Howitzer

Armament - 152mm howitzer.
Maximum Effective Range - 24,000 meters.
Combat Weight - 28 metric tons.
Engine - V-12, 520–580 horsepower diesel.
Armor - 15mm hull, 20mm turret.
Crew - 4 on board plus 2 in separate ammunition-carrying vehicle.
Basic Load of Ammunition - 40 152mm howitzer rounds.
Secondary Armament - None.
Fire Control System - Direct fire sight and panoramic telescope.
Armor-Piercing Capability in Direct Fire - 800mm of armor.
Rate of Fire - 4 rounds per minute.

United States

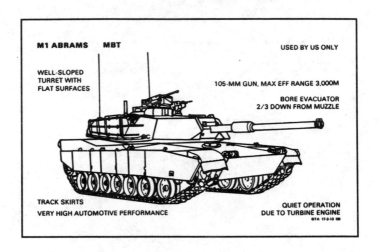

M1 Main Battle Tank

Armament - M68 105mm rifled cannon.

Combat Weight - 60 tons.

Main Gun Maximum Effective Range - 2,500 meters.

Engine - 1,500 horsepower Avco-Lycoming diesel turbine.

Armor - Classified Chobham-type armor.

Crew - 4: commander, gunner, loader, and driver.

Basic Load of Ammunition - 55 rounds.

Fire Control System - Laser range finder and thermal imaging sights. The thermal imaging sights on the M1 can be used day and night and provide a marked advantage over Soviet systems in acquiring targets.

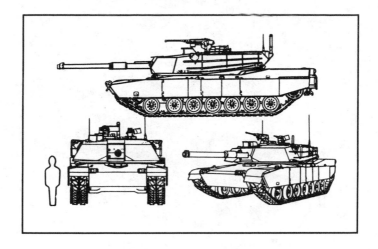

M1A1 Main Battle Tank

Armament - M256 120mm smoothbore hypervelocity cannon.

Combat Weight - 68 metric tons.

Main Gun Maximum Effective Range - 3,000 meters.

Engine - 1500 horsepower Avco-Lycoming diesel turbine.

Armor - Special multilayer-type armor. Best armor of any tank in the world.

Crew - 4: commander, gunner, loader, and driver.

Basic Load of Ammunition - 40 rounds.

Fire Control System - Laser range finder and thermal imaging sights. The thermal imaging sights on the M1A1 can be used day and night and provide a marked advantage over Soviet systems in acquiring targets.

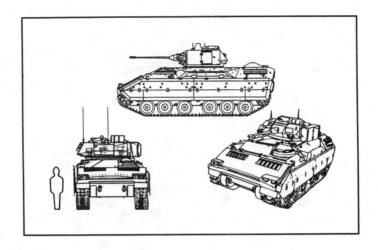

M2, Bradley Infantry Fighting Vehicle

Armament - 25mm automatic cannon, 2-shot TOW missile launcher.

Combat Weight - 22 metric tons.

Main Weapons' Maximum Effective Range - 25mm cannon, 1,500 meters; TOW (ATGM), 3,750 meters.

Engine - Cummins VTA-903 400-horsepower diesel.

Armor - Spaced laminate armor capable of defeating 14.5mm machine gun fire at its frontal arc. The M2/M3 has better armor than the Soviet BMP.

Crew - 3: commander, gunner, and driver plus 6-man infantry squad.

Basic Load of Ammunition - 25mm: 300 ready (usually broken down into 75 rounds armor piercing and 225 rounds high explosive) /600 stowed. TOW (ATGM launcher): 2 in launcher/5 stowed.

Secondary Armament - 7.62mm machine gun coaxially mounted with the 25mm cannon.

Fire Control System - Optical range finder and thermal imaging sights. The thermal imaging sights on the Bradley can be used day and night and provide a marked advantage over Soviet systems in acquiring targets.

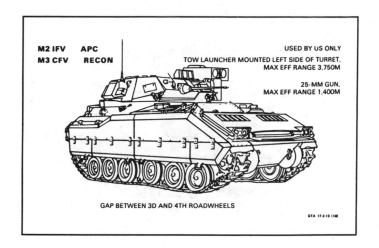

M3, Bradley Cavalry Fighting Vehicle

Armament - 25mm automatic cannon, 2-shot TOW missile launcher.

Combat Weight - 22 metric tons.

Main Weapons' Maximum Effective Range - 25mm cannon, 1,500 meters; TOW, 3,750 meters.

Engine - Cummins VTA-903 400-horsepower diesel.

Armor - Spaced laminate armor capable of defeating 14.5mm machine gun fire at its frontal arc. The M2/M3 has better armor than the Soviet BMP.

Crew - 3: commander, gunner, and driver plus 2 dismounted scouts.

Basic Load of Ammunition - 25mm: 300 ready/1,200 stowed. TOW: 2 in launcher/10 stowed.

Secondary Armament - 7.62mm machine gun coaxially mounted with the 25mm cannon.

Fire Control System - Same as M2 Bradley infantry fighting vehicle. Optical range finder and thermal imaging sights. The thermal imaging sights on the Bradley can be used day and night and provide a marked advantage over Soviet systems in acquiring targets.

FIST-V

Armament - 7.62mm M60 machine gun.

Combat Weight -13 metric tons.

M60 Machine Gun Maximum Effective Range - 900 meters.

Engine - GMC Model 6V53 215-horsepower diesel.

Armor - Aluminum alloy, 38mm maximum, 12mm minimum (effective in stopping 7.62mm and smaller bullets.)

Crew - 3: driver, vehicle commander, and fire support officer.

Basic Load of Ammunition - 2,000 rounds of 7.62mm, plus whatever can be stowed.

Laser Designator and Optical Sights - Used for calling artillery and mortar fires. The laser designator can direct special laser-guided artillery projectiles. (The U.S. military name for these laser-guided artillery shells is Copperhead.)

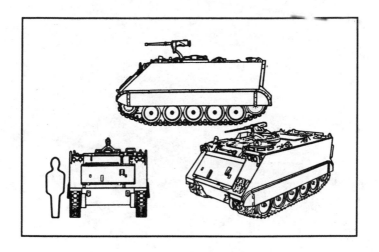

M113 (APC)

Armament - .50-caliber machine gun.

Combat Weight - 13 metric tons.

M2 Machine Gun Maximum Effective Range - Approximately 1,000 meters.

Engine - GMC Model 6V53 215-horsepower diesel.

Armor - Aluminum alloy, 38mm maximum, 12mm minimum (effective in stopping 7.62mm and smaller bullets.)

Crew - 2: driver and vehicle commander. Can carry up to 11 infantry soldiers (very cramped) in the back.

Basic Load of Ammunition - 2,000 rounds of .50 caliber, plus whatever can be stowed in lieu of troops.

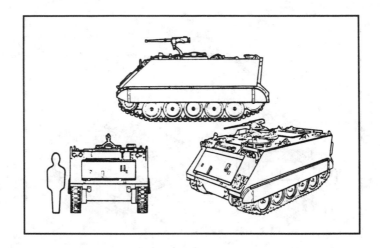

M106A1 Mortar Carrier

Armament - 4.2-inch (107mm) M30 mortar.
Maximum Effective Range - 5,650 meters.
Combat Weight - 12 metric tons.
Engine - 6V53 turbo-charged 215-horsepower diesel.
Armor - Aluminum alloy, 38mm maximum, 12mm minimum (effective in stopping 7.62mm and smaller bullets.)
Crew - 2 (driver and vehicle commander) plus 4.
Basic Load of Ammunition - 88 mortar rounds; 2,000 .50 caliber.
Secondary Armament - .50-caliber machine gun.
Fire Control System - n/a.
Armor-Piercing Capability in Direct Fire - Will not penetrate.
Rate of Fire - 10 mortar rounds per minute.

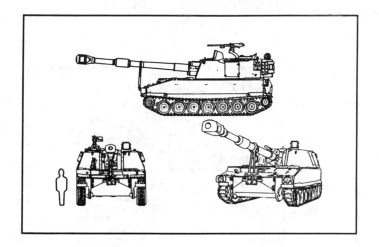

M109A1 155mm Self-propelled Howitzer

Armament - 155mm howitzer.
Maximum Effective Range - 18,000 meters.
Combat Weight - 24 metric tons.
Engine - 8V71T turbo-charged 405-horsepower inline diesel.
Armor - 38mm maximum in the turret.
Crew - 4 on board plus 2 in separate ammunition-carrying vehicle.
Basic Load of Ammunition - 28 howitzer rounds.
Secondary Armament - .50-caliber machine gun.
Fire Control System - Direct fire sight and panoramic telescope.
Armor-Piercing Capability in Direct Fire - 800mm of armor.
Rate of Fire - 2 rounds per minute.

Appendix B

U.S. Unit Organizations

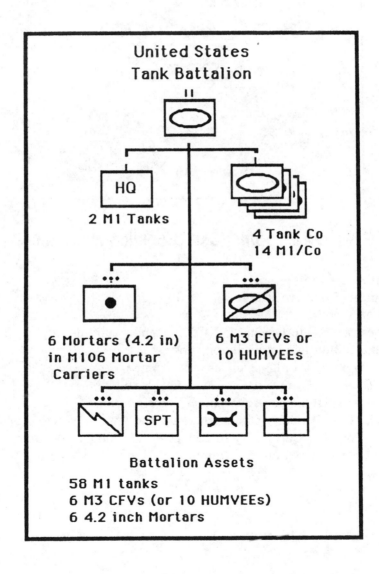

United States
Tank Battalion

HQ

2 M1 Tanks

4 Tank Co
14 M1/Co

6 Mortars (4.2 in)
in M106 Mortar
Carriers

6 M3 CFVs or
10 HUMVEEs

SPT

Battalion Assets

58 M1 tanks
6 M3 CFVs (or 10 HUMVEEs)
6 4.2 inch Mortars

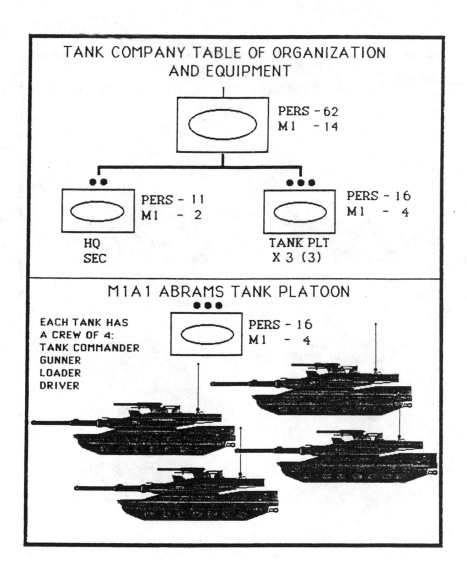

TANK COMPANY TABLE OF ORGANIZATION
AND EQUIPMENT

PERS – 62
M1 – 14

PERS – 11
M1 – 2

HQ
SEC

PERS – 16
M1 – 4

TANK PLT
X 3 (3)

M1A1 ABRAMS TANK PLATOON

EACH TANK HAS
A CREW OF 4:
TANK COMMANDER
GUNNER
LOADER
DRIVER

PERS – 16
M1 – 4

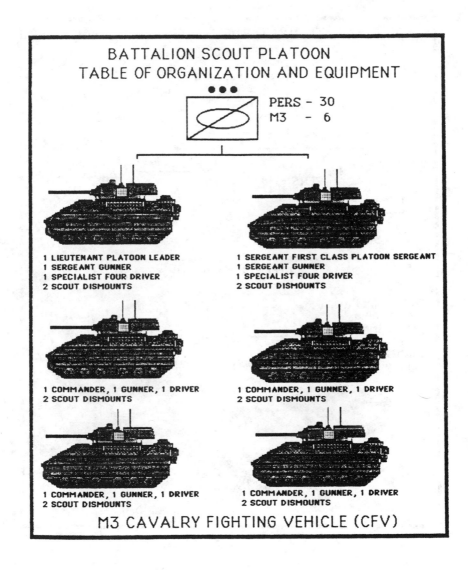

BATTALION SCOUT PLATOON
TABLE OF ORGANIZATION AND EQUIPMENT

PERS – 30
M3   – 6

1 LIEUTENANT PLATOON LEADER
1 SERGEANT GUNNER
1 SPECIALIST FOUR DRIVER
2 SCOUT DISMOUNTS

1 SERGEANT FIRST CLASS PLATOON SERGEANT
1 SERGEANT GUNNER
1 SPECIALIST FOUR DRIVER
2 SCOUT DISMOUNTS

1 COMMANDER, 1 GUNNER, 1 DRIVER
2 SCOUT DISMOUNTS

1 COMMANDER, 1 GUNNER, 1 DRIVER
2 SCOUT DISMOUNTS

1 COMMANDER, 1 GUNNER, 1 DRIVER
2 SCOUT DISMOUNTS

1 COMMANDER, 1 GUNNER, 1 DRIVER
2 SCOUT DISMOUNTS

M3 CAVALRY FIGHTING VEHICLE (CFV)

Appendix C

Threat Unit Organizations

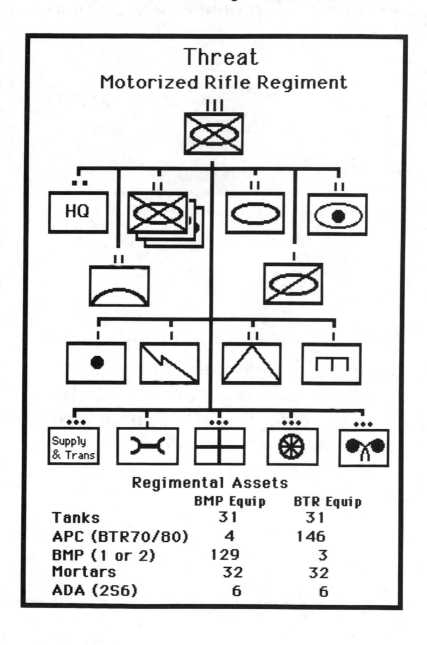

Threat
Motorized Rifle Regiment

Regimental Assets	BMP Equip	BTR Equip
Tanks	31	31
APC (BTR70/80)	4	146
BMP (1 or 2)	129	3
Mortars	32	32
ADA (2S6)	6	6

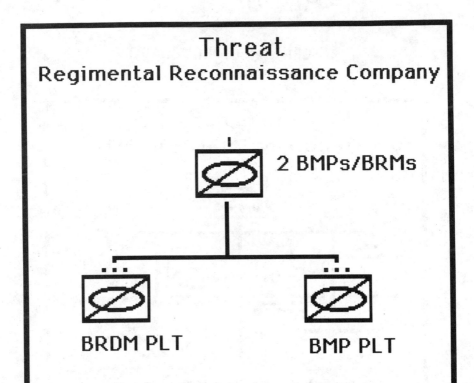

Threat
Regimental Reconnaissance Company

2 BMPs/BRMs

BRDM PLT

BMP PLT

The Regimental Reconnaissance Company is designed to conduct detailed reconnaissance on at least two of the regiment's primary routes of advance. Its equipment includes BMPs, BRDMs and up to three motorcycles.

Appendix D

Troop-Leading Procedures

The troop-leading procedures have been used by generations of U.S. soldiers. The 1942 edition of FM 101–5, the *Staff Officers Field Manual*, described them as follows: "First, make an estimate of the situation. Then develop a plan to execute the decision. Next, by means of an order, issue instructions. Finally, supervise to ensure that the operation is executed according to plan." Simple and direct. The troop-leading procedures were designed for use by a commander with limited staff. With them, commanders have a logical process to make speedy battlefield decisions.

The troop-leading procedures are the basis for the command and control process in the United States Army. These procedures are designed for use by commanders at the small-unit level. They provide a handy guide to planning, coordinating, executing and supervising tactical operations. The troop-leading procedures represent an effective method which has a long tradition in the U. S. Army. Follow the troop-leading procedures. They work. Not following these procedures almost always creates problems.

The troop-leading procedures are the basis for planning and preparation for commanders without staffs (company level and below) and for those with staffs when they do not have time to assemble them. The commander does a rapid estimate of the situation with the other members of the tactical command post. A quick radio update is provided, and vital information is transmitted over the radio. The commander gathers his leaders and passes information either by radio or face-to-face on terrain that overlooks the area of operations.

The troop-leading procedures are as detailed—or as simple—as time allows. The commander plays the central role in this process. The commander's decisions are based on his analysis of the factors of METT-T and comparisons of feasible courses of action, war-gaming, and his personal judgment. The troop-leading procedures can occur in almost any sequence, with several actions taking place simultaneously. Some actions, such as reconnoitering, may begin early and be repeated as often as required.

Appendix D

U.S. Army Field Circular 71–6, *Battalion and Brigade Command and Control*, dated 1 March 1985, stressed that the "troop-leading procedures form the basic framework the commander routinely uses to make timely decisions and supervise the execution of the mission. Staff input during this process will be accomplished as time and the situation permit." Doctrine does not restrict the use of the troop-leading procedures to commanders only. They are clearly intended, however, for the leader or commander who does not have staff.

The habitual use of the troop-leading procedures by commanders without staffs will aid in the subordinate's implicit understanding of the commander's decision-making process. This implicit understanding is very important in speeding up the commander's decision cycle since a commander without a staff—primarily the company commander and platoon leader—has very little time for the decision-making process. Experience proves that the determined application of the troop-leading procedures reduces friction and saves time. The troop-leading procedures are shown here.

Troop-leading procedures

1. Receive the mission
2. Issue a warning order
3. Make a tentative plan
    a. Estimate of the situation
     I. Detailed mission analysis (step 1)
     II. Develop situation and courses of action (step 2)
       - Enemy situation (enemy courses of action)
       - Terrain and weather (OCOKA = *O*bservation and fields of fire, *C*over and concealment, *O*bstacles, *K*ey terrain, and *A*venues of approach)
       - Friendly situation (troops and time available)
       - Courses of action (friendly)
     III. Analyze courses of action—war-game (step 3)
     IV. Compare courses of action (step 4)
     V. Decision (step 5)
    b. Expand selected course of action into a tentative plan
4. Start movement
5. Reconnoiter
6. Complete plan
7. Issue plan
8. Supervise and refine the plan

Receive the mission

The first step is to receive the mission. The best situation is for the commander to receive his mission in person from his higher commander, but often the mission is received over the radio. If possible, the order is issued overlooking the ground where the action will take place. If this is impractical, maps, sketches and terrain models should be used. No matter how the mission is received, it is critical to get a clear understanding of the higher commander's intent and also that of the next higher commander. Minutes spent understanding the commander's intent can save hours of planning time.

The commander should next analyze the mission using the factors of METT-T (mission, enemy, terrain and weather, troops, and time available). The first step in this process is to plan the available time. Time is the common factor of the battlefield. To emphasize the importance of time in military operations, it is useful to reverse the location of the time analysis in METT-T to T-METT. T-METT is explained as follows:

a. **Time available** - Without an initial time plan it is easy to get so involved in the decision-making process that the commander loses track of time and wastes precious minutes.

Time drives the planning and execution of all military operations. Backward planning and ruthless enforcement of the time plan are the keys to effective time management. The commander must make the most of his available time by starting reconnaissance units moving as soon as possible and by disseminating as much preliminary information as possible to allow subordinate units to begin planning and preparing.

The backward planning technique starts with the final planned action and progresses backward to the present time. Starting with the time for the crossing of line of departure (offensive battle), or the time when the defense must be established (defensive battle), the time plan includes the unit's major tasks. The time of the battle action (crossing the LD, or the time to be set and ready to defend), battle update briefing (BUB), orders issue, reconnaissance, and initial movement should be listed in the time plan.

Commanders must enforce the time plan. The goal is to give the subordinate unit enough daylight to conduct planning, reconnaissance, and preparation prior to the start of combat operations. It does more harm than good to present a "perfect" plan to subordinate units if they do not have the time to disseminate their own orders and prepare.

b. Mission - The mission is what the unit is tasked to do. The mission is restated to contain the elements WHO, WHAT, WHERE, WHEN and WHY. The mission from the higher commander is restated in a clear, concise statement of the task to be accomplished.

c. Enemy - Who is the enemy (unit, size, type)? Enemy forces are evaluated by their doctrine (how they fight) and known enemy information (what is out there opposing the friendly force). The goal of this analysis is to determine the enemy's intent and his most-likely courses of action.

d. Terrain and weather - The terrain is analyzed for its military application and for its effect on both friendly and enemy courses of action. The weather is considered for the same reasons.

e. Troops - Units measure their combat power two echelons down. Brigade commanders, therefore, must consider the number of companies they can employ. Battalion commanders consider the number of platoons. The analysis of the friendly forces available is essential to establishing what a unit can do. A tired battalion, reduced to less than three companies, cannot fight in the same fashion as a fully rested, full-strength unit.

Issue the warning order

Warning orders are partial orders which are issued to gain time. They are critical to effective parallel planning. Warning orders get your forces moving in the right direction as you continue to develop the plan. They allow the preparation to get started. A clear warning order saves time and focuses the planning effort. Warning orders are issued over the radio or given orally overlooking the area of operations.

Make a tentative plan

The commander conducts his estimate of the situation, determining the specified and implied tasks and selecting the mission-essential tasks. A commander with a staff then issues his commander's guidance. Based upon the commander's guidance, the staff develops courses of action. A commander without a staff must complete this mental process himself.

The commander must decide his intent early in the process. This is a critical element of the commander's guidance. The commander's intent is his stated vision for the operation. It must define the **object** (the purpose of the action), the **reason** (the end state with respect to the relationship among the force, the enemy, and the terrain), and the **importance** (how the end state will be achieved by the force as a whole, and how far the force should go to achieve it).

The commander now war-games the options for the deployment of his forces and determines his best course of action. War-gaming is a mental process of visualizing each step of the battle, considering friendly and enemy actions and counteractions. He starts the war-gaming by looking at the enemy in detail. "Where will the enemy attack from?" "Where do I want to kill him?" These are the types of questions that are asked based upon the enemy's capabilities. A thorough understanding of the enemy, his tactics, organization, and weapons capabilities is essential to developing a tentative plan.

The intelligence preparation of the battlefield (IPB) plays an important part in war-gaming. The IPB is a crucial step in developing an effective combat order. Through IPB, the commander develops a clear picture of the battlefield, the courses of action available to the enemy commander, actions that disclose what the enemy is likely to do and decision points for key friendly actions. These decision points require a specified action to occur (a counterattack, or the firing of an artillery mission for instance) on order or as directed in the operations order.

The commander then compares courses of action and chooses one. The best course of action is always that which offers the greatest flexibility during the execution of the mission. To maintain maximum flexibility, the commander should develop branch plans. By developing branch plans as a part of the initial planning, the commander creates the agility necessary to operate in an environment of limited information.

Begin movement

Movement should begin as soon as possible to position the force to execute the mission. In some cases, early movement will be critical if long marches to the area of operations are required. The commander can often order his unit to move while he is receiving orders from the higher commander. He may also designate his second in command to move the force while he continues planning and conducts reconnaissance.

Reconnoiter

The commander must focus his reconnaissance to gain the information he needs to execute his branch plans. Nothing can take the place of a good reconnaissance. Reconnaissance demands careful planning. The commander must issue specific objectives to each of his subordinate leaders and specify a time and place to meet with them to discuss the results of the reconnaissance. The commander will then wargame any changes these results have made on the tentative plan. If possible, the commander should choose a site for this meeting that allows the group to observe the terrain over which they will fight.

Complete the plan

The process of refining the concept continues as more information about the enemy, terrain, and weather is gathered by the commander and his staff. The task organization, fire support plans, combat service support, surveillance, communication, and command and control measures are finalized. Coordination with adjacent, supporting, and higher headquarters is effected.

Most importantly, the commander ensures that branch plans are an integral part of the completed effort. Actions are taken to compensate for any disadvantage associated with the chosen course of action, and contingency plans are fully developed. These branch plans build flexibility into the selected course of action and allow the commander to act decisively against enemy weaknesses as they are discovered on the battlefield.

Israeli soldiers have a saying which emphasizes their belief in flexibility: "plans are merely a basis for changes." The Israelis generally make several branch plans and put these alternative plans on their overlays. If the situation changes, they will still achieve their commander's original intent by radioing a code word to execute one of the branch plans. This technique greatly increases agility. Branch plans allow a commander to act on the latest intelligence. Branch plans permit flexibility and the opportunity to get inside the enemy's decision cycle.

Issue the order

The ideal operations order is simple, clear, and issued in time for subordinate commanders to fully brief and rehearse their missions with their subordinates. The friction of battle will quickly eat away at available planning time. Ideally, the commander should issue his orders orally. Oral orders are faster. Effectiveness is a matter of practice. Maps, sketches, and overlays are critical to communicating the plan effectively. Even in warfare, a picture is still worth a thousand words.

Oral orders can be issued over the radio or in person. As a minimum, an oral order requires an accurately drawn overlay. Subordinate commanders copy this overlay from their commander's map. Accurate map overlays are essential in synchronizing the movements and actions of the force. Without them, directions given over the radio would be very difficult.

If possible, the commander issues his order from a vantage point overlooking the terrain of the area of the operation. If this is not possible, the commander should use visual aids such as terrain models or sketches to help explain his plan clearly.

After the order is issued, the commander has his subordinate commanders conduct an oral backbrief of the plan. The backbrief is the final check by the commander to insure that his intent is clearly understood. It also allows the commander to war-game possible enemy countermoves and the actions that counter those moves. Each subordinate commander should listen to each of the backbriefs to assist in synchronizing battle actions. This procedure insures that subordinate commanders will know the entire plan before they return to their units. It strengthens their ability to continue the mission if the commander becomes a casualty. Ideally, backbriefs are conducted while overlooking the terrain with all commanders, fire support officers, and key staff present.

Lastly, the commander issues a time check to synchronize everyone's actions. A misunderstanding over the difference of a minute can lose a battle!

Supervise and refine

The commander and his staff must supervise and inspect preparations prior to combat. The preparations include coordination, reorganization, fire support, engineer activities, maintenance, resupply, and movement. Rehearsals are conducted for both the maneuver and fire plans. Emphasis by commanders above the company level must be placed on the supervision of items that require coordination between units of the same size.

Information derived from reconnaissance will cause the plan to change. Tactical planning must be oriented on the enemy. This means that a commander must do whatever it takes to discover where the enemy is. The size and composition of the friendly reconnaissance effort must be a METT-T decision. Reconnaissance must be a central part of the plan. If the unit's reconnaissance forces are not sufficient to accomplish the reconnaissance mission, they must be reinforced by other units. The reconnaissance is focused to gain the critical information that will help the commander decide the best way to accomplish his mission.

Refinement of the plan is a continual process. The reconnaissance determines which branch plan the commander executes during the battle. Branch plans are executed when the reconnaissance discovers information on critical enemy weaknesses.

Once the battle starts, the commander makes the decisions necessary to give his force an advantage over the enemy. If communication is interrupted, subordinates are expected to act without active supervision, based upon their best judgment and their understanding of the commander's intent. To do nothing when the situation demands action is a sure way to surrender the initiative to the enemy.

Appendix E

Tank Fighting Positions

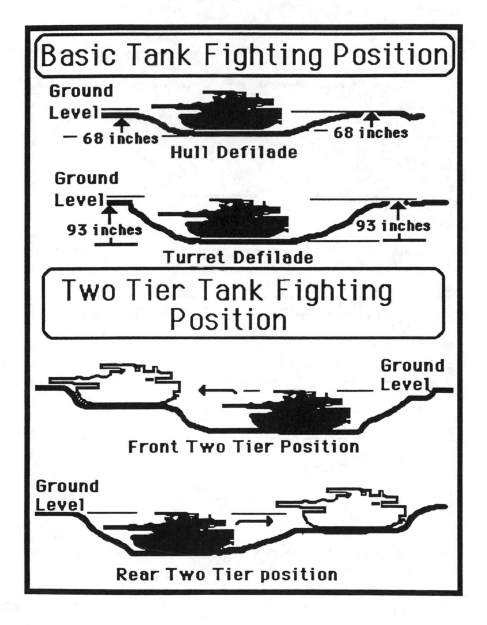

Basic Tank Fighting Position

Ground Level
— 68 inches   — 68 inches
Hull Defilade

Ground Level
93 inches   93 inches
Turret Defilade

Two Tier Tank Fighting Position

Ground Level

Front Two Tier Position

Ground Level

Rear Two Tier position

Appendix F

Order Formats

	WARNING ORDER	
AS OF _____		UNIT_____

¹ADDRESSES

²CHANGES TO TASK ORG

³PROBABLE MISSION

4 INTENT

⁵EARLIEST TIME OF MOVE: A)_____ B) SP_____ C)_____

⁶MOVEMENT INSTR

⁷RECON INSTR

8 OPORD A)TIME_____ B) PLACE_____ | **9 MOPP LEVEL** CURRENT_____ ANTICIPATED_____

¹⁰SPECIAL EQUIPMENT

¹¹SPECIAL INSTRUCTIONS

PLATOON OPERATIONS ORDER FORMAT FOR AIRLAND BATTLE

TASK ORGANIZATION (DESCRIPTION OF HOW YOUR UNIT IS ORGANIZED TO FIGHT)

1. SITUATION:
   A. ENEMY FORCES
   B. FRIENDLY FORCES
   C. ATTACHMENTS/ DETACHMENTS
   D. COMMANDER'S INTENT OF THE COMMANDERS TWO ECHELONS ABOVE YOUR LEVEL OF COMMAND

2. **MISSION: A CLEAR STATEMENT OF WHAT THE UNIT IS TO DO (usually defined in terms of the enemy, not the terrain)**

3. EXECUTION:
   A. CONCEPT OF THE OPERATION: CLEARLY STATE YOUR INTENT (The acid test of the leader's intent is for his subordinates to act correctly even if communications are lost and the situation changes, making the initial order inappropriate.)
   B. DESIGNATE THE MAIN EFFORT AND ANY LIMITING INSTRUCTIONS
   C. SUBORDINATE MISSIONS: DESIGNATE WHAT SUBORDINATE UNITS MUST DO (usually described in terms of the enemy, not the terrain)
   D. COORDINATING INSTRUCTIONS (Timings, MOPP level, etc.)

4. SERVICE SUPPORT
   A. CLASS I (food & water), CLASS III (fuel), CLASS IV (barrier material), and CLASS V (ammunition)
   B. MAINTENANCE COLLECTION POINT AND PROCEDURES
   C. MEDICAL EVACUATION AND PROCEDURES

5. COMMAND AND SIGNAL
   A. COMMAND (location and chain of command)
   B. SIGNAL (to include frequencies and procedures to change frequencies if you are jammed)

GLOSSARY

Alternate Position - The position given to a weapon, unit, or individual to be occupied when the primary position becomes untenable or unsuitable for carrying out its task. The alternate position is located so that the individual can continue to fulfill his original task.

Assembly Area - An area in which a force prepares or regroups for further action.

Attack - An offensive action characterized by movement supported by fire.

    Deliberate Attack - An attack planned and carefully coordinated with all concerned elements, based on thorough reconnaissance, evaluation of all available intelligence and relative combat strength, analysis of various courses of action, and other factors affecting the situation. It generally is conducted against a well-organized defense when a hasty attack is not possible or has failed.

    Frontal Attack - An offensive maneuver in which the main action is directed against the front of the enemy forces, and over the most direct approaches.

    Hasty Attack - An offensive operation for which a unit has not made extensive preparations. It is conducted with the resources immediately available in order to maintain momentum or to take advantage of the enemy situation.

    Main Attack - The principal attack or effort into which the commander places the bulk of the offensive capability at his disposal. An attack directed against the chief objective of the battle.

    Supporting Attack - An attack designed to hold the enemy in position, to deceive him as to where the main attack is being made, to prevent him from reinforcing the elements opposing the main effort, and/or to cause him to commit his reserves prematurely at an indecisive location.

Avenue of Approach - An air or ground route of an attacking force of a given size leading to its objective or to key terrain in its path.

Axis of Advance - A general route of advance, assigned for the purposes of control, which extends toward the enemy. An axis of ad-

320

vance symbol graphically portrays a commander's intention, such as avoidance of built-up areas or envelopment of an enemy force. It follows terrain for the size of the force assigned to the axis. A commander may maneuver his forces and supporting fires to either side of an axis of advance, provided the unit remains oriented on the axis and the objective.

Base of Fire - Fire placed on an enemy force or position to reduce or eliminate the enemy's capability to interfere by fire and/or movement of friendly maneuver elements. It may be provided by a single weapon or a grouping of weapon systems.

Battle Position (BP) - A defensive location oriented on the most likely enemy avenue of approach from which a unit may defend or attack. Such units can be as large as battalion task forces and as small as platoons. A unit assigned a BP is located within the general outline of the BP.

BMNT - Before morning nautical twilight.

CEOI - *See* Communications Electronic Operating Instruction.

Checkpoint - A predetermined point on the ground used as a means of coordinating friendly movement. Checkpoints are not used as reference points in reporting enemy locations.

Clear Enemy in Zone - A requirement to eliminate organized resistance in an assigned zone by destroying, capturing, or forcing the withdrawal of enemy forces that could interfere with the unit's ability to accomplish its mission.

Close Air Support (CAS) - Air action against hostile targets that are in close proximity to friendly forces. The action requires detailed integration of each air mission with the fire and movement of those forces.

Coil - An arrangement of vehicles forming a circle.

Combat Multiplier - Supporting and subsidiary means that significantly increase the relative combat strength of a force while actual force ratios remain constant. Examples of combat multipliers are economizing in one area to mass in another, surprise, deception, camouflage, electronic warfare, psychological operations, and terrain reinforcement.

Commander's Intent - Commander's vision of the battle—how he expects to fight and what he expects to accomplish. The acid test of understanding the commander's intent is for the subordinate to act in concert with the commander's desires in a situation where

Glossary

the circumstances are different from those foreseen at the time the plan was issued and the commander cannot be reached for a decision.

Communications Electronic Operating Instruction (CEOI) - A listing of all frequencies, call signs, and signal operating instructions for a unit for a specific period of time.

Company Team - A team formed by attachment of one or more nonorganic tank, mechanized infantry, or light infantry platoons to a tank, mechanized infantry, or light infantry company either in exchange for or in addition to organic platoons.

Concealment - The protection from observation or surveillance.

Concept of Operations - A graphic, verbal, or written statement in broad outline that gives an overall picture of a commander's assumptions or intent in regard to an operation or a series of operations; includes at a minimum the scheme of maneuver and fire support plan. It is described in sufficient detail for the staff and subordinate commanders to understand what they are to do and how to fight the battle without further instructions.

Coordinating Point - A control measure that indicates a specific location for the coordination of fires and maneuver between adjacent units. They usually are indicated whenever a boundary crosses the forward edge of the battle area (FEBA), and may be indicated when a boundary crosses report lines or phase lines (PLs) used to control security forces. In NATO, physical contact between adjacent units is required.

Counterattack - Attack by a part or all of a defending force against an enemy attacking force, for such specific purposes as regaining ground lost or cutting off or destroying enemy advance units, and with the general objective of regaining the initiative and denying to the enemy the attainment of his purpose in attacking. In sustained defensive operations, it is undertaken to restore the battle position (BP) and is directed at limited objectives.

Cover - Natural or artificial protection from enemy observation.

Covered Approach - (1) Any route that offers protection against enemy observation or fire. (2) An approach made under the protection furnished by other forces or by natural cover.

Cross Attachment - The exchange of subordinate units between units for a temporary period. Example: A tank battalion detaches a tank company that is subsequently attached to a mechanized infantry battalion, and the mechanized infantry battalion detaches a mechanized company that is then attached to the tank battalion.

CVC Helmet - Crew vehicle crewman helmet. Each CVC helmet has a microphone and earphones to allow intercom and radio communications. Vehicle crew members wear the CVC helmet on the vehicle to communicate with other crew members and to talk over the radio.

Dead Space - An area within the maximum effective range of a weapon, surveillance device, or observer that cannot be covered by fire and observation from a given position because of intervening obstacles, the nature of the ground, the characteristics of the trajectory, or the limitations of the pointing capabilities of the systems.

Decisive Engagement - An engagement in which a unit is considered fully committed and cannot maneuver or extricate itself. In the absence of outside assistance, the action must be fought to a conclusion and either won or lost with the forces at hand.

Decisive Terrain - Key terrain is decisive terrain if it has an extraordinary impact on the mission. Decisive terrain is rare and will not be present in every mission. To designate terrain as decisive is to recognize that the successful accomplishment of the mission, whether offensive or defensive, depends on seizing or retaining it. The commander designates decisive terrain to communicate its importance in his concept of operations, first to his staff and, later, to subordinate commanders.

Defilade - Protection from hostile observation and fire provided by an obstacle such as a hill, ridge, or bank. To shield from enemy fire or observation by using natural or artificial obstacles.

Defile - A narrow passage that tends to constrict the movement of troops.

Direct Fire - Fire directed at a target that is visible to the aimer or firing unit.

Direction of Attack - A specific direction or route that the main attack or the main body of the force will follow. If used, it is normally at battalion and lower levels. Direction of attack is a more restrictive control measure than axis of advance, and units are not free to maneuver off the assigned route. It is usually associated with infantry units conducting night attacks, or units involved in limited visibility operations, and in counterattacks. (In NATO, referred to as an attack route.)

Glossary

Direction of Fire - The direction on which a cannon or missile is laid. It represents the direction to the most significant threat in the target area.

Displace - To leave one position and take another. Forces may be displaced laterally to concentrate combat power in threatened areas.

DPICM - Dual-purpose improved conventional munitions.

Dominant Terrain - Terrain which, because of its elevation, proportions, or location, commands a view of and may offer fields of fire over surrounding terrain.

Economy of Force - The allocation of minimum-essential combat capability or strength to secondary efforts, so that forces may be concentrated in the area where a decision is sought. *A principle of war*.

EENT - Early evening nautical twilight.

Engagement Area - An area in which the commander intends to trap and destroy an enemy force with the massed fire of all available weapons. Engagement areas are routinely identified by a target reference point in the center of the trap area or by prominent terrain features around the area. Although engagement areas may also be divided into sectors of fire, it is important to understand that defensive systems are not designed around engagement areas, but rather around avenues of approach. Engagement areas and sectors of fire are not intended to restrict fires or cause operations to become static or fixed; they are used only as a tool to concentrate fires and to optimize their effects.

FASCAM (Family of Scatterable Mines) - A scatterable mine field, composed of antitank or antipersonnel mines, delivered by artillery.

Field of Fire - The area that a weapon or a group of weapons may effectively cover with fire from a given location.

Fire Sack - Soviet term for engagement area. Kill zones for armored formations.

Fire and Movement - The simultaneous moving and firing by men and/or vehicles. This technique is primarily used during the assault of enemy positions.

Fire Support Plan - A plan on how fire support will be used to support an operation. It should include a portion for each means of fire support involved.

FIST (Fire Support Team) - In fire support operations, a team comprised of a team chief (field artillery lieutenant) and the necessary additional personnel and equipment required to plan, request, co-ordinate, and direct fire support efforts for company-sized units.

Forward Edge of the Battle Area (FEBA) - The forward limit of the main battle area (MBA). Used in the defense.

Fragmentary Order (FRAGO) - An abbreviated form of an operation order (OPORD) used to make changes in missions to units and to inform them of changes in the tactical situation.

Front - The lateral space occupied by an element measured from the extremity of one flank to the extremity of the other flank. The unit may be extended in a combat formation or occupying a position, depending on the type of operation involved. Typical fronts are given in kilometers/meters as follows:

Unit	Offense	Defense
U.S. Tank Platoon	100–400 m	500 m
U.S. Mechanized Infantry Platoon	100–400 m	500 m
U.S. Tank Company	1 km	1–2 km
U.S. Tank Battalion	5–7 km	7–13 km
Soviet Tank Platoon	100–400 m	300 m
Soviet Motorized Rifle Platoon	100–400 m	500–600 m (Security Zone)
Soviet Motorized Rifle Platoon	100–400 m	300 m (Main Defense Belt)
Soviet Motorized Rile Company	600–800 m	500–1,000 m
Soviet Motorized Rifle Battalion	1–2 km	3–7.5 km

Frontage - The width of the front plus that distance beyond the flanks covered by observation and fire by a unit in combat.

Gap - Any break or breach in the continuity of tactical dispositions or formations beyond effective small arms coverage.

Grid Coordinates - The left-right (west-east) and top-bottom (north-south) values of a grid that designate the location of a specific point on a map. Coordinates usually are expressed to the nearest 100, 10, or 1 meter, with the numerical designations combined into a single expression. Example: 329378 (nearest 100 meters); 32943785 (nearest 10 meters), or 3294837853 (nearest 1 meter).

Group of Targets - Two or more targets on which fire is desired simultaneously. A group of targets is designated by a letter-number-letter combination or a code name.

Glossary

Hull Down - The positioning of an armored vehicle so that the muzzle of the gun/launcher is the lowest part of the vehicle exposed to the front.

HVAPFSDS - Hypervelocity, armor-piercing, fin-stabilized, discarding sabot.

Intelligence Preparation of the Battlefield (IPB) - A systematic approach to analyzing the enemy, weather, and terrain in a specific geographic area. It integrates enemy doctrine with the weather and terrain as they relate to the mission and the specific battlefield environment. This is done to determine and evaluate enemy capabilities, vulnerabilities, and probable courses of action.

Key Terrain - Any locality or area the seizure, retention, or control of which affords a marked advantage to either combatant.

Limit of Advance - An easily recognized terrain feature beyond which attacking elements will not advance.

Line of Contact (LC) - A general trace delineating the location where two opposing forces are engaged.

Line of Departure (LD) - A line designated to coordinate the commitment of attacking units or scouting elements at a specified time. A start line.

Line of Departure is Line of Contact (LD/LC) - The designation of forward friendly positions as the LD when opposing forces are in contact.

Maneuver - The movement of forces supported by fire to achieve a position of advantage from which to destroy or threaten destruction of the enemy. *A principle of war.*

Mass - (1) The concentration of combat power at the decisive time and place. *A principle of war.* (2) To concentrate or bring together fires, so as to mass fires of multiple weapons or units. (3) The military formation in which units are spaced at less than normal distances and intervals.

Mine Field - An area of ground containing mines laid with or without a pattern.

Mission, Enemy, Terrain, Troops, and Time Available (METT-T) - The phrase or acronym used to describe the factors that must be considered during the planning or execution of a tactical operation. Example considerations are:

Mission. The who, what, when, where, and why of what is to be accomplished.

Enemy. Current information concerning the enemy's strength, location, disposition, activity, equipment, capability, and a determination as to the enemy's probable course of action.

Terrain (includes weather). Information about vegetation, soil type, hydrology, climatic conditions, and light data is analyzed to determine the impact that the environment can have on current and future operations for both enemy and friendly operations.

Troops. The quantity, level of training, and psychological state of friendly forces, to include the availability of weapons systems and critical equipment.

Time Available. The time available to plan, prepare, and execute operations is considered for both enemy and friendly forces.

Mission Oriented Protective Posture (MOPP) - A flexible system for protection against a chemical attack devised to maximize the unit's ability to accomplish its mission in a toxic environment. This posture permits maximum protection from chemical agent attack without unacceptable reduction in efficiency. The five levels of MOPP are:

MOPP LEVEL	Over Garment	Protective Boot	Mask/Hood	Gloves
0	***	***	Carried	***
1	Worn*	Carried	Carried	Carried
2	Worn*	Worn	Carried	Carried
3	Worn*	Worn	Worn**	Carried
4	Worn	Worn	Worn closed	Worn

*   Worn open or closed based on temperature.
**   Mask/hood zipper may be open or closed, as required.
*** Readily available to the individual (that is, within work area, vehicle, fighting position).

Movement Technique - Manner of traversing terrain used by a unit (such as traveling, traveling overwatch, and bounding overwatch). The likelihood of enemy contact determines which of the following techniques are used:

Traveling. A movement technique used when speed is necessary and contact with enemy forces is not likely. All elements of the unit move simultaneously, with the unit leader located where he can best control.

Glossary

Traveling Overwatch. A movement technique used when contact with enemy forces is possible. The lead element and traveling element are separated by a short distance, which varies with the terrain. The trailing element moves at variable speeds and may pause for short periods to overwatch the lead element. It keys its movement to terrain and the lead element. The trailing element overwatches at such a distance that, should the enemy engage the lead element, it will not prevent the trailing element from firing or moving to support the lead element.

Bounding Overwatch. A movement technique used when contact with enemy forces is expected. The unit moves by bounds. One element is always halted in position to overwatch another element while it moves. The overwatching element is positioned to support the moving unit by fire or fire and movement.

Objective - (1) The physical object of the action taken (for example, a definite terrain feature, the seizure and/or holding of which is essential to the commander's plan, or the destruction of an enemy force without regard to terrain features). (2) The principle of war that states that every military operation should be directed toward clearly defined, decisive, and attainable objectives.

Offense - A combat operation designed primarily to destroy the enemy. Offensive operations may be undertaken to secure key or decisive terrain, to deprive the enemy of resources or decisive terrain, to deceive and/or divert the enemy, to develop intelligence, and to hold the enemy in position. Offensive operations include deliberate attack, hasty attack, movement to contact, exploitation, pursuit, and other limited-objective operations. The offensive is undertaken to seize, retain, and exploit the initiative, and, as such, is a principle of war.

Operation Order (OPORD) - A directive issued by a commander to subordinate commanders for effecting the coordinated execution of an operation; includes tactical movement orders.

Operation Overlay - Overlay showing the location, size, and scheme of maneuver/fires of friendly forces involved in an operation. As an exception, it may indicate predicted movements and locations of enemy forces.

Orders Group - A standing group of key personnel requested to be present when a commander at any level issues his concept of the operation and his order.

Overwatch - (1) A tactical technique in which one element is positioned to support the movement of another element with immediate direct fire. (2) The tactical role of an element positioned to support the movement of another element with immediate direct fire.

Passage of Lines - Passing one unit through the positions of another, as when elements of a covering force withdraw through the forward edge of the main battle area, or when an exploiting force moves through the elements of the force that conducted the initial attack. A passage may be designated as a forward or rearward passage of lines.

Phase Line (PL) - A line used for control and coordination of military operations. It is usually a recognizable terrain feature extending across the zone of action. Units normally report crossing PLs, but do not halt unless specifically directed. PLs often are used to prescribe the timing of delay operations.

Primary Position - A place for a weapon, a unit, or an individual to fight, which provides the best means to accomplish the assigned mission.

Priority of Fires - Direction to a fire support planner to organize and employ fire support means according to the importance of the supported unit's missions.

Priority Target - A target on which the delivery of fires takes precedence over all the fires for the designated firing unit/element. The firing unit/element will prepare, to the extent possible, for the engagement of such targets. A firing unit/element may be assigned only one priority target.

Reverse Slope - A position on the ground not exposed to direct fire or observation. It may be a slope that descends away from the enemy.

Reverse Slope Defense - A defense area organized on any ground not exposed to direct fire or observation. It may be on a slope that descends away from the enemy.

Scatterable Mine - A mine laid without regard to classical pattern that is designed to be delivered by aircraft, artillery, missile, ground dispenser, or hand thrown.

Sector - An area designated by boundaries within which a unit operates and for which it is responsible. Normally, sectors are used in defensive operations.

Secure - To gain possession of a position or terrain feature, with or without force, and to deploy in a manner that prevents its destruction or loss to enemy action.

Glossary

Seize - To clear a designated area and obtain control of it (physically occupy it).

Start Point (SP) - A clearly defined initial control point on a route at which specified elements of a column of ground vehicles or flight of aircraft come under the control of the commander having responsibility for the movement.

Strongpoint - A key point in a defensive position, usually strongly fortified and heavily armed with automatic weapons, around which other positions are grouped for its protection.

Support Force - Those forces charged with providing intense direct overwatching fires to the assault and breaching forces.

Suppression - Direct and indirect fires, electronic countermeasures (ECM), or smoke brought to bear on enemy personnel, weapons, or equipment to prevent effective fire on friendly forces.

Tactical Operations Center (TOC) - The element within the main command post (CP) consisting of those staff activities involved in sustaining current operations and in planning future operations. Staff activities are functionally grouped into elements or cells. Units at battalion level and above normally have a TOC.

Target Overlay - An overlay showing the locations of friendly artillery units, targets, boundaries, and fire support coordination measures. It enables the fire support coordinator (FSCOORD) to view graphically all targets planned in support of the maneuver force and to determine the best fire support agency to engage the listed targets.

Task Organization - A temporary grouping of forces designed to accomplish a particular mission. Task organization involves the distribution of available assets to subordinate control headquarters by attachment or by placing assets in direct support (DS) or under the operational control of the subordinate.

TC - Tank commander.

Terrain Analysis - The process of interpreting a geographic area to determine the effect of the natural and man-made features on military operations.

Turret Down - A vehicle is in a turret-down position when the entire vehicle is behind cover but the commander can still observe to the front from the turret hatch or cupola.

"V" - An arrangement of vehicles or personnel that may be used when the enemy situation is vague and the leader requires firepower to the front and flanks.

Warning Order - A preliminary notice of an action or order that is to follow. Usually issued as a brief oral or written message. It is designed to give subordinates time to make necessary plans and preparations.

Wedge - A formation of vehicles or personnel that (1) permits excellent fire to the front and good fire to each flank; (2) facilitates control; (3) permits sustained effort and provides flank security; (4) lends itself readily to fire and movement; (5) is often used when the enemy situation is vague and contact is imminent.

Withdrawal - A retrograde operation in which a force in contact with the enemy frees itself for a new mission.

Zone - The area of responsibility for offensive operations assigned to a unit by the drawing of boundaries.

Decision Chart

Enter each section number as you select it. Victory is the objective, and whatever path achieves it is correct; but obviously it is more efficient to win in a relatively small number of choices without repeatedly having to go back and start over. Consider your choices carefully.

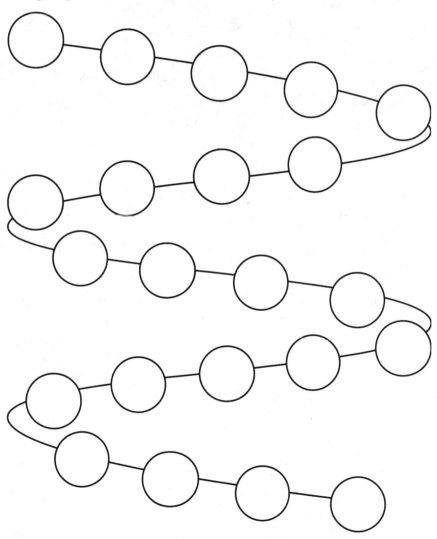

Decision Chart

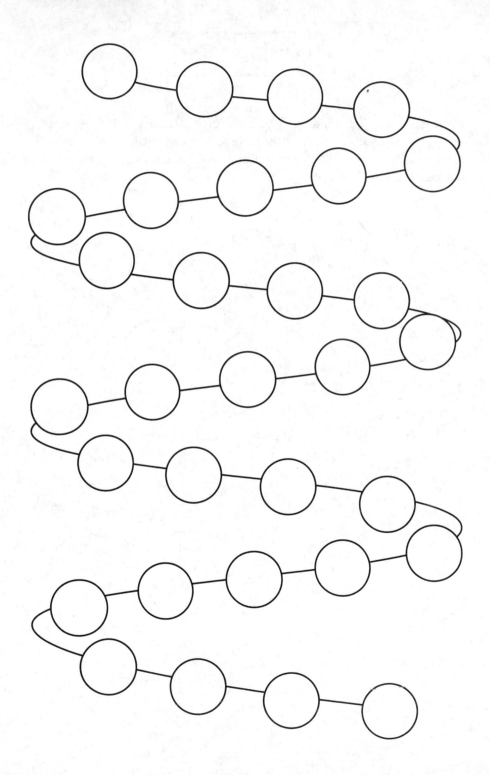

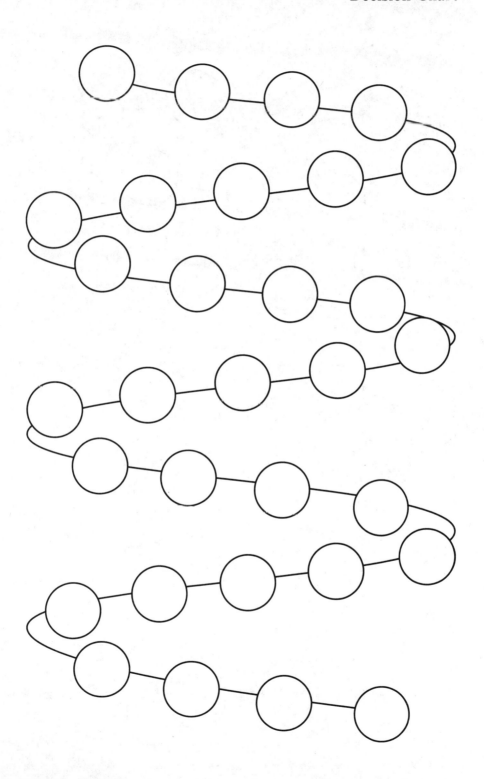

Decision Chart

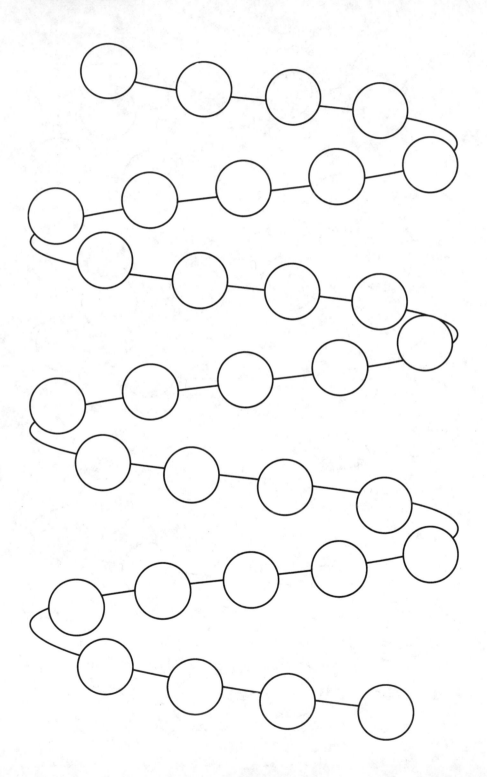

Decision Chart

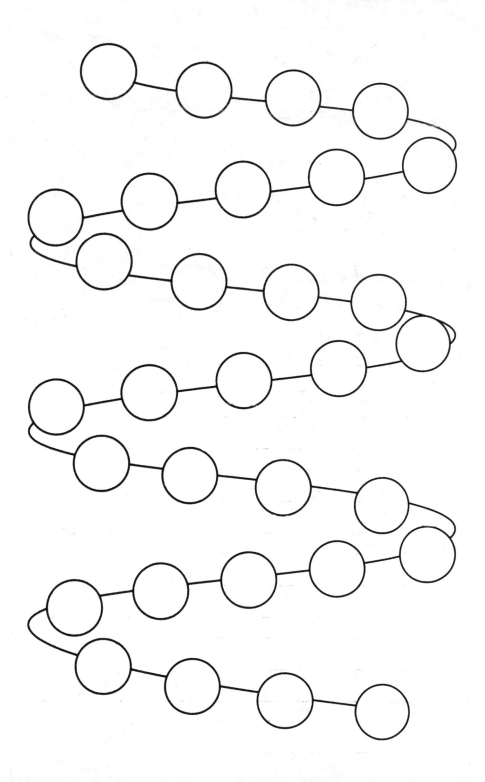

Decision Chart

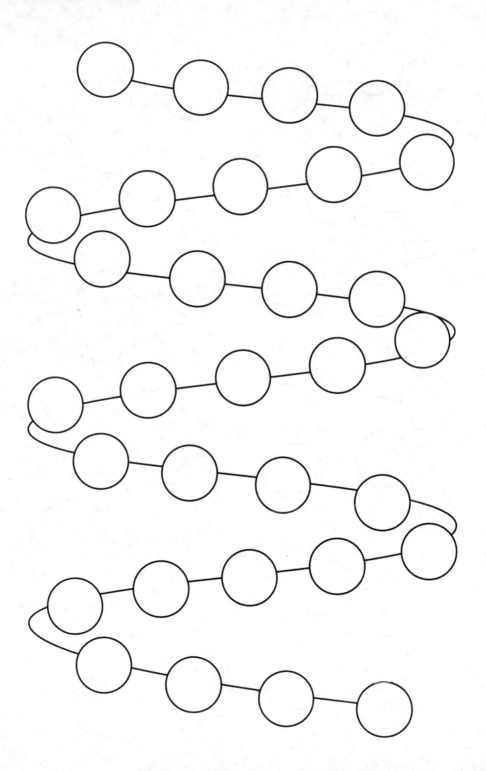

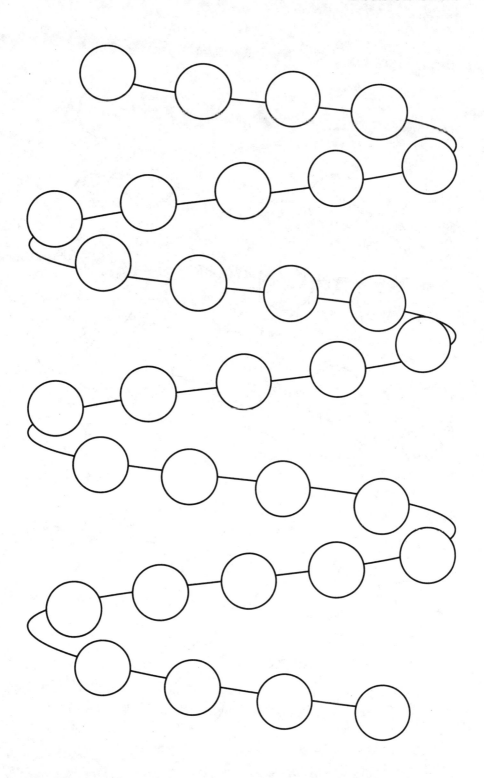

Decision Chart

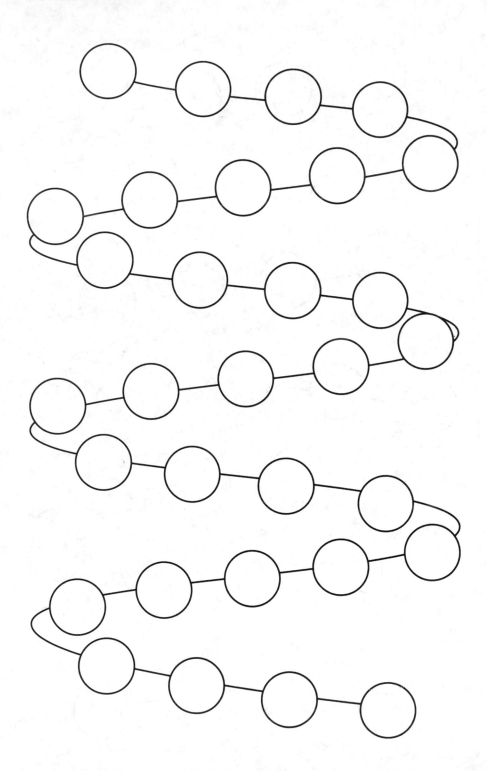

Related Titles of Interest from Presidio ★ Press

Call for our current catalog
Order Toll Free 1-800-966-5179, or write P.O. Box 1764, Novato, CA 94948-1764
Prices are current as of 1 December 1991 but are subject to change

Abrams: A History of the American Main Battle Tank, Vol II by R.P. Hunnicutt 0-89141-388-X, cloth, 8.5x11, 716 photos, 320 pages, $60.00

Art of Maneuver by Robert R. Leonard 0-89141-403-7, cloth, 6x9, maps, 288 pages, $24.95

August 1944: The Campaign for France by Robert A. Miller 0-89141-316-2, cloth, 6x9, photos, maps, 300 pages, $17.95

Bill Mauldin's Army: Bill Mauldin's Greatest World War II Cartoons by Bill Mauldin 0-89141-159-3, paper, 8.5x11, 412 drawings, 384 pages, $14.95

Common Sense Training: A Working Philosophy for Leaders by Lt. Gen. Arthur S. Collins, Jr., USA (Ret.) 0-89141-067-8, paper, 6x9, 252 pages, $9.95

Defense of Hill 781: An Allegory of Modern Mechanized Combat by James McDonough 0-89141-310-3, cloth, 6x9, maps, 212 pages, $18.95

Dragons at War: 234th Infantry in the Mojave by Daniel P. Bolger 0-89141-246-8, cloth, 6x9, photos, maps, charts, 360 pages, $18.95

Firepower: A History of the American Heavy Tank by R.P. Hunnicutt 0-89141-304-9, cloth, 8.5x11, photos, illustrations, 224 pages, $40.00

Forward Into Battle: Fighting Tactics from Waterloo to the Near Future by Paddy Griffith 0-89141-413-4, cloth, 6x9, 228 pages, $24.95

Great Captains Unveiled: From Genghis Khan to General Wolfe by Sir Basil H. Liddell-Hart 0-89141-377-4, cloth, 6x9, 280 pages, $24.95

Infantry Attacks by Erwin Rommel 0-89141-385-5, cloth, 6x9, 288 pages, $24.95

Leaders and Battles: The Art of Military Leadership by William J. Wood 0-89141-185-2, cloth, 6x9, maps, 336 pages, $24.95

Lost Victories by Erich von Manstein 0-89141-130-5, cloth, 6x9, photos, maps, 1 diagram, 584 pages, $24.95

Military Lessons of the Gulf War Edited by Bruce W. Watson 1-85367-103-7, cloth, 6x9, photos, 256 pages, $24.95

No Victor, No Vanquished: The Yom Kippur War by Edgar O'Ballance 0-89141-017-1, cloth, 6x9, maps, photos, 384 pages, $24.95

On Strategy: A Critical Analysis of the Vietnam War by Harry G. Summers, Jr., Col. of Infantry 0-89141-156-9, cloth, 6x9, 1 map, 240 pages, $18.95

On the Banks of the Suez: An Israeli General's Personal Account of the Yom Kippur War by Avraham "Bren" Adan 0-89141-043-0, cloth, 6x9, maps, photos, 480 pages, $24.95

Patton: A History of the American Main Battle Tank, Vol I by R.P. Hunnicutt 0-89141-230-1, cloth, 8.5x11, 1,222 b&w illustrations, 464 pages, $60.00

The Rise and Fall of an American Army: U.S. Ground Forces, Vietnam: 1965-1973 by Shelby L. Stanton 0-89141-232-8, cloth, 6x9, photos, maps, 428 pages, $22.50

The Russo-German War, 1941-45 by Albert Seaton 0-89141-392-8, cloth, 6x9, 590 pages, $37.50

Small Unit Leadership: A Commonsense Approach by Col. Dandridge M. (Mike) Malone, USA (Ret.) 0-89141-173-9, paper, 6x9, illustrations, 180 pages, $8.95

Treat 'Em Rough: The Birth of American Armor, 1917-20 by Dale E. Wilson 0-89141-354-5, cloth, 6x9, photos, maps, 242 pages, $24.95

Vietnam at War: The History 1946-1975 by Lt. Gen. Phillip B. Davidson, USA (Ret.) 0-89141-306-5, cloth, 6x9, maps, photos, 848 pages, $27.50